CW01635085

Morality in the Philosophy of Thomas Hobbes

Cases in the Law of Nature

In this book, S. A. Lloyd offers a radically new interpretation of Hobbes's Laws of Nature, revealing them to be not egoistic precepts of personal prudence but rather moral instructions for obtaining the common good. This account of Hobbes's moral philosophy stands in contrast to both divine command and rational choice interpretations. Drawing from the core notion of reciprocity, Lloyd explains Hobbes's system of "cases in the law of nature" and situates Hobbes's moral philosophy in the broader context of his political philosophy and views on religion. Offering ingenious new arguments, Lloyd defends a reciprocity interpretation of the Laws of Nature through which humanity's common good is secured.

S. A. Lloyd is professor of philosophy, law, and political science at the University of Southern California. Lloyd is the author of *Ideals as Interests in Hobbes's "Leviathan": The Power of Mind over Matter.*

Morality in the Philosophy of Thomas Hobbes

Cases in the Law of Nature

S. A. LLOYD
University of Southern California

CAMBRIDGE
UNIVERSITY PRESS

CAMBRIDGE
UNIVERSITY PRESS

32 Avenue of the Americas, New York NY 10013-2473, USA

Cambridge University Press is part of the University of Cambridge.

It furthers the University's mission by disseminating knowledge in the pursuit of education, learning and research at the highest international levels of excellence.

www.cambridge.org
Information on this title: www.cambridge.org/9781107629899

© S. A. Lloyd 2009

This publication is in copyright. Subject to statutory exception and to the provisions of relevant collective licensing agreements, no reproduction of any part may take place without the written permission of Cambridge University Press.

First published 2009
Reprinted 2011
First paperback edition 2013

A catalogue record for this publication is available from the British Library

Library of Congress Cataloguing in Publication data

Lloyd, S. A., 1958–
Morality in the philosophy of Thomas Hobbes: cases in the law of nature / S. A. Lloyd.
p. cm.
Includes bibliographical references and index.
ISBN 978-0-521-86167-0 (hardback)
1. Hobbes, Thomas, 1588–1679 – Ethics. 2. Ethics, Modern – 17th century.
3. Natural law – History – 17th century. I. Title.
B1248.E7L56 2009
171′.2–dc22 2008036400

ISBN 978-0-521-86167-0 Hardback
ISBN 978-1-107-62989-9 Paperback

Cambridge University Press has no responsibility for the persistence or accuracy of URLs for external or third-party internet websites referred to in this publication, and does not guarantee that any content on such websites is, or will remain, accurate or appropriate.

For Anastasya Cactus-Butt, Isabella Fairy-Face, and Bobby-Alexander Lloyd-Damnjanovic, and for the one who made them possible and actual.

Contents

Preface

> [T]hey that have written of justice and policy in general, do all invade each other and themselves with contradictions. To reduce this doctrine to the rules and infallibility of reason, there is no way, but, first, put such principles down for a foundation, as passion, not mistrusting, may not seek to displace; and afterwards to build thereon the truth of *cases in the law of nature* (which hitherto have been built in the air) by degrees, till the whole have been inexpugnable.
>
> (*Elements of Law*, Dedicatory Epistle, emphasis added)

This is a book about Hobbes's moral philosophy. It examines his "Laws of Nature" because Hobbes insisted that "the science of them is the true and onely moral philosophy".[1] Hobbes terms the conclusions of moral philosophizing once Laws of Nature have been brought to bear on specific practical questions "cases in the law of nature", hence the book's title. I used to think that Hobbes did not have any genuine moral philosophy. My reason for thinking so was not the reason offered by many commentators in support of the same conclusion, namely,

[1] *The Collected English Works of Thomas Hobbes*, edited by Sir William Molesworth (11 vols., London 1839–1845), volume III, 146; T 110. References to the Molesworth collected edition will appear as EW, followed by volume number and page number. *Leviathan* appears in EW III. Richard Tuck's revised student edition of *Leviathan* (Cambridge, 1996) helpfully contains a concordance with the Molesworth edition to which I shall be referring and with the popular Macpherson edition (London, 1990). When referring to *Leviathan*, I cite the EW page followed by the Tuck edition (abbreviated T) page.

that Hobbes's egoistic psychology leaves no room for the possibility of genuinely moral motivation for action. That view rests, I believe, on an incorrect characterization of the psychology of Hobbesian men. Rather, I thought that Hobbes saw his political philosophy as needing no moral philosophy to undergird it. According to Hobbes's explicit chart of the sciences in chapter 9 of *Leviathan,* civil philosophy is a distinct science of political rights and duties derived from the concept of commonwealth – which is the concept of an artificial (man-made) entity – and thus not a branch of natural philosophy, while ethics – which Hobbes describes as a branch of science concerning consequences of the passions of men – is a part of natural philosophy.[2] Because I am not tempted to view political philosophy as merely a specific application of moral philosophy, I saw nothing problematic in Hobbes's treating civil philosophy as an autonomous science. More importantly, I thought the political philosophy I understood him to offer had an impressive coherence and sufficiency despite having no dependence on, nor contribution to make to, moral philosophy proper.

I interpreted Hobbes's political philosophy as intended to argue that recurrent social disorder results from people's resisting their government in pursuit of what I termed "transcendent interests" – interests for the sake of which they are willing to sacrifice their lives, if necessary.[3] Many interests may be transcendent in this way: interests in securing the good of our children, in furthering the realization of substantive moral ideals such as liberty or justice or human rights, in defending one's country – even interests in defending our honor or reputation may be transcendent for any given person. Hobbes was primarily concerned with the social disorder that results from men's

[2] EW III, 72–73. Hobbes calls "natural" those creations that issue from God's art, characterizing nature as "the art whereby God hath made and governs the world". "Artificial" are those things made by the art of man, for instance, automata such as watches, as well as such things as poems, monetary systems, and universities. "*Art*", Hobbes writes in the introduction to *Leviathan,* "goes yet further, imitating that rational and most excellent work of nature, *man.* For by art is created that great LEVIATHAN called a COMMONWEALTH, or STATE, in Latin CIVITAS, which is but an artificial man; though of greater stature and strength than the natural, for whose protection and defence it was intended" (EW III, ix; T 9).

[3] S. A. Lloyd, *Ideals as Interests in Hobbes's Leviathan: The Power of Mind over Matter* (Cambridge, 1992); hereafter cited as *IAI,* followed by page number.

acting on transcendent religious interests in doing what they believe to be their religious duty, and in seeking to obtain the eternal reward promised to those faithful who fulfill their religious duties, and to avoid divine punishment for failing to fulfill them. Hobbes analyzed the English Civil War as largely the result of transcendent religious interests, in some cases manipulated by those ambitious of worldly power. Because subjects willing to risk death in the service of their religious or other interests cannot usually be compelled to civil obedience by the state's threats to punish them corporally or capitally, the instability generated by transcendent interests poses a particularly difficult problem for Hobbes's project of discovering the principles by which the commonwealth might be made to remain stable indefinitely. The idea of motivation by transcendent interests, which may have seemed to some who read my interpretation of Hobbes's political theory when it was first presented in 1992 a strange and unlikely explanation for socially disruptive behavior, has sadly become, after September 11th, 2001, and the suicide bombings of recent years a widely recognized and increasingly studied phenomenon.[4] Although historians and dramatists have from ancient times forward documented the power of transcendent interests, I believe that Hobbes was the first philosopher to offer a systematic philosophical analysis

[4] The notion has entered the realm of public and foreign policy debates. For instance, in his *New York Times* column of September 18, 2002, on U.S. policy toward Iraq's Saddam Hussein, Thomas L. Friedman called attention to the potential social disruption effected by those with what I call transcendent interests: "What worries Americans are not the deterrables like Saddam. What worries them are the 'undeterrables' – the kind of young Arab-Muslim men who hit us on 9/11, and are still lurking. Americans would pay virtually any price to eliminate the threat from the undeterrables – the terrorists *who hate us more than they love their own lives,* and therefore cannot be deterred" (emphasis added). Freidman's "undeterrables" act on a transcendent interest, although how precisely to characterize that interest is open to dispute.

David Braybrooke's notion of "interest-transcending motivations" as motives that lead people to act in disregard of their interests in the service of higher causes is a related but narrower notion than the notion of transcendent interests I attribute to Hobbes as interests for the sake of which one is willing to risk and if need be sacrifice one's natural life. These latter may (and Hobbes thinks typically do) include men's larger self-interests in procuring their own salvation, or honor, or reputation.

of civil disorder generated by transcendent interests. And I argued that Hobbes developed a powerful original political theory capable of addressing the problems to stability within one's society posed by the transcendent interests of one's fellow citizens. Hobbes addressed in particular the transcendent religious interests of his fellow subjects, but the method he pursued in doing so has much broader application, and makes Hobbes studies of perhaps greater importance today than ever before.[5]

I argued that Hobbes thought the disorders internal to civil societies generated by transcendent interests can be reliably avoided only if subjects are persuaded that they have, what they can see in their own terms to be, sufficient reason for political obedience. Hobbes aimed to offer a confluence of reasons – prudential, moral, and religious – for political obedience, in the hope that this confluence would motivate most of the people most of the time to obey, thus ensuring sufficient compliance for the perpetual maintenance of effective domestic social order. Such a solution requires a serious engagement with the beliefs that support and express disruptive transcendent interests, which Hobbes undertakes in the half of *Leviathan* devoted to discussion of Judeo-Christian religion, and the equivalent portions of his earlier works on civil philosophy.

Of course, no interpretation of Hobbes as addressing the recurrent social disorder that ensues from action on transcendent interests will make sense if men cannot be motivated to act in any way they recognize as threatening to their survival. Traditionally, interpretations of Hobbes's philosophy have attributed just such a narrowly prudential psychology to Hobbesian agents: The desire for bodily self-preservation systematically (some claim necessarily) overrides all other motives and desires in any nonpathologically functioning human being. Hence, healthy men are incapable of having or acting on transcendent interests. If true, this must defeat the sort of

[5] One measure of Hobbes's philosophical importance is how often his work is used to address the most pressing concerns of the time during which his interpreter is writing. For instance, during the Cold War, Gregory Kavka saw in Hobbes's theory useful direction for designing a deterrence strategy that might avoid nuclear annihilation. See the essays collected in Kavka's *Moral Paradoxes of Nuclear Deterrence* (Cambridge, 1987).

interpretation I have proposed, depending as it does on motivations men cannot have. Those interpreters who believe Hobbes thought aversion to bodily death is the dominant motivation of human nature have adduced Hobbes's treatment of the Laws of Nature as a main support for their interpretation. They suppose that Hobbes considers the Laws of Nature to be normative precepts justified by their instrumental relation to the temporal self-preservation of the agent who follows them. Why, they ask, would Hobbes treat moral norms as mere strategies for securing self-preservation unless he thought their normativity depended upon their being so treated? And why would he think their normativity depended on their securing bodily self-preservation unless he believed that men will not act otherwise than their concern for temporal bodily self-preservation dictates? For instance, one interpreter writes that "there is only one way that it could be true that these laws of nature are exceptionlessly binding precepts: we must ascribe to Hobbes the standard view that all persons have the dominant desire for self-preservation.... Since the laws of nature are formulated with the aim of self-preservation in mind, it must be this end that is desired most powerfully by all Hobbesian agents", and concludes that "Hobbes' account of the moral law is the strongest evidence in Hobbes' texts in favor of the standard interpretation of Hobbes' view on the evil of death".[6]

By insisting on a narrowly prudential interpretation of Hobbes's Laws of Nature, these sorts of traditional interpretation merely beg the question against the transcendent interests interpretation. It is true that if the traditional interpretation of the Laws of Nature is correct, Hobbes was inconsistent to have acknowledged, as he unquestionably did, that men have transcendent interests; and he should not have been aiming to offer an account of civil disorder and its remedy in terms of transcendent interests, as I have argued he did. But it is equally true that if the transcendent interests interpretation is correct, Hobbes could not have held the account of the Laws of Nature traditionally attributed to him. Perhaps it has not occurred to many to question whether the traditional understanding of Hobbes's Laws of Nature as rules for the temporal preservation of the agent who follows

[6] Mark C. Murphy, "Hobbes on the Evil of Death", *Archiv für Geschichte der Philosophie* 82 (2000): 36–61, 44–46.

them is correct. Having pursued this question I have concluded that the traditional understanding of Hobbes's Laws of Nature is fundamentally flawed, and that this crucial misunderstanding reverberates throughout Hobbes interpretation, causing interpreters to attribute to Hobbes an overly simplistic psychology that cannot accommodate transcendent interests, and a correspondingly impoverished moral theory. So long as the traditional interpretation of Hobbes's Laws of Nature as mere precepts of personal preservation is allowed to stand, condescending interpretations of Hobbes as having offered a political theory threatened with insignificance by its reliance on a false human psychology will muster support from what they allege to be Hobbes's moral philosophy. Unless this understanding of the Laws of Nature is overturned, even those interpreters who are prepared to admit that Hobbes recognized transcendent interests and are persuaded that Hobbes was concerned to address those interests will find themselves in the uncomfortable position of having to attribute to Hobbes a theory that is internally incoherent, or else ambivalent, confused, intentionally deceptive, or inadequately developed. I do not find any of these alternatives attractive. Showing why they are not compelling requires addressing the assumptions from which they spring at their source, in how we understand Hobbes's conception of the Laws of Nature.

Thus the main motivation for the present investigation of Hobbes's moral philosophy is to provide an alternative to the traditional interpretation of Hobbes's Laws of Nature that shows how those laws support, rather than undermine, the *transcendent interests interpretation* of Hobbes's political philosophy. But in the course of arguing the case for that thesis, I learned something that surprised me very much: Hobbes *does* have a distinctive, original, and philosophically attractive moral philosophy, a philosophy not only worth considering on its own merits, but one that helps us to think critically about our own contemporary dispute between reasonability and rationality accounts of morality. Time spent with Hobbes is never wasted, and having continued to study him, I now believe that just as he first articulated significant philosophical ideas for which Locke and Hume received credit, so did he offer an early articulation and defense of the idea Rawls has termed "the reasonable" and Scanlon "reasonableness" ordinarily traced to Kant.

So the present study is offered with two objectives in mind. The primary one is to defend the *transcendent interests interpretation* of Hobbes's political philosophy by showing the internal coherence and philosophical attractiveness of the broader theory comprised of Hobbes's moral and political philosophies. The second is to enable us to see that Hobbes did make an original contribution to moral philosophy, which, once we recognize it, provides a useful resource for thinking about the post-Kantian moral landscape that concerns us today.

Portions of the argument of Chapter 6 appeared in "Hobbes's Self-Effacing Natural Law Theory", *Pacific Philosophical Quarterly* 82, nos. 3 & 4 (September 2001): 285–308. A portion of the argument of Chapter 7 appeared in "Coercion, Ideology, and Education in Hobbes's *Leviathan*", in Andrews Reath, Barbara Herman, and Christine M. Korsgaard, eds., *Reclaiming the History of Ethics: Essays for John Rawls* (Cambridge, 1997), pp. 36–65. And a portion of the argument of Chapter 8 appeared in "Contemporary Uses of Hobbes's Political Philosophy", in Jules L. Coleman and Christopher W. Morris, eds., *Rational Commitment and Social Justice: Essays for Gregory Kavka* (Cambridge, 1998), pp. 122–149.

I have many people to thank for their help in developing the ideas and arguments of this study. Stephen Darwall, John Deigh, Bernard Gert, Kinch Hoekstra, A. P. Martinich, and Thomas Pogge have provided consistently illuminating critical feedback on many aspects of the argument through several versions. David Braybrooke, Gerald Gaus, and A. P. Martinich gave me very useful comments on the entire penultimate version of the book; and David Lyons gave me particular help with the arguments of Chapter 4. I have learned a great deal from discussions with members of the Southern California Law and Philosophy Group, including Carl Cranor, Barbara Herman, Pamela Hieronymi, Aaron James, Herb Morris, Chris Nattichia, Calvin Normore, Andy Reath, and Seanna Schiffrin, but most especially from Steve Munzer, who has not only helped me to think about Hobbes, but also to become a somewhat better writer. I am lucky to have at U.S.C. a group of colleagues who have provided me an unfailing stream of support and constructive criticism: My special thanks to Ed McCann (who in addition to his critical expertise generously gave me his set of Molesworth's *Collected English Works of Hobbes*), Scott Altman, Marshall Cohen, John Dreher, Steve Finlay, Greg Keating,

Janet Levin, Ed McCaffrey, Kadri Vihvelin, and Gideon Yaffe, whose insightful criticism has strengthened the argument at several points. My research assistant, Daniel Considine, has been a tremendous help. I learned from all the participants at the University of Pennsylvania's Law and Philosophy conference on social contract theory, organized by Heidi Hurd and Michael Moore, but owe particular thanks to Claire Finkelstein, Gerald Gaus, David Gauthier, Chris Morris, Gerald Postema, and Geoff Sayre-McCord. I have also profited from discussions with David Boonin, Pasquale Pasquino, John Simmons, Peter Vanderschraaf, Jeremy Waldron, Garrath Williams, and Donald Wilson. My treasured friend Greg Kavka's continuing voice in my ear helped me, particularly in Chapter 4, to refine my discussion of desire-based interpretations. Most of all I owe a debt of gratitude to Zlatan Damnjanovic for more than a decade of constructive, challenging engagement with the arguments of this book, and for organizing his life to support my efforts.

Introduction

> The *end* or *scope* of philosophy is, that we may make use to our benefit of effects formerly seen; or that, by application of bodies to one another, we may produce the like effects of those we conceive in our mind, as far forth as matter, strength, and industry will permit, for the commodity of human life.... [T]he utility of moral and civil philosophy is to be estimated, not so much by the commodities we have by knowing these sciences, as by the calamities we receive from not knowing them.
>
> (EW I, 7–8; *Elements of Philosophy*, Sec. 6–7)

Civil philosophy, which Hobbes claimed to have invented, has its point and purpose in teaching humankind how to live in peace. While we cannot always control the actions of neighboring nations, we can, Hobbes taught, so organize our own society that we may maintain peace among ourselves, and best hope to defend against outsiders. The benefits of maintaining a bastion of domestic peace and stability are so many and so precious that one might hardly think they need advertising; but Hobbes lived in a time that called out for reminding men that learning, progress, arts and sciences, comfort and plenty, society, civilization, and the very preservation of humanity are worth the price we must pay for them. That price is significant, for it usually involves requiring us to do many things that we do not want to do. It requires us to obey laws that do not make exceptions for us, to squelch our impulse to demand that our private judgment order the common business; to defer to what we judge to be the inferior reasons of other men; often to tolerate what we regard as the inefficiency, stupidity, offensiveness, and sometimes even the wrongful, sinful, or heretical actions of our compatriots. It requires us to swallow indignities and insults, and to accept less than we think we deserve. It requires us to obey our society's laws even though we see the ends we care most about promoting go unpromoted by our society, and to accept punishment for trying to promote those ends contrary to what we regard as the bad laws of our society. Peace requires that we treat our own judgment with a degree of detachment, as one judgment among many, to be discounted if need be for the sake of peace. Considering these costs, how can domestic peace be worth the price it demands from those who must sustain it?

Had men been simpler creatures, caring only for their survival and rudimentary comfort, the price to them of securing peace would be negligible. A simple showing that survival requires peace, and peace requires obedience to political authority, would suffice to maintain domestic stability because there would be no costs of peace to be weighed and balanced against the good it secures. Without concerns for religious causes and moral principles, for honor and achievement, and the myriad attachments and affections that affect our decisions about how we will act, a simple instrumental argument for political submission would be good enough. This fact explains, I suspect, the enduring appeal of those interpretations of Hobbes's civil philosophy that take it to have presupposed a simple, biologically based egoistic preoccupation with personal survival. For what simpler argument for political submission could there be than one purporting to demonstrate that the dominant end of human nature requires political submission?

For better or for worse, we are not such simple creatures, a fact Hobbes recognized and crafted his political philosophy to accommodate. Unlike bees and ants and other naturally sociable creatures who enjoy hard-wired consensus in judgment, we naturally exercise idiosyncratic private judgment, compete for honor and precedence, find fault in others, and strive to control their actions. We are tempests of swirling, altering, often warring allegiances and impulses, whose potentially destructive tendencies may be either moderated and contained or exacerbated, depending upon the social environment we impose on ourselves. As Hobbes thinks of it, the problem for civil philosophy is to discover the principles that must be observed if domestic peace is to be achieved and maintained. The problem for moral philosophy is to show how such principles are properly normative for us, making claims on us that we ought to honor and can be motivated to honor. If men as we are have many interests that pull against or trump our interest in peace, how can the sacrifices required in order to secure peace be made normative for us? Hobbes develops a moral philosophy that successfully solves this problem.

The solution depends in the first instance upon a perceptive appreciation of the complex constellation of motives required in order to move men to resist the governments that could otherwise secure domestic peace. To motivate rebellion, men must be discontented with their lot in life, but that alone is not enough. They must further have hope of success in improving their lot by throwing off or replacing their government. Even together these motives will not suffice to raise rebellion. Because, as Hobbes plausibly insists, we will not rebel unless we believe that we are morally justified in doing so, a showing or "pretense" of right is a third necessary condition for rebellion.[1] Most people will live with an unsatisfactory political regime, even when they might be capable of overthrowing it, if they believe that insurrection would be *wrong*. This is an important insight, and it distinguishes the seditious or rebellious resister of concern to civil philosophy from the mere criminals who burden every society. Civil war generally requires persons of conscience on both sides, whose belief in the justness of their cause animates the risks and sacrifices they undergo. Hobbes's recognition that we care so profoundly that our actions be justifiable has a seismic effect on the way he addresses the problem of social disorder, for it means that there is no hope to maintain a perpetual peace without finding a workable formula to address the thorniest questions of right and wrong. This puts moral philosophy front and center in the project of securing civil peace.

Religion, in particular, complicates this project enormously, by supplying a potentially independent source of normative claims that must be reconciled with morality if moral philosophy is to play the role Hobbes assigns it in decisively justifying compliance with

1 *Elements of Law* II.8.1.

the conclusions of civil philosophy. Indeed, religion provides a rich resource for justificatory rationales for political insurrection capable of satisfying the "pretense of right" condition for motivating rebellion. Hobbes consistently presents the Laws of Nature, which he equates with "the true moral philosophy", as articulating those of God's requirements most certain to all of us who have not enjoyed the benefit of a direct revelation from God Himself. The pronouncements of revealed religion we take on hearsay evidence or mere authority from those who claim that God has spoken to them immediately; but God's natural law is discoverable by each of us immediately through a mere exercise of our natural reason, allowing us to assure ourselves of its claim on our obedience. By attempting to confer God's imprimatur on the conclusions of moral philosophy, Hobbes seeks to consolidate normative support for the principles of social stability uncovered by political philosophy. Political philosophy then completes the task of reconciliation by showing that Scripture, properly interpreted, confirms the conclusions of moral philosophy.

The point of departure of Hobbes's moral philosophy is our shared conception of ourselves as rational agents. From our common definition of man as rational, Hobbes argues that we won't count a person as rational unless he can formulate and is willing to offer, at least *post hoc,* what he regards as justifying reasons for his conduct (and beliefs). But to offer some consideration as justifying one's action commits one to accepting that same consideration as justifying the like actions of others, *ceteris paribus.* (Nothing counts as a reason for doing a particular action unless it counts as a reason for doing actions of the same general type all else equal.) So one acts against reason when one does what one would judge another unjustified in doing.

From this reciprocity constraint, formally derived as a theorem of reason, Hobbes proceeds to argue that any rational agent ought to submit to government. Because we would judge it unreasonable of others to whom we have no special obligations to condemn us for directing our actions by our own private judgment rather than deferring to theirs, the reciprocity theorem requires us to grant a universal right of private judgment. Yet, if men disagree in their judgments, as we can see that they do, a condition of universal self-government by private judgment will be a condition of perpetual irresoluble contention and conflict. Such a condition thwarts men's effective pursuit of their ends (whatever those ends may be) and is, for this reason, something any rational agent must, *qua* rational agent, be concerned to avoid. Because the reciprocity theorem rules out asymmetrical solutions that would grant unequal rights to exercise private judgment, the only alternative to universal private judgment sanctioned by reason is joint submission to authoritative arbitration of disputes. Because such submission makes possible an environment in which agency may be effectively exercised, it accords with reason that we submit to authoritative arbitration. A sovereign is in its essence an authoritative arbitrator of disputes, with the associated rights necessary if arbitration is to eliminate contention. In this way the reciprocity theorem of reason conjoined with the requirements of effective agency (no matter the agent's ends) dictates that we submit to sovereign authority.

The theory Hobbes presents finds a crucial resource in our human desire to justify ourselves – our actions, motives, and beliefs – in the courts of private conscience and public opinion, and before God. We hold ourselves superior to lesser animals on account of our reason. When reason condemns our actions, we experience shame, and a sense of degradation. We care very much that our actions be, and be seen to be, justified. But that sort of justification by reason depends upon a willingness to offer, and also to accept, various considerations as generally justifying types of actions. Although we may disagree about which considerations justify which types of actions, no one who claims the respect due to a human being can refuse to grant that whatever sorts of actions he judges to be "against reason" (unreasonable) when done by others do not lose that character *simply* because done by himself, apart from any further reference to some germane distinguishing status or circumstance he may occupy.

The Laws of Nature articulate practical applications of Hobbes's moral philosophy, and these twenty or so rules detail the many things men are to do or refrain from doing, and the virtues they must cultivate, if they are to behave toward their fellows as reason requires, in a way that sustains human society and civil life. But it is striking that these rules, neither individually nor taken together, actually direct men to set up and submit to government. Considering that Hobbes's political philosophy argues that submission to an absolute political authority is necessary for the perpetual maintenance of peace, it is nothing short of astonishing that the moral philosophy unfolds and terminates without directing submission to such an authority.

Commonly, interpretations of Hobbes wave hands at this apparent lapse, supposing that somehow the moral requirement that we give up our right to everything entails the political requirement that we give up our right to anything, that we submit to absolute sovereignty. The various Laws of Nature Hobbes articulates do require that we submit to arbitration of disputes, that we keep promises, be grateful, modest, fair, and the like. Hobbes offers no obvious argument to the effect that any of these are, or even collectively add up to, a submission to an absolute sovereign. Yet he evidently believes that they do. Thus there remains a mystery as to how the moral philosophy expressed in the Laws of Nature is meant to provide an argument for subjection to an absolute political authority.

Here again the reciprocity theorem provides the answer. It offers a resource for making simple arguments for complex conclusions that could not otherwise be defended. If we would fault our fellows for defecting from obedience to the political authority that protects us both, according to their own private preferences, then neither may we, in reason, do so. If we would fault others for not agreeing with us on equal terms to submit to a common law and a common arbitration of disputes, then we must so submit when others are also willing. If we would demand that others obey our sovereign in order to secure our safety, then we cannot in reason exempt ourselves from obedience. And similarly in many more cases, to be discussed, where Hobbes offers arguments to discharge the antecedents of these conditionals. Hobbes's achievement is to derive our common- (moral) sensical commitment to reciprocity as a requirement of reason, then to organize its implications into a comprehensive, defensible, and attractive moral philosophy through his discussion of "cases in the law of nature".

This book unfolds the interpretation just sketched in the following manner: Part One, entitled *Moral Philosophy, Method and Matter,* introduces the content and casuistry of Hobbes's Laws of Nature in Chapter 1, then sets out Hobbes's complex conception of human nature in Chapter 2, a psychology I defend as realistic. These provide the data that any plausible interpretation of Hobbes's moral philosophy must successfully reconcile. Part Two, on the movement

From Psychology to Moral Philosophy, considers how a moral philosophy of the content Hobbes lays down could prove properly normative for people having the psychology Hobbes describes, including ourselves. Chapter 3 clarifies the definition and unifying function of the Laws of Nature, arguing, in opposition to consensus opinion among Hobbes scholars, that these are correctly conceived as rules for securing the common good of humanity generally in sustaining decent communities rather than merely rules for the personal profit of the agent who follows them. Chapter 4 critically considers derivations of the Laws of Nature offered by the main schools of interpretation – which I classify as offering desire-based, duty-based, or definitional derivations. Chapter 5 offers my own reconstruction of a definitional derivation, which I term the *reciprocity interpretation* of Hobbes's moral philosophy, and argues that this interpretation secures the normativity of Hobbes's Laws of Nature for ordinary people in a way consistent with his stated methodology, while incorporating the virtues of other approaches and avoiding some of their more significant failings. Part Three, *From Moral Philosophy to Civil Philosophy,* includes Chapter 6 offering an explicit derivation of the duty to undertake political obligation under the Law of Nature, along with an analysis of the relation between civil law and natural law, and a reconciliation of the concepts of liberty, law, and obligation in Hobbes's system. I argue that Hobbes espoused a *self*-effacing natural law theory, supported by an interesting conception of the *hierarchy of responsibility* among those in authority and those subject to their authority. Chapter 7 considers how Hobbes addresses the sorts of characters unsuited to civil obedience – fools, hypocrites, zealots, and dupes – and assesses the success of his recommendations for minimizing the incidence and effectiveness of these problematic character-types. By showing that a society regulated by his recommended principles is likely to constrain the formation of problematic character-types, Hobbes makes the case that a society ordered by his principles would be self-sustaining and stable. Chapter 8 seeks to display the unity of practical wisdom within Hobbes's system on the reciprocity interpretation of his moral philosophy and the transcendent interests interpretation of his political philosophy, by indicating how his moral philosophy of cases in the Laws of Nature is connected with his interpretation of Christian religion and his civil philosophy. It concludes by assessing some contemporary uses of Hobbes's political philosophy, and proposes a new research program drawing on Hobbes's insights and method.

The argument of the book employs a layered, fugue-like method of introducing interpretive elements, then returning in several successive chapters to provide new considerations in their support and development. Most of these elements are introduced in Chapter 1 as claims (without defense yet) intended to outline a coherent framework for systematizing Hobbes's discussions of his many different cases in the Laws of Nature. But because Hobbes is offering a system involving many mutual dependencies, his justifications for particular components of that system cannot fully be argued in separate, linear segments one at a time. My exposition seeks to follow the spiraling method we see within and across Hobbes's many reworkings of the various elements of his moral philosophy, rather than imposing the neater, but ultimately hopeless, method of defending fully in isolation each component element. This approach necessarily involves repeated consideration of key texts through several chapters. Chapter 8 orders all of these texts (as finally interpreted) in a unified system. Readers who wish to preview the overall shape of the system may prefer to skip from Chapter 1 directly to Chapter 8, then return to Chapter 2 through 7 for the supporting arguments.

I should say something about the way I deploy Hobbes's earlier and later texts. I know of no Hobbes interpreter who both clearly articulates and faithfully adheres to a strict priority rule for which of Hobbes's texts trumps all others when they seem to conflict.[2] Because I take a holistic approach to the interpretation of Hobbes's moral and political philosophies, I consider evidence from across Hobbes's writings; but it would be fair to say that usually I look to the earlier works for clarification of his concern or impulse, and to the later works for refinement and correction of positions and arguments. Still

[2] Bernard Gert seems to come closest to doing so, but at the price of ascribing to Hobbes an enormous amount of inconsistency, and some quite implausible views. A. P. Martinich sees no need to prioritize Hobbes's texts, because, as he argues, it is a mistake to believe that Hobbes had a single consistent theory. See Bernard Gert, "Hobbes and Psychological Egoism", *Journal of the History of Ideas* 28 (1967): 503–520; "Hobbes's Psychology", in Tom Sorell, ed., *The Cambridge Companion to Hobbes* (Cambridge, 1996), 157–174; and A. P. Martinich, *Thomas Hobbes* (London, 2005).

I recognize that Hobbes's conceptions of human motivation and the problem of social disorder alter with his own maturity and the historical disorders his writings span, and so the concerns of the earlier works cannot be taken as wholly authoritative. Conversely, in some instances Hobbes's efforts to improve his arguments in response to particular criticisms, events, or methodological considerations do more harm to his theory than good; and so the refinements of the later works cannot be taken as wholly authoritative. I take seriously his Latin *Leviathan* and use it as an aid in interpreting certain corresponding passages in his English *Leviathan.* Like all other interpreters, I seek to focus attention on the sets of passages that ground the interpretation I find most plausible. I do, however, attend particularly to the strongest passages that may seem to count against my preferred interpretation; and in Chapter 4 I charitably reconstruct and then critique several of the most important competing schools of interpretation. But, of course, my primary intention in this work is to construct and make plausible the reciprocity interpretation of Hobbes's moral philosophy. Traditional desire-based interpretations have defenders enough to mount a response to my critique and positive alternative without my attempting to imagine anticipatorily what that might be.

The reciprocity interpretation of Hobbes's moral philosophy requires numerous adjustments in widely held prior assumptions about the meaning of Hobbes's particular doctrines and his specific intentions. Although this interpretation is built from all the same elements that figure into any interpretation of Hobbes's normative theory, the interpretive adjustments I urge in each case, taken together, require a "duck-rabbit" style shift in our perception of Hobbes's moral and political theories. Like now seeing a pair of human faces where before one saw only a classical vase, the familiar Hobbes is replaced by a more complex, but at the same time more human, picture. To some this may seem a shocking shift that would deprive Hobbes of his place in history as the principal protagonist of psychological and ethical egoism, as the first to mount a serious, although failed, argument to prove the narrow rationality of morality. Indeed it does, if correct. But it most certainly does not undermine his title to have initiated modern moral philosophy, and in a way that makes his work not just of continuing, but rather increasing, importance some 350 years later. Hobbes's analysis of social conflict, of the ineradicability of transcendent interests, of the irresolubility of disagreement in private judgments, of the connection between reason and moral judgment, and of the centrality of our self-conceptions to our motivations, and his identification of a small but sturdy basis upon which social peace might nonetheless be forged – these are the contributions that earn Hobbes his proper place in our Pantheon.

PART ONE

MORAL PHILOSOPHY, METHOD AND MATTER

1

Moral Judgments

> The laws of nature are immutable and eternal... [a]nd the science of them, is the true and only moral philosophy...and therefore the true doctrine of the laws of nature, is the true moral philosophy.
>
> (EW III, 145–146; T 110)

"The laws of nature", Hobbes writes, "are the sum of *moral* philosophy".[1] An investigation into Hobbes's moral philosophy must therefore be concerned to understand those Laws of Nature. What it is for something to be a law of nature, how such laws are discovered, in what consists their normativity, what is their relation to personal prudence, divine command, and virtuous character, and how they direct submission to political authority – these are some of the questions that will have to be answered in the course of explicating Hobbes's moral philosophy. But it will be useful to begin by setting aside these questions while we briefly lay out the actual content of the norms Hobbes terms "Laws of Nature" and the casuistry of these laws – the conclusions Hobbes reaches from applying them in particular cases. These moral judgments form the data, or raw material, of Hobbes's moral philosophy, and one who has never looked carefully at the many "cases in the law of nature" Hobbes discusses may be surprised to realize how very many questions Hobbes thought could be settled by these laws. Also surprising is his ingenuity,

[1] EW II, 49; *De Cive* 3.32. References to *De Cive* are cited first by EW volume and page number, then by chapter and section number for those using different editions.

subtlety, and occasional perversity in applying the Laws of Nature to particular cases. Once we have a vivid sense of the moral judgments Hobbes believes justified as or under Laws of Nature, along with an understanding of the universality and fixity of those judgments, we will be well situated to take on the more difficult question of how the Laws of Nature would have to be understood in order for it to be possible that such judgments can be normative for Hobbesian men, and, as Hobbes hopes we will recognize, for us as well.

Hobbes famously insisted that all of what he calls the Laws of Nature may be captured "in these words, *quod tibi fieri non vis, alteri ne feceris: do not that to others, you would not have done to yourself*".[2] Gregory Kavka suggested that Hobbes erred in saying that the Golden Rule summarizes his Laws of Nature, and that the precept that actually summarizes Hobbes's laws is "do unto others as they do unto you". Kavka termed his revised precept "the Copper Rule" on the ground that "it glitters less brightly as an inspiring ideal of moral conduct than does the Golden Rule".[3] But Hobbes consistently and insistently presented his Laws of Nature as applications of the traditional Golden Rule, and I'll explain in due course why he was correct to do so.[4] Because Hobbes's precept articulates a kind of reciprocity requirement, and because he argues that the Laws of Nature are theorems of reason, I will refer to his precept as "the reciprocity theorem", or for short, "reciprocity".

Hobbes identifies this principle variously as the "core" or "sum" of the "Law of Nature", and sometimes simply as the Law of Nature itself. He offers various formulations of reciprocity, supposing them to be equivalent, as prohibiting

- Doing what one would not have done to oneself[5]
- Doing what one thinks unreasonable to be done by another to oneself[6]

[2] EW II, 45; *De Cive* 3.26; also EW III, 144; T 109.

[3] Gregory S. Kavka, *Hobbesian Moral and Political Theory* (Princeton, NJ, 1986), 347.

[4] In Chapter 4 I offer a critical examination of Kavka's interpretation of the Laws of Nature, explaining why I believe mistaken his substitution of the Copper Rule for Hobbes's own formulation, and I show in Chapter 5 how Hobbes derives the Golden Rule, or, as I shall refer to it, *the reciprocity theorem.*

[5] "The laws of nature... have been contracted into one easy sum... and that is, *Do not to another, which thou wouldest not have done to thyself*" (EW III, 144; T 109).

[6] "*Do not that to another, which thou thinkest unreasonable to be done by another to thyself*" (EW III, 258; T 188).

- Doing what one would not approve in another[7]
- Reserving to oneself any right one is not content should be reserved to all the rest[8]
- Allowing to oneself that which one denies to another[9] and correlatively as commanding that
- Whatsoever you require that others should do to you, that do ye to them[10] and that
- We love others as ourselves.[11]

Hobbes identifies the requirement that we love others as ourselves with a fairness requirement that we each apply some or other uniform set of standards to everyone, without exempting ourselves from the rules or judgments we apply to others. He writes,

> [T]hat same equity, which we proved in the ninth place to be a law of nature, which commands every man to allow the same rights to others they would be allowed themselves, and which contains in it all the other laws besides, is the same which Moses sets down (Levit. xix. 18): *Thou shalt love thy neighbour as thyself.* And our Saviour calls it *the sum of the moral law*.... But to love our neighbour as ourselves, is nothing else but to grant him all we desire to have granted to ourselves.[12]

Reciprocity is a rational constraint on justifiable, that is, *blameless*, action. Certainly, the various notions Hobbes uses in the effort to call our attention to the core requirement of natural law – disapproval,

7 EW III, 279–280; T 202–203.

8 EW III, 141; T 107; EW II, 39; *De Cive* 3.14.

9 EW III, 494; T 344.

10 EW III, 118; T 92. See also EW IV, 104 (*Elements of Law* I.4.2) for an application of this principle: "*Whatsoever right any man requireth to retain, he allow every other man to retain the same*".

11 "*Thou shalt love thy neighbor as thyself*...is the natural law, having its beginning with rational nature itself" (EW II, 263–264; *De Cive* 17.8). "[T]he law of nature, which is also the moral law, is the law of the author of nature, God Almighty... [f]or the sum of God's law is, *Thou shalt love God above all, and thy neighbour as thyself;* and the same is the sum of the law of nature, as hath been showed" (EW IV, 224; *Elements of Law* II.10.7). Cf. EW II, 57 (*De Cive* 4.12) and EW IV, 113 (*Elements of Law* I.5.6): "*Thou shalt love thy neighbour as thyself*...which is...so to be understood, as that a man... should esteem his neighbour worthy all rights and privileges that himself enjoyeth; and attribute unto him, whatsoever he looketh should be attributed unto himself: which is no more, but that he should be humble, meek, and content with equality".

12 EW II, 57; *De Cive* 4.12. Cf. EW II, 39; *De Cive* 3.14: the ninth Law of Nature dictates "that what rights soever any man challenges to himself, he also grant the same as due to all the rest".

judging unreasonable, iniquitous, or unacceptable, being unwilling to allow – are not fully equivalent. But they do all convey our judgment of what I will call the *unjustifiability* of the actions they characterize, and this is the judgment Hobbes sees as salient. Men express this judgment in their ascriptions of moral fault or blame. When we behave in a way we fault others for behaving, our action lacks vindication, is unjustifiable, or is to use Hobbes's phrase, "contrary to reason".[13] Of course, this apparently simple assertion raises at least as many questions as it answers. We will want to know how, exactly, the relevant actions are to be described. On what grounds, precisely, are our judgments of unreasonableness, inequity, or blameworthiness to be made? And how, considering the diversity of men's judgments and sensibilities, could such a principle be expected to yield a single set of moral norms applicable to every agent? And, of course, we will need to know precisely how Hobbes derives this "theorem" as a requirement of reason. We will work through Hobbes's answers to these and other questions in subsequent chapters. For now, we simply note that reciprocity is the central principle of Hobbes's moral philosophy from which are derived the various cases in the Law of Nature he discusses, either directly, or by means of subsidiary principles themselves derived from reciprocity.

Reciprocity suggests a test for discerning whether one's actions comport with the Law of Nature, namely, that the agent imagine herself on the receiving end of the action she proposes to perform and consider whether from that vantage point she would fault the action as unreasonable:

> [T]here is an easy rule to know upon a sudden, whether the action I be to do, be against the law of nature or not... [namely] [*t*]*hat a man imagine himself in*

[13] As I'll show in Chapter 5, Hobbes's notion of contrariety to reason is broad, encompassing unreasonableness as well as mere irrationality. I use the more familiar term 'unjustifiability' to express this broad notion of contrariety to reason. When Hobbes himself uses the terms 'justify' and 'justified', he is speaking of vindicating as innocent of wrongdoing, as when he writes of sovereigns that "they will all of them justify the war by which their power was at first gotten, and whereon, as they think, their right dependeth", requiring men's "approbation" of their action (EW III, 706; T 486) or of having accepted one's plea of innocence of wrongdoing, as when Hobbes writes that "man is then also said to be justified when his plea, though in itself insufficient, is accepted; as when we plead our will, our endeavour to fulfil the law, and repent us of our failings, and God accepteth it for the performance itself" (EW III, 600; T 413).

the place of the party with whom he hath to do, and reciprocally him in his. Which is no more but a changing, as it were, of the scales.[14]

[T]he rule by which I said any man might know, whether what he was doing were contrary to the law or not, to wit, what thou wouldst not be done to, do not that to another; is almost in the self-same words delivered by our Saviour . . .[15]

[For a man in a quiet mind] there is nothing easier for him to know, though he be never so rude and unlearned, than this only rule, that when he doubts whether what he is now doing to another may be done by the law of nature or not, he conceive himself to be in that other's stead. Here instantly those perturbations which persuaded him to the fact, being now cast into the other scale, dissuade him as much. And this rule is not only easy, but is anciently celebrated in these words, *quod tibi fieri no vis, alteri ne feceris: do not that to others, you would not have done to yourself.*[16]

Some of Hobbes's applications of the reciprocity that lies at the core of all of the Laws of Nature and their particular cases are surprisingly liberal. For instance, he insists that the efforts of missionaries to alter religion in another country are prohibited by the Law of Nature, and this, despite the fact the proselytizer believes he is doing good by his action. Why? Because "he does that which he would not approve in another, namely, that coming from hence, he should endeavour to alter the religion there".[17] This application of reciprocity is striking, because it resists the parochial description of the agent's action as one of teaching "true religion" or "saving souls", in favor of the least abstract description of the action that members of *both* societies, *disagreeing* over the value of the proposed missionary work, might be expected to converge upon, namely, that it is an instance of coming from one place and trying to alter the religion in another place. We will not approve the efforts of foreigners to alter our religious beliefs, not least because of the civil strife any effective such effort would surely cause among defenders of the former religion and advocates for the new. In this case Hobbes applies his reciprocity theorem to the action under the least

[14] EW IV, 107; *Elements of Law* I.4.9. Cf. EW II, 44–45; *De Cive* 3.26: this rule lets us determine whether our actions "may be done by the law of nature or not" (EW II, 61–62; *De Cive* 4.23); and the famous formulation from *Leviathan,* EW III, 144–145; T 109–110.

[15] EW II, 61–62; *De Cive* 4.23.

[16] EW II, 44–45; *De Cive* 3.26.

[17] EW III, 280; T 103.

abstract description of it – "endeavouring to alter the religion" – that *all* affected by the very action may be expected to accept as correct. Men disagree about which religious teachings are true. They disagree about what conversions are salvationary. But they can agree at least that the action under assessment is one of attempted religious conversion. Notice that this degree of abstraction in contested cases is itself a requirement of reciprocity, if we cannot think it reasonable of others with whom we disagree to insist upon their own parochial description of the action whose permissibility is at issue. For if we would fault them for insisting on their contentious preferred action description, then neither may we insist on our own.[18]

RECIPROCITY AND THE RIGHT OF NATURE

Of course, this requirement has its costs. Like the liberal who cannot take his own side in an argument, the reasonable man of Hobbes's moral theory must allow that should he insist upon being held blameless in relying on his own private judgment, he must allow that others are equally justified in trusting to their own private judgments, even while seeing the disasters that threaten to attend making such allowances. Reason's demand that consideration of reciprocity must constrain our actions compels us to afford to all those not subject to prior obligations – that is, all those in what Hobbes calls "the condition of mere nature" – a right to act on their own best judgment of how to act in matters that affect their vital interest, for we cannot think it reasonable for others to whom we owe nothing special to demand that we shall defer to their judgment of how we shall act in matters of vital interest to ourselves. Thus, reciprocity grounds Hobbes's famous "Right of Nature". "For", as Hobbes argues,

> if it be against reason, that I be judge of mine own danger myself, then it is reason, that another man be judge thereof. But the same reason that maketh another man judge of those things that concern me, maketh me also judge of that that concerneth him. And therefore I have reason to judge of his sentence, whether it be for my benefit, or not.[19]

[18] I discuss this feature of Hobbes's moral theory, and the problems it raises, in Chapter 5.

[19] EW IV, 83; *Elements of Law* I.1.8.

This application of reciprocity grants that allowing each to judge in her own case is, in the absence of any prior obligation to subordinate one's judgment to the judgment of others, only reasonable. But the consequences of allowing that are profoundly disturbing, for when each person is permitted license to judge all actions, and to act on her own private judgment of all actions, a terrible prospect of irresoluble contention arises. Should it turn out that our private judgments fail to converge, the state of universal unlimited private judgment Hobbes refers to as a condition of mere nature, may well become a condition of widespread conflict – a war of all against all. On this basis Hobbes insists, "[I]f every man would grant the same liberty to another, which he desires for himself, *as is commanded by the law of nature;* that same natural state would return again, in which all men may by right do all things; which if they knew, they would abhor, as being worse than all kinds of civil subjection whatsoever".[20]

It is difficult not to be alarmed by this audacious account of the claim of reason, which generates from the most basic requirement of reasonableness or fair play a condition that no rational agent can fail to abhor because in that condition no one can expect to exercise effective agency in pursuit of any of her ends. But this account, which inverts the traditional view of the relation between Hobbes's Right of Nature and his Law of Nature, allows Hobbes to argue plausibly that the greater the scope of private judgment over disputed matters, the lesser men's prospects for achieving their ends in action, for the efforts of each will throw up obstacles that impede the contrary efforts of others.[21] This suggests a *continuum* notion of the state of nature, which makes specific sets of normative relations (conditions) more or less states of nature depending upon the scope and extent of legitimate private judgment in them. Universal individual private judgment over all matters (the condition of mere nature) lies at one extreme, in which the price of perfect freedom is the complete

[20] EW II, 135, emphasis added; *De Cive* 10.8. Cf. EW IV, 164; *Elements of Law* II.5.2: "if every man were allowed this liberty of following his conscience … they would not live together in peace an hour". The solution, of course, is to show men that reason requires that they settle for the more limited liberty they would be content to let everyone else retain, a degree of civil liberty under government.

[21] In his mildest language, Hobbes describes this mutual interference as men's "irregular jostling, and hewing one another" (EW III, 308; T 221).

abolition of conditions necessary for effective agency directed toward any end whatsoever (including, but by no means limited to, security of life, limb, liberty, or property). This, any rational agent must abhor. A condition of private judgment among the heads of numerous small families, while less extremely individualistic, is hardly more conducive to the effective exercise of agency, there being still in that condition numerous other individuals and heads of families who have the right, ability, and desire to act in ways that impede the realization of one's own projects.[22] Civil war provides another instance of a state of nature, not only because the warring factions may interfere with the actions of each other and anyone else, but because, although members of competing parties may indeed have obligations of obedience to their respective leaders, the general public must employ private judgment to decide which if any faction to obey, issuing in widespread *de facto* private judgment, and interference with people's pursuit of their life plans.

As surprising as this may sound, even under certain forms of political society, a state of nature may continue to obtain, just to the degree that those forms invite the use of private judgment. If the essential rights of sovereignty are limited,[23] private judgment will be required to determine whether the limits have been overstepped. Some other body could be designated to decide that issue, but, Hobbes argues, that would be either to seat unlimited sovereignty in that other body (otherwise we get a useless regress of limited bodies), or else to divide the essential rights of sovereignty. But if the essential rights of sovereignty are divided, and those who possess them disagree on the policy to be pursued, the prospect of a stalemate paralyzing effective

[22] Hobbes thinks this is of all empirically realizable states of nature the one that ascribes a right of unlimited private judgment to the largest number of individuals. Because children owe obligations of obedience to those who sustain them (usually their parents), a state of perfectly universal individual private judgment can be conceived only by considering men, counterfactually, as if they had "sprung up like mushrooms" full grown, without any obligations of obedience to anyone. I elaborate this argument in the following chapter.

[23] The essential rights of sovereignty are those without which a government cannot effectively perform its function (under the Law of Nature) of securing domestic peace and national defense. They include rights of legislation, adjudication of disputes, enforcement of decisions, taxation and the right to wage war. See *Leviathan,* chapter 18.

government, or of a civil war to resolve the issues, requires again ordinary citizens to exercise private judgment in deciding which, if either, of the contenders to obey, or whether to fend for themselves in the face of a paralysis of effective government.[24] Divided and limited forms of government institutionalize avenues for the exercise of private judgment, and thus effect an incomplete removal from the state of nature, with all of its uncertainties and obstacles to the effective pursuit of our ends. They are, of course, usually much better than the condition of mere nature because in them there are many fewer agents entitled to exercise private judgment that may interfere with the agency of the rest, and whether such forms will or will not become practically problematic depends upon empirical variables such as the range and frequency of policy disagreements; it is certainly not Hobbes's view that states in which sovereignty is divided or limited in any way *necessarily* collapse into civil war or the condition of mere nature. But once we understand the argument from effective agency for restricting the scope of private judgment, we will see that *the degree of restriction of private judgment that provides subjects with maximum scope for pursuit of their ends will coincide with a system of unified sovereignty, properly exercised.*

Perhaps more surprising still, the very reasons we have for deciding to escape the condition of mere nature will motivate us to resist subjection to a totalitarian state. What is problematic about a condition of unbridled universal private judgment is that it largely negates our powers of agency, because so many others can be expected to deprive us of needed resources, throw up obstacles to our plans, attempt to harness us to theirs, and so on. But so too may the constraints of a totalitarian state void our powers of agency, in which case a totalitarian state will be objectionable for the same reason. In chapter 21 of *Leviathan,* Hobbes expresses a plausible skepticism that any state, however oppressive, could *entirely* void subjects' liberty to do what they have the will and capacity to do:

> [S]eeing there is no commonwealth in the world, wherein there be rules enough set down, for the regulating of all the actions, and words of men; as being a thing impossible: it followeth necessarily, that in all kinds of actions

[24] These arguments are developed in more detail in *IAI,* chapter 2.

by the laws, praetermitted, men have the liberty, of doing what their own reasons shall suggest, for the most profitable to themselves.... In cases where the sovereign has prescribed no rule, there the subject hath the liberty to do, or forbear, according to his own discretion. And therefore such liberty is in some places more, and in some less; and in some times more, in other times less, according as they that have the sovereignty shall think most convenient.[25]

Hobbes also opines, in chapter 18 of *Leviathan,* that under any form of government the greatest inconvenience that "can possibly happen to the people *in general,* is scarce sensible, in respect of the miseries, and horrible calamities, that accompany a civil war, or that dissolute condition of masterless men" in a condition of mere nature.[26] But these are factual, not conceptual, claims. Whether or not Hobbes is correct to be confident that no state could possibly regulate all our actions, or make people in general more miserable than they would be in a condition of lawless conflict, it is clear that, according to Hobbes's theory, as a state increasingly encroaches upon the realm within which subjects can pursue their ends, the advantage of civil society over the various states of nature correspondingly diminishes. If, *pace* Hobbes's sunny empirical claims, the state's interference with subjects' pursuit of their ends *did* rival the degree of interference of the condition of mere nature, we would expect Hobbesian rational agents not only to be increasingly indifferent as between those two conditions, but – most importantly – increasingly motivated to risk rebellion (to "reshuffle the deck", as Hobbes says) in hopes of increasing their scope of effective agency by establishing a better government. This is a fact about the way men are actually motivated on the assumptions of Hobbesian psychology.[27]

Of course, Hobbes denies that subjects have any *right* to rebel against even an oppressive government, so long as it is effective in securing domestic peace and national defense, a view that will attract our critical scrutiny later on. And Hobbes insists that subjects are to defer to the judgment of their sovereign as to the propriety of its exercises of power. Here I am simply noting that as the difference

[25] EW III, 199 and 206; T 147 and 152.
[26] EW III, 170, emphasis added; T 128.
[27] That psychology is the subject of Chapter 2.

in what matters to us (namely, being able to act effectively to serve our ends) between the condition of mere nature and civil society collapses, so too does our motivation to yield civil obedience, as Hobbes recognizes. Because our motive, as rational agents, in transferring a portion of our right of private judgment to the public is to increase the effectiveness of our agency, we have no reason to transfer more to the public than is optimal for securing that end, and will indeed, if we are rational, resist pressures to do so. It is in this way that Hobbes sets the proper exercise of sovereign power, and the desirable range of subjects' rights, much closer to what we judge to be proper than to the authoritarian extreme generally attributed to Hobbes. We'll see concretely the limits of these powers in a moment, when we consider what reciprocity tells us about the duties of sovereigns.

The present suggestion is that the state of nature is a continuum notion that lies in a segment along a larger continuum of the scope of private judgment, as does the continuum notion of civil authority. Imagine a line, the leftmost point of which represents the condition of universal private judgment over all issues (the condition of mere nature), and the rightmost point of which represents the condition of entirely singular private judgment, in which a single person[28] judges every issue for all subjects (the perfectly totalitarian sovereign). As we move from left to right we diminish the scope of private judgment, by constricting either the number of individuals who may exercise it, or the range of issues over which it is exercised, or both. From its origin we move to savage government by small families, to tribal or feudal systems, to civil wars, to political systems of divided and/or limited government, until we arrive at the Archimedean point of Hobbes's adequately authorized and properly operating sovereign.[29]

[28] This need not be a natural person, or a single-member artificial person, e.g., a monarch. An artificial person such as a sovereign assembly would do just as well. On persons, see *Leviathan,* chapter 16.

[29] Notice that while heads of households or lords may enjoy "absolute" power over their own subjects, the fact that they may find themselves in irresoluble contention with so many other heads of households and lords makes savage and tribal or feudal *systems* kinds of states of nature. Of course, if any parent or lord heads an operation so strong that it and its members cannot be credibly threatened by outsiders, he or she would then count as the sovereign of a small commonwealth, and not part of any savage or feudal system. Although Hobbes *defines* a sovereign as an entity that possesses all the essential rights of sovereignty, he is fully aware that

We then continue rightward to invasive regimes, oppressive regimes, and totalitarian regimes according to the degree and extent to which private judgment is disallowed in ways unnecessary for securing the public good, manifesting an improper exercise of sovereignty. It is sometimes suggested that Hobbes's political ideal lies at the furthermost right-hand point. But that makes no sense, once we see why Hobbesian men care to move from left to right along this continuum. The purpose of the exercise is to determine the point at which each may best expect to make effective his agency, that is, to achieve his ends, considering the same desire in others. This optimal point turns out to be what defines the proper exercise of sovereign authority in a well-run commonwealth, according to Hobbes. As sovereigns exceed this use of authority, and encroach on the domain of what Hobbes terms "harmless liberty", they take up points on the continuum that collapse the rational preference for government over anarchy. At the limit the perfectly totalitarian state – could there be such a thing – has no meaningful advantage over the condition of mere nature, because both must be equally abhorred by any who care to make their agency effective, as all rational persons must, according to Hobbes.[30] As the improper exercise of political authority increasingly nullifies individual agency, what we were thinking of as a line bends in on itself, so that the condition of mere nature and the condition under the perfectly totalitarian sovereign become contiguous points on the circle with respect to the expanse allowed for effective exercises of our agency. For Hobbes's theory of sovereignty to provide a solution to the problem of constraining mutual interference, the political

many governments that have existed have not met the conditions for sovereignty, and have consequently failed (EW III, 195; T 145). See also his discussion of "mixt government" in *Leviathan* chapter 29, EW III, 318; T 288, and those governments that do not enjoy absolute power (EW III, 309; T 222). Cf. *Elements of Law,* part 2, chapter 1, paragraph 13.

30 This position is consistent with Hobbes's insistence that "the sovereign power…is as great as possibly men can be imagined to make it" and "the consequences of the want of it…are much worse" (EW III, 194–195; T 144–145.) Men are to construct the most powerful sovereign they possibly can, not to imagine that the sovereign is more powerful than they can possibly make it; because it is "a thing impossible" to construct a sovereign that can control every aspect of all subjects' lives, the strongest sovereign men can make will fall short of the perfectly totalitarian sovereign and still allow greater scope for agency than a condition of mere nature. How much more depends on whether that power is properly exercised.

ideal it recommends must stop far short of the sort of totalitarian authoritarianism that voids agency. It needs to stop the wheel with both anarchy and totalitarianism at the bottom, and the Hobbesian fully authorized and properly executing sovereign at the top. It can, in fact, do this; but seeing how requires a long argument, of which we are only at the beginning.

RECIPROCITY AND THE DUTY TO SUBMIT TO GOVERNMENT

To return to reciprocity, once Hobbes derives the necessary unacceptability to any rational agent of living in a condition in which everyone has a right to everything, the duty to quit that condition of universal private judgment (the state of nature) by submitting to political authority follows straightforwardly. If, as Hobbes argues, a condition of universal private judgment (such as reciprocity insists must be allowed if any are to be granted the Right of Nature) entails a condition in which everyone must be allowed a right to everything, rational agents must will the abridgment of that condition. Most desirable, from the point of view of the agent, would be to retain her own right of private judgment while requiring others to give up theirs. But reciprocity rules out any such asymmetrical solution. Instead, abridging a universal right to act according to private judgment will involve taking some questions out of the purview of private judgment for everyone, and submitting them to arbitration by a public judgment.[31] A sovereign/government/political authority is nothing more than the repository of public judgment, empowered to make that judgment effective in regulating conduct. Thus reason, making appeal to reciprocity, requires submission to government.

If reciprocity requires that all subjects equally submit their private judgments to an authoritative public judgment, why does it not require the same of sovereigns? The sovereign *is* the authoritative public judgment in a commonwealth. To say that reciprocity requires the sovereign to submit to public judgment is to say that it is required to submit

[31] An alternative way of abridging the universal Right of Nature would be to leave all questions within the purview of private judgment, but take some people's judgments out of consideration; but reciprocity rules out this asymmetric possibility.

to its own judgment, a requirement of no practical significance.[32] To require the sovereign to submit to any *other* judgment than its own would be to require, contrary to reciprocity, something of it that is not required of any subject, namely, that it submit to someone else's merely *private* judgment. As the source of authoritative public judgment on *all* questions, the sovereign must, as a conceptual matter, retain the right to judge questions concerning itself; and reciprocity licenses this because each party to the originating covenant would fault the others for refusing to join in the creation of a sovereign for their mutual benefit. Reciprocity also requires the sovereign to execute its functions (fulfill its sovereign role) in the way it would wish to see those functions executed were it subject to them, as we shall see in a moment. Reciprocity does not require that sovereigns be subjects (a conceptual incoherence on Hobbes's view) nor more generally that all persons take on the same roles and corresponding responsibilities.[33] But reciprocity may constrain how a sovereign by institution is selected: If we would fault others for insisting that their preference determine the choice of sovereign, then neither may we insist that our preference should determine the choice, but should instead select the sovereign through some mutually agreeable procedure (Hobbes suggests a vote of the majority).[34]

32 The sovereign has the authority to make or repeal any law, issue any decree or immunity, decide any controversy. As natural persons, the members of a sovereign assembly are subject to the laws passed by the majority in that assembly, but the sovereign assembly is not; and although as a natural person, a monarch could be said to be subject to the commands she issues as an artificial person (assuming she does not exempt herself from the scope of the legislation), the fact that she has authority to repeal the law, subsequently interpret it to exempt herself, or pardon herself for any violation of it, makes her subjection of no practical significance. The sovereign is, in this sense, above the civil law. However, none of this entails that a sovereign may not violate the natural law requirements of reciprocity in how it fashions laws, decrees, immunities, and pardons. These are subject to moral, although not legal, constraints.

33 How reciprocity applies to the differentiation of roles is discussed in Chapter 5.

34 "A *Common*-wealth is said to be *Instituted,* when a *Multitude* of men do Agree, and *Covenant, every one, with every one,* that to whatsoever *Man,* or *Assembly of Men,* shall be given by the major part, the *Right* to *Present* the person of them all... every one, as well he that *Voted for it,* as he that *Voted against it,* shall *Authorise* all the Actions and Judgements, of that man, or Assembly of men" (EW III, 159; T 121; cf. EW III, 162; T 123). See also Hobbes's remark in EW II, 74 (*Philosophical Rudiments* vi.2) that in a sovereign assembly the will of the majority is to be taken for the sovereign will.

HOW MUCH AUTHORITY MUST BE PUBLIC?

Were one to inhabit a state of nature and to think it blameworthy of others not to join oneself in submitting to government upon equal terms, reciprocity would require one to join with willing others in transferring to a public authority that portion of private judgment one thinks it must have in order to secure peace and defense, and be content with the same degree of residual liberty of private judgment one is willing to allow to others. This requirement is just Hobbes's second Law of Nature, "*that a man be willing, when others are so too, as far-forth, as for peace, and defense of himself he shall think it necessary, to lay down this right to all things; and be contented with so much liberty against other men, as he would allow other men against himself*".[35]

Still, if we renege on our authorization to a public arbitrator of the right to judge controversies whenever we dislike the outcome of that arbitration, or reserve a right to act on our own private judgment when the public arbitrator's decision goes against our interests or values, we void our prior transfer of the right of judgment. To act in this way sustains a condition of universal private judgment that only continues contention. For this reason we cannot be willing that others should retain the right to take back their private judgment, and so, reciprocity disallows us from reserving that right to ourselves. Thus, Hobbes derives his third Law of Nature: "From that law of Nature, by which we are obliged to transfer to another, such rights, as being retained, hinder the peace of mankind, there followeth a third [law of nature]; which is this, *that men perform their covenants made:* without which, covenants are in vain".[36]

For those of us already living under a government that is effective in protecting us, Hobbes can urge the duty of political obedience on the simple ground provided by reciprocity itself. If we cannot be willing that others should exempt themselves from obeying the authority who without obedience cannot secure the protection we enjoy, then under reciprocity, neither may we legitimately exempt ourselves from obedience. In general, to enjoy the benefits of our fellow subjects' obedience without ourselves obeying is contrary to the requirement

35 EW III, 118; T 92.
36 EW III, 130; T 100.

of reciprocity, which licenses only symmetrical behaviors, and never such asymmetrical arrangements as when some free-ride on the cooperation of others. The condition of mere nature, in which all are granted the right to be judge and jury over all matters, is one conceptual possibility under reciprocity; that all submit equally to a public judgment that supersedes the private judgment of each is another possibility under reciprocity. What is not possible under that theorem is the asymmetrical outcome that only some retain rights that they deny to others.[37]

RECIPROCITY AND THE TRUE LIBERTIES OF SUBJECTS

If what reciprocity requires us to give up is just the degree of private judgment that we would have others give up, and if what it permits us to retain is just the degree of freedom to act on our own private judgment that we are willing to grant to others as well, a series of applications of reciprocity will carve out the set of retained liberties Hobbes terms the true liberties of subjects. We must balance our desire that others should give up their liberty to act in ways that may undermine social order against our desire to retain a realm of blameless liberty in certain matters of crucial importance to us.

Hobbes supposes that in order to rule effectively, the state must have authority of life and death (subject only to the constraints of the Law of Nature) over subjects. On this supposition, although each of us would rather that the sovereign not have the right to kill us, our recognition that our safety depends on its possessing the right to kill others when it deems that necessary for public safety requires, under reciprocity, that we grant it authority of life and death over ourselves as well. The sovereign's use of this right is, of course, limited by reciprocity, for "they who thus kill men, although by right given them

[37] One may wonder whether it might not be at least narrowly rational to give up more than others if they demanded this as a condition of entering into a commonwealth, or to demand more sacrifice from others as a condition of one's own participation. Interpreters who wish to attribute to Hobbes a conception of reason that involves only narrow rationality and to square it with Hobbes's insistence on fully equal and reciprocal terms of submission to political authority will need to explore those questions. Such questions lose interest once reciprocity is seen to be an exceptionless constraint on action in accordance with reason. This point is elaborated in Chapter 5.

from him that hath it, yet if they use that right otherwise than right reason requires, they sin against the laws of nature, that is, against God".[38] But because effective rule does not require that anyone kill himself at the state's command (for it may kill him if it wishes), and because we may find ourselves unable to force ourselves to obey such a command, we would judge it unreasonable to blame us for refusing such a command. And if we would judge it unreasonable for others to fault us for refusing to kill ourselves on command, then neither may we fault others for refusing to do so. But actions or refusals to act for which no one can reasonably be faulted comprise the true liberty of a subject, that is, "what are those things, which though commanded by the sovereign, he may nevertheless, without injustice, refuse to do". Thus, it belongs to the true liberty of a subject to refuse "to kill, wound, or maim himself; or not to resist those that assault him; or to abstain from the use of food, air, medicine, or any other thing, without which he cannot live; [and even though commanded] yet hath that man the liberty to disobey".[39] Hobbes further asserts that one has the liberty to refuse to do any dishonorable action – such as executing his own father – so long as others can perform that action just as well without dishonor, a position easily explained by appeal to reciprocity. For it would be unreasonable to fault a man for failing to do something so extraordinary that is not necessary for the society's security that he personally do it, and that, in any case, he cannot reasonably be relied upon to be able to bring himself to do.[40]

[38] EW II, 83; *De Cive* 6.13.

[39] EW III, 204; T 151.

[40] In *Bethemoth* Hobbes considers whether a subject must obey the king's command that he with his own hands execute his judicially condemned father, and concludes that he need do so only if the command takes the form of a *general law* published prior to the condemnation of one's father, *and* one has elected to remain in the kingdom after the publication of that law. Evidently Hobbes thinks it would be unreasonable to fault one for refusing to obey a merely personal order to execute one's father, or even a general law requiring that, unless one had had the chance to depart the kingdom before the issue arose in his own case. (Although, of course, he is liable to punishment if he refuses to obey.) If we suppose that to remain in the kingdom is to warrant that one would be able to bring oneself to execute one's judicially condemned father if called upon to do so, it then would be reasonable to fault such a person for refusing to do so in the event, explaining why he then has no liberty to refuse. This position is analogous to Hobbes's view that we may fault those who enroll as soldiers for running from battle even though we would usually excuse such conduct in others, for

Hobbes's mention of dishonorable actions raises the issue of transcendent interests, those interests in pursuit of which a person is willing to risk or even to sacrifice her life. In general, Hobbes argues, it is unreasonable to fault any person for refusing to do what he would rather die than do, at least when the state is granted authority to kill the disobedient, and the job is either unnecessary for the survival of the commonwealth, or others may be found who can do it. "[T]he command may be such", writes Hobbes, "as I would rather die than do it"; and "as no man can be bound to will being killed, much less is he tied to that which to him is worse than death".[41] Under reciprocity, our judgment that when the state can secure the public good without our compliance and may punish our disobedience, it is unreasonable to fault us for refusing to obey commands to do things that we would rather die than do, requires we grant this same immunity to others. A liberty even against the sovereign's command that none can be faulted for exercising is a "true" liberty.

Subjects enjoy other liberties that do not rise to the level of "true" liberties as defined here. Hobbes rightly points out that the vast majority of subjects' liberties are those granted by the silence of the law, such as the extensive liberties that may be left to us to decide on our own occupation, diet, hairstyle, place of residence, marital status, and recreations, within limits. These harmless liberties are again justified by reciprocity, for how could it be reasonable to fault us for engaging in those harmless activities the law allows? And if we are not to be faulted, then neither may we fault others, and all are to be granted the liberty to engage in such activities. To act according to our own private judgment across the range of activities immaterial to maintaining social order as these are determined by law is a liberty we would judge it unreasonable to be faulted for retaining, and so reciprocity grants this liberty to all.

presumably those who enlist in the military are warranting that they will remain sturdy in the face of mortal threats. Thus, his view here on executing one's father is a refinement, rather than a retraction, of his principled stance in *Leviathan*. See EW, VI, 227; *Behemoth*, part I. Further, even when the command falls under preexisting legislation, if the subject regards executing his father as a fate worse than death, it will also be unreasonable to fault him for refusing to comply, as I explain in the following paragraph.

41 EW II, 82; *De Cive* 6.13. Cf. EW II, 83; *De Cive* 6.13.

Even Hobbes's distinction between obligation *in foro interno* and *in foro externo* is explicable by appeal to Hobbes's reciprocity theorem. Hobbes maintains that we are required to observe the Laws of Nature in our actions (as opposed to merely in conscience) only toward those who are not harming us by their failure to do so. This passage is usually interpreted in line with a thin egoistic psychology as claiming that we need observe the Laws of Nature only when it is not dangerous, and is profitable to us, to do so. But that is not Hobbes's position. He writes,

> These laws of nature...in case they should be observed by some, and not by others, would make the observers but a prey to them that should neglect them, leaving the good both without defence against the wicked, and also with a charge to assist them.... Reason therefore, and the law of nature over and above all these particular laws, doth dictate this law in general, *That those particular laws be so far observed, as they subject us not to any incommodity, that in our own judgments may arise, by the neglect thereof in those towards whom we observe them.*[42]

If others neglect to observe particular laws toward us, then we need observe those laws toward them only to the extent that we do not believe our unilateral observance will harm ourselves. This is a far cry from being told we may treat others as they in fact treat us, or that we need not follow the Laws of Nature whenever doing so would disadvantage us. I understand Hobbes to be saying that we are to observe the Laws of Nature toward those who observe them toward us, even should it disadvantage us to do so. And we are to observe the Laws of Nature, even toward those who do *not* observe them toward us, the only exception being in those particular cases in which we judge our doing so harmful to ourselves. This exception is justified by reciprocity: Because it would be unreasonable to fault us for refusing to assist the wicked in harming us (that is, because we would fault others for faulting us for refusing to aid the wicked in harming us), all must be granted the right to withhold such aid from the wicked in those circumstances. When we do not judge that any incommodity to us will arise from observing these laws toward those who do not themselves observe them, we are bound to act in

[42] EW IV, 107–108; *Elements of Law* I.4.10.

accordance with them still.[43] Hobbes is thus not espousing Kavka's "Copper Rule" that one treat others as they treat oneself, but rather the more robust rule that one refrain from actions one would disapprove in others.[44]

Why does Hobbes not grant everyone the right to flout the Laws of Nature toward any who have failed to observe them toward any other person? Perhaps he thinks that we would judge it unreasonable for those whom we have never harmed, to place us beyond the pale of moral consideration (as they do by refusing to observe the Laws of Nature toward us), on hearsay evidence from others who allege that we have violated the Laws of Nature against themselves or others. Those accusers may be mistaken, or lying. Such an attitude does seem unreasonable. And Hobbes may well be right to hold that the mere fact that others act wrongly gives one no permission to act wrongly oneself (two wrongs don't make a right), except when acting better than those others would aid them in victimizing oneself.

WHO IS THE LEGITIMATE RULER?

In an artful twist, Hobbes holds that the legitimate ruler for a person is the ruler he would fault his fellow subjects for failing to obey. Hobbes's argument in his *Elements of Law* that "to whose dominion we require our fellow subjects to yield obedience for our good, his

[43] This position is compatible with Hobbes's claim in *Leviathan* that in the imaginary extreme case in which "*no man else*" is "modest and tractable, and perform[s] all he promises", a person who observed the requirements of the Law of Nature toward those ne'er-do-wells would be doing nothing but making himself "a prey to others", that is, assisting the wicked – since they are *all* wicked because failing to observe any of the Laws of Nature toward himself – in harming himself by their injustice, iniquity, intractability, and so on (EW III, 145; T 110).

[44] This is the traditional Golden Rule, which Hobbes asserts captures his Laws of Nature, stated negatively. George Shelton recognized the centrality of the Golden Rule to Hobbes's theory in his *Morality and Sovereignty in the Philosophy of Hobbes* (New York, 1992). There he writes, "As Hobbes's references to the golden rule indicate, his second Law of Nature is a version of that rule which, in essence, is the principle of reciprocity. The formation of any human group requires an understanding on this basis. It is the key to society and the key to Hobbesian political theory" (49; cf. 75). Although I agree with Shelton that reciprocity is at the center of Hobbes's moral theory, I do not agree that the particular moral theory in which Shelton centrally locates reciprocity was actually Hobbes's, for reasons discussed in Chapters 4 and 5.

dominion we acknowledge to be legitimate by that very request"[45] appeals implicitly to reciprocity, for his conclusion would not follow unless we assume that we must, as Hobbes has insisted, do what we require of others. Hobbes offers an almost caricaturist application of reciprocity in his insistence in *De Homine* that because we would not approve of disobedience in subjects were we sovereign, we as subjects must not disobey our sovereign:

> God himself, because He hath made men rational, hath enjoined the following law on them, and inscribed it in all hearts: that no one should do unto another that which he would consider inequitable for the other to do unto him. In this precept are contained both universal justice and civil obedience. For who would not judge it inequitable, if he were constituted by the people with the highest sovereignty in the state, in order to rule and to issue laws, for his laws to be spurned, or his authority overlooked, not to mention disputed, by any subject whatsoever? Therefore, if, when you were a king, you judged this to be inequitable, would you not have, in law, a most certain rule for your actions?[46]

This argument provides one suggestion for how Hobbes understood the Law of Nature to dictate civil obedience. Here Hobbes derives the requirement of obedience directly from reciprocity using his role-changing test, without mediation of any other Laws of Nature such as the precepts directing covenant-keeping or peace-seeking. He says explicitly of equity, which is an articulation of reciprocity, that "in this precept are *contained* both universal justice and civil obedience". We consider a more attractive derivation of the requirement of civil disobedience from reciprocity in Chapter 5.

RECIPROCITY AND THE DUTIES OF SOVEREIGNS TOWARD SUBJECTS

Once having established reciprocity as a requirement of reason, and so as a Law of Nature, Hobbes can use it to delimit the justifiable actions of governments. The Law of Nature requires sovereigns to advance, to the best of their abilities, the welfare of the people who

[45] EW II, 192; *De Cive* 14.12.

[46] Bernard Gert, ed., *Man and Citizen: Thomas Hobbes* (Indianapolis, 1991), 73.

have reposed trust in them. This theorem unequivocally requires that any sovereign pursue the good of its subject people:

THE OFFICE of the sovereign, be it a monarch or an assembly, consisteth in the end, for which he was trusted with the sovereign power, namely the procuration of *the safety of the people;* to which he is obliged by the law of nature, and to render an account thereof to God, the author of that law, and to none but him. But by safety here, is not meant a bare preservation, but also all other contentments of life, which every man by lawful industry, without danger, or hurt to the commonwealth, shall acquire to himself.[47]

Now all the duties of rulers are contained in this one sentence, *the safety of the people is the supreme law*.... [It is] their *duty* in all things, as much as possibly they can, to yield obedience unto right reason, which is natural, moral, and divine law. But because dominions were constituted for peace's sake, and peace was sought after for safety's sake; he, who being placed in authority, shall use his power otherwise than to the safety of the people, will act against... the laws of nature.... [H]e hath fully *discharged* himself, if he have thoroughly endeavoured by wholesome constitutions to establish the welfare of the most part, and made it as lasting as may be; and that no man suffer ill, but by his own default, or by some chance which could not be prevented.... But by *safety* must be understood, not the sole preservation of life in what condition soever, but in order to its happiness.[48]

Sovereigns are to pursue the good of their subjects. What constitutes that good? According to reciprocity, no sovereign may rightly – that is, justifiably, in accordance with right reason – rule in a way that he would fault, were he subject to that same sort of rule, as unreasonable given the ends he would have had in submitting himself to government. Understanding the contours of rightful rule thus requires reflection on the ends for which subjects wish to see government imposed on their fellows, and so (by reciprocity) the sovereign's adoption of ruling policies that promote rather than frustrate those same ends. This has some very interesting implications for how much

47 EW III, 322; T 231. Cf. EW IV, 213; *Elements of Law* II.9.1: "the duty of a sovereign consisteth in the good government of the people.... [W]hen [his acts] tend to the hurt of the people in general, they be breaches of the law of nature... and consequently, the contrary acts are the duties of sovereigns, and required at their hands to the utmost of their endeavour, by God Almighty, under pain of eternal death". See also EW IV, 214; *Elements of Law* II.9.1: "the general law for sovereigns, *That they procure, to the uttermost of their endeavour, the good of the people*"; and EW II, 168, 80–81 note, and 101–102; *De Cive* 13.4, 6.13, and 7.14.

48 EW II, 166–167; *De Cive* 13.2–4; cf. EW III, 335; T 239.

control sovereigns may properly exert over the lives of subjects, which I shall mention momentarily. But here we should consider the specific constraints Hobbes thinks his Law of Nature imposes on sovereigns in how they pursue the good of their subjects, as they consider various cases in the Law of Nature. Hobbes writes, "The benefits of subjects, respecting this life only, may be distributed into four kinds. 1. That they be defended against foreign enemies. 2. That peace be preserved at home. 3. That they be enriched, as much as may consist with public security. 4. That they enjoy a harmless liberty".[49] We can see by this passage that the sovereign has several distinct duties. What direction does the Law of Nature give us in determining how they are to be fulfilled? Let us take them in turn.

National Defense

"God made Kings for the people", and because the king "is to answer to God Almighty for the safety of the people", he "to that end is intrusted with the power to levy and dispose of the soldiery".[50] With respect to the first duty of national defense, Hobbes holds that it is obligatory for the sovereign to provide for both spies and armies, in order to be both forewarned and forearmed:

> [P]rinces are, by the law of nature, bound to use their whole endeavour in procuring the welfare of their subjects: it follows, that it is not only lawful for them to send out spies, to maintain soldiers, [etc.]; but also not to do thus is unlawful....For rulers are bound according to their power to prevent the evils they suspect.[51]

Reciprocity easily explains this duty. It is plausible that had he been a subject, the prince would reasonably have faulted his ruler for not doing everything possible to prevent anticipated evils, and so is, by application of reciprocity, himself bound to pursue the safer course.

Further, the Law of Nature imposes on the sovereign a duty to avoid unnecessary wars, for war is dangerous and costly, and so not

49 EW II, 169; *De Cive* 13.6.
50 EW VI, 13–14.
51 EW II, 171; *De Cive* 13.8.

to be undertaken unless it significantly serves at least one of the four components of *salus populi* enumerated earlier. Hobbes writes,

> [C]ontained in that supreme law, *salus populi*, is their defense; and consisteth partly in . . . the avoiding of unnecessary wars. For such commonwealths, or such monarchs, as affect war for itself, that is to say, out of ambition, or of vain-glory, or that make account to revenge every little injury, or disgrace done by their neighbours, if they ruin not themselves, their fortune must be better than they have reason to expect.[52]

Wars conducted from any motive other than the procuring of one of the proper ends of government are morally suspect. It is worth noting that wars to improve other peoples, when their improvement is not necessary for our defense, will be morally impermissible just insofar as we would think it unreasonable of them to wage war on our state in order to improve us.

Domestic Peace

With respect to the requirement of securing domestic peace, the Law of Nature requires fair adjudication of disputes, proper practices of punishment, and the fair distribution of public burdens. First, sovereigns must judge contested cases fairly and impartially, and they must be sure all their appointed subfunctionaries do so as well, and set up special panels to review complaints against those appointees. Hobbes writes,

> The law of nature therefore gives this precept to supreme commanders, that they not only do righteousness themselves, but that they also by penalties cause the judges, by them appointed, to do the same; that is to say, that they hearken to the complaints of their subjects; and as oft as need requires, make choice of some extraordinary judges, who may hear the matter debated concerning the ordinary ones.[53]

Partiality is also to be rooted out, for the sovereign, considering "the trust reposed in him, and for the equality which the law of nature

[52] EW IV, 219–220; *Elements of Law* II.9.9. As we'll see in Chapter 7, the fault of Hobbes's infamously unjust "Foole" is partly that he counts on fortune better than he has reason to expect.

[53] EW II, 181; *De Cive* 13.17.

requireth him to consider in the parties, he violateth that law, if for favour, or hatred to either party, he give other sentence than he thinketh right".[54] If the sovereign finds that a judge has, through ignorance or corruption damaged a subject, he must, under the Law of Nature requiring equity, provide a remedy to the injured subject.[55]

In addition to fair adjudication of disputes, the Law of Nature requires an equitable practice of punishment, and, Hobbes insists, one that is forward looking rather than merely vengeful: "[T]he law of nature commands... supreme commanders, that in taking revenge and punishing they must not so much regard the past evil as the future good; and they sin, if they entertain any other measure in arbitrary punishment than the public benefit".[56]

Because no good can come to the commonwealth from punishing the innocent, this seventh Law of Nature forbids punishing the innocent, as does the fourth Law of Nature forbidding ingratitude or the returning of evil for good, and the eleventh requiring equity, or the equal distribution of justice.[57] "Natural equity", writes Hobbes,

[54] EW IV, 106; *Elements of Law* I.4.7.

[55] EW VI, 26.

[56] EW II, 179; *De Cive* 13.16. In Leviathan this constraint on civil punishments is articulated in Hobbes's seventh Law of Nature requiring "*that in revenges,* that is, retribution of evil for evil, *men look not at the greatness of the evil past, but the greatness of the good to follow*.... For this law is consequent to the next before it, that commandeth pardon, upon security of the future time. Besides, revenge without respect to the example, and profit to come, is a triumph, or glorying in the hurt of another, tending to no end;... and glorying to no end, is vain-glory, and contrary to reason, and to hurt without reason, tendeth to the introduction of war; which is against the law of nature; and is commonly styled by the name of *cruelty*" (EW III, 140; T 106–107). From this law it would follow that a civil sovereign should exercise mercy and the power of pardon when he can do so without harm to the commonwealth.

[57] EW III, 304; T 219. One might doubt the claim that no good can come from punishing the innocent. Hobbes's sovereign is authorized to inflict whatever harms on individuals he sincerely deems necessary for the public good, whether they fall under judicial punishment or not; such harms while injuries are not injustices. However, Hobbes is not willing to include such inflictions of harms on known innocents for the greater good within the practice of punishment. A punishment practice that did include such inflictions – Rawls termed such a system "telishment" – would undermine public confidence in the justice of punishment, decrease its deterrent effects and undermine its capacity to function as a price system, and increase fear, uncertainty, and feelings of victimization. In addition to these bad effects of a system of telishment, such a system would violate the constraints of equity, gratitude, and avoidance of cruelty imposed by the Law of Nature. For these reasons Hobbes rejects a system of justice that would permit punishment of

"commands that equal transgressions be equally punished".[58] The Law of Nature forbids the sovereign to inflict greater punishments than are prescribed by the laws, or punishments for actions that were not illegal at the time they were performed, or to inflict punishment upon any who have not been first been found guilty in a court of law.[59] We can see reciprocity at work in the background of Hobbes's explanation of the wrongness of punishing more severely than the law advertises:

> [T]he end of punishment is not to compel the will of man, but to fashion it, and to make it such as he would have it who hath set the penalty.... If therefore the legislator doth set a less penalty on a crime, than will make our fear more considerable with us than our lust, that excess of lust above the fear of punishment, whereby sin is committed, is to be attributed to the legislator, that is to say, to the supreme; and therefore if he inflict a greater punishment than himself hath determined in his laws, *he punisheth that in another in which he sinned himself*.[60]

Just as the sovereign would fault others if they punished him for their own sins (who wouldn't fault such unfair behavior?), reciprocity prohibits him from acting in that manner, and so punishments should be administered no more severely than advertised.

Another element of good government for domestic peace is the fair distribution of public burdens. Equity requires that those who benefit equally should equally share the burdens of producing that benefit, and no one should be burdened beyond bearing. This has implications for the structure and form of taxation. Hobbes writes,

> To remove therefore all just complaint, it is the interest of the public quiet, and by consequence it concerns the duty of the magistrate, to see that the public burthens be equally borne.... Now it is the law of nature... that every man in distributing right to others, do carry himself equal to all. Wherefore

the innocent, even though there might be particular cases in which good could come from inflicting "punishment" on an innocent whom the state intentionally misrepresented as guilty. For a discussion of telishment and the distinction between the justification of a practice and the justification of an action falling under a practice, see John Rawls, "Two Concepts of Rules", *Philosophical Review* 64 (1955): 3–32.

58 EW II, 180; *De Cive* 13.16.

59 EW III, 298–300; T 214–216.

60 EW II, 180, emphasis added; *De Cive* 13.16.

rulers are, by the natural law, obliged to lay the burthens of the commonweal equally on their subjects.[61]

Hobbes argues that the requisite equity prescribed by the Law of Nature requires taxation on consumption rather than on earnings,[62] and that taxation be strictly proportional to benefit.[63] Furthermore, taxes should be kept as low as is compatible with the sovereign's fulfilling his duties under the Law of Nature.[64]

Prosperity

Sovereigns, Hobbes writes, "would sin against the law of nature, (because against their trust, who had committed that power unto them), if they should not study, as much as by good laws could be effected, to furnish their subjects abundantly, not only with the good things belonging to life, but also with those which advance to delectation".[65] Limiting taxation to the smallest amount needed to secure the public good contributes to domestic peace by limiting the discontent of subjects aggrieved to part with their goods, for "great exactions, though the right thereof be acknowledged, have caused great seditions".[66] But appropriate taxation is also a part of the sovereign's duty to promote

[61] EW II, 173; *De Cive* 13.10.
[62] EW II, 173–174; *De Cive* 13.11; EW IV, 216; *Elements of Law* II.9.5.
[63] Hobbes writes at EW IV, 216–217; *Elements of Law* II.9.5: "there is a *proportionably* to every man's ability, and there is a *proportionably* to his benefit by commonwealth: and this latter is it, which is according to the law of nature. For the burdens of the commonwealth being the price that we pay for the benefit thereof, they ought to be measured thereby. And there is no reason, when two men equally enjoying, by the benefit of the commonwealth, their peace and liberty, to use their industry to get their livings, whereof one spareth, and layeth up somewhat, the other spendeth all he gets, why they should not equally contribute to the common charge. That seemeth therefore to be the most equal way of dividing the burden of public charge, when every man shall contribute according to what he spendeth, and not according to what he gets. And this is then done, when men pay the commonwealth's part in the payments they make for their own provision". Less important for our purposes than whether Hobbes was right about the most equitable form of taxation is to recognize that for Hobbes, the determination of correct tax policy requires prosecution of a case in the Law of Nature – an application of the Law of Nature to a set of empirical assumptions.
[64] EW IV, 201; *Elements of Law* II.8.2.
[65] EW II, 168; *De Cive* 13.4.
[66] EW IV, 201; *Elements of Law* II.8.2.

prosperity and subjects' enrichment, the third of his four kinds of benefits to subjects of their submission to government. Some tax revenues should be used to provide a social safety net that provides work for those who are able to work, and support for those who are not able to work; for to leave men to the hazard of uncertain private charity is contrary to the duty of a sovereign under the Law of Nature.[67] Public policy must encourage not just labor by public employment and laws against idleness,[68] but also thrift, by forbidding superfluous consumption, by good trade regulation, and by supporting the useful arts and sciences, such as farming, fishing, navigation, mechanics, and the mathematical sciences.[69]

Interestingly, Hobbes insists that increasing wealth by preying on other nations "is not to be brought into rule and fashion".[70] This conclusion may be the result of a direct but implicit application of reciprocity, for surely we would fault other nations that can provide for their own needs through industry and thrift to elect instead to sack our own, and so are forbidden by the Law of Nature so to behave ourselves. Suspicion that reciprocity is at work here is reinforced by Hobbes's striking position that if population pressures compel it to colonize foreign territories, the sovereign must, under the Law of Nature, restrain colonial settlements so that they do not extinguish native populations or deprive them of their means of preservation, even if it could gain by doing so.[71]

Liberty

Although legislation is necessary to secure domestic peace, I have not discussed earlier what the Law of Nature requires of the sovereign in the general exercise of legislative authority, because that issue cannot be treated separately from a discussion of the proper scope of subjects' liberty under the Law of Nature. In legislating, "to leave man as much liberty as may be, &c. is the duty of a sovereign by the law of nature".[72]

[67] EW III, 334; T 239.
[68] EW II, 177; *De Cive* 13.14.
[69] EW II, 177–178; *De Cive* 13.14; EW IV, 215; *Elements of Law* II.9.4.
[70] EW II, 177; *De Cive* 13.14.
[71] EW III, 335; T 239. I discuss this case at greater length in Chapter 3.
[72] EW IV, 215, marginal summary; *Elements of Law* II.9.4.

But how much liberty is that? It turns out to be the largest amount of liberty compatible with the maintenance of peace, "nor doth the law of nature command any divesting of other rights, than of those only which cannot be retained without the loss of peace".[73] We saw that because a condition of unrestricted private liberty (the universal liberty to act on private judgment) in fact impedes the effective exercise of our agency as we cross purposes and thwart one another's plans, justle and hew, we must, as rational agents, will its abridgment. But by reciprocity, we must accept the same degree of abridgment of our own liberty that we would fault others for refusing to cede together with us. Each of us must judge it unreasonable of others to refuse to cede all those liberties whose retention is inimical to peace, understood as an ordered condition that makes effective agency generally possible; but at the same time each of us must also think it unreasonable of others to fault us for refusing to accept greater limitations on our liberty than are necessary for peace, because, after all, we value peace instrumentally, for the sake of more effectively pursuing our ends. Because our interest is precisely in obtaining the conditions best suited for facilitating our agency in pursuit of whatever our ends may be, we can have no reason to prefer a condition in which all our actions are constrained by the state with nothing left to our own private judgment to the anarchic condition of mutual interference created by universal private judgment. Neither of these is desirable from our perspective as rational agents. The point of balance between these competing judgments of reasonableness should mark out the domains of proper legislation (that which accords with reason) and harmless liberty, and this is what we see.[74] Hobbes writes,

> [L]aws were not invented to take away, but to direct men's actions; even as nature ordained the banks, not to stay, but to guide the course of the stream.

[73] EW IV, 103–104; *Elements of Law* I.4.2.

[74] I'll be offering more extended arguments for this claim in Chapter 5, with supporting considerations offered in Chapter 2. It should be remembered that although every law the sovereign makes is legitimate (because subjects authorize all the sovereign does in his capacity as sovereign, hence no law can be "unjust"), not every law is proper. Laws that cross the duties of sovereigns as given by the natural law requiring reciprocity fail to accord with reason, and are thus improper. That is, such laws express an improper exercise of sovereign authority, which, if done willingly, is iniquity and an injury to God. Such transgressions are to be judged and punished only by God. These points are elaborated in the Chapter 6 discussion of Hobbes's *hierarchy of responsibility*.

The measure of this liberty is to be taken from the subjects' and the city's good. Wherefore, in the first place, it is against the charge of those who command and have the authority of making laws, that there should be more laws than necessarily serve for good of the magistrate and his subjects.... [S]upreme commanders are bound to preserve [harmless liberty] for their subjects by the laws of nature.[75]

And again in *Leviathan*,

A good law is that, which is *needful*, for the *good of the people*, and withal *perspicuous*....For the use of laws...is not to bind the people from all voluntary actions; but to direct and keep them in such a motion, as not to hurt themselves....And therefore a law that is not needful...is not good....Unnecessary laws are not good laws; but traps for money.[76]

Hobbes suggests that it is best that unless the reasons for prohibiting some activity are fairly intuitive, the civil law should not prohibit it because otherwise people would be prone to accidentally violating the laws through ignorance, as if "to entrap their harmless liberty", which, as we see in the earlier passage, sovereigns are required by the Law of Nature to preserve for their subjects.[77] In terms of reciprocity, we would judge it unreasonable to be faulted for failing to adhere to norms we could not know we were supposed to, because the law was neither discernible through an exercise of our reason, nor explicitly promulgated.

If legislation is confined to such fairly obvious restrictions on liberty, we should not expect greatly intrusive micromanagement of individuals' affairs. Hobbes evidently believes that subjects are not in any real danger of finding their liberty unreasonably constrained in civil society, not just because the Law of Nature forbids this, but also because

[S]eeing there is no commonwealth in the world, wherein there be rules enough set down, for the regulating of all the actions, and words of men; as

[75] EW II, 178–179; *De Cive* 13.15. Hobbes goes on to tie this liberty to the need for judicial integrity we noted earlier: "It pertains therefore to the harmless and necessary *liberty* of subjects, that every man may without fear enjoy the rights which are allowed him by the laws. For it is in vain to have *our own* distinguished by the laws from *another's,* if by wrong judgment, robbery, or theft, they may be again confounded. But it falls out so, that these do happen where judges are corrupted" (EW II, 180; *De Cive* 13.17).

[76] EW III, 335–336; T 239–240.

[77] EW II, 179; *De Cive* 13.15.

being a thing impossible: it followeth necessarily, that in all kinds of actions by the laws praetermitted, men have the liberty, of doing what their own reasons shall suggest, for the most profitable to themselves... such as is the liberty to buy, and sell, and otherwise contract with one another; to choose their own abode, their own diet, their own trade of life, and institute their children as they themselves think fit; and the like.[78]

This belief that it is impossible for governments to regulate all men's actions allows Hobbes to endorse the saying that "it is better to live where nothing is lawful, than where all things",[79] consistent with my earlier contention that as government control diminishes the scope for effective agency, the rational agent becomes increasingly indifferent as between that state and anarchy, the condition of mere nature, and becomes increasingly tempted to seek a change of government. Hobbes believed that total governmental control was *not* possible (nor is a condition in which *literally nothing* is lawful), but the total breakdown of governmental control *is* possible, and is not infrequently actual. Hobbes makes clear that the Laws of Nature justify only a limited sphere of proper governmental operation. I'll return to this point shortly.

Although no greater restriction on personal liberty than what is necessary for peace and order is licensed by Hobbes's Laws of Nature, there are some restrictions on personal liberty that he believes are necessary to that end. He argues for restrictions on sex and marriage, including laws against incest, so that sexual and marriage practices are not "prejudicial to the improvement of mankind"; to omit to legislate concerning such important matters as sex and marriage "is against the law of natural reason in him, that hath taken into his hands any portion of mankind to improve".[80] This stance on laws regulating sex and marriage seems to extend the idea of the public good in ways not prefigured in his discussion of the main modes of benefiting subjects.

He also argues that it is against the Law of Nature for princes to permit factions, which Hobbes characterizes as unions of subjects into pacts or leagues bound by covenants of obedience to some

78 EW III, 199; T 147–148.
79 EW IV, 233; *Of Liberty and Necessity* (Epistle to the Reader).
80 EW IV, 214–215; *Elements of Law* II.9.3.

authority other than the civil sovereign, without the sovereign's authorization. Members of such unions may have divided loyalties and conflicting obligations. This constraint on the freedom of subjects to form factions is necessary, for "those princes who permit factions, do as much as if they received an enemy within their walls: which is contrary to the subjects' safety, and therefore also against the law of nature".[81]

Doctrine and Religion

Hobbes insists that it also belongs to the sovereign's office of procuring the good of subjects that he regulates doctrine, primarily through education, and also public religion. Education in true doctrines is crucial to domestic stability because some erroneous doctrines provide a misguided pretext for rebellion, and "in the well-governing of opinions, consisteth the well-governing of men's actions, in order to their peace, and concord".[82] Hobbes asserts that the sovereign's job of procuring the good of the people "should be done... by a general providence, contained in *public instruction, both of doctrine, and example;* and in the making and executing of good laws, to which individual persons may apply their own cases".[83] Proper education is absolutely necessary if the sovereign is to fulfill his duty of securing the good of the people because "There are certain doctrines wherewith subjects being tainted, they verily believe that obedience may be refused to the city, *and that by right they may, nay ought, to oppose and fight against princes and dignities*".[84]

Hobbes lists as one of the three conditions necessary to motivate rebellion what he calls "pretense of right", by which he means the sense that one can give a principled moral or religious justification for one's rebellion.[85] Without pretense of right, even discontented men who think their rebellion might succeed will not attempt it (itself

[81] EW II, 176; *De Cive* 13.13. Cf. his discussion of irregular systems and private leagues in *Leviathan,* chapter 22.

[82] EW III, 164; T 124. Cf. Hobbes's discussion of "the poison of seditious doctrines" in *Leviathan,* chapter 20.

[83] EW III, 322–323, emphasis added; T 231.

[84] EW II, 79n; *De Cive* 6.11, emphasis added.

[85] EW IV, 200; *Elements of Law* II.8.1.

a surprising allegation that we will investigate in the next chapter).[86] The sorts of doctrines Hobbes thinks dangerous function in this role, and so he sees regulation of doctrine as essential to maintaining civil peace, as the sovereign is duty-bound under the Law of Nature to do. Because he thinks all of these destabilizing doctrines false, and demonstrably false by right reasoning, Hobbes is not in the least conflicted about requiring the sovereign to prohibit their being taught, and to teach true, stability reinforcing doctrines in their stead.[87] In *Leviathan* he writes,

> [I]t is annexed to the sovereignty, to be judge of what opinions and doctrines are averse, and what conducing to peace.... And though in matter of doctrine, nothing ought to be regarded but the truth; yet this is not repugnant to regulating the same by peace. For doctrine repugnant to peace, can no more be true, than peace and concord can be against the law of nature.... It belongeth therefore to him that hath the sovereign power, to be judge, or constitute all judges of opinions and doctrines, as a thing necessary to peace; thereby to prevent discord and civil war.[88]

It may seem that Hobbes is equivocating between conceptual repugnance and causal repugnance in his claim that doctrines repugnant to peace cannot be true. It would seem that whether a doctrine is true, and what it causes, must be altogether separate questions. In fact, because doctrines without normative implications are causally inert, the *only* kinds of doctrines that *can* be causally repugnant to peace are those that state or imply a normative demand or permission. If the doctrine states or implies a false normative demand or permission, then the doctrine is false. Once Hobbes has demonstrated the truth of the proposition that we ought to settle peace (i.e., that settling peace is required under the Law of Nature) he is entitled to the conclusion that any doctrine that has normative implications

86 This position can be made compatible with Hobbes's claim, quoted earlier, that "great exactions, though the right thereof be acknowledged, have caused great seditions" if we suppose that discontent with these large taxes causes subjects to find some justifying pretext for sedition *other than* a claim that the sovereign has no right to levy such taxes (e.g., that he is wrong to carry out the war for which they are being taxed).

87 We will critically examine Hobbes's system of education and its role within his political theory in Chapter 7.

88 EW III, 164–165; T 124–125.

inconsistent with that proposition is false. Hence doctrines causally repugnant to peace (on account of their normative implications) cannot be true. The sorts of doctrines Hobbes is alluding to are "seditious doctrines" such as those discussed in chapter 29 of *Leviathan,* "that every private man [may permissibly] judge of good and evill actions [even those falling under civil law]", and that "whatsoever a man does against his conscience is sinne". These doctrines have been interpreted to imply that subjects ought or may permissibly act on their own private judgment in defiance of public authority; but this implication contradicts an implication of the demonstrable truth that we ought to settle peace.

Religious contention is a most serious threat to domestic stability, and so it is the sovereign's duty to settle a public convention governing religious profession and practice, and make sure that religious doctrines are not interpreted in ways that make them antithetical to civil obedience, for "What", Hobbes asks, "can be more pernicious to any state, than that men should, by apprehension of everlasting torments, be deterred from obeying their princes, that is to say, the laws; or from being just?"[89] More than that, Hobbes argues, if we desire that our commonwealth should be of a religion, which requires that it observe a uniform public worship, reciprocity requires that we defer to the sovereign's judgment (as the public arbitrator of disputes) as to what form that public worship should take.[90] Quite apart from these practical considerations, Hobbes takes it to be a failure of sovereign duty not to do what the sovereign sincerely believes necessary for securing his subjects' eternal good. "Forasmuch", Hobbes writes, "as eternal is better than temporal good, it is evident, that they who are in sovereign authority, are by the law of nature obliged to further the establishing of all... they believe

[89] EW II, 155–156; *De Cive* 12.5.

[90] EW II, 222; *De Cive* 15.17: "subjects can transfer their right of judging the manner of God's worship, on him or them who have the sovereign power. Nay, they must do it; for else all manner of absurd opinions concerning the nature of God, and all ridiculous ceremonies which have been used by any nations, will be seen at once in the same city. Whence it will fall out, that every man will believe that all the rest do offer God an affront; so that it cannot be truly said of any, that he worships God; for no man worships God, that is to say, honours him outwardly, but he who doth those things, whereby he appears to others for to honour him". Cf. EW III, 355 (T 252–253), on public worship, and the discussion of it in *IAI,* 117–118.

the true way thereunto. For unless they do so, it cannot be said truly, that they have done the uttermost of their endeavour [for the good of the people]".[91] This is a bold claim, the defense of which requires appeal not only to Hobbes's Law of Nature but also to his argument for a hierarchy of responsibility linking subjects to sovereigns and sovereigns to God. I won't lay out this argument until Chapter 6, but note here the striking fact that Hobbes takes the duties imposed on sovereigns by the Law of Nature to extend as far as attempting to secure the prospects of their subjects in the afterlife. This explains the caveat in Hobbes's enumeration of the types of benefits to be provided to subjects in the passage with which we began, for you'll recall that there Hobbes remarked that these are the "benefits of subjects, *respecting this life only*".[92]

Provision for the Future Good

Finally, the Law of Nature requires that a sovereign provide for the continuing good of her subjects upon her death. The vicissitudes of fortune and uncertainties of this mortal life being what they are, we rightly fault those whose duty it is to ensure our security when they do not make provision for its continuation beyond their death. Hence the enduring appeal of such practices as procuring godparents, life insurance, and living trusts. Under the Law of Nature, a sovereign owes it to subjects to provide for their security beyond his death. One aspect of this requirement is the provision of an organized succession, for a sovereign "is bound by the *law of nature*... *of not returning evil for good,* prudently to provide that by his death the city suffer not a dissolution"[93] by establishing an effective mechanism for the seamless transfer of power from government to government. Here Hobbes mentions the duty of gratitude imposed by the fourth Law of Nature (itself derived using reciprocity), in an argument that relies implicitly on the assumption that subjects do good to their ruler by obeying her rule. But the same conclusion can be more directly derived from reciprocity by observing that had the sovereign been in the subject's

91 EW IV, 214; *Elements of Law* II.9.2.
92 EW II, 169, emphasis added; *De Cive* 13.6.
93 EW II, 103; *De Cive* 7.16.

place, he would have thought it blameworthy that his sovereign should have neglected to make such provision.

Many more details could be added to the emerging picture of the moral constraints on legitimate governmental law and policy imposed by Hobbes's reciprocity principle and the end of government it establishes, by considering more of these applications of reciprocity, which Hobbes calls "cases in the law of nature". I shall not do more than present this basic overview of the many implications for proper government Hobbes saw his reciprocity theorem to have, because my present aim is only to give a flavor for how Hobbes wields his reciprocity theorem. It is the pivot of his moral theory, from which he spins out much more elaborate and extensive moral casuistry than is generally recognized. However, I conjecture that were we to bring our own questions of appropriate legislation and policy to Hobbes's standard, successive applications of reciprocity would yield legal norms that were not in any great tension with our own moral intuitions and considered convictions of equity. Of course, the fact that Hobbes's theory rules out inequitable laws as improper provides no practical *guarantee* that actual sovereigns would never legislate iniquitously. No theory guarantees conformity with its own requirements, nor precludes corrupt, unjustifiable departures from its requirements. Still, Hobbes's reputation for having endorsed a tyrannical dictatorship not subject to any moral constraints is entirely undeserved, and results from confusing Hobbes's position on the scope of sovereign authority (unlimited) with his position on the moral limits on its proper exercise imposed by the Law of Nature (and judged and enforced only by God.) Those who oppose absolute monarchy think the king will "take all, spoil all, kill all.... Will he, to please one or some few, spoil all the rest? First, though by right... he may do it, yet he can not do it justly, that is, without breach of the natural laws and injury against God".[94] Hobbes's political theory

94 EW II, 80–81n; *De Cive* 6.13. Although Hobbes here uses the term 'justly', he probably means in accordance with the natural law requiring equity. In *Leviathan* he distinguishes 'injustice' – the not keeping of covenant – from 'iniquity' – violation of a fundamental natural law of fairness. Having made no covenant with subjects, sovereigns do no wrong by "unjustly" not keeping to any covenant with subjects not to take all, spoil all, and kill all. But they nonetheless do wrong in such taking, spoiling, and killing by acting iniquitously. However, if we assume that the

does not license iniquitous behavior in a sovereign, and, as we shall see, his psychological theory explains why those who behave iniquitously should expect to be overthrown, despite the moral prohibition on revolution.

RECIPROCITY AND CONSENSUAL OBLIGATIONS

The Laws of Nature in Hobbes's system are best understood as imposing upon us a set of natural duties, as distinct from obligations.[95] The Laws of Nature make a claim on all humans possessing normal powers of reason, regardless of whether they have consented to be bound by them or even acknowledged them. Our duty to refrain from cruelty, for instance, does not depend on our having previously agreed to do so. In contrast, obligations result from voluntary undertakings, such as covenants and promises, under certain circumstances. No voluntary undertaking in violation of natural law can create an obligation, nor can a new undertaking incompatible with a prior obligation create an obligation. But voluntary undertakings prohibited neither by natural law nor by existing obligations can create obligations, when background institutions providing for their enforcement are in place. In Hobbes's system, obligations are morally underwritten by the natural duty "that men perform their covenants made" (the third Law of Nature). And the third Law of Nature is itself underwritten by reciprocity, for our readiness to fault others for reneging on their

king has covenanted (say, through his baptism) to obey God's laws, he does violate that covenant in acting iniquitously, hence acting unjustly and with injury against God. In *A Dialogue Between A Philosopher & A Student Of The Common Laws of England* Hobbes's philosopher says "There may indeed in a statute-law, made by men, be found iniquity, but not injustice", explaining that "iniquity [is] the transgression of the law of reason", and that "the King is not bound to any other law but that of equity" (EW VI, 25–26). Cf. EW II, 102 (*De Cive* 7.14), where Hobbes writes, "in a monarchy, if the monarch make any decree against the laws of nature, he sins himself; because in him the civil will and the natural are all one". In sovereign assemblies, as we have in aristocratic and democratic systems, only those members who vote in favor of decrees against the Laws of Nature sin. We will examine Hobbes's view on responsibility in Chapter 6.

95 For an illuminating discussion of this distinction, see John Rawls's account, following H. L. A. Hart and R. B. Brandt, in *A Theory of Justice* (Cambridge, MA, 1971), 113–115. His account is surprisingly similar to Hobbes's, particularly with respect to its insistence that valid obligations depend upon background institutions, and that obligations are normally owed to definite individuals.

valid promises requires us to acknowledge the duty not to renege on our own.

The possibility of creating obligations *de novo* through consent or covenant expands the range of reason's requirements, and can alter its requirements, so that actions that were before morally indifferent become either morally required or impermissible. Because it is contrary to reason to violate our valid covenants, this being prohibited by the third Law of Nature, it may be against reason for some people to perform actions that others may perform blamelessly. This is the meaning of Hobbes's observation that "consent and covenant may so alter the cases, which in the law of nature may be put, by changing the circumstances, that that which was reason before, may afterwards be against it; and yet is reason still the law".[96] In marrying, for instance, the person who was before at liberty to consort sexually with anyone, becomes blameworthy for any extra-marital relations;[97] and by enlisting in the military (an example from Hobbes), a man gives up his previous right to plead fear as an excuse for running from battle. Because voluntarily assumed obligations can alter the moral requirements on individuals, it is, practically speaking, impossible to determine in advance all of the cases in the Law of Nature, and this leaves Hobbes's moral philosophy with a kind of openness and underdetermination characteristic of all plausible moral theories.

However, Hobbes's stance that voluntary undertakings create obligations only if they run contrary to neither natural laws nor prior valid obligations implies that when sovereigns erroneously grant away powers that disable them from securing the safety of the people, those grants do not create valid obligations. Hobbes writes,

> [K]ings that grant such liberties, are bound to make them good, so far as it may be done without sin: but if a King find that by such a grant he be disabled to protect his subjects, if he maintain his grant, he sins; and therefore may, and ought to take no notice of the said grant. For such grants, as by error or false suggestion are gotten from him, are, as the lawyers do confess, void and of no effect, and ought to be recalled. Also the King, as is on all hands confessed, hath the charge lying upon him to protect his people against foreign

[96] EW IV, 108–109; *Elements of Law* I.4.11.

[97] Alternatively, one might understand marriage as transforming the person who was before culpable for having any sexual relations into one who may permissibly engage in them with his spouse.

enemies, and to keep the peace betwixt them within the kingdom: if he do not his utmost endeavour to discharge himself thereof, he committeth a sin, which neither King nor Parliament can lawfully commit.[98]

This means that the obligations of sovereigns are always to be ascertained by looking first to their duty under the Law of Nature to provide for the security, prosperity, and harmless liberty of their people, and discounting any voluntary pacts in tension with that duty.

It is interesting to note that although in Hobbes's system obligations arise only through voluntary undertakings, we do have a natural duty to undertake some obligations. We are duty bound (by reciprocity) to undertake those obligations that we require others to undertake, or fault for not undertaking. In particular, the Law of Nature requires us to undertake political obligation, because our insistence that others should do so for the sake of our own safety and agency requires that we so submit as well.[99] Hobbes's infamous "Foole" says that it is not against reason "to make, or not make" covenants according only to how they benefit oneself particularly; but Hobbes aims to prove that it *is* against reason not to make a covenant of political submission, because no rational agent can will that his fellows should be permitted to operate according to their own various private judgments outside of any ordered political system, and so one has a duty to join with willing others in forging and maintaining such a system.

Because Hobbes regards reciprocity as the hub of all moral reasoning, it would be surprising were he not to employ it in his personal as well as political moral reasoning. We find that he does. In his *Considerations Upon the Reputation, &c. of Thomas Hobbes* (written as a letter to John Wallis, D.D.), he writes, "if tenderness of conscience be a good plea, you must give Mr. Hobbes also leave to plead tenderness of conscience to his new Divinity, as well as you".[100] This passage

[98] EW VI, 16.

[99] Even the person subsequently elected sovereign by the majority in a covenant instituting a commonwealth is understood to have first consented along with all the others to stand to the majority's choice of sovereign, whomever it should be, or else be excluded from the resulting commonwealth. Similarly, heirs to existing sovereigns in ongoing commonwealths are until their succession under the same duties of political obligation as other subjects. As noted above, the Laws of Nature impose a special political obligation to ensure the safety, prosperity, and liberty of subjects generally on those who occupy the role of sovereign.

[100] EW IV, 431; *Considerations upon the Reputation, &c. of Thomas Hobbes.*

makes implicit appeal to reciprocity, as does his query, "[W]ith what equity can it be denied [Mr. Hobbes] to repeat your manifest and horrible crimes, for all you have been pardoned; when you publish falsely pretended faults of his, and comprehended in the same pardon?"[101] Wallis can't reasonably deny that what's good for his goose is as good for Hobbes's gander.[102]

THE LAWS OF NATURE

In addition to the various cases in the Law of Nature we have sampled, Hobbes enumerates a number of specific Laws of Nature. Hobbes varied slightly his presentation and numbering of the Laws of Nature across the versions of his political philosophy. Kavka offers a helpful summary of those laws as they appear in chapters 14 and 15 of *Leviathan* by stating what each is for or against:[103]

1. For peace
2. For mutual and reciprocal surrender of natural rights
3. Against injustice, that is, against violating obligations
4. For gratitude
5. For accommodating others (including giving up one's luxuries for their necessities)
6. For pardoning offenses of those who repent and offer assurance of future good conduct
7. Against punishing for revenge
8. Against declaring contempt or hatred for others
9. For acknowledging others as one's natural equals

[101] EW IV, 416; *Considerations upon the Reputation, &c. of Thomas Hobbes.*

[102] Speaking more literally, Hobbes's actual stance on human treatment of at least some animals also appears to make appeal to an idea of reciprocity. Because fierce predators will not refrain from hunting us, we cannot be faulted for seeking to kill them. This is permitted under the Law of Nature, even without confirmation by divine positive law, because otherwise "it were a hard condition of mankind, that a fierce and savage beast should with more right kill a man, than the man a beast" (*Elements of Law* II.3.9). Hobbes speaks of "irrational creatures", but because he elsewhere asserts that some animals exhibit prudence, it must be because of some other sort of reason that animals lack. It may be that Hobbes thinks precisely that what they lack is the capacity to constrain their behavior to conform with the requirements of reciprocity.

[103] Kavka, *Hobbesian Moral and Political Theory*, 343.

10. Against claiming for oneself rights that one denies to others
11. For equity by judges
12. For common use of resources that cannot be divided
13. For alternating use, or assignment by lot, of what cannot be used in common
14. For primogeniture or first seizure as a form of natural lottery in distributing goods
15. For safe conduct for mediators
16. For submitting controversies to an arbitrator
17. Against being a judge in one's own case
18. Against using arbitrators who are partial
19. For using witnesses to settle controversies of fact.

This summary omits some subtleties needed to show these laws to be instances of reciprocity, and that Hobbes stresses – for instance, the first law requires that a man pursue peace to the extent he believes he can achieve it with others, and the second law requires him to lay down only those rights he thinks it necessary for peace and defense that others should lay down. In Chapter 5 we will examine how the most important of these Laws of Nature are derived from Hobbes's reciprocity theorem, and how that theorem itself is derived. But Kavka's summary is a useful guide to the basic idea of each of the laws Kavka mentions.

However, Kavka's list omits several important Laws of Nature. The first is, of course, the "sum" of the Laws of Nature, that is, reciprocity.[104] It also omits "the law of nature over and above all these particular laws" dictating when the laws oblige only *in foro interno,* as well as all those Laws of Nature that forbid actions tending in the first instance to the destruction of particular men rather than to the destruction of mankind in general, such as the law against drunkenness.[105] A permission to use and to kill nonhuman animals also is "of the law of

[104] EW III, 144; T 109; EW III, 153; T 117; *Elements of Law,* part 1, chapter 17.10.

[105] It turns out, however, that this law, which I discuss in Chapter 3, is justified by appeal to the consideration that drunkenness and "all other parts of intemperance" destroy the rational faculty and hence degrade our capacity to govern our actions in accordance with others of the Laws of Nature. In this way drunkenness does tend to the destruction of men other than the inebriate, at least in the second if not the first instance.

nature".[106] Crucially, Kavka's list omits the law Hobbes articulates in *Leviathan*'s review and conclusion:

> To the laws of nature, declared in Chapter XV. I would have this added, that every man is bound by nature, as much as in him lieth, to protect in war the authority, by which he is himself protected in time of peace.... And though this law may be drawn by consequence, from some of those that are there already mentioned; yet the times require to have it inculcated, and remembered.[107]

This law is striking in its insistence that everyone (that is, every person who has a Right of Nature to preserve their own body, which every normal adult woman and man does, and perhaps also children of some ages) is required by the Law of Nature to do the utmost within their abilities to protect the sovereign, no matter how risky, nor how suboptimal this may be for their pursuit of self-interest. And the argument for this final law is mysteriously elliptical. Hobbes asserts that this law is an implication of others of the Laws of Nature, and charges that no one who asserts a right to preserve himself can consistently deny a duty to aid (to the utmost of his abilities) in resisting destruction the power that has (formerly) preserved him.[108] It is difficult to imagine how this law might be understood as a prudential dictate of individual rational self-interest, considering that it requires fighting, and prohibits running away, lying low, switching sides, and any number of strategies that may, in the circumstances, promise greater personal safety to individuals than fighting for their sovereign. This law raises a puzzle about how Hobbes could have understood his Laws of Nature to be straightforward reliable precepts of prudence that necessarily operate to the personal profit of the agent who follows them.

I shall propose a simple solution to this puzzle in Chapter 3. For now it is enough to have registered the very many Laws of Nature and cases in the Law of Nature that Hobbes seeks to justify under

[106] See note 105 above.

[107] EW III, 703; T 484. Although Kavka mentions this requirement, he does not identify it as a Law of Nature. See Kavka, *Hobbesian Moral and Political Theory*, 425.

[108] Hobbes's language is "For he that pretendeth a right of nature to preserve his own body, cannot pretend a right of nature to destroy him, by whose strength he is preserved: it is a manifest contradiction of himself" (EW III, 703; T 484).

his moral philosophy. Before we can sensibly assess his casuistry, we need pertinent information about his moral psychology. What is he supposing about the nature of human moral agents? What are their concerns and perceived constraints, how do they reason, and what are the external constraints they must satisfy to count as competent moral agents? We begin this part of our inquiry by considering Hobbes's views on human nature.

2

Moral Judges: Human Nature and Motivation

> How rare, men with the character to praise a friend's success without a trace of envy, poison to the heart – it deals a double blow. Your own losses weigh you down but then, look at your neighbor's fortune and you weep. Well I know, I understand society, the flattering mirror of the proud.
>
> (Aeschylus, *Agamemnon*, 818–824)

Our task in this chapter is to lay out those essential features of the psychology of Hobbesian agents that we will need to understand for our subsequent investigation of how Hobbes's Laws of Nature are dictates of right reason for such agents, and how men can be motivated to follow those laws and to grant them the sort of normative authority Hobbes assigned them. Hobbes has not infrequently been taken to have ascribed to humankind a simple egoistic psychology according to which men's primary aversion must be to their own violent bodily death, and all of their voluntary actions aimed at avoiding their own death or securing the means for avoiding it (notwithstanding occasional lapses of prudence due to vain-glory).[1]

[1] This interpretation is captured in the joke (whose author is unknown to me) "Why did the chicken cross the road?" Thomas Hobbes: Forre therre Bee bvt twoe Cawses thatte myght yndvce an Fowle orre Chyckenne too bestyrre Ytselfe ande ventvre fromme yts Farmyarde vnto ye Roade ande there-acrosse: And thee Fyrste of svch Cawses bee thatte whyche wee calle Hvngerre, ande ye Seconde bee thatte whyche men doe calle Vayneglorie.

The persistence of this attribution to Hobbes of a human psychology, conceded on all sides to be too oversimplified to be plausible as an accurate description of actual human psychology, is intriguing.[2] For although Hobbes does sometimes say things that suggest the simple one-note view, the rest of what he says reveals a remarkably rich, complex, and insightful conception of human psychology. Unfortunately, this complex picture is also messy, thwarting efforts to use it in establishing Hobbes's political conclusions by means of the simple arguments often attributed to him, for instance, syllogisms concluding that absolutism is justified as the necessary means to satisfying men's dominant end of self-preservation. Perhaps it is this difficulty that explains the persistence of our attribution to Hobbes of an impoverished psychological theory. We are surer of Hobbes's political conclusions than we are of his moral theory or psychology, and so select versions of both of the latter, no matter their intrinsic demerits, that make it easiest for us to reach his political conclusions.

The danger in ascribing to Hobbes an overly simplistic psychology is that doing so forces a distortion of his moral theory that then forms a false foundation for his political arguments. Like a bad game of "telephone", the initial errors are compounded as they are passed along, until the end result bears little resemblance to Hobbes's authentic view. We achieve a systematic Hobbes, but one whose political conclusions are supported by an implausible moral theory dictated by an unrealistic characterization of human psychology.

Of course, Hobbes's fledgling efforts to describe a deterministic physical mechanism that might ground a reductionist account of psychological phenomena invites the kind of overly simple psychology some of his modern commentators have attributed to him. His idea that we are averse to those stimuli that cause a decrease in our vital motion (which is said to be experienced as pain), averse in proportion to the magnitude of the decrease, has suggested to some that we would have to be most averse to death, understood as the cessation of

[2] For instance, Jean Hampton insists that for Hobbes, "the desire for self-preservation is the strongest of them all", but then criticizes Hobbes as "crude and overly simplistic" for making that psychological assumption. *Hobbes and the Social Contract Tradition* (Cambridge, 1986), 15, 17.

all vital motion, as being the most painful of all experiences.[3] It thus provides a theoretical foundation for assigning alpha status to men's aversion to death.

Hobbes himself does not actually offer the argument just described, but something close to it can be cobbled together from different remarks in *Human Nature* and in *De Corpore Politico*.[4] There are, however, a number of problems with the argument, which may explain why (even if he had earlier offered it, which I doubt) it does not appear in *Leviathan*. Hobbes stated his intention to build his system on securely established premises confirmed by experience, yet it is not explained how the living could actually know that death is the most painful of experiences, never having had that experience, nor how those not acquainted with Hobbes's pioneering theory would have any reason to expect that death should be the most painful of experiences. Ordinary observation suggests that it is not. If dying is so painful, how can people die in their sleep, never so much as awakened by the pain? Why do the tortured breathe a sigh of relief when they die? And if decreases in vital motion are supposed to be experienced as painful, and thus to trigger aversion in proportion to the decrease, how is it that those addicted to damaging substances continue to desire and pursue them as their vital motions deteriorate, even to the point of death? If we are averse to stimuli that decrease our vital motions *because* we experience the decrease as painful – that is, if what we are averse to is simply pain – why assume that we would prefer a prolonged life in pain to the cessation of pain a quick death could bring?

More importantly than these defects in the argument attributed to Hobbes, Hobbes's rudimentary physiology cannot explain, nor did Hobbes think it could, how for any actual case mental phenomena like thoughts, beliefs, passions, and judgments of permissibility or of duty arise out of prior states of the body and the world, nor

3 Hobbes writes in the *Elements of Law* that in losing life we expect "the greatest of bodily pains in the losing" (I.14.6), and Mark Murphy interprets this to mean that "if death involves the worst of all bodily pains, and so we desire to avoid that which is painful, then death would be that to which we have the most powerful aversion"; "Hobbes on the Evil of Death", *Archiv für Geschichte der Philosophie* 82 (2000): 36–61, 42–42.

4 See *Human Nature,* part I, chapter VII, sections 1 and 2 (EW IV, 31) and *De Corpore Politico,* part I, chapter I, section 6 (EW IV, 83).

how they in turn affect vital motion. Hobbes's sketchy physiology offers no guidance in predicting or explaining how the many such factors at work interact to produce even the simplest human action. To observe this is not in any way to criticize Hobbes, since we still cannot do this satisfactorily. But it is important to recognize that Hobbes offers his materialistic reductionism as an educated conjecture about what will eventually be shown, if science progresses, to underlie our experience, rather than as a foundation from which he builds up his specific conception of human nature, his moral philosophy, or his civil philosophy. Hobbes's mechanism cannot ground those philosophies because, as he insists, "the principles of natural science ... are so far from teaching us any thing of God's nature, *as they cannot teach us our own nature,* nor the nature of the smallest creature living".[5] Believing that then existing natural science cannot teach us our own nature, yet recognizing the necessity of an account of human nature to serve in the civil science Hobbes insisted he had sufficiently demonstrated, notwithstanding the inadequacy of natural science, Hobbes could not have intended to confine his psychological theory to those phenomena explicable by his rudimentary natural science.

Instead, Hobbes believed that moral and civil philosophy can proceed without knowledge of the underlying physical mechanisms of psychological phenomena; it can be adequately grounded on human nature as this is revealed by *experience and introspection.* He writes: "I saw that, grounded on its own principles sufficiently known by experience, [the third section on civil government] would not stand in need of the former sections [on body and man]"[6] and "[W]hen I shall have set down my own reading [of human nature] orderly, and perspicuously, the pains left another, will be only to consider, if he also find not the same in himself. *For this kind of doctrine admitteth no other demonstration*".[7] Hobbes banks the success of his reading of human nature on our being able to recognize, as introspectively indubitable,

5 EW III, 354, emphasis added; T 252. Cf. EW II, 217; *De Cive* 15.15. I offer evidence for the independence in Hobbes's theory of moral and civil philosophy from mechanistic materialism in Chapter 8.

6 EW II, xx; *De Cive* (Preface to the Reader).

7 EW III, xii, emphasis added; T 11.

those few psychological premises upon which his moral and political philosophies rely.[8]

Because one barrier to recognizing the complexity of Hobbes's psychological theory is the perception that he thought fear of violent bodily death to be the key motive force in human behavior – a necessary, overriding, and determinative consideration – I will begin by discussing the case against that claim. But my chief reason for doing so is to counteract the prejudice that the Laws of Nature *could not but be* about and in the service of self-preservation, because Hobbes took the individual's desire for self-preservation to be (1) blameless, (2) inescapable, and (3) systematically overriding. I'll offer reasons for thinking that while (1) is true of Hobbes's view, (2) is for most practical purposes false, and (3) is a demonstrable falsehood frequently noted as such by Hobbes himself. I will then go on to consider several others of the most important ends, interests, and motivations of agents as Hobbes describes them, and discuss how these must converge for men to be motivated to rebel against the state.

SELF-PRESERVATION

Hobbes is adamant, at least in his earlier writings on human nature, that all persons "by necessity of nature" desire most of all to preserve their lives – that is, their natural living bodies. This language diminishes to the point of having been altogether eliminated by the time he writes *Leviathan* – itself an interesting fact that suggests he did not take his theory to depend on it – but it reemerges in *De Homine*,[9] and his early language is so strong that any interpretation must make sense of it. He writes, for instance, that, considered in the natural condition, "every man is desirous of what is good for him, and shuns what is evil, but chiefly the chiefest of natural evils, which is death; and this he doth by a certain impulsion of nature, no less than that whereby a

[8] An instance of this sort of appeal to our experience occurs in Hobbes's discussion in chapter 13 of *Leviathan* inviting every man to confirm his conclusions by "considering with himself" the attitudes he exhibits when arming himself, locking his doors and chests, and the like.

[9] *De Homine* was published after *Leviathan;* I do not know precisely when the relevant passages for *De Homine* were written.

stone moves downward",[10] and "necessity of nature maketh men to will and desire *bonum sibi,* that which is good for themselves, and to avoid that which is hurtful; but most of all, the terrible enemy of nature, death"[11] and "[reason] teaches every man to fly a contra-natural dissolution, as the greatest mischief that can arrive to nature".[12]

These and other similar passages show Hobbes believed that "natural men", or men considered with respect to none but the properties they have "from nature", have a strong, possibly overriding impulse to try to save themselves from death. One assumes that Hobbes means to be speaking of normal adults, not those terminally ill, suffering from great physical burdens, or worn out from life, since he readily admits that the burdens of life may make some men count death a good,[13] nor those too immature or disabled to understand or fear the prospect of death. The thought is that a normal healthy adult, considered just as he or she is "from nature", desires most of all to avoid death, and perhaps even fashions his or her life around that desire.

Some refinement is needed here. It is not clear that Hobbes actually believed this of women, whom he may have noticed had always accepted grave risks to their self-preservation in carrying and giving birth to children, and in caring for them (and others) through the unhappily ordinary challenge posed by deadly contagious illnesses. Although the texts do not allow us to settle the question, I believe he would have analyzed women's disposition to assume such risks as effects of what he terms "natural affection" rather than as some sort of unnatural cultural imposition, or systematic human pathology.[14] Thus the question arises whether it is correct to contend that Hobbes

[10] EW II, 8; *De Cive* 1.7. Cf. EW II, 36; II, 17 (*De Cive* 3.9; 2.3); and IV, 88 (*Elements of Law* I.2.3).

[11] EW IV, 83; *Elements of Law* I.1.6.

[12] EW II, vii; *De Cive* (The Epistle Dedicatory).

[13] He writes, "the pains of life can be so great that, unless their quick end is foreseen, they may lead men to number death among the goods" (Gert, *Man and Citizen,* 48–49).

[14] Indeed, the notion of pathology is not available to Hobbes here, because he thinks of "madness" (pathology) as deviation from the ordinary; and if women form roughly half of the population and typically do engage in such behaviors, those behaviors will not be sufficiently extraordinary to license condemning them as pathological. Sometimes Hobbes speaks of madness as fixation on a single passion that drives out the claims of all others, but by that criterion, a fixation on the fear of death trumping all other desires would itself be a form of madness!

believed all people naturally care most for preserving their lives. The most minimal, conservative refinement we can make to the view that Hobbes thought that death avoidance is our overriding natural end is to interpret him as having meant to claim that, not death avoidance generally, but only avoidance of bodily death *by violence* is our foremost end by nature.[15] Such an interpretation would allow us to accept as nonpathological mothers who behave as they typically do, while nonetheless maintaining that avoiding whatever leads to their *violent* deaths is the strongest natural imperative. The more plausible thesis would be that men's greatest natural aversion is to being killed in a violent manner.

One worry about this position is that it is difficult to understand why people should be more averse to dying by violence than they are to dying in childbirth or from disease, starvation, exposure, or other natural deprivations. It is not as if violent death need be necessarily more painful than death from these other causes; our experience shows that some elect violent death just in order to avoid the prolonged pain of a natural death. What reason could there be for positing any systematic *natural* discrimination among violent and nonviolent causes of death? Nor does it seem that the general category of *violent* death should be especially significant to the civil philosophy Hobbes aimed to defend; people die untimely traumatic deaths in earthquakes, floods, famines, shipwrecks, travel accidents, foreign invasions, and wars abroad; but Hobbes does not take civil philosophy to concern how to avoid those deaths. Civil philosophy addresses only the avoidance of civil war or domestic conflict and its devastations. But if, despite these difficulties, we attribute to Hobbes the view that people are, by nature, overridingly averse just to violent death at the hands of others in their own community, we must offer some explanation of why this particular desire should be acknowledged as *natural*. My own suggestion, developed in Chapter 5, is that it will make sense to call it natural insofar as

[15] Leo Strauss suggested that Hobbes's complete disinterest in medicine indicated that he took men to be concerned, not with death, but only with violent death at the hands of others. See *The Political Philosophy of Hobbes* (Chicago, 1952), 16–17. A. P. Martinich doubts Strauss's claim that Hobbes was not interested in medicine, noticing that he observed dissections (of deer) by Dr. William Harvey and by William Petty and was a friend of other physicians, including Charles Scarborough; *Hobbes: A Biography* (Cambridge, 1999), 218.

we believe that people should not be faulted for acting on it. Hobbes seeks to build his argument only from premises that "passion not mistrusting" will allow, and no premise requiring general self-sacrifice to our murderous neighbors would enjoy the requisite confidence. *Desires are natural when actions on them are licensed by natural law.*

What is the force of the observation that men naturally desire to avoid violent death? Clearly not that it disables men from taking risks with their lives, for Hobbes defines the familiar virtue of courage as "the contempt of wounds and death, when they oppose a man in the way to his end".[16] It is worth noting that Hobbes saw us as having other desires "from nature", for example, the desires for food, for air, and for sexual relations with members of the opposite sex. Like the desire to avoid violent death, these desires will move us in many cases. But must they *determine* our actions? Just as gravity causes a stone to move downward, in the absence of countervailing forces, so the aversion to death will cause men to resist death in the absence of countervailing forces. But surely that does not suffice to guarantee that men will always seek to avoid death, any more than the operations of gravity preclude a stone's moving upward if, say, it is carried up a flight of stairs in one's pocket. Indeed, we are as subject to the force of gravity as is the stone, but this does not prevent us from rationally and willfully acting against it, by climbing stairs, jumping rope, flying in planes, or blasting off into weightlessness in rocket ships. Men typically do create countervailing forces to thwart the effectiveness of their natural impulses. Despite its naturalness, the impulse toward sexual relations may be successfully resisted in the service of a commitment to monogamy or celibacy or prudence or care for reputation, by any number of means ranging from distancing oneself from temptation to inviting social censure to voluntary castration. And similarly, while the natural impulse to breathe makes it impossible to kill oneself by holding one's breath, one can counteract the effects of these natural impulses by swimming out very far into a body of water, or tying a heavy weight to one's body before jumping in. By such means men can and routinely do thwart their natural impulses by imposing upon themselves countervailing forces. So knowledge of

[16] *Elements of Law* I.9.4.

men's desires "from nature" won't enable us in general to predict with any accuracy what they will actually do.

This obvious point invites the question what the fact, supposing Hobbes to be correct, that the desire to avoid being violently killed is the overriding end of men "by nature" can tell us about its importance to men "by culture"? For many (although by no means all) of the reasons we have for electing to create countervailing pressures against our natural impulses are the product of our acculturation – of our social practices, roles and sensibilities, moral beliefs, religious beliefs, and idiosyncrasies of our upbringing and training.

This question would lack interest were culture optional for humans, or atypical of human life. But, as Hobbes acknowledges, *we are all men by culture.* Even those few who inhabit the state of nature, for instance, the "savages of America", are shaped by their upbringing within families (which may include servants and slaves as well as parents and children) and the practices of what Hobbes calls *natural religion.* We are all born into highly elaborate ongoing societies, the forces of which shape our dispositions and ends in the most profound ways imaginable. As Hobbes tells us in *Behemoth,* the Ethiopian kings willingly obeyed commands from their priests to die, such is the power of culture over nature,

> For the priests...when they have a mind to it, send a messenger to the King to bid him die, for that the Gods have given such order, and that the commandments of the immortals are not by any means to be neglected by those who are, by nature, mortal....Therefore in former times the Kings did obey the priests, not as mastered by force and arms, but as having their reason mastered by superstition.[17]

This is an example of motivation by what I have elsewhere called *transcendent interests,*[18] interests that the agent takes to trump the requirements of bodily self-preservation or narrow prudence, and I'll take up this sort of interest again in a moment. What's worth noting here is that Hobbes does not dispute that the Ethiopian kings, all

[17] EW VI, 281; *Behemoth* II. Cf. EW VII, 74; *Decameron Physiologicum* I.

[18] See *IAI,* especially chapters 6 and 8. That people are motivated by such interests is an empirically observable fact, as Hobbes notes. Which such interests can be defended as reasonable is a separate question, and Hobbes treats that question on a case-by-case basis, as we'll see.

men by nature, were able to act against the natural necessity of the desire to resist violent death on account of their acculturation. While they, along with more admirable sorts such as true Christian martyrs and noble men of "generous natures", may present extreme cases of the phenomenon of formation by nurture, all actual men exhibit the effects of acculturation to some degree. In his *De Homine* discussion of men's "dispositions and manners", Hobbes writes that "men's inclinations toward certain things, arise from a six-fold source: namely from the constitution of the body, from experience, from habit, from the goods of fortune, from the opinion one hath of oneself, and from authorities. When these things change, dispositions change also".[19]

Particularly important among these influences on men's motivational impulses is *habit*, since it is "because of this, that those things that offend when new (that is, those things that man's nature initially resists) more often than not whet that same nature when repeated; and those things that at first are merely endured soon compel love".[20] Daredevils may come to love danger; addicts may come to love poisonous substances; those habituated to conquest may come to love combat, despite the fact that all of these practices invite self-destruction and were, initially, contrary to nature. We can test this claim ourselves by considering that over a prolonged period, anything one does everyday becomes "natural" and affects one's inclinations and one's well-being for better or for worse.

One's particular *social experience* is also strongly formative, because "it is by the rod that boys' *dispositions toward all things* are shaped as parents and teachers wish".[21] This is an exceedingly strong statement

[19] Gert, *Man and Citizen*, 63.
[20] Ibid., 64–65.
[21] Ibid., 65, emphasis added. Hobbes offers the rearing of children as an example of investing labor in something that we can form in accordance with our purposes: "For *cultus* signifieth properly, and constantly, that labour which a man bestows on anything, with a purpose to make benefit by it. Now those things whereof we make benefit, are either subject to us, and the profit they yield, followeth the labour we bestow upon them, as a natural effect; or they are not subject to us, but answer our labour, according to their own wills. In the first sense the labour bestowed on the earth, is called *culture;* **and the education of children, a *culture* of their minds**" (EW III, 348, bold emphasis added; T 248). Hobbes contrasts this with the second case, in which "men's wills are to be wrought to our purpose, not by force, but by complaisance".

of the power of nurture over nature, and this power is to be exercised not only by the rod, but also by example, for

> it must be understood, first, not only how much fathers, teachers, and tutors of youths must imbue the minds of youths with precepts which are good and true, but also how much they must bear themselves justly and in a righteous manner in their presence, for the dispositions of youths are not less, but much more disposed to bad habits by example than they are to good ones by precept.[22]

Education turns out to be a further crucial determinant of men's dispositions, for "the actions of men proceed from their opinions; and in the well-governing of opinions, consisteth the well-governing of men's actions, in order to their peace, and concord"[23] and "[T]he common people's minds [if not already 'scribbled over' by others] … are like clean paper, fit to receive whatsoever by public authority shall be imprinted in them".[24]

We are all at least as much creatures of our cultural nurture as we are of our abstract human nature. Hobbes tells an amusing but memorable story to this effect in a passage in which he is seeking to naturalize a kind of aberrant behavior by showing it to be more plausibly the result of human passions than of demonic possession. He tells the story of a group of maidens who (for whatever reason) thought it fashionable to commit suicide by hanging themselves. Interestingly, Hobbes is not the least exercised by their suicides. Instead, he is concerned to show that we needn't posit any diabolical intervention to account for this. His proof:

> [T]here reigned a fit of madness in another Grecian city, which seized only the young maidens; and caused many of them to hang themselves. This was by most then thought an act of the Devil. But one that suspected, that contempt of life in them, might proceed from some passion of the mind, and supposing they did not contemn also their honour, gave counsel to the magistrates, to strip such as so hanged themselves, and let them hang out naked. This, the story says, cured that madness.[25]

[22] Gert, *Man and Citizen*, 67–68.
[23] EW III, 164; T 124.
[24] EW III, 325; T 233.
[25] EW III, 65; T 56. Recall that Hobbes defines madness simply as an unusually high degree of passion (EW III, 62; T 54).

Our first conclusion then, is that to agree that humans have some strong – even overwhelming when occurrent – impulses by nature is not to concede that none can act otherwise than those impulses occurrently dictate, since, like Ulysses having himself bound to the mast before overwhelmed by the Sirens' song, we often make prior provision to thwart them. The second is that we cannot read off from what is true of all men "by nature" *anything* about what will be true of all (or even any) men by culture, that is, of any men we know or need to accommodate in our political theory. Socialized men are the products of their raw material – their "natural natures" if it makes sense to speak in that way – transformed, possibly beyond recognition – by experience, education, habit, example, and social indoctrination. Seeing this enables us to appreciate how far some err in claiming that for Hobbes, "human beings are not in any fundamental way products of their social environment".[26]

There is yet a third reason to reject any claim that Hobbes's attribution to men of an overriding natural desire for self-preservation can serve as the foundation of a political philosophy intended to motivate men as they really are, in particular, Hobbes's readers. Very many real people have *transcendent interests,* interests for the sake of which they are willing to risk or even accept the certainty of untimely death. First among such interests in Hobbes's day might seem to be the interest in achieving eternal life – salvation. It may be true that all men most desire their temporal bodily self-preservation "by nature", while being equally true that no Christian most cares about his temporal body's marginally longer survival. We all die sooner or later, as Antigone famously noted.[27] What matters to the Christian is how to live and die in a way that does not undermine his eligibility for union with God or a better life hereafter. There can be no question that Hobbes not only acknowledges, but acknowledges as *proper,* men's prioritization of eternal life over temporal, bodily self-preservation. For instance, he writes, "*eternal life* is a greater reward than the *life present;* and *eternal*

[26] Hampton, *Hobbes and the Social Contract Tradition,* 11.

[27] "Die I must, I've known it all my life – how could I keep from knowing – even without your death-sentence ringing in my ears.... But if I had allowed my own mother's son to rot an unburied corpse – that would have been an agony! This is nothing. And if my present actions strike you as foolish, let's just say I've been accused of folly by a fool" (Sophocles, *Antigone,* 512–524).

torment a greater punishment than the *death of nature*"[28] and "[I]f [the sovereign's] command be such as cannot be obeyed, without being damned to eternal death; then it were madness to obey it".[29]

With respect to these passages, one may understand Hobbes to be saying that an interest in some extended notion of self-preservation (not the limited interest in bodily survival previously postulated) trumps the narrow bodily interest we've been considering. It is quite true that Hobbes took eternal life, or what I have elsewhere called considerations of "special prudence",[30] to trump considerations of natural preservation in keeping one's current body alive. And it seems reasonable to suppose that Hobbes's attitude here results from thoughtful consideration of the way people behave. So he writes, "That the fear of God's wrath doth expel corporeal fear, is well said...and proveth strongly, that fear of the greater evil may necessitate in a man of courage to endure the lesser evil"[31] and "[T]he fear of darkness and ghosts, is greater than other fears".[32]

Recognizing the claims of religion on men is of the first importance for understanding how they are motivated, because

> it is impossible a commonwealth should stand, where any other than the sovereign hath a power of giving greater rewards than life, and of inflicting greater punishments than death. Now seeing *eternal life* is a greater reward than the *life present;* and *eternal torment* a greater punishment than the *death of nature;* it is a thing worthy to be well considered...for what offenses, and against whom committed, men are to be *eternally tormented;* and for what actions they are to obtain *eternal life*.[33]
>
> For Christ hath said it, **nay even nature itself dictates**, that *we should not fear them who slay the body, but cannot kill the soul; but rather fear him, who can cast both soul and body into hell* (Matth. x. 28). Neither is any man so mad, as not to

[28] EW III, 437; T 307.
[29] EW III, 585; T 403.
[30] See *IAI,* 151–157.
[31] EW V, 289; *Liberty, Necessity, and Chance* XX.
[32] EW III, 317; T 227.
[33] EW III, 437; T 306–307. Also EW II, 78 (*De Cive* 6.11): "if one command somewhat to be done under penalty of natural death, another forbid it under pain of eternal death,... it will follow that... the city itself is altogether dissolved. For no man can serve two masters; nor is he less, but rather more a master, whom we believe we are to obey for fear of damnation, than he whom we obey for fear of temporal death".

choose to yield obedience rather to them who can remit and retain their sins, than to the powerfulest kings.[34]

Even the most self-obsessed person has reason to obey God in preference to his fellow men, because "Man cannot kill a soul; for the man killed shall revive again. But God can destroy the soul and body in hell, as that it shall never return to life".[35]

Not only do these passages make clear that Hobbes believed that men may have a transcendent interest in securing their eternal prospects for the sake of which they may rationally choose even a violent bodily death, but they enable us to appreciate the utter implausibility of the standard interpretation of Hobbes as having argued that mere governmental force can reliably maintain social order. On that interpretation, Hobbes is said to have held that we can achieve enduring social order simply by creating a sovereign to coerce, by credible threats of physical force, our compliance with his laws. Indeed, such a solution might have some hope of succeeding did people care most to avoid bodily death. But because Hobbes insists that they do not, and further insists that men will disobey the political authority that without their obedience cannot secure civil peace whenever they believe their religion requires it of them, Hobbes's theory will have to address men's religious beliefs if it is to solve the problem of recurrent social disorder. In particular, it will have to show that, properly understood, true religion never requires disobedience to civil authorities; and if it can show that true religion and our prospects for salvation actually require us to obey the civil authorities, it will have found a way to turn men's transcendent interests into a force for peace and stability, rather than remaining a resource for social disorder.[36] This fact explains why Hobbes devotes a substantial portion of each of his political works to a detailed discussion of religious doctrine and practice, expanding his treatment of religion through each successive political work, until it occupies fully half of *Leviathan*. So the fact that men's actions are

[34] EW II, 284, bold emphasis added; *De Cive* 17.25. "For every man, if he be in his wits, will in all things yield that man an absolute obedience, by virtue of whose sentence he believes himself to be either saved or damned" (EW II, 317 [*De Cive* 18.14]). Cf. EW II, 293; *De Cive* 17.27.

[35] EW IV, 352; *An Answer to Bishop Bramhall.*

[36] A sketch of the argument is provided in Chapter 8. I lay out Hobbes's full arguments for these conclusions in *IAI,* chapter 3.

not reliably determined by their natural desire to avoid violent death has tremendous ramifications for how we must understand Hobbes's analysis of recurrent social disorder and his proposed remedy for it.

Still, not all resistance to natural urges is dictated by fear of God's wrath. Concerns for honor, reputation, justice, and liberty also appear in Hobbes's writings; and the transcendent claims of ordinary love of children and other family, friends, and social causes find room in Hobbesian psychology. In response to Bishop Bramhall's assertion that the cases of Moses, Saint Paul, and the Decii provide counterexamples to Hobbes's claim that the object of men's voluntary actions is their own good, Hobbes writes,

> the two former did what they did for a good to themselves, which was eternal life; and the Decii for a good fame after death. And his Lordship also, if he had believed there is an eternal happiness to come, or thought a good fame after death to be anything worth, would have directed all his actions towards them, and have despised the wealth and titles of the present world.[37]

Hobbes here again acknowledges that men can act for ends beyond their own temporal preservation, seeing not just salvation but also posthumous honor as their primary good. That many men will resist their fear of death on account of their sense of honor, or concern for reputation (unmistakably evident in their willingness to duel, which exercised Hobbes), affection for others or out of indignation is indicated in Hobbes's insistence that "[M]ost men would rather lose their lives (that I say not, their peace) than suffer slander"[38] and "[A] son will rather die than live infamous and hated of all the world [for executing a parent]"[39] and "[M]ost men choose rather to hazard their life, than not to be revenged".[40] Further, men take up arms against constituted authority on grounds that it is violating the requirements of liberty, or of justice. Hobbes knew, as do we, that any of these concerns may prove *transcendent.*

Between the defeasibility of the natural aversion to violent death, its susceptibility to cultural modification, and its subordination to the

[37] EW IV, 378; *An Answer to Bishop Bramhall.*

[38] EW II, 38; *De Cive* 3.12. Some would also rather die than acknowledge their own wrongdoing (*Elements of Law* I.9.6).

[39] EW II, 83; *De Cive* 6.13.

[40] EW III, 140; T 107.

satisfaction of transcendent interests, it is easy to see how Hobbes could have ascribed this aversion to natural men while not having seen it as determining men's conduct. What is more difficult to understand is why he insisted upon it, when it does so little work in predicting or explaining human behavior. The answer lies in his ideas about the requirements of a normatively sound moral theory. Such a theory will be justified to those subject to it, making only those demands upon them that they can view as reasonable. Here the fact of the natural desire to avoid untimely death becomes important, because while it may not be true that each person cares most about avoiding bodily death, it is highly probable that people would judge a moral theory that systematically required them to sacrifice their lives to be unreasonable. People are not to be required to behave as if their survival meant nothing to them, and to be subject to blame and moral censure for wanting to resist death.[41] That is too much to ask of men, who, while rational animals, are nonetheless animals, subject to the demands of their animal nature, who cannot be sure that they would, in the face of a mortal threat, even be capable of squelching their impulse to defend themselves. Hobbes insists throughout his writings that, absent special obligations, the effort to defend one's life must be accounted blameless. To condemn a man for acting from this impulse, considering its naturalness, is to condemn him simply for being a man; and it is also to self-conceitedly criticize God for having made men with the nature he did.[42] This is why

> Among so many dangers therefore, as the natural lusts of men do daily threaten each other withal, to have a care of one's self is so far from being a matter scornfully to be looked upon.... It is therefore neither absurd nor reprehensible, neither against the dictates of true reason, for a man to use all his endeavours to preserve and defend his body.... But that which is not

[41] Indeed, we may presume that a man who cares nothing at all for his life is, to some extent, not *compos mentis*. Hobbes writes, "I conceive not how any man can bear *animum felleum,* or so much malice towards himself, as to hurt himself voluntarily, much less to kill himself. For naturally and necessarily the intention of every man aimeth at somewhat which is good to himself, and tendeth to his preservation. And therefore, methinks, if he kill himself, it is to be presumed that he is not *compos mentis,* but by some inward torment or apprehension of somewhat worse than death, distracted" (EW VI, 88 [*A Dialogue of the Common Laws*]).

[42] Hobbes writes: "[That men are] wicked by nature...cannot be granted without impiety" (EW II, xvi [*De Cive,* Preface to the Reader]).

contrary to right reason, that all men account to be done justly, and with right.[43]

As this passage clearly illustrates, Hobbes's insistence that all men naturally and strongly desire their bodily preservation is in the service of the normative claim that we *ought to allow as justified* actions done from this motive. We can hardly help interfering with one another in ways that are hurtful, so unless we will make every human action a sin, that is, a crime against God's natural law, we should acknowledge self-defense as morally permissible, *ceteris paribus:* "That which is done out of necessity, out of endeavour for peace, for the preservation of ourselves, is done with right, *otherwise every damage done to a man would be a breach of the natural law, and an injury against God*".[44] Hobbes's concern in establishing the naturalness of a strong impulse toward self-preservation is, I suggest, only to ground his claim that actions sincerely meant in defense of one's life are not to be judged blameworthy. At the end of this chapter we will consider why this question of blameworthiness looms so large for Hobbes.

Had Hobbes intended to mount his argument on the basis of sheer self-preservation, we might have expected him to boast of his own remarkable longevity.[45] He did live, after all, for ninety-one years, through a period of terrific civil strife, and one would have expected that approaching his death bed he would have patted himself on the back for having survived so long and so well, if indeed he valued and believed everyone else also values self-preservation above all else. Hobbes wrote his own epitaph, which turns out to be quite surprising. Consider:

> Here lies Tom Hobbes whose philosophy taught
> That survival is all men do care for or ought.
> Obey to stay safe (the King's laws, though they chafe)
> Ere we're damned, civil peace we'll have bought.

[43] EW II, 8–9; *De Cive* 1.7.

[44] EW II, 46n, emphasis added; *De Cive* 3.27n.

[45] If staving off death is the goal of human life, those who do it longest ought to be the winners of life's "race". However, when Hobbes explicitly analogized life to a race, he asserted that it had no other goal than "being foremost", satisfaction being taken in progress toward whatever we desire farther than our competitors (*Elements of Law* I.9.21).

Here lies *Leviathan*'s author who thought
God's commandments, truth, justice we must count for naught
When weighed in the scales against saving our tails
Self-survival is all should be sought.

Living ninety-one years without children or wife
Thomas Hobbes' foremost love was his own mortall life.
Through thick and through thin
He saved his dear skin
What prouder achievement amid civil strife?

This is not the verse Thomas Hobbes chose for his gravestone. Instead, he took pride in his *virtue* and his *learning*. This is what he wrote: "Here are buried the bones of Thomas Hobbes of Malmesbury, who for many years served two earls of Devonshire, father and son. He was a virtuous man and his reputation for erudition both at home and abroad is well known".[46] That this is what Hobbes wished to be remembered for is quite a remarkable fact.

THE STATE OF NATURE AND "NATURAL MAN"

Although Hobbes talks about the desires and inclinations men have "from nature", he does not suggest that any of these are or must be the strongest motivating forces for men as we know them. In the case of the desire for self-preservation, I've argued that while this desire is neither inescapable nor overriding, Hobbes stresses the naturalness of this desire in order to justify his premise that it is unreasonable to blame others for seeking to defend their lives (from which, as we'll see, he goes on to argue that we ought to grant to each man a right to do what he sincerely judges necessary for his own preservation). But the more general question arises, why does Hobbes have us consider a state of "mere nature", rather than just the ordinary state of men in civil societies, unless he means to give theoretical primacy to the characteristics men have merely "from nature"? What would be the point of positing a state of nature unless to single out men's *pre-social* characteristics as especially significant for justifying his subsequent political conclusions?

[46] Quoted in Martinich, *Hobbes: A Biography*, 356.

It is understandable that readers have supposed Hobbes intended the state of nature to describe the condition of presocial, natural men possessing only those qualities they have "from nature" and not from culture, or from social interaction.[47] It is sensible to think that if Hobbes seeks to justify social arrangements by demonstrating that they would be agreed to by those who are to become subject to them, he would have to begin from a condition in which people's attitudes are not already formed by prior social interactions. And he describes the natural condition as one of "no Society", in which life is "solitary".[48]

Nevertheless, this natural supposition that the state of nature is a presocial state in which are considered only the dispositions men have "from nature" is incorrect. The state of nature is rather a state in which men are taken to have *no obligations to obey one another or to defer to one another's judgment.* This is a narrow and specific constraint that is compatible with men's interacting, cooperating, and socializing in all sorts of familiar ways. They can make friends and take lovers, give and accept help, compete and cooperate, preach, proselytize and believe, and interact in every other way that does not presuppose or create obligations of submission to others.[49] What Hobbes is asking us to imagine is the condition of people like us were they to have no political obligations, as if they had not yet committed to any engagements, undertakings, promises, contracts, or covenants to obey or submit to the judgment of others.[50] We are to imagine not natural

47 Jean Hampton goes to a lot of trouble drawing distinctions that she then uses to assert this interpretation of the state of nature, writing that "it was important for Hobbes that an initial premiss of his argument be that human beings are not in any fundamental way products of their social environment" (*Hobbes and the Social Contract Tradition*, 11).

48 EW III, 113; T 89. Of course, if life were *literally* solitary, no children would be conceived, infants would die at birth, and there would be no warfare or conflict. But life does lack the solidarity and society (with a capital "S") on a large scale that only political organization can create.

49 Such interaction will not preclude the state of nature's being a state of war, because any effective mechanism for resolving disputes and enforcing decisions is lacking. In fact, these sorts of interactions may create new sources of conflict.

50 This is not to suggest that men in the state of nature have no natural duties toward one another – duties of gratitude or fairness, for instance; the eternal and immutable Law of Nature does impose such duties of conscience on men even in a state of nature. Rather, Hobbes distinguishes natural duties from obligations, the latter being optional, voluntary undertakings by which we become "bound by our

men, for there are no natural men, but socialized men were we to suppose them free from any political obligations to others. Would these men find that reason recommends that they undertake political obligation? This conception of the state of mere nature as a condition in which men have no obligations of obedience is actually the more obvious starting point for a theory designed to justify political obligation by appeal to hypothetical agreement than is the condition of presocial natural men, because the more like us men in the state of nature are, the stronger the case that *we* should care about what *they* would take reason as requiring of them.

This interpretation of the state of nature as a condition of ordinary, socialized men from which has been abstracted away all of their political obligations is compatible with Hobbes's text. In speaking of the Right of Nature, Hobbes speaks of the state of nature as "the bare state of nature, or before such time as men had engaged themselves by any covenants or bonds".[51] Prior to undertaking any special obligations of obedience to one another, men have no duty to submit to one another's judgment about how to act; each is as entitled to exercise and act on his own private judgment, including his private judgment of good and evil, as any other.[52] So this conception of the state of nature as a state in which men have no political obligations to one another explains why Hobbes also says it is characterized by the universal right of private judgment: "so long as a man is in the condition of mere nature... as private appetite is the measure of good, and evil".[53]

Hobbes thus characterizes the condition of mere nature as a condition in which none has an obligation to obey anyone else. But this is not to say that there can be no other obligations in that condition. Hobbes holds that we may voluntarily assume an obligation to perform any action, so long as that action is both permissible and possible, simply by undertaking (vowing, promising, contracting, covenanting, etc.) to do it. For instance, one can obligate oneself to obey

own act", artificial bonds morally underwritten by our natural duty to perform our covenants.

51 EW II, 9–10; *De Cive* 1.10.

52 I will show in Chapter 5 that this entitlement is ultimately derived from the Law of Nature, rather than a postulate prior to or independent of the Law of Nature.

53 EW III, 146; T 111.

the divine positive law alleged by someone who claims to be divinely inspired, even though he cannot know that law to be true, and even if he does not actually believe it: "For if the law declared, be not against the law of nature, which is undoubtedly God's law, *and he undertake to obey it, he is bound by his own act;* bound I say to obey it, but not bound to believe it".[54] In this instance one is pledging to obey the message, not the messenger as an authority. Hobbes considers the condition of mere nature in order to determine what our lives would be like absent our undertaking specifically *political* obligations.

Consider then the bit of text that has induced so many commentators to ascribe to Hobbes the intention to fix a presocial, radically individualist, state of nature as his starting point:[55] "Let us return again to the state of nature, and consider men as if but even now sprung out of the earth, and suddenly, like mushrooms, come to full maturity, without all kind of engagement to each other".[56] If one took this passage in isolation, one might easily suppose that "without all kind of engagement to each other" is intended to track the notion "without any social interaction of any sort". But the evidence just reviewed shows that when Hobbes spoke of "engagement" he meant specifically the undertaking of obligations of obedience, and not some generic idea of unspecified interaction.

We can confirm our interpretation by attending to how this undeniably peculiar suggestion that we do political philosophy best by considering men *as if they were mushrooms* actually fits with Hobbes's other remarks about men's generation and the obligations that flow from that. (A serious concern, in light of the fact that it is difficult to see the appeal of a hypothetical contract theory that insists that we should adopt the arrangements that we would, had we been mushroom-men, find attractive.) Hobbes insists that children must be assumed to have undertaken obligations of obedience toward their parents,

54 EW III, 273, emphasis added; T 198.

55 For example, Hampton points to this text to support her claim that "Gauthier is right to find in Hobbes's theory a very strong brand of individualism, one that regards individual human beings as conceptually prior . . . to *all* social interactions" (Hampton, *Hobbes and the Social Contract Tradition*, 6).

56 EW II, 108–109; *De Cive* 8.1. Cf. EL xxii.2: "Considering men therefore again in the state of nature, without covenants or subjection one to another, as if they were but even now all at once created male and female" (EW IV, 149 [*Elements of Law* II.3.2]).

as recompense for their parents' having nourished and reared them. He writes:

> [S]eeing the infant is first in the power of the mother, so as she may either nourish, or expose it; if she nourish it, it oweth its life to the mother; and is therefore obliged to obey her, rather than any other; and by consequence the dominion over it is hers.... For it ought to obey him by whom it is preserved; because... every man is supposed to promise obedience, to him, in whose power it is to save, or destroy him.[57]

This entails that all children should be regarded as under obligations to their mothers or to whomever else they owe their preservation – which implies that no children, at least of still-living parents, can be without obligations, nor can be part of the state of nature, if this is properly understood as a state of persons without any obligations. And here Hobbes confirms our expectation (when he answers his hostile critics' charge that, on his account, a son does his father no injury in killing him) by writing "I have answered, that *a son cannot be understood to be at any time in the state of nature,* as being under the power *and command* of them to whom he owes his protection *as soon as ever he is born,* namely, either his father's or his mother's, or him that nourished him; as is demonstrated in the ninth chapter".[58]

Sons and daughters (although grown children of living parents) are *not and never have been* in a state of nature, and they have not been *precisely because* they are under obligations to their parents. This confirms our interpretation that Hobbes's state of nature is defined by the absence of political obligation. This further explains why, in order to imagine a state of nature, we must conceive people as "sprung out of the earth, and suddenly, as mushrooms come to full maturity". Only such entities could possibly be supposed *not* to have undertaken obligations to their parents. In order for men to have no obligations at all, they'd have to have been spontaneously, and without care from others, sprung up – just like mushrooms, as Hobbes says.[59]

[57] EW III, 187–188; T 140.

[58] EW II, 10n., emphasis added; *De Cive* 1.10n.

[59] It is interesting that Robert Filmer, in his 1652 critique of *Leviathan, Observations on Mr. Hobbes's Leviathan: Or his artificial Man: A Commonwealth,* section 3, perfectly grasps that Hobbes's mushroom analogy is intended to signal the absence of prior obligation. He objects to Hobbes's theory on the ground that it requires that we deny what Filmer regards as the "truth of the history of creation", that men are

Unless it excludes prior obligations, the state of nature cannot serve the role Hobbes assigns it in his civil philosophy. Civil philosophy seeks to derive political obligation, that is, the duties and rights of subjects, and the duties and rights of sovereigns, from the definition of a commonwealth.[60] Hobbes's philosophical method dictates that the definition of a thing must include its method of generation. Thus Hobbes aims to derive political conclusions from the method by which commonwealths are generated. But to discern the generation of anything, we must consider how it could have come into being from a state in which it was not. If we are concerned to explain political obligation by reference to the institution from which it follows, we must begin by considering a condition in which no such institution, hence no such obligation exists. This requires consideration of a condition without political obligation. If we follow Hobbes in calling such a condition the state of nature, or the condition of mere nature, we may easily see why Hobbes is compelled to lay down the counterfactual assumption that men in that state were sprung up like mushrooms. We will see in Chapter 5 how this assumption affects Hobbes's derivation of his Laws of Nature. But what we are missing is full-blown men, with all those socialized features that are not the product of relations of political obligation.

DESIRE, GOOD, AND WILL

There is a long tradition of interpreting Hobbes as a psychological egoist who held that the only motive of voluntary human action is the desire for good for oneself – that men can be motivated to act only by considerations of what conduces to their interest "in themselves" as opposed to satisfying interests "of themselves". The idea is that men can be moved to act only by consideration of what advances

born and reared up into obligations to parents. He writes: "I cannot understand how [Hobbes's] right of nature can be conceived without imagining a company of men at the very first to have been all...sprung out of the earth without any obligation to one another.... [T]he scripture teacheth us otherwise". Quoted in Johann P. Sommerville, ed., *Robert Filmer: Patriarcha and Other Writings* (Cambridge, 1991), 187–188. Filmer may be missing the point of the exercise, but he does correctly understand Hobbes's intention to imagine the state of nature as a condition without prior obligations of obedience.

60 EW III, 72; T 61. Cf. *IAI*, chapter 2.

those of their ends that are self-directed – their personal reputation, or health, or wealth, or happiness (or in its most extreme version, just their physical survival) – but either have no care for, or at least cannot be motivated to act by their care for, what advances ends that are not self-regarding – say, the welfare of others, or the good of the nation, or species, except insofar as those ends promote their self-regarding ends of survival, reputation, health, wealth, and happiness. Hobbes's mechanistic materialism is usually cited in support of this view, by an argument that because alterations in our vital motions form the basis for our appetites and aversions, and appetites and aversions determine our actions, voluntary actions must be directed toward increasing our vital motions. Gauthier articulates this view when he writes: "From this account of vital and voluntary motion, it follows that each man seeks, and seeks only, to preserve and to strengthen himself. A concern for continued well-being is both the necessary and the sufficient ground of human action. Hence man is necessarily selfish".[61]

The most philosophically refined treatments of this question decisively show that Hobbes was not a psychological egoist in the sense of one who holds that men's voluntary actions necessarily pursue a self-regarding object of desire.[62] Even if our desires do have physical correlates in our vital motions, and even if they are laid down by our vital motions, it does not follow that the object of desire is an increase in vital motion. We may experience an increase in vital motion when we aid the needy without it being true that we aid them in order to experience that increase in vital motion.[63] Further, Hobbes's texts will not bear interpreting him as espousing psychological egoism. He recognizes the existence of such passions as benevolence, which he defines as "desire of good to another", and makes plain that men do seek to the good of

[61] David Gauthier, *The Logic of 'Leviathan': The Moral and Political Theory of Thomas Hobbes* (Oxford, 1969), 7.

[62] Especially fine are Bernard Gert's and Greg Kavka's treatments. See Gert's Introduction to *Man and Citizen* and Gregory S. Kavka, *Hobbesian Moral and Political Theory* (Princeton, NJ, 1986).

[63] Hampton has a very nice discussion of this point in which she asks: "And why distort the phenomena by saying that what I *really* want when I go after the alleviation of another's pain is the alleviation of my own distress? I may or may not be conscious of the physiological sources of desire, but I do know what I desire, and this is the distinction Hobbes's psychology respects" (Hampton, *Hobbes and the Social Contract Tradition*, 23–24).

others in such passages as this (sadly misogynistic) remark that "love... is understood in two ways;... it is called one kind of love when we wish ourselves well, and another when we wish well to others. Therefore a male neighbor is usually loved one way, a female another; for in loving the former, we seek his good, in loving the latter, our own".[64]

Although Hobbes did not espouse psychological egoism, his language invites that misunderstanding. He consistently holds that men's actions are determined by their desires, and that they desire what is good to themselves – that the object of a man's will is what is good to himself. We must then inquire how such language is sensibly interpreted in a nonegoistic manner. One way to do so is to interpret Hobbes as saying that men "call good" whatever they happen to desire, and thus are correctly said to "desire their good", by which is meant what they deem good. This position is, of course, compatible with their desiring things that are in fact harmful to themselves, as when they are mistaken about the properties of the desired object. Acknowledging this, Hobbes holds that while we apply the term 'good' to what we desire, we desire what *appears* good to us, whether it actually is good or not. Men cannot desire what they deem the greater of evils, but they can desire things whose achievement is, and is seen by them to be, in the particular case incompatible with their natural preservation or narrow self-interest – things like saving a child, exacting revenge, embracing martyrdom, or choosing an honorable death over a dishonorable life. There is no constraint on the content of men's desires and so on what they can deem good. All Hobbes's remarks on desire and the good establish is that men will *call* "good" all and only those things they desire, and correlatively, that they desire what appears to them to be good.

This position does not, however, tell us anything about what things Hobbes thought actually *are* good, nor about what Hobbes takes the meaning of 'good' to be. Hobbes is often interpreted as a value subjectivist on the basis of the position just discussed, but that position is nothing more than an observation about our actual tendency to use evaluative language to signal personal desires, rather than an endorsement of that tendency. Hobbes insists that the meaning of a word depends upon agreement in the community of speakers. And

64 Gert, *Man and Citizen*, 60.

while people may call the things they desire 'good', they do not think that 'good' means 'what I desire', nor even 'desired by the speaker'. People argue over whether something is or is not good, believing themselves to have a genuine disagreement. They think that things that are good are so independently of their being desired, their goodness being at least one of the things that explains why they are desired. The community of speakers would *deny* that good is a synonym for being desired, even while granting that people do often make that corrupt use of the term.

Furthermore, men's tendency to use evaluative terms in this way – to call good what they desire, and evil whatever they are averse to – is (although predictable) *highly problematic,* according to Hobbes. It creates systematic contention over what is good or evil, rendering argument that begins from assertions of goodness useless, for the most part. It makes terms like 'good' and 'evil' of *inconstant signification,* both because the differing desires of different men will preclude these terms having a fixed meaning across the community, and because instability of the individual's own desires over time will make his own use of those terms of inconstant.[65] This will be true even though "the nature of that we conceive, be the same", and "therefore such names can never be true grounds of any ratiocination".[66] Our tendency to use evaluative terms this way encourages the use of private judgment, which creates serious conflict. It misleads men into thinking that the *proper measure* (or rule for discerning) of good and evil is their own liking or disliking, rather than the Law of Nature, or their sovereign's judgment. That Hobbes *disapproves* of this subjective use of evaluative terms appears plainly in his criticism of Greek philosophy:

Their moral philosophy is but a description of their own passions. For the rule of manners, without civil government, is the law of nature; and in it,

[65] See, e.g., EW II, 196; *De Cive* 14.17: "Such is the nature of man, that every one calls that *good* which he desires, and *evil* which he eschews. And therefore through the diversity of our affections it happens, that one counts that *good,* which another counts *evil;* and the same man what now he esteemed for *good,* he immediately looks on as *evil:* and the same thing which he calls *good* in himself, he terms *evil* in another". Cf. EW III, 146 (T 110–111), emphasis added: "divers men, differ.... Nay, the same man, in divers times, differs from himself; and one time praiseth, that is, calleth good, what another time he dispraiseth, and calleth evil: *from whence arise disputes, controversies, and at last war*".

[66] EW III, 28 and 29; T 31.

the law civil, that determineth what is *honest* and *dishonest*, what is *just* and *unjust*, and generally what is *good* and *evil*. Whereas they make the rules of *good* and *bad*, by their own *liking* and *disliking*: by which means, in so great diversity of taste, there is nothing generally agreed on; but every one doth, as far as he dares, whatsoever seemeth good in his own eyes, to the subversion of commonwealth.[67]

We should be careful here. To say that 'good' does not mean 'is desired by me' or 'is desired by the speaker' is not to say that 'good' has nothing whatsoever to do with desiring, or that it is a concept unrelated to human attitudes. It is often true that in calling something good we betray or communicate our desire for or approval of that thing – just as is the case when we call something lucky – and this would remain true even though 'good' did not mean 'is desired by me'. Hobbes held that words are "marks" to ourselves of our ideas (private language is possible) and "signs" used to communicate our ideas to others. But nothing in his linguistic theory precludes the possibility that we use words that mean one thing to communicate something else, for instance, our approval or disapproval. (It is easy to see how this works by observing our contemporary use of a term like "bitch".) Hobbes illustrates this point when he notes that 'heresy' "signifies no more than private opinion", but "has only a greater tincture of choler", and so is used to convey our disapproval or aversion to those private opinions with which we disagree.[68] So it does not follow from the fact that 'good' does not mean "is desired" that our use of 'good' does not communicate our desires. Moreover, there would be nothing peculiar in holding that to call something good is to say that it is *desirable*, in the sense of *possessing worthiness of being desired*, which meaning ascription, while not identifying goodness with being actually desired, nonetheless cannot be understood without recourse to our human practices of valuation. It is thus a coherent position to maintain that 'good' means, properly, "worthy of being desired", but that men apply the term 'good' to whatever they actually desire, and in doing so reveal their desires. And so it is possible that Hobbes affirmed an objective conception of goodness, while highlighting

67 EW III, 669; T 461.

68 EW III, 90; T 73. Cf. EW IV, 387–388 (*Concerning Heresy*), and IV, 101 (*Elements of Law* I.3.11).

men's improper and harmful tendency to take their own desires as the measure of goodness.

Granting this interpretation, the question remains how we ought to understand Hobbes's remarks that evaluative terms like good and evil are "ever used with relation to the person that useth them: there being nothing simply and absolutely so".[69] If that does not mean that things are good or bad only as being desired or eschewed by the speaker, what does it mean? I suggest that Hobbes's contention that nothing is "simply and absolutely" good should be understood as asserting a fact about the logical form of evaluative propositions about goodness, namely, that "x is good" means "x is a good F", where each speaker fixes the actual reference of F through the lens of his desires or interests. One says of something that it is good having in mind a particular notion of the kind of thing it is a good instance of, and this notion may easily vary from speaker to speaker. When I say "this brick is good", I am speaking in shorthand for a claim of the sort "this brick is a good F" – piece of material for the wall, doorstop, piece of found art, implement for bashing the skull of my adversary, example of the dictionary definition of a brick, etc. – and which of these predicates fixes the reference of the term depends upon the purposes and interest of the person using the term.[70] This is the sense in which 'good' is ever used in relation to the person using the term – it is used in relation to the purpose the individual has in mind. But this does not undermine the objectivity of goodness claims. It just reveals how opaque they are.[71] We can see the logical form of goodness ascriptions in Hobbes's explanatory illustration of the claim that nothing is simply and absolutely good: "Nor is there any such thing as absolute goodness, considered without relation: for even the goodness which we apprehend in God Almighty, is *his goodness to us*".[72] To say that God – who might have been thought the best candidate for intrinsic goodness – is good is to say that he is a good provider for us,

[69] EW III, 41; T 39. Cf. EW II, 47 (*De Cive* 3.31), and IV, 32 (*Human Nature* 7.3).

[70] To say of a thing that it is "inconsiderable" – expressing our attitude of "contempt", is to say that it is irrelevant to one's present purpose.

[71] David Boonin-Vail argues in a different way for a similar conclusion in his *Thomas Hobbes and the Science of Moral Virtue* (Cambridge, 1994), 61.

[72] EW IV, 32; *Human Nature* 7.3.

or a good caretaker or custodian or benefactor: It is certainly not to say that we "desire God".[73]

This interpretation allows x's goodness to be discoverable by reason in virtue of its falling under a general concept, as Hobbes's account of reason as a cognitive capacity requires. (And it is worth remembering that Hobbes thinks we can discover by our exercise of reason that at least this one thing – peace – is good.) We can determine the truth of a claim about a particular only by subsuming it under a universal concept, or "definition" in Hobbes's parlance. So for the truth of a proposition of the form "x is good" to be determinable by reason, it must be possible to bring x under some general term; and the fact that which general term it is to be subsumed under depends upon the speaker's intention does not in any way compromise the possibility of bringing it under some such concept. Subjective uses of 'good' merely to signal the speaker's desire sever the connection with reason, and so make claims about goodness in principle irresoluble. Hobbes, purporting to adjudicate such claims, believes them to be resoluble in principle, although seldom in fact because of men's tendency to use their desires as criteria for goodness. This is why a sovereign arbitrator to set standards against which goodness claims are to be judged is needed.

We should thus take at face value Hobbes's claim that men call the things they desire good, as a mere observation about how people use 'good', and not an endorsement of it. Even from this thin, uninteresting premise it will follow, however, that men will their (apparent) good. Men call good what they desire, and the will, for Hobbes, is just the desire – the appetite or aversion – a man acted on in acting as he did; thus men will what they desire, and so will what they deem good (or the lesser of evils). Hobbes consolidates this chain of reasoning with the pithy remark that "whatsoever a man would, it therefore seems good to him because he wills it".[74] There is nothing in any of this to indicate any substantive constraint on the ends that men can desire, deem good, or will.

73 Nor, in saying "God is good" are we simply saying God gives us what we desire. God permits good men to suffer adversity (which they do not desire) as Hobbes notes both generally and in Job's case specifically, but is still called good.

74 EW II, 10; *De Cive* 1.10.

THE COMPLEX MOTIVATIONS OF HOBBESIAN AGENTS

Hobbesian men act in pursuit of their desires, but a host of factors affect what it is that men desire, as we noted earlier in our discussion of socialized human nature. Chief among these is the way in which they are educated, for Hobbes insists that the actions of men proceed from their opinions,[75] and education is an important determinant of opinions. Common people's minds, "unless they be tainted with dependance on the potent, or scribbled over with the opinions of their doctors, are like clean paper, fit to receive whatsoever by public authority shall be imprinted in them".[76] Hobbesian men are thus highly *malleable* through education.

Part of what makes education so potent, however, is that men are *credulous*, which makes them *easily manipulable*, "[s]o easy are men to be drawn to believe any thing, from such men as have gotten credit with them; and can with gentleness, and dexterity, take hold of their fear, and ignorance".[77] A susceptibility to manipulation is shared by virtually all men, "[f]or such is the ignorance and aptitude to error generally of all men...as by innumerable and easy tricks to be abused".[78] This clearly implies that men are opaque to one another, unable to detect the true intentions of others to deceive them before the fact, and this to such a degree that "the characters of man's heart, blotted and confounded as they are with dissembling, lying, counterfeiting, and erroneous doctrines, are legible only to him that searcheth hearts", with most men "for the most part deceived, by too much trust, or by too much diffidence".[79] And thus, to deceive a man is "a very easy matter to do".[80]

This means that men can reasonably expect to have some success in manipulating others to their own ends; and one very effective way

[75] See, for example, EW III, 164 (T 124), where he writes: "the actions of men proceed from their opinions; and in the well-governing of opinions, consisteth the well-governing of men's actions, in order to their peace, and concord".

[76] EW III, 325; T 233.

[77] EW III, 103; T 82.

[78] EW III, 434; T 304.

[79] EW III, xi–xii; T 10. Cf. III, 92; T 74. The fact of men's opacity to one another constrains how Hobbes's famous reply to the Foole may plausibly be interpreted, as we shall see in our Chapter 7 discussion of Kavka's interpretation.

[80] EW III, 434; T 304.

of manipulating others is through the use of rhetoric. Much has been written about Hobbes's attitude toward rhetoric,[81] but at least all agree that Hobbes viewed rhetoric as very dangerous in the wrong hands. What matters for our present purpose of fixing Hobbes's human psychology is that rhetoric operates by exploiting our natural credulity, for rhetoric is "that art of words, by which some men can represent to others, that which is good, in the likeness of evil; and evil, in the likeness of good; and augment, or diminish the apparent greatness of good and evil; discontenting men, and troubling their peace at their pleasure".[82] Rhetoric enables men to cause the credulous to change their beliefs and the corresponding desires that ground action; and "impudence", Hobbes writes in *Behemoth,* "is the goddess of rhetoric, and carries proof with it. For what ordinary man will not, from so great boldness of affirmation, conclude there is great probability in the thing affirmed?"[83]

Several further features of human nature will be important for our subsequent investigation into how the Laws of Nature can be normative and motivationally efficacious for Hobbesian men. Men are prone to develop religious beliefs. The psychological features that incline men toward religious belief – anxiety about their futures, ignorance of how nature operates, and curiosity about how effects are caused, among others – are so natural and pervasive that they "can never be so abolished out of human nature, but that new religions may again be made to spring out of them, by the culture of such men, as for such purpose are in reputation".[84] Furthermore, Hobbes argued that an exercise of natural reason inquiring into the causes of our experience brings us to conclude that God, understood as an eternal, uncaused ultimate cause, exists. This means that religious beliefs are likely to persist in any society, potentially competing with other normative claims on society's members. Showing how the Laws of Nature can be normative for men will thus require a demonstration that these laws do not require that men give up all religious belief, although it may

[81] David Johnston, *The Rhetoric of 'Leviathan': Thomas Hobbes and the Politics of Cultural Transformation* (Princeton, NJ, 1986), and Quentin Skinner, *Reason and Rhetoric in the Philosophy of Hobbes* (Cambridge, 1996), are examples.

[82] EW III, 157; T 119–120.

[83] EW VI, 250; *Behemoth* II.

[84] EW III, 105; T 83.

require certain rationalizing modifications in the content of religious beliefs.[85]

Men aspire to dominion over others, "that is to say, to rule and reign over them; which is a thing, that all men naturally desire".[86] This desire is easy to understand considering Hobbes's view that power requires eminence, and rule over others both expands one's own powers and reduces the number of competitors. But failing dominion, men's love of liberty – of being uncrossed in doing what they will to do – disinclines them to accepting rule by others, "[f]or there are very few so foolish, that had not rather govern themselves, than be governed by others".[87] They are unwilling to give up self-government by their own private judgment unless compelled to do so by the prospect of an even greater burden than that of deferring to the judgment of another.

Hobbes variously characterizes men as self-partial, short-sighted, self-important beings that desire novelty,[88] and as subject to feelings of hate, lust, and envy. The greater part of men are prone to either ambition and covetousness, or else sloth and indolence, and sometimes a combination. Most important, men are *prideful:* apt to take their own reason for right reason, apt to insist that their own judgment is authoritative, to believe that they enjoy God's special favor, and that they are wiser, wittier, more discerning, and more virtuous than others. It is because of men's pervasive pride that Hobbes names his political masterpiece for *Leviathan,* king over all the children of pride, explaining,

> Hitherto I have set forth the nature of man, whose pride and other passions have compelled him to submit himself to government: together with

85 The ineradicability of religious belief, given the persistence of its root sources and of men's incentives for cultivating religious belief in others, poses an insurmountable obstacle to the viability of interpretations of Hobbes's political philosophy that claim Hobbes's strategy for social stability is to get men to give up any religious belief in a higher power or a life beyond the present so as to transform them into the narrow egoists they would need to become in order for civil obedience to be securable by state threats of physical coercion. One such view can be found in Johnston, *The Rhetoric of Leviathan.*

86 EW III, 424; T 297.

87 EW III, 141; T 107. Cf. EW III, 153, 689, 572; T 117, 475, 394–395.

88 For example, EW III, 314; T 225: "the constitution of man's nature, is of itself subject to desire novelty". People do have a "natural inclination" toward their children and members of the opposite sex (EW III, 187; T 140).

the great power of his governor, whom I compared to *Leviathan*, taking that comparison out of the two last verses of the one-and-fortieth of *Job;* where God having set forth the great power of *Leviathan*, calleth him king of the proud.[89]

This pridefulness drives them to demand that others acknowledge their superiority, thus "[a]ll men naturally strive for honour and preferment",[90] and "ambition and greediness of honours cannot be rooted out of the minds of men".[91] Their desire to be honored by others may be so great that they are willing to risk their very lives to gain that honor, "to dare and do anything" in its pursuit: "For what was it but an honourable name with posterity, which the Decii and other Romans sought after; and a thousand others, who cast themselves upon incredible perils?"[92]

Men take others' disagreement with them as a sign of disrespect, as impugning their judgment, and "[a]ll the world knows that such is the nature of men, that dissenting in questions which concern their *power*, or *profit*, or *pre-eminence of wit*, they slander and curse each other".[93] When they cannot win from others the admiration they seek, or at the very least an acknowledgment of their noninferiority, men are likely to try to extract it from others by force, since "life itself, with the condition of enduring scorn, is not esteemed worth the enjoying".[94] The role of pride in the complex constellation of forces directing human action must not be underestimated.

MOTIVATING REBELLION, REASON AND THE DESIRE FOR SELF-JUSTIFICATION

Because he was chiefly concerned to reveal how commonwealths might enjoy perpetual domestic stability, Hobbes thought it important

89 EW III, 307; T 220–221.
90 EW II, 160; *De Cive* 12.10.
91 EW II, 175; *De Cive* 13.12. Rousseau criticized this attribution in his *Discourse on the Origin of Inequality* as a twisted, rather than proper, form of *amour propre*. The desire to be accepted as an equal is proper to self-love, while the desire to assert superiority over others is not.
92 EW II, 318; *De Cive* 18.14.
93 Ibid.
94 EW IV, 101; *Elements of Law* I.3.11.

to discuss what he took to be the motives that lead men to rebel against their existing government. He writes:

> To dispose men to sedition, three things concur. The first is discontent; for as long as a man thinketh himself well, and that the present government standeth not in his way to hinder his proceeding from well to better, it is impossible for him to desire the change thereof. The second is pretense of right; for *though a man be discontent, yet if in his own opinion there be no just cause of stirring against, or resisting the government established, nor any pretence to justify his resistance, and to procure aid, he will never show it.* The third is hope of success; for it were madness to attempt without hope, when to fail, is to die the death of a traitor. Without these three, discontent, pretence, and hope, there can be no rebellion: and when the same are all together, there wanteth nothing thereto, but a man of credit to set up the standard, and to blow the trumpet.[95]

The first and last of these are easy enough to understand. Men who are contented with the present regime will not be motivated to undertake the burdens and risks of attempting regime change. Why should they? And if they see no hope of affecting a change of regime, then even if they are discontent, they will think any effort at revolution futile, and will see no point in assuming its risks and burdens. It is the further condition Hobbes describes as necessary for rebellion that is really interesting. Hobbes insists that men will not rebel unless they believe they are morally justified in doing so, that their cause is just and righteous, or at least that they can mount a plausible moral case in support of their resistance. Even discontented men who can expect to succeed will nonetheless not revolt unless they believe they can *justify* their action. This is a very striking position, which invites the question, Why is pretense of right so important to men?

Hobbes held that humans care deeply about justifying themselves to others.[96] This is not because they have any particular desire to avoid making others unhappy by their actions, although justification does require attention to the effects on others of one's actions, and there is nothing in Hobbes's theory that rules out men's having such a desire. But the importance of justifying one's actions is not that it pleases others for us to do so. On the contrary, Hobbes explicitly recognizes

95 EW IV, 200–201, emphasis added; *Elements of Law* II.8.1.
96 EW IV, 218; *Elements of Law* II.9.8.

that our felt need to justify our actions brings us into conflict with those who favor an alternative course, or who refuse to accept our proposed justification, and creates some of the most acute hostilities, hostilities we will prefer to suffer rather than to give up our claim to being justified. And he laments that sovereigns by conquest bring unnecessary instability to the state by insisting upon justifying their route to power, writing, "they will all of them justify the war, by which their power was at first gotten, and whereon, as they think, their right dependeth, and not on the possession... wherein whilst they needlessly think to justify themselves, they justify all the successful rebellions that ambition shall at any time raise against them, and their successors".[97]

The fact that men will try to justify themselves even when doing so negatively affects their other interests suggests that the desire for self-justification is a matter of personal pride, or vanity. This is surely part of the story, but it is not the whole truth. The desire for justification may be also a matter of wanting to be *worthy* of other's esteem, and decent in our own eyes and in the sight of God. Men may be fearful that God will condemn them for acting unjustifiably, and desire to avoid that condemnation. And it may be that the desire for self-justification depends upon no further desire but is simply built in to the human design, a possibility I shall discuss momentarily. Whatever the proper account, the fact remains that men do care, very much, about justifying themselves, and are loath to harm others unless they feel they may rightfully do so. (This fact explains why Hobbes is concerned to establish the *Right of Nature,* that actions necessary for self-defense are to be granted to be justified.) Especially to undertake something as potentially harmful as sedition, men will need to feel justified in doing so. Because such justification is a necessary condition for rebellion, a "thing necessary [for stable domestic order], is the

[97] EW III, 706; T 486. Garrath Williams argues that Hobbes takes men to be "normatively demanding creatures" who "seek endorsement of our standards for action from those around us" in "Normatively Demanding Creatures: Hobbes, The Fall and Individual Responsibility," *Res Publica* 6, no. 3 (2000): 301–319, 307. I agree with him, although he takes a somewhat more negative view of Hobbesian men's need for self-justification than I do, noting its destructive potential while not discussing, as I stress, its positive potential as a source of motivation to sociable behavior.

rooting out of the consciences of men, all those opinions which seem to justify and give pretense of right to rebellious actions".[98] Hobbes's strategy for preventing civil disorder is to undermine the necessary conditions for rebellion, importantly by depriving men of the ability to justify rebellion. His moral philosophy carries out this task, and helps to undermine men's discontent with being governed, by showing them how much less desirable are the alternatives.

It is helpful in thinking about Hobbes's insistence on the importance to men of self-justification to consider his remarks on madness. What is wrong with the person who is mad? He suffers from an "overvehemence" of passion, from a greater degree of one or another passion than is "usually seen in others". But why is this a problem? Why, in particular, does this overvehemence of passion disable reason? The answer is that madness is passion so vehement that it blots out one's concern to justify oneself to others.[99] Reason, as I shall argue in Chapter 5, is the faculty of *judgment,* whose function is to judge the justifiability of actions (and the warrant of beliefs). What gives motivational force and regulative priority to the conclusions of reason is our desire to justify ourselves. Because we want to be in the right, we will willingly act on our desires only when reason approves our course of action as justifiable. The mad person acts against reason – no matter how well he instrumentally fits means to his mad ends – because his degraded ability to care about justifying his actions severs his actions from his reason, as a wheel without a gear. This analysis makes sense of Hobbes's declaration that "[t]he passion, whose violence, or continuance, maketh madness, is either great *vain-glory;* which is commonly called *pride,* and *self-conceit;* or great *dejection* of mind".[100]

When we are overly prideful or conceited, we feel it beneath us to have to justify our actions to others; and when we are greatly dejected, hopeless and depressed, we just cannot afford to care about doing so, or may already have given up any hope of doing so. In either case we are not moved to put our reason to work to assess the justifiability of our actions. As Hobbes puts the point in *De Homine,* "[e]xcessive

98 EW IV, 218; *Elements of Law* II.9.8.

99 This analysis is at odds with that of Bernard Gert, who believes that Hobbes thought the problem with madness is that it interferes with our pursuit of natural (bodily) preservation, which, in Gert's view, is the end reason dictates to men.

100 EW III, 62; T 54. Cf. EW IV, 57–59; *Human Nature* 10.9–11.

self-esteem impedes reason; and on that account it is a perturbation of the mind.... The contrary emotion is excessive diffidence".[101] It is striking that the two examples of prideful madness Hobbes offers are of persons who believe themselves to be God, or to be divinely inspired.[102] Since God need not justify his actions, as Hobbes makes plain in his own analysis of the meaning of the Biblical story of Job,[103] one who believes himself to be God, or to be in the "supernatural know" by the special grace of God will feel precisely that he is exempted from the requirement of justifying himself to his fellow men. Because the *deployment* of our crucial judging faculty of reason depends upon our caring to justify ourselves, that desire is paramount in Hobbesian psychology, and any perturbation of desires that demotes it is thus deemed pathological. To care for any single thing to the exclusion even of caring to justify ourselves as reasonable is a kind of madness.

The singular importance of the human desire for self-justification may appear fanciful, until we recognize how it is connected to our faculty of reason, and consider what is the significance of our status as reasoning creatures. Many lesser animals share with us the capacity to fit means to desired ends, and so perform instrumental reasoning in that sense. But without the faculty of judgment, we would be no more capable than they of deciding whether it is appropriate to act on the various ends we happen to have. Without the faculty of judgment, our doings would be entirely determined by our instincts, drives, and desires (in conjunction with external environmental conditions). Our voluntary actions would be more properly described as happenings than as doings. The relevant contrast is not between philosophical voluntarism and determinism of the will, since Hobbes is famous for his early development of a compatibilist position, according to which all human doings are determined by prior causes, but many of these are nonetheless voluntary actions for which we may rightly be held responsible. It is, rather, a contrast between being a

101 Gert, *Man and Citizen,* 60.

102 EW III, 63–64; T 55.

103 See, for example, EW III, 347; T 247–248. In *Liberty and Necessity* Hobbes writes, "the power of God alone without other helps is sufficient *justification* of any action he doth.... That which he does, is made just by his doing it; just, I say, in him, though not always just in us" (EW IV, 249).

distinctively *human* being, whose actions, while strictly determined, are nonetheless determined by his human faculty of judgment as well as his animal passions, and being a creature whose doings are driven by instincts or desires alone. Hobbes correctly notes that to accept a picture of ourselves that ascribes to us a faculty of reason that merely serves ends without judging the suitability of serving them is to degrade ourselves to the level of lesser animals. When the madman loses his reason, he becomes no different from, and certainly no better than, the rabbit he eats, or the tiger who eats him.

Hobbes thinks that we will and ought to care very much to claim our birthright as "rational animals". "God", writes Hobbes, "because He hath made men rational, hath enjoined…on them" the Law of Nature, which, as we shall see, limits what actions men may legitimately perform to satisfy their desires, and which desires they can be justified in acting upon.[104] Were men to lack the faculty of judgment, or were they to have it, but be unable to put it to work in deliberation (which requires its representation in the form of an appetite or aversion), they could not be properly said to be the authors of their action, or culpable for their behaviors, any more than are lesser animals. And so Hobbes writes that "children, fools, and madmen that have no use of reason, may be personated by guardians, or curators; but can be no authors, during that time, of any action done by them, longer than, when they shall recover the use of reason, they shall judge the same reasonable".[105]

The suggestion here is that only if one can judge an action reasonable, which ability requires the use of reason, can one be assigned responsibility for it (whether the action is one's own or done in one's name by one's representative); and madmen lack this ability. (Presumably, as I've argued, it is because their overvehement passion blocks the desire for self-justification that motivates the exercise of judgment that they cannot access the reasoning faculty they nonetheless have.) To be demoted from the community of responsible agents, as the madman is because he cannot exercise judgment, would be experienced as degrading by any human being who enjoys that ability. More degraded still may be the position of the person who can

[104] Gert, *Man and Citizen*, 73.
[105] EW III, 150; T 113.

exercise judgment, but doesn't care enough about acting justifiably, and for avoiding appropriate blame and censure, for that desire to determine his actions. Because he is responsible for his actions, his loss of stature is a consequence of self-degradation, which will elicit shame in any who value their special status as human.

We will see in due course how the concern to justify one's actions provides a source of normativity for Hobbes's Laws of Nature. But first, with this richer picture of Hobbesian psychology in hand, and keeping in mind the extensive casuistry of the Laws of Nature we earlier surveyed, let us take a fresh look at our musty default assumptions about the definition and function of Hobbes's Laws of Nature. Are those laws really just advice to the agent about how to preserve herself?

PART TWO

FROM PSYCHOLOGY TO MORAL PHILOSOPHY

3

The Law of Nature: Definition and Function

> [I]f they sin against right, they do, as much as in them lies, abolish human society and the civil life of the present world.
>
> (EW II, 152)

An account of Hobbes's Laws of Nature adequate to explain how agents can be motivated to adhere to the normatively inescapable requirements Hobbes speaks of as the Laws of Nature will ideally provide plausible answers to five distinct questions:

First: What is the definition of a Law of Nature?
Second: What function ultimately unifies the particular rules Hobbes enumerates under the term "the Laws of Nature"?
Third: How are the Laws of Nature normative for agents? That is, what makes their demands binding on us?
Fourth: What can be expected to motivate our compliance with the normative demands of the Laws of Nature?
Fifth: What is the metaphysical status of the Laws of Nature? Are they divine commands, precepts of individual prudence, rule-egoistic principles, freestanding natural duties, or yet something else? And are they literally laws?

Most discussions of Hobbes's Laws of Nature have tended to conflate these questions, particularly the first with the second, the second with both the third and fourth, and the third with both the fourth and the fifth. I suspect that what explains much of this eliding of useful distinctions is that it has seemed obvious to many commentators that the Laws of Nature are, essentially or by definition, instructions for promoting the agent's own preservation or profit, and it is their serving that function that grounds their normativity and motivational efficacy.[1]

My primary concern in this chapter is to challenge the little-considered default answer to the second question: What function *ultimately unifies* the particular precepts Hobbes speaks of as the Laws of Nature? Hobbes makes clear that these precepts all tend to promote peace, but because commentators typically do not see peace as an end in itself, nor believe that Hobbes saw it so, they look for a more basic function these precepts promoting peace ultimately serve. So do I. It has seemed obvious to many that this function is and must be the self-preservation of the individual agent who is to follow those precepts, or the self-interest of the individual agent. I understand why this has seemed obvious to others, but it is no longer obvious to me, and, in fact, I have come to believe that it is false. I shall argue that the only end *reliably* served by the Laws of Nature is *the common good, or the good of humanity generally,* and not the preservation or profit of the individual agent who is to follow those laws, and that for this reason, among others, it is actually the function of securing humanity's good that ultimately unifies Hobbes's Laws of Nature.

I shall not address in this chapter the further questions of what grounds the normativity of those laws, what motivates men to comply with them, or what is their metaphysical status. These are large

[1] For instance, David Boonin-Vail writes: "the laws of nature aim at promoting the self-preservation of the agent who follows them" (*Thomas Hobbes and the Science of Moral Virtue* [Cambridge, 1994], 141). According to Kavka, "[Hobbes's] definition of natural law in all three political works makes it evident that these laws are fundamentally rules of *prudence*" (*Hobbesian Moral and Political Theory* [Princeton, NJ, 1986], 360), a position David Gauthier argued in *The Logic of 'Leviathan'* (Oxford, 1969). A. P. Martinich states in *The Two Gods of Leviathan* (Cambridge, 1992) that "the content of Hobbes's law [of nature]... concerns one's own self-preservation" (116) and that "Hobbes derives the content of his laws of nature from features of self-interest" (122); "the content of... the laws of nature is to defend oneself by any means one can" (110). In the Introduction to his edition of *Leviathan* (Indianapolis, 1994), Edwin Curley writes "the prescriptions [of the Laws of nature] are conditional on, and justified by, your interest in self-preservation" (xxxii). See also Quentin Skinner, *Reason and Rhetoric in the Philosophy of Hobbes* (Cambridge, 1996), 320–321, and Jean Hampton, *Hobbes and the Social Contract Tradition* (Cambridge, 1986).

questions whose answers depend on a prior reconstruction of Hobbes's derivation of the Laws of Nature, my preferred version of which will not be laid out until Chapter 5. However, I shall here engage the first question, as to what is the definition of a Law of Nature, arguing against the common presumption that Hobbes defined a Law of Nature as a precept forbidding an agent to do what is destructive of his own preservation and requiring him to pursue his preservation. Because this presumption has led some commentators to assert that the ultimate function of the Laws of Nature could not but be the individual agent's preservation, it is necessary to my subsequent argument that I explain my reasons for thinking this presumption about how Hobbes defined a Law of Nature is mistaken.

DEFINING A LAW OF NATURE

Identifying Hobbes's definition of the Law of Nature turns out to be more difficult than one might have expected, given his stated commitment to a method that begins from definitions of key concepts, and the centrality to Hobbes's political theory of the concept of the Law of Nature. Part of the difficulty is that Hobbes articulates several apparent definitions, or candidates for a definition, of a Law of Nature that are nonequivalent. Another problem is that he often interjects further observations about what a Law of Nature does, about how we value it, about why we speak of it in the terms we do, and about what uses are made of it, into the sentences in which he is ostensibly defining a Law of Nature. Both of these difficulties contribute to the widespread belief that Hobbes defined a Law of Nature as a norm that directs the self-preservation of the agent. As indicated, I shall argue that this belief is false. And until it is corrected, it will continue to tempt us to conclude that no matter what else Hobbes may say, his moral philosophy must be essentially egoistic because he defines the Laws of Nature that lie at the core of that philosophy as rules for securing the agent's preservation.

Candidate Definitions

Hobbes points out more than once that the definition of a Law of Nature is contested, but what is surprising, considering his concern to settle proper definitions of the concepts he is using, is that his own formulations across several works of the definition of a Law of Nature differ dramatically. In *De Corpore Politico,* Hobbes remarks that "there can therefore be no other law of nature than reason, nor no other precepts of *natural law,* than those which declare unto us the ways of peace, where the same may be obtained, and of defense where it may not".[2] In *Philosophical Rudiments Concerning Government and Society,* Hobbes writes,

the *law of nature,* that I may define it, is the dictate of right reason [i.e. the peculiar and true ratiocination of every man concerning those actions of his, which may either redound to the damage or benefit of his neighbours] conversant about those things which are either to be done or omitted for the constant preservation of life and members, as much as in us lies.[3]

And later in that work, "The natural laws, namely, those…deduced from the dictates of reason…which pertain to the discharge of the duties of men one toward the other"[4] and "the laws of nature are nought else but the dictates of reason"[5] and "those which we call the laws of nature…are nothing else but certain conclusions, understood by reason, of things to be done and omitted".[6]

In the English *Leviathan* of 1651, Hobbes offers this candidate for a definition:

A LAW OF NATURE, (*Lex Naturalis,*) is a Precept, or generall Rule, found out by Reason, by which a man is forbidden to do, that, which is destructive of his life, or taketh away the means of preserving the same; and to omit, that, by which he thinketh it may be best preserved.[7]

2 EW IV, 87.
3 EW II, 16.
4 EW II, 210.
5 EW II, 44.
6 EW II, 49.
7 I quote from Richard Tuck's edition of *Leviathan* (1996), 91, because his edition includes a comma after the word 'do' in the phrase "forbidden to do, that, which is destructive of his life", and a comma after the word 'omit' in the phrase "and to omit, that, by which he thinketh it may be best preserved", as does the earlier edition of C. B. Macpherson (London, 1968), 189. The corresponding passage in EW III, 116–117, deletes this comma, as does Curley's edition, 79, which also deletes the next comma after the word 'that' in each phrase. I find these commas to be of substantive interest, for reasons that will become clear below. Kavka has pointed out that this apparent definition contains prohibitions on both subjectively

However, in the Latin *Leviathan* of 1668, Curley's translation shows Hobbes to have altered the comparable passage to read "A LAW OF NATURE (*lex naturalis*) is a precept or general rule, found out by reason, by which a man is forbidden to do that which seems to him to tend to his own loss".[8] In both the earliest and the latest published candidate definitions Hobbes makes no specific mention of self-preservation, preferring to speak of securing what tends to peace or to our good or avoiding what tends to our loss more generally or what seems to us to do so. No two of these candidate definitions are equivalent.

The Strict Definition: What a Law of Nature "Is"

Despite the striking divergence among these candidate definitions, they do share a simple common core, namely, that *a Law of Nature is a rule found out by reason.* I suggest that this is actually the strict definition of *a* Law of Nature; to be *a* Law of Nature is to be a rule, found out by reason (by which Hobbes means correct reasoning). Among

described actions and objectively described actions: we are forbidden both to omit to do what *we think* will best preserve our life (whether or not our thinking is correct), and also forbidden to do what is objectively destructive or disabling (even though we may mistakenly believe that it is not destructive or disabling). Because what we think may well diverge from what is so, these two requirements may pull apart, threatening the coherence of this definition, supposing that every clause in the sentence is to be taken as part of the definition of a Law of Nature. Those who wish to include every clause within the definition will have to devise some way of rendering it coherent unless they are content to do without it in mounting their own arguments.

[8] Curley, 79. In his edition Curley notes the evidence from Hobbes's verse autobiography that he began writing *Leviathan* in Latin. If so, we cannot be sure that Hobbes altered this passage rather than simply failed to correct it when importing his earlier work into a later complete Latin *Leviathan* (if he did import it). But three Latin editions postdating the English *Leviathan* were published during his lifetime, the last two in England (Curley translates from the latter of these); and it is difficult to believe, given his fastidiousness and mental acumen and his interest in having his views understood, that Hobbes could have been unaware of the error and unintentionally allowed it to stand from decades earlier (G. A. J. Rogers and Karl Schuhmann in their critical edition of *Leviathan* [Bristol, 2003] have argued that Hobbes had nothing to do with the second and third Latin editions of *Leviathan;* but that stills leaves the first.) I am therefore prepared to take it seriously as a revision of the more famous passage in the *Leviathan* of 1651. A. P. Martinich has suggested to me that a slightly more literal rendering of the Latin is that a Law of Nature is a general rule, found out by reason "by which it is prohibited to do that which will seem to himself to tend to his own injury".

the passages seeming to confirm this suggestion is his argument that it is a Law of Nature that a man not weaken the power from which he has demanded or willingly accepted protection, for this prohibition "is a dictate of natural reason, *and consequently* an evident law of nature".[9]

Because he insists that *the* Laws of Nature (the specific set of laws he enumerates and discusses) are moral laws, and morality concerns social behavior, we can also say that the Laws of Nature range over a certain sort of *action*, namely *action that affects others.* They are rules, as Hobbes puts it, "concerning those actions of [a man] which may either redound to the damage or the benefit of his neighbors". We know that Hobbes understood morality to concern what men owe to each other because, for instance, in speaking of the Ten Commandments, Hobbes writes: "Some of them were indeed the laws of nature, as all the second table... [and] The second table containeth the duty of one man towards another".[10]

While it is true of all of the particular norms Hobbes lists under the heading of the Laws of Nature that they concern our behavior toward others, this limited scope should not be taken as part of the definition of a Law of Nature, and indeed it does not appear as an explicit element of all of the candidate definitions. We can understand *a* Law of Nature as simply a rule found out by reason, and *the* Laws of Nature, or *the* Law of Nature identified by Hobbes in the context of an investigation of moral philosophy, as those among such rules that concern our behavior toward others.[11] This latter understanding is suggested by Hobbes's further explanation of why these rules are called Laws of Nature and moral laws: "*The laws mentioned*...are called the laws of nature, for that they are the dictates of natural reason, and also moral laws, because they concern the manners and conversation of men, one towards another".[12]

[9] EW III, 260; T 190; emphasis added.

[10] EW III, 513–514; T 357.

[11] This interpretation allows that a precept discovered by reason forbidding intemperance could be *a* Law of Nature even if it were not included within the set of precepts treating our duties toward others. Not all rationally discoverable precepts need concern social interactions. In fact some will be laws of arithmetic, and others laws of geometry.

[12] EW IV, 111, emphasis added.

The particular rules Hobbes lists are termed *natural* laws because they are discovered through the exercise of the natural faculty of reason. They are spoken of as *moral* laws because they concern morality, which is the duty men owe to one another. Of course, not all natural laws are moral laws. (Galileo's law of free fall is a natural, but not a moral, law.) But because Hobbes is working out (in these texts we are discussing) a moral philosophy, he can take understanding of that context for granted in discussing the Laws of Nature. So long as the context into which Hobbes introduces his definition of a Law of Nature makes clear that we are talking about rules for interacting with others, his definition of a Law of Nature need not contain the scope restriction needed to pick out only the Laws of Nature he is discussing. Hobbes does not include the stipulation that the laws concern social interaction within his definition, but rather exports it to the framing context that governs the scope of the term "Law of Nature" as it appears in his moral philosophy. In explaining why these particular laws are termed moral laws, Hobbes conforms to a pattern of expression he uses to discuss other features of the Laws of Nature that are quite clearly no part of the definition of a Law of Nature. So while it is true that *the particular* laws Hobbes enumerates when discussing the Laws of Nature do all concern actions that affect others, it is preferable to say that what *a* Law of Nature *is*, by definition, is a rule found out by correct reasoning.

Being and Being Called

Just as Hobbes explained why the Laws of Nature are spoken of as moral laws, so he also takes care to explain why these particular natural laws are called *laws:* "[L]aw, properly, is the word of him, that by right hath command over others. But yet if we consider the same theorems, as delivered in the word of God, that by right commandeth all things; then are they properly called laws".[13] According to the present analysis, that the Laws of Nature are divine commands is no part of their definition. This is not in itself to deny divine command interpretations of the Laws of Nature, for it remains true that Hobbes insists that Scripture confirms that God commands us to observe the norms

[13] EW III, 147; T 112.

Hobbes has enumerated as the Laws of Nature, and so that Hobbes maintains that the Laws of Nature are in fact divinely commanded. But a Law of Nature is not *defined* as a divine command found out by reason. Rather, in the quoted passage Hobbes is explaining why these rules *are termed* "laws", just as he earlier explained why they are termed "natural", and why termed "moral". He is offering to show how his analysis of these norms can comfortably accommodate our familiar way of speaking of them. And pointing out that they may properly be called laws when we consider them as commands of God, as Hobbes argues we should, will serve to *multiply men's motives* for following them. That reason recommends them is one motive for following them; that we are divinely commanded to follow them is another, at least for the believer. The multiplication of motives is desirable from Hobbes's point of view, so we should not wonder if we see him adducing as many, and as compelling, additional motives for compliance as he can muster.[14]

Doing, Being, and Being Called

The Laws of Nature are precepts discovered by correct reasoning about those of our actions that affect others. But what the specific rules Hobbes discusses as falling under this definition *do* is promote peace. That is, they enable men to avoid or to remedy social discord, thereby making possible "human society and civil life in the present world".[15] Perhaps, had the world been differently constituted, they would not do so, but as it is, the rules reason identifies for governing relations with others in fact serve to promote peace. This fact about what they do explains "wherein consists their goodness" and "how they come to be praised". Here again Hobbes is attaching to his definition considerations explaining why we speak of these laws the way we do. It follows simply from Hobbes's premises – that we call "good" whatever we desire, and desire peace (being averse to its opposite, war), that we call peace good, as do we also the Laws of Nature that are the "ways or means of peace".[16]

[14] I describe Hobbes's general strategy of multiplying motives for political obedience by offering what I call a confluence of reasons for obedience in *IAI*, 88–98.

[15] EW II, 152.

[16] Hobbes writes, "all men agree on this, that peace is good, and therefore also the way, or means of peace, which, as I have shewed before, are... the laws of nature, are good" (EW III, 146; T 110).

Their goodness "consists" – to use our parlance – in their relation to peace.[17] Again, it follows simply from Hobbes's premises – that we praise what we deem good, deem good what we desire, and desire that the conditions that secure and sustain peace obtain – that we praise the Laws of Nature (for what they do is sustain those conditions). The Laws of Nature "come to be praised, as the means of peaceable, sociable, and comfortable living".[18] Note that because the preservation or profit of some individuals may be an evil to others, men's praising the Laws of Nature is not likely to be on account of the contribution of those laws to the preservation and profit of the agent who follows them, for then men would be praising those laws for securing an end they deem undesirable, namely, the profit of their adversaries. Further, it follows from the fact that vice is the contrary of virtue, that we deem virtuous those qualities in others that please us, and that it pleases us that others have and act on the qualities that sustain peace, that in the case of the Laws of Nature, "their transgression is not properly to be called a crime, but a vice".[19] We thus condemn transgressions of the Laws of Nature as vicious because we desire that others follow the norms that do what the Laws of Nature in fact do.

Although it is no part of the definition of a Law of Nature that it promote peace, the Laws of Nature that concern those actions of ours that affect others do promote peace, and this fact explains why we praise them and view them as good. Were we to fail to distinguish what a Law of Nature is from what Laws of Nature do and how they are spoken of, we would be saddled even so far with a cumbersome complex definition nowhere to be found in any of the candidate definitions, to wit: "*X* is a law of nature if and only if *X* is a divinely commanded precept discovered by correct natural reasoning concerning our behavior towards others that is praised and called good because it promotes peace". But the predicament worsens once we attempt to include within the definition of a Law of Nature not only what the

[17] EW II, 48–49: Hobbes writes of previous moral philosophers "[f]or since they could not observe the goodness of actions to consist in this, that it was in order to peace, and the evil in this, that it related to discord, they built a moral philosophy wholly estranged from the moral law, and unconstant to itself".

[18] EW III, 146–147; T 111.

[19] Curley, *Leviathan*, 99n14.

Laws of Nature do and how we speak of them but also what further ends we can achieve by means of those rules.

Being, and Being That by Which Something Else Is Achieved

A brick is defined as a baked clay block, but it can be used to build a wall or hold open a door or weight a stack of papers or bash the skull of an adversary. A rabbit is a burrowing animal of the family Leporidae, but it may be used as a source of food or fur or companionship, or as a decorative Easter accessory or a particularly demonic instrument of torture against a despised neighboring gardener. Botulinum Toxin A is defined as the nerve toxin produced by the soil-borne bacterium *Clostridium botulinum,* but it can be used to staunch sweating and relax wrinkles. In general, what a thing "is" is not to be identified with what may be done "by means of" that thing. While what a thing is will, of course, constrain what may be done by means of it, and suggest certain uses, standard human purposes also play a large role in how things – independently defined – are deployed. We do not and should not include within the definition of a thing every desired effect that may be achieved by use of that thing.

This is an obvious point, but it applies to rules as well as to more tangible things like bricks and bunnies and Botox. Take tax law. Not everything that can be done by means of a tax law, nor even everything that is usually done by a tax law, belongs to the definition of a tax law. Even if it is true that redistribution of wealth from middle class to very rich is often accomplished by means of tax laws, we would not take such redistribution to be part of the *definition* of a tax law. The definition is independent of many of the functions actually or probably served. Naturally, our personal interests will partially determine how rules defined independently of those interests are nonetheless used; and the fact that a rule can be used to advance our personal interests may increase its palatability and our willingness to comply with and enforce it. This suggests that if it can be shown that some important personal interest is served by means of those Laws of Nature Hobbes has identified, our motives for compliance with reason's requirements are again multiplied, and adherence to them made more secure.

Were Hobbes's Laws of Nature to be *defined* as prohibiting every destructive behavior and compelling all behavior believed to be constructive, every single dangerous action would be a violation, and every single helpful thing would be strictly required by the Law of Nature. This would be too ridiculous to bear consideration. The Laws of Nature would prohibit not just actions inimical to *peace,* but narrowly dysfunctional actions among men in multitudes like selling foods containing transfats or requiring each person to join her local bowling team for the benefits of healthful weight-bearing exercise. The Law of Nature is supposed to regulate social interaction in fundamental ways, and a definition that construes the Law of Nature as so oppressive in its particularity would fail to do that.

With this in mind, I conjecture, Hobbes emphasizes that by means of adhering to the Laws of Nature, many agents will enjoy an increased chance of escaping injury at the hands of others. Of course, some will be the victims of random or passionate or otherwise unreasoned crimes, or of others' accidentally harmful actions; and some few will enjoy positions or have ends that make adherence to the Laws of Nature suboptimal for them. And all remain obliged by the Law of Nature to "protect their protection", that is, their sovereign, in time of war – a risky and oft times fatal requirement. But in general, for most people much of the time, the *general implementation* of the Laws of Nature will create an *environment* in which they can best secure their self-interest. What a Law of Nature *is* is a rule of reason; what the Laws of Nature *do* is promote peace. But *by means of the general implementation of the laws,* a man may improve his prospects for avoiding harm at the hands of his fellows. While this last is no part of the definition of a Law of Nature, it is an undeniably attractive talking point for multiplying motives for adherence to the set of natural laws that promote and sustain peace.

This interpretation receives support from Hobbes's peculiar, but persistent, formulation of a Law of Nature as a rule of reason "*by which* a man is forbidden to do, *that,* which" (in the general formulation of the Latin *Leviathan*) "seems to him to tend to his own loss". As radically as Hobbes changes the definition of a Law of Nature between the English and the Latin *Leviathan*'s in the passage under discussion, he retains his puzzling "by which..., that, which ..." locution, and this fact is worthy of attention. Hobbes *could* be saying a Law of Nature is a rule found out by reason; by means of which rule a man is forbidden himself to do some type of action, which type of action when performed by others seems to him to threaten his interests. So, for example, supposing that a man will think people's retaining their right to all things threatens his interests (as Hobbes has argued he should), then the rule found out by reason requiring that this right not be retained will be one which forbids him to do *that* – namely, retain the right to all things – which people's doing seems to him to threaten his interests. In subsequent chapters I shall return to this possible interpretation of Hobbes's statement. For now, the point to notice is the narrow one that on this interpretation, the Laws of Nature might often be successfully used to serve what is, from the agent's point of view, the desirable function of furthering his self-interest, even though this possible use of them does not belong to their definition, nor to any account of what they systematically do.

Thus there is no *necessity* that we construe Hobbes's definition of a Law of Nature as a rule that enjoins either self-preservation or self-interest more generally. And there is good reason not to, if we think of those passages that seem to be offered as definitions of a Law of Nature as what promotes self-interest by analogy with Hobbes's professed model for demonstration, geometry. Recall that geometry is Hobbes's model science, and model for rational demonstration generally. He opines that had the moral philosophers discharged their commission as well as did the geometers, humanity would have been spared the devastations of civil war. Hobbes aspires to give moral philosophy the demonstrative warrant of right reasoning from correct definitions or indubitable axioms that he believes geometry to enjoy.

Consider then geometrical theorems (rules found out by reason concerning the qualities of figures from the proportions of lines and angles).[20] The theorems of geometry may serve for land survey, to measure the size of vessels, and for other practical tasks of directing actions according to our ends; but the theorems of geometry are *not*

[20] Hobbes characterizes geometry as "addition and subtraction in lines, figures... angles, proportions" (EW III, 30; T 32). Cf. EW I, 71, 73, 87, where Hobbes emphasizes that geometry concerns "the ways of simple motion". We might define Hobbes's Euclidean geometry as rules describing the properties of objects extended in space disregarding all properties other than those preserved under rigid motions.

defined as those rules that serve the individual agent's practical purposes. For any given individual, his interest in the theorems of geometry, or their normativity for him given his interest, or his motivation to observe them, may well depend on his practical purposes and desired ends; but those facts have nothing to do with the definition of a theorem of geometry. A theorem of geometry is a truth collected by right reasoning governing the use of geometrical terms described independently; a theorem of geometry *does* describe the properties and relations of geometrical objects; and a theorem of geometry may be *used* to serve any number of important human purposes. Clearly, these three features of a geometrical theorem are distinct, and certainly not all parts of the definition of a theorem of geometry.

We can appreciate this point by considering how we would regard a purported definition of a law of geometry that strictly paralleled what most commentators take as a definition of the (moral) Law of Nature. Assuming a context of discussion that exports the scope constraint (that geometrical laws are concerned with geometrical notions) to the position of a qualifier on the definition (as I have argued his moral Laws of Nature definition did), the definition of a law of geometry strictly analogous to Hobbes's statement in the English *Leviathan* in the third paragraph of chapter 14 would be the following:[21] "A LAW OF GEOMETRY…is a precept or general rule, found out by reason, by which a man is forbidden to do, that, which is inimical to sound land surveying practices or takes away the means of performing the same; and to omit, that, by which he thinketh they may be best performed".

In this case we would not be remotely tempted to construe the clauses following "by which" as parts of the definition of "a theorem of geometry". We would understand that two things are being communicated; the definition of a theorem of geometry – "a precept of general rule found out by reason [concerning geometrical objects independently defined]" – and what such theorems imply for a particular issue we care about. For instance, while it is quite true that

[21] EW III, 116–117; T 91: "A LAW OF NATURE (*lex naturalis*) is a precept or general rule, found out by reason, by which a man is forbidden to do that, which is destructive of his life, or taketh away the means of preserving the same; and to omit that, by which he thinketh it may be best preserved".

should one deny a certain theorem of geometry, for instance, the congruence of alternate interior angles formed by a transversal cutting across two parallel lines, one will be doing something, which thing is inimical to sound land surveying practices and taking away the means of performing the same (and so we shouldn't do *that*), this does not imply that *serving* surveying practices is part of the *definition* of a geometrical theorem, nor any element of the derivation of this particular one.

I suggest that the same error is committed by those who treat as belonging to the definition of a Law of Nature observations about the interests the Laws of Nature may be used to forward. This category mistake has been particularly pernicious within the interpretation of Hobbes's moral philosophy, for it has led to commentators to assume without argument that the ultimate function of the Laws of Nature *must be* to promote the preservation or profit of the individual agent because Hobbes *defined* a Law of Nature as a rule that promotes the preservation or profit of the agent. If, as I've argued, he did not, the question what function ultimately unifies the Laws of Nature will have to be decided on its own merits, on the basis of evidence and argument. We turn now to a consideration of that question.

THE ULTIMATE FUNCTION OF THE LAWS OF NATURE

What function – the common good of mankind or the agent's good – ultimately unifies the particular rules Hobbes enumerates as the Laws of Nature? This inquiry is motivated in part by a minor mystery: If Hobbes intended to justify his political conclusions in terms of the agent's self-interest, why did he insist across some thirty years of writings on employing the highly distorting language of natural law? Traditional conceptions of natural law understood that law to be directed to the *common* good, or the good of *humanity*, and not only to the narrow self-interest of the individual.[22] Natural law was thought to approve an individual's pursuit of self-preservation, but without a doubt talk of natural law carried a presumption that securing the

[22] For instance, Aquinas had defined law as "an ordinance of reason for the common good, promulgated by him who has care of the community" (*Summa Theologica*, part 1–2, Q 90, art. 4).

common good was the proper function of the Law of Nature. Hobbes elected to hitch his cart to this natural law tradition. Why would Hobbes call upon a tradition in which the good of the human *community* is understood to be central for the purpose of presenting an entirely agent-centered theory of normative requirements?[23]

The simplest solution to this minor mystery is that Hobbes *wasn't* intending to offer a novel individualistic theory – that he actually was thinking of the Laws of Nature as functioning to secure mankind's common good in the same way as his natural law predecessors had supposed them to do, but saw the advantage to be gained by emphasizing how these rules might be used to advance the agent's self-interest. Perhaps he thought of them as rules for securing the fundamental needs and interests of human communities, or of mankind generally, the agent's interests included, rather than as fundamentally the personal voice of individual narrow self-interest. I'll now investigate that possibility by asking which is more plausible as an interpretation of Hobbes's argument: That the Laws of Nature reliably realize the narrow self-interest of any agent who follows them? Or that they reliably secure a common human good (and thereby *also* tend, although only contingently and not fully reliably, to secure the good of the agent)? I'll call the first of these possibilities the "self-interest account" of the Laws of Nature; the second, "the common good account".[24]

[23] Johann P. Sommerville provides an elegant brief overview of the natural law tradition Hobbes inherited, while noting that "much of the peculiarity of Hobbes' political theory arises from the emphasis that he placed on self-preservation"; *Thomas Hobbes: Political Ideas in Historical Context* (New York, 1992), 33. Although Sommerville himself believes that Hobbes "grounded his whole system upon individual self-preservation" (37), understood as a duty owed to God (33), he remarks that "the special status [Hobbes] gave to self-preservation... flew in the face of one of the most widely accepted beliefs of his contemporaries", namely, that men are naturally sociable (39). As Sommerville notes, other natural law theorists (e.g., Aquinas) had held that men seek the preservation of their whole species (34). Presumably they are naturally sociable in other ways as well, their natural impulses grounding natural laws directing their pursuit of those natural sociable ends. It is puzzling then that, had Hobbes thought that the ultimate function of the Laws of Nature is to secure the narrow self-interest of the agent, he would have adopted natural law discourse to express that view, knowing that it carried this unwanted baggage.

[24] The common good account claims that the Laws of Nature reliably secure the shared good of communities of interacting agents ("men in multitudes") rather than the distinct goods of individual agents. But insofar as distinct communities

Overt Text

We must now revisit some of the passages we looked at earlier in the context of determining Hobbes's definition of a Law of Nature, but this time with the intention to discern his stance on whether it is the individual agent's good or rather mankind's good that provides the ultimate unifying function of the Laws of Nature. In the English *Leviathan,* Hobbes asserts that "A LAW OF NATURE...is a precept...by which a man is forbidden to do that, which is destructive of his life, or taketh away the means of preserving the same; and to omit that, by which he thinketh it may be best preserved".[25] This looks like strong evidence for the self-interest account, as does the parallel passage in his later Latin *Leviathan:* "A Law of nature is a precept... by which a man is forbidden to do that which seems to him to tend to his own loss". This still looks narrowly self-interested, if no longer preservation-centered.

However, other passages appear to favor the common-good account. Consider this passage from *Philosophical Rudiments* asserting that the right to all things had to be given up: "[R]eason, namely, dictating that they must forego that right *for the preservation of mankind;* because the equality of men among themselves...was necessarily accompanied with war; and with war joins *the destruction of mankind*".[26] Michael Silverthorne's translation of the corresponding passage in *De Cive* is this: "[A]t the dictation of reason, that right had to be given up for the preservation *of the human race.* For the inevitable consequence of men's being equal...was war, and the consequence of war is *the ruin of mankind*".[27]

(say, nations or peoples) interact with one another, the common good account also implies that the Laws of Nature reliably secure the good of mankind, for Hobbes tells us that the Laws of Nature govern the relations of commonwealths, and that the Law of Nature is the proper law of nations. I shall thus suppose that whatever secures the common good, also secures the good of humanity generally, when the different communities into which humanity is organized are interacting. I am grateful to Kinch Hoekstra for discussion on this point.

[25] Cf. EW II, 16, quoted above.

[26] EW II, 206–207, emphasis added.

[27] Richard Tuck and Michael Silverthorne (eds.), *On the Citizen* (Cambridge, 1998), 173. Tuck notes that "Hobbes himself never repudiated the book, despite having published *Leviathan* four years later, and he proudly reprinted it in his collected works (in Latin) in 1668, alongside a Latin translation of *Leviathan*" (ix). If Tuck is

Lest we imagine that Hobbes may be using the term 'mankind' idiosyncratically as a synonym for 'the agent', he had already counterposed these: "it is easily judged how disagreeable a thing to the preservation *either of mankind, or of each single man,* a perpetual war is".[28] A concern for the good of humanity generally appears clearly here: "[L]aw was brought into the world for nothing else, but to limit the natural liberty of particular men, in such manner, as they might not hurt, but assist one another, and join together against a common enemy".[29]

Because there is textual support for each of these two interpretations, the bare language of Hobbes's remarks on the subject of the Laws of Nature will not suffice to settle the issue between them. To be sure, Hobbes often discusses the Laws of Nature as rules for promoting peace among men, but both interpretations can understand peace to be of purely instrumental value. This is not to say that the fact that Hobbes took peace to be of instrumental value cannot help us to decide between the self-interest and common good accounts, for it may be that peace better serves one of these ends than the other. Any plausible interpretation will have to square with Hobbes's insistence that the Laws of Nature are "immutable and eternal.... For it can *never* be that war shall preserve life, and peace destroy it".[30] But we need not think of peace as an end in itself.

correct, this passage is evidence that Hobbes all along held that the problem with war is its harm to humanity generally, thus implying that the value of the Laws of Nature forestalling war is their securing the good of humanity.

[28] EW II, 12, emphasis added. Silverthorne translates the parallel passage in *De Cive,* "One may easily see how incompatible perpetual *War* is with the preservation of the human race or of individual men" (Tuck and Silverthorne, *On the Citizen,* 30).

[29] EW III, 254; T 186. The Laws of Nature are "rules which conduce to the preservation of *man's life on earth*" (EW III, 134–135; T 103); "These are the laws of nature, dictating peace, for a means of the conservation of *men in multitudes*", which Hobbes contrasts with "other things tending to the destruction of *particular men*" (EW III, 144; T 110, emphases added). Those other rational dictates not concerned with social interactions can, of course, satisfy the formal definition of a Law of Nature as a rule found out by reason (as do geometrical theorems and Galileo's law of free fall), but that does not argue for including them among the set of rules Hobbes terms "the" Laws of Nature as spoken of by the moral philosophers. However, I shall argue that they are not themselves laws, but rather other "things which the law of nature hath forbidden".

[30] EW III, 145; T 110 emphasis added.

Our question, then, is whether what ultimately unifies the function of the Laws of Nature is that they secure the common good (good of humanity generally), or rather that they secure the self-interest (including self-preservative interest) of the agent who follows them. Of course, it is a difficult and subtle matter to devise tests that could help us decide this question, because no universally binding rule could be thought to secure the interests of humanity generally that did not also secure the interests of (at least most of) the agents following it (at least most of) the time. Nor could rules that all must follow be good for mankind if following them harmed most people. So we would expect rules that are good for humanity to be good for most individual agents, much of the time. One question, then, will be whether Hobbes's text supports the self-interest account's claim that Laws of Nature must, and so do, *always* secure the interest of the agent who is to follow them, or whether they *sometimes* direct actions against the self-interest of *some* of the persons required to follow them (as the humanity account implies that they could). That is, can the Laws of Nature ever require an agent to act against her own greatest self-interest?

Clarifying and Motivating the Common Good Account

In order to make clearer the distinction between the two accounts, let me offer a possibly useful analogy. Suppose we think of Hobbes's Laws of Nature by analogy with "rules for the preservation of airline passengers in case of unintended landings" (aka, crashes). Consider such rules; taking into account the conditions generally required for human survival, they are aimed at preserving the maximum number of passengers in the event of a crash and are formulated to accommodate problems of interaction imposed by the copresence and thus cooperation or interference of other passengers. These rules typically include such directives as "Remain calm and quiet. Follow the instructions of the flight attendants. Crouch low to the floor (to reduce smoke inhalation). Leave your belongings behind, and proceed in an orderly fashion, without pushing or shoving, toward the nearest exit". It is perfectly plausible that should passengers follow such rules as these in the event of a crash, more lives will be preserved than would be were they to follow any alternative set of rules, or to act each on his or her own judgment or impulse. These rules create, for any given crash, an *environment* optimally conducive to human survival. Those rules could thus exemplify "rules for the preservation of passengers in general". This would be a common good account, akin to the one I have proposed for understanding Hobbes's Laws of Nature.

But is it plausible to say of each passenger that *he,* in the event of a crash, can expect to best preserve *his* life by being herded along with the others? What if he is very far from an exit, there are slow-moving octogenarians or injured passengers in his path, and the plane is on fire? Does he really maximize his own prospects by following the airline's general "passenger preservation" rules?

Apparently, corporate America thinks not (according to tabloid exposés of how they coach their executives). It advises its frequent-flyer executives that they should obtain seats near an exit (which is obviously not a universally generalizable rule), carry individual smoke inhalation masks, and then should, in the event of a crash, *get off the plane as fast as possible by any means necessary,* including pushing out of the way or climbing over all passengers located between them and the exits. Corporate America sees that the dictates of individual prudence *diverge* from "rules for the preservation of men in multitudes".

The general point suggested by this analogy is that it does not follow from the fact that a rule, if generally followed, would preserve the maximum number of people, that conforming to the rule will best preserve the individual agent. This obvious point helps us to see the common good account as genuinely distinct from the self-interest account.

But here, proponents of the self-interest view may object that Hobbes cannot maintain any such distinction, even should he wish to, because he holds that an individual is not required to do the actions dictated by the Laws of Nature whenever it would "procure his own certain ruin" to do so.[31] If individuals are released from their duty to be just, grateful, merciful, tractable, and so on, whenever doing so would certainly destroy them, then, concludes the objection, that must be so because the Laws of Nature are essentially dictates of individual self-preservation. If one need not follow them when they do

[31] EW III, 145, T 110.

not serve one's self-interest, they must be in their essence dictates *of* self-interest.

There is no question of Hobbes's commitment to the view that individuals are not required to act as the Laws of Nature dictate when doing so would procure their own certain ruin.[32] But it certainly does not follow from this that the Laws of Nature must be rules directing individuals to preserve themselves, or rules justified by reference to the interests of the agent. We can infer *nothing* about the essential purpose of a rule from facts about the conditions under which it is suspended. Consider another analogy: One justification for requiring citizens to sit on juries is that trial by a jury of one's peers best realizes justice in a democracy. It is true that a showing of "extreme financial hardship" excuses one from jury duty, but this does not imply that the essential purpose of jury duty is to promote the financial well-being of the jurors. (If that were so, jurors should be permitted to accept bribes as well!) When jury service would compromise the self-preservation of a juror, he is excused; but the essential aim of jury service is to contribute to the justice, and thus common good, of society. Similarly, when adhering to the Laws of Nature would "procure one's certain ruin", one is excused from doing so; but the Laws of Nature need not be essentially rules of individual self-preservation. They might just as easily be rules for the preservation, or common good, of mankind generally.

Hobbes does acknowledge men's natural right to do what they sincerely judge necessary for their preservation, but it is important to remember that this right is quite limited and, as I will argue in Chapter 5, is a right itself derived from the Law of Nature. The summary formulation of the Laws of Nature is not to treat others in any

[32] In *Leviathan* he writes, "The laws of nature oblige...to the putting them in act, not always. For he that should be modest, and tractable, and perform all he promises, in such time, and place, where no man else should do so, should but make himself a prey to others, and procure his own certain ruin, contrary to the ground of all laws of nature, which tend to nature's preservation" (EW III, 145: T 110). Notice, though, that Hobbes is willing to excuse people from obedience to the Laws of Nature only to avoid their own certain destruction, and not to procure lesser gains or to avoid lesser harms. The excuse does not extend to interests other than avoiding "certain ruin". In less extreme cases, we are bound to obey the Laws of Nature even when doing so is not in our narrow self-interest. I provide textual evidence to support this suggestion below.

way we would think it unreasonable of them to treat us. Because we would think it unreasonable of others to blame us for defending our lives – something which in any case we may not be able to restrain ourselves from doing – the Law of Nature requires us to grant others that same right. To harm others in pursuit of what we *sincerely believe to be necessary* for our preservation is blameless under the Law of Nature. But this right is not a blank check, and it *never* permits us to harm others in the ways the Laws of Nature forbid in pursuit of ends less pressing than our very survival. It is in this way that the Laws of Nature *always* bind *in foro interno* – in the court of conscience – and anything we do against them in bad faith is sin, a violation of God's law, for which God will hold us accountable.

Still, it might be thought that had Hobbes held a common good account of the Laws of Nature, he should not have allowed any self-preservation suspension condition on them at all, for wouldn't humanity's interests be better served if each man were always required to adhere to all the laws *in foro externo,* no matter how others behave, and even at the sacrifice of his life, in order to avoid warfare that threatens the common good? But this would be a mistake. This would not prevent warfare, but only increase the incidence of one-sided warfare (of the opponents' will to contend by battle). The suspension condition provides a deterrent to would-be aggressors, and an inducement to cooperation, both of which help to secure the peaceful conditions that benefit humanity. Were men to be duty-bound not to resist aggression, they would invite aggression, and we could expect much more violence and insecurity overall than under Hobbes's suspension condition, thus compromising the good of humanity. So the common good account fares no worse than the self-interest account in accommodating Hobbes's suspension condition.[33]

There is another, facile, objection to the common good account. It might be asserted that the Laws of Nature could be justified only by reference to the agent's personal interest because Hobbesian men are psychological egoists, incapable of being motivated (hence, by the principle "ought implies can" of being duty-bound) to do anything not recommended by self-interest, or to act on any ground other than self-interest. As I noted n Chapter 2, recent studies have decisively shown

[33] Kinch Hoekstra alerted me to this possible objection.

that Hobbes's texts do *not* support this attribution of psychological egoism.[34] Because the foundational assumption of this objection is less tenable than the common good account it is intended to preclude, I mention the objection only to set it aside.

Finally, I want briefly to sketch how Hobbes understands the idea of the "common good", because it may seem to us that the notion of individual self-interest enjoys a conceptual transparency that the notion of "the interests of humanity", or of the common good, does not. What "interests" or common good does, or could, humanity have?[35]

This much about Hobbes's view is clear: If *anything* is contrary to the common good, the *mode of life suffered in the state of nature is*. So we can think of the common good as (at a minimum) the benefits that distinguish the state of men under civil government from the miserable form of life in a state of nature. These are primarily the benefits of peaceable, organized, sociable, and comfortable living within a community. Peaceable living offers increased security of life and limb, and freedom from gnawing fear; organized sociable living provides the benefits of culture, civilization, and fellowship that depend on political relationships; "commodious living" involves comfort, variety, and plenty. In *De Cive,* Hobbes contrasts life outside of the commonwealth, with life within it: "[O]ut of it, there is a dominion of passions, war, fear, poverty, slovenliness, solitude, barbarism, ignorance, cruelty; in it, the dominion of reason, peace, security, riches, decency, society, elegancy, sciences, and benevolence".[36]

It is fair, then, to characterize Hobbes's conception of the common good as the enjoyment of peace, security, riches, decency, society, elegancy, sciences, and benevolence – in short, to use his own phrase, of "peaceable, sociable, and comfortable living". This characterization of humanity's interests seems adequately intelligible. Maintaining "human society and the civil life of the present world" would be the ends toward which the Laws of Nature aim on the common good account, and not, as on the self-interest view, merely the self-preservation or self-interest of the individual agent. We can see a graphic representation

[34] See, for instance, the Introduction in Bernard Gert, *Man and Citizen: Thomas Hobbes* (Indianapolis, 1991).

[35] I am indebted to John Dreher for raising this worry, and for his very helpful discussion with me about it.

[36] EW II, 127.

of the contrast between a condition securing the common good and the condition of mere nature in the frontispiece to Hobbes's *De Cive* (Figure 3.1). In it the condition of mere nature, or liberty, is represented by a half-naked savage presiding over a land of forts and inhabitants chasing one another with bows and arrows. The condition under

FIGURE 3.1. Frontispiece to *De Cive*, 1642.

civil law, in contrast, shows a civilized figure holding scales of justice presiding over a happy and prosperous land of farms and interesting cities and churches.

To appreciate the appeal of this account of Hobbes's conception of the interests of humanity, notice that the problem with a "state of nature", which Hobbes defines in *Leviathan* as a state in which "private judgment" is the measure of good and evil, is that in it our interests in peaceable, sociable, and comfortable living cannot be realized: Commodious living is undercut by the withering of "industry", of "culture of the earth", of "navigation", of "use of commodities that may be imported by the sea", of "commodious building", and for want of "instruments of moving and removing such things as require much force". Without commonwealths, humanity cannot enjoy the benefits of social cooperation that produce "knowledge of the face of the earth", any "account of time", the arts" and "letters", and, generally, "society".[37] Moreover, without a social system of organization within commonwealths, individuals would find themselves in "continual fear, and danger of violent death". This would make people's lives not only likely short, but also and importantly, "solitary" (i.e., not even weakly social), "poor" (i.e., not commodious), and "nasty and brutish" (i.e., uncultured, uncivilized, and unfitting for a human being). Organization into commonwealths supplies the deficiencies of the state of nature. Thus it is in humanity's interest to abide by norms that best secure the stability of commonwealths, or civil life. These are the norms articulated by Hobbes's Laws of Nature.

An Argument for the Common Good Account from the Implausibility of the Alternative

Because both the self-interest and the common good interpretations agree that Hobbes viewed the Laws of Nature as requirements of peace, each must mount a case that peace is required in order to secure the end it claims it to be the ultimate function of the laws to serve. Thus the common good account must claim that pursuing

[37] EW III, 113; T 89. I understand this to mean not just company (as opposed to solitude), but an organized society with differentiation of complementary roles – what Rawls termed a "social union".

peace always best secures the interest of humanity, while the self-preservation account must insist that peace always best promotes the interests of the agent bound by the rules (that is, that each individual's interests are best served by pursuing peace). My first argument in favor of the humanity account addresses the implausibility, including textual implausibility, of this latter claim.

Hobbes wrote that "all men agree on this, that peace is good, and therefore also the way, or means of peace, which...are...the laws of nature, are good".[38] Yet to say this, that peace is good "in the conversation, and society of mankind" as being "conformable... to reason, in the actions of common life",[39] and thus that the Laws of Nature "come to be praised, as the means of peaceable, sociable, and comfortable living", is evidently not to say that every agent values peace as a means to satisfying his personal interest. Hobbes recognized, what we see clearly, that peace is unfortunately not always in the rational self-interest, even the long-run rational self-interest, of every agent. Many agents in Hobbes's world *stand to fare better by destabilizing the peace* than by adhering to the Laws of Nature that promote it: "needy and hardy" men who will benefit from disruption of the prevailing social order, men ambitious of military command or other office, potent or popular men whom others will protect,[40] the wealthy and powerful who can privately command defenses, religious zealots who care more for their cause than they do for peace or their narrow self-interest, and even, on occasions, sovereigns, who may rationally hope to enrich themselves and their people by foreign wars. When so many stand to gain by violating the Laws of Nature, the position that the Laws of Nature promote the interest of all bound by them seems quite indefensible.

Hobbes explicitly discusses some types who fare better by violating the Laws of Nature – those who hope to make a living by war, or come out better off because of it: "[N]eedy men, and hardy, not contented with their present condition; as also, all men that are ambitious of military command, are inclined to continue the causes of war; and to stir up trouble and sedition: for there is no honour military but

38 EW III, 146; T 111.

39 Ibid.

40 And who can extort money or preferments from the state as a condition for desisting from their disruptive actions. See EW III, 338; T 241.

by war; nor any such hope to mend an ill game, as by causing a new shuffle".[41] There is no suggestion in this passage or elsewhere that Hobbes thinks such people are making *errors* in reasoning; he seems to acknowledge that for them there is no more rational way to their ends than to "reshuffle the deck" – to force a new deal – to stir up trouble in ways the Laws of Nature forbid. Such men may reasonably expect to fare better by disrupting the status quo than by maintaining it. Yet while their violations of the Laws of Nature may profit them, they nonetheless contribute to the destabilization of social order, contrary to the interests of humanity generally, for which reason the Law of Nature condemns them.

Nor are these marginal characters. In his history of the English Civil War, Hobbes names them among the important agents of that disorder:

> Sixthly, there were a *very great number* that had either wasted their fortunes, or thought them too mean for the good parts they thought were in themselves; and *more there were,* that had able bodies, but saw no means how honestly to get their bread. These *longed for a war,* and hoped to maintain themselves hereafter by the lucky choosing of a party to side with, and consequently did for the most part serve under them that had greatest plenty of money.[42]

Others who may sometimes stand to gain by violating the Laws of Nature include *powerful persons* – those with extraordinary wealth, or large followings. These people may quite rationally aim to extract greater than equal benefits from others (thus violating the second, eighth, and ninth Laws of Nature) while still deterring retaliation by threat of their superior power. Hobbes cites the case of Julius Caesar, who "having won to himself the affections of his army, made himself master both of senate and people" as an instance of how "this proceeding of popular, and ambitious men" in violation of natural law,[43] *can indeed* bring them personal gain, and is thus to be guarded against.[44] Hobbes notes that

> it happeneth *commonly,* that such as value themselves by the greatness of their wealth, adventure on crimes, upon hope of escaping punishment, by corrupting public justice, or obtaining pardon by money or other rewards.

41 EW III, 86–87; T 71.
42 EW VI, 168, emphases added.
43 Especially against the first, second, and third Laws of Nature.
44 EW III, 320–321; T 230.

And that such as have multitude of potent kindred; and popular men, that have gained reputation amongst the multitude, take courage to violate the laws, from a hope of oppressing the power, to whom it belongeth to put them in execution.[45]

Although Hobbes does not say so here, it must be as obvious to him as it is to us that often the hopes of such people are realized, and that it cannot always have been irrational for them to have expected the benefits they actually obtained. As he notes in *De Homine,* "Riches, if immense – certainly as Lucullus defined the wealthy man as one that can support an army on his own – are useful. For they are *almost certain* protection".[46] Thus the observation that the wealthy and powerful may rightly judge that they stand to gain by violating the Laws of Nature is fully compatible with Hobbes's insistence, in the famous "Foole" passage,[47] that one who violates the Laws of Nature acts irrationally even when his iniquity turns out to benefit him, because he could not have foreseen the turn of events that enabled him to snatch victory from the jaws of defeat. At least some among the powerful and wealthy *can* foresee the happy outcome, because they enjoy "almost certain" immunity from their violations of natural law, and thus do not act as fools in pursuing their narrow self-interest at the expense of others.

Hobbes warns that selecting good counselors is difficult precisely because people do expect to benefit from disrupting peace:

The most able counsellors, are they that have least hope of benefit by giving evil counsel, and most knowledge of those things that conduce to the peace,... [yet it] is a hard matter to know who expecteth benefit from public troubles; but the signs that guide to a just suspicion, is the soothing of the people in their unreasonable, or irremediable grievances, by men whose estates are not sufficient to discharge their accustomed expenses.[48]

In general, Hobbes recognizes the possibility of what he calls "successful wickedness".[49] Unhappiness is not always the punishment

[45] EW III, 283; T 205, emphasis added.

[46] Gert, *Man and Citizen,* 49, emphasis added. Lest we think such people too few to be of great importance, Hobbes continues, "Moderate wealth, to those willing to use it for protection, is also useful; for it acquires friendships; friendships, moreover, are protection".

[47] EW III, 132–133; T 102.

[48] EW III, 339; T 242.

[49] EW III, 132; T 102.

of vice, at least not in this world. Hobbes acknowledges that for all we can tell, the wicked do prosper,[50] but argues that nonetheless success does not *justify* wickedness.[51] No violation of the law can be justified by the fact that the violator *successfully profits,* because were the bindingness of laws to be judged by their personal effects on individuals, the security of men generally would suffer. Hobbes writes:

> [M]en, from having observed how in all places, and in all ages, unjust actions have been authorized, by the force, and victories of those who have committed them... have thereupon taken for principles... *that examples of former times are good arguments of doing the like again;* and many more of that kind: which being granted, no act in itself can be a crime, but must be made so, not by the law, but by the success of them that commit it; and the same fact be virtuous, or vicious, as fortune pleaseth; so that what Marius makes a crime, Sylla shall make meritorious, and Caesar, the same laws standing, turn again into a crime, to the perpetual disturbance of the peace of the commonwealth.[52]

In the passage just quoted Hobbes is talking about positive laws, but there is no reason to think his argument would be any different for natural laws, especially since he insists that the natural law is always a part of civil law.[53] Hobbes's point is that if we take the stand that what the law is (i.e., that what norms bind us) depends on what happens to profit us as individuals, then law will differ from person to person and over time, causing never-ending disruption to peace. Hobbes condemns that stance, and it is a perfectly plausible explanation of his

[50] Hobbes writes, "This question, *why evil men often prosper, and good men suffer adversity,* has been much disputed by the ancient, and is the same with this of ours, *by what right God dispenseth the prosperities and adversities of this life;* and is of that difficulty, as it hath shaken the faith, not only of the vulgar, but of philosophers, and which is more, of the Saints, concerning the Divine Providence" (EW III, 346; T 247). He argues, not that rogues are made to pay in the end, thus making successful wickedness impossible; rather, that God's actions are justified by his irresistible power and not by our ideas of justice.

[51] Machiavelli famously argues that successful wickedness is an oxymoron; he praises as virtues successful violations of moral conventions, especially when they serve to secure political power. (In fairness to Machiavelli, he does value political power as a means to *salus populi* and the glory of the state, so it might be argued that for Machiavelli as well as for Hobbes, virtuous acts are those that secure the good of men generally.)

[52] EW III, 281–282; T 204.

[53] "The law of nature, and the civil law, contain each other, and are of equal extent.... The law of nature therefore is part of the civil law in all commonwealths of the world" (EW III, 253; T 185).

condemnation that natural law requires us to act in ways that provide for the general good of humanity, from which we are excused for no self-interested end less urgent than immediate survival. Individuals do sometimes profit from violating the Laws of Nature, but personal profit cannot be the standard for right conduct set down by law.

Another important class of persons who might reasonably expect to gain by violating the Laws of Nature at least some of the time is sovereigns. Although Hobbes insists that sovereigns have reason not to pilfer or abuse their subjects ("the good of the sovereign and people, cannot be separated"),[54] it seems that it would be often in their interest to violate the Laws of Nature when dealing with foreign states. Sovereigns certainly are bound by the requirements of the Laws of Nature in their treatment of foreign states: "[T]he law of nations, and the law of nature, is the same thing.... And the same law, that dictateth to men that have no civil government, what they ought to do, and what to avoid in regard of one another, dictateth the same to commonwealths, that is, to the consciences of sovereign princes and sovereign assemblies".[55]

Yet the sovereign of a very powerful nation may rationally expect to gain by waging an offensive war for plunder (not self-defense) against another nation too weak to make effective resistance. Hobbes writes that "because there is no territory under the dominion of one commonwealth, except it be of very vast extent, that produceth all things needful for the maintenance, and motion of the whole body... [the commonwealth does] supply these wants at home, by importation of that which may be had abroad, either by exchange, or *by just war*".[56] Since within Hobbes's system there can be no injustice between sovereigns unless they have undertaken special agreements toward one another, all wars not forbidden by prior treaty agreements will be just. "The definition of INJUSTICE", Hobbes writes, "is no other than *the not performance of covenant*. And whatsoever is not unjust, is *just*".[57] So it follows from Hobbes's premises that a sovereign can be violating the Laws of Nature in prosecuting a just war, so long as he does not judge

[54] EW III, 336; T 240.
[55] EW III, 342; T 244.
[56] EW III, 232–233; T 171, emphasis added.
[57] EW III, 131; T 101.

that war strictly necessary for self-defense. Because he may reasonably expect to gain by engaging in such a war against a wealthy but weak opponent, strict adherence to the Laws of Nature will not always be in the sovereign's interest.

And even in the case of domestic matters, it would be hard to maintain that sovereigns can *never* rationally expect to profit by actions that violate the Laws of Nature, for instance, in maintaining an advantage against their domestic rivals. The show trial of an unpopular minister may, in some circumstances, effectively stave off rebellion. And because a sovereign monarch is not only an "artificial person", whose interests are identical with the interest of the people, but also a "natural person" with distinct interests, a violation of the natural law contrary to the common good may nonetheless serve his personal interests, as, for instance, King David's iniquitous action to make Bathsheba a widow arguably did. Here common sense and experience must overrule Hobbes's hopeful protestations.

Perhaps the most important case of a class of persons who may systematically hope to benefit from violating the Laws of Nature, which maintain peaceful stability, is the case of religious zealots. Hobbes is enormously exercised by these persons. These "seducers of the people" are "everywhere the same: they would fain be absolute governors of all they converse with; and have nothing to plead for it, but that where they reign, it is God that reigns, and nowhere else".[58] They willingly sacrifice peace for their cause. Some are after temporal power to reorder the world in the way their religion dictates; Hobbes says that in the English Civil War, "The mischief proceeded wholly from the Presbyterian preachers, who...preached up the rebellion powerfully... to the end that...as they thought, seeing politics are subservient to religion, they might govern".[59]

Others disrupt peace because they are concerned to do what they believe necessary to secure their personal eternal prospects, and "through fear of offending God, transgresses the commandments of the commonwealth".[60] "[N]o man can serve two masters", writes

[58] EW VI, 372–373.

[59] EW VI, 363. He also faults Independents, Adamites, Quakers, Fifth Monarchy Men, and Anabaptists as co-fomenters of the Civil War.

[60] EW III, 343; T 245.

Hobbes, "nor is he less, but rather more a master, whom we believe we are to obey for fear of damnation, than he whom we obey for fear of temporal death".[61] Hobbes concedes that "when the commands of God and man shall differ, we are to obey God, rather than man",[62] and that if a sovereign's "command be such as cannot be obeyed, without being damned to eternal death; then it were madness to obey it";[63] but he argues that we have reasons for thinking God never commands us to violate the Laws of Nature, or to disobey the sovereign whom those Laws of Nature direct us to obey.

Nonetheless, Hobbes recognized the indisputable fact that some religious folk *do* believe that they will gain by violating the Laws of Nature: "There be some that...will not have the law of nature, to be those rules which conduce to the preservation of man's life on earth; but to the attaining of an eternal felicity after death; to which they think the breach of covenant may conduce".[64] Hobbes, who concedes that "there is no natural knowledge of man's estate after death; much less of the reward that is then to be given to breach of faith",[65] is in no position to provide a positive refutation of their belief. Theirs may be a sort of wishful thinking, or the result of erroneously believing that God has issued different directives to them than those for the mass of mankind, and so they may be mistaken in thinking they stand to gain personally from violating the Laws of Nature; but Hobbes cannot prove them mistaken. He cannot prove that God has not spoken to them immediately and supernaturally, he cannot prove that God will not reward their violations of natural laws, and so he cannot prove that those violations are against their self-interest. What Hobbes can do is plausibly argue that violations of natural law disrupt the peace of humanity, and that such disruption harms mankind generally, as the common good account of the Laws of Nature contends. And because, although some truths may be beyond the grasp of natural reason, none are *contrary* to those revealed by natural reason,[66] so anyone to whom God has not spoken immediately and supernaturally

[61] EW II, 78.
[62] EW IV, 171.
[63] EW III, 585; T 403.
[64] EW III, 134–135; T 103.
[65] EW III, 135; T 103.
[66] EW III, 360; T 255.

should not trust the claim, should any zealot make it, that violating the Laws of Nature is in the interest of humanity, for this contradicts the conclusions of natural reason.

Finally, we should take notice of another, quite different sort of case of persons who may not do best by adhering to the Laws of Nature. It seems plausible that very many people living under an oppressive and threatening regime, especially if it is understaffed and disorganized, may reasonably judge their narrow self-interest best served by violating the requirements of maintaining peaceful stability – the worse off they are, the more they stand to gain by "reshuffling the deck". It seems wrong to suppose that the possibility of their being harmed should war result will always weigh more with them than their prospects for gain. These "defensive" or "reactive" violations of the Laws of Nature present a plausible case for divergence between the requirements of preserving peace and those of promoting individual self-interest.

The existence of this set of persons raises a larger question that might be thought to challenge the common good account as well as the self-interest account, namely, is peace really always in the best interests of humanity? Peace at any price? If peace is not always in humanity's interests, wouldn't that fact count against interpreting the Laws of Nature (which, on Hobbes's assumption, do reliably contribute to peace) as essentially norms to secure the good of mankind?

My own intuition is that "peace at any price" would *not* be in the interests of mankind. But I don't think Hobbes is committed to the view that it is. I'll describe a two-pronged argument available to Hobbes for answering our imagined objection. First, Hobbes might plausibly have argued that, except in really extreme cases, over the longest run, peace is indeed better for humanity than its alternatives: either outright war or perpetual insecurity. Even a somewhat oppressive peace allows people the security to cultivate many sources of satisfaction, and may provide the benefits of a cultured and commodious life. (Hobbes certainly never envisioned the totalitarian states that make this objection so lively for us.)[67] If a particular action required

[67] Indeed, quite the contrary. Hobbes asserts that sovereigns can hope to exercise very little control over the daily lives of most subjects: "For seeing there is no commonwealth in the world, wherein there be rules enough set down, for the regulating of all the actions, and words of men; as being a thing impossible: it followeth necessarily, that in all kinds of actions by the laws praetermitted, men have the

by the Laws of Nature fails to help existing humanity, it is nonetheless reasonable to imagine that pursuing the policy of adhering to the Laws of Nature will best profit humanity overall and in the long run. For instance, losses to the present generation may be more than outweighed by gains to future generations, or present apparently profitable violations may set precedents for future violations whose results will be disastrous for humanity.[68]

But what about the extreme case of a brutally oppressive state that threatens the very survival of much of its own population? Could the Laws of Nature require subjects to preserve a brutally oppressive peace? And, if so, could that possibly be imagined to conduce to even the longest-run interests of humanity?

The second prong of the reply I claim Hobbes has available addresses this extreme case. It notes that the notion of a "brutally oppressive peace" is of doubtful coherence within the Hobbesian worldview. Hobbes held that serious oppression – that is, severe violations of the Laws of Nature by the sovereign in his treatment of his subjects – would sooner or later lead to rebellion and active warfare, even if not justified. Men might be wrong to rebel, but they will. He writes: "[M]en that are once possessed of an opinion, that their obedience to the sovereign power will be more hurtful to them than their disobedience, *will* disobey the laws, and thereby overthrow the commonwealth, and introduce confusion and civil war".[69] But Hobbes defines peace as only the time during which there is

liberty, of doing what their own reasons shall suggest, for the most profitable to themselves" (EW III, 199; T 148). But it is interesting that while these brutally repressive regimes with which we are familiar were bad for the preservation prospects of individuals, many of them nonetheless effectively advanced science, technology, and the arts, which advancement belongs as a part to Hobbes's conception of the common good.

68 Hobbes advances this latter consideration in his argument against violating covenants in hopes of gaining political power: as for the "instance of attaining sovereignty by rebellion; it is manifest, that though the event follow, yet...because by gaining it so, others are taught to gain the same in like manner, the attempt thereof is against reason" (EW III, 134; T 103). Even successful rebellion is against reason, because successful rebellion encourages further rebellions. This works to the disadvantage of more than just the persons overthrown; it works to the disadvantage of the collective, whose interests are better served by peace than by perpetual insecurity or warfare.

69 EW III, 537; T 372, emphasis added.

"assurance" against war,[70] so on Hobbes's assumption that severe oppression causes rebellion, a "brutally oppressive peace" would have to be a state of assurance against war in the face of the inevitability of rebellion. "Brutally oppressive peace" is thus a contradiction in terms, within Hobbes's conceptual framework. So peace at the "price" of brutal repression is not a possibility.

This stance is compatible with the claim that peace really is always in the best interests of humanity, and that when following the Laws of Nature will not procure the ruin of the agent, he ought to follow them, as required by the good of humanity. The latter prong of the reply works only against the extreme case, and not against lesser cases of mild or sporadic oppression; but when combined with the plausible argument that with only such lesser abuses to fear, peace really is better for humanity in the long run than either war or perpetual insecurity, Hobbes has available an adequate reply to the objection we have been considering. Although peace need not be in the narrow self-interest of each and every agent, it does seem plausible that it is in the interests of mankind generally.

In summary, when we consider how very many sorts of person may *rationally* expect to gain by violating some of the Laws of Nature on some occasions, the self-interest account's contention that the Laws of Nature dictate peace *qua* necessary means to the self-interest of each agent becomes doubtful. And it is striking that the groups enumerated – the rich and powerful, sovereigns, the ambitious, the needy, the oppressed, and those with pressing religious agendas – are not some irrelevant fringe; these groups comprise the most politically active sector of society. If Hobbes's concern is with preserving social order, and if the Laws of Nature are supposed to be means for doing that, then Hobbes had better not have understood those laws in any way that exempts this politically active sector from obedience to them. The fact that under the self-interest interpretation *all* of these groups would have to be exempted from obedience to the Laws of Nature, because those do not promote their self-interests, strongly suggests that Hobbes cannot have intended to endorse that account.

To conclude this section, it may be useful to notice that our observation that peace is not in the personal interest of every agent is

70 EW III, 113; T 88.

compatible with Hobbes's remark that "all men agree on this, that peace is good, and therefore also the way, or means of peace... the laws of nature, are good".[71] All agree that peace is good because all agree that "a war of all against all" is bad, and thus that peace, being the condition of surety against such a war, is good. But this consensus in no way implies that peace is the *only* good, let alone the *best good* for every agent. Each calls 'good' whatever she desires;[72] and although everyone desires peace as a means to *an* end of her own (namely, the end of self-preservation and commodious living), any given individual may also desire *other* things, for instance, salvation, or liberty, or honor, or revenge, or relief from misery, or the good of her children, and may desire them more than peace, or more even than self-preservation, and she may sometimes rationally expect to obtain them by violating the requirements for peace. So if its instrumental relation to self-preservation or self-interest is to account for the importance of peace (and of the Laws of Nature), those whose most important interests are not best served by peace will have no reason to conform, even *in foro interno,* to the Laws of Nature. Thus, the universal acknowledgment of peace as a good does not detract from the present criticism of the self-interest account that to conform with Hobbes's stance on the bindingness of the Laws of Nature, it must assert that peace is in the greatest ("all things considered") self-interest of every agent, an assertion Hobbes's texts absolutely cannot be made to support.

Hobbes's Specific Rationales for Specific Laws of Nature

We saw earlier that Hobbes's text does not support the self-interest account's claim that peace is necessarily in the self-interest of every agent, a claim that was to explain how rules for securing peace (the Laws of Nature) could be understood to be dictates of individual prudence. But the self-interest account could remain viable if it could be shown that there are other, more direct ways in which adherence to the Laws of Nature contributes to the narrow self-interest of every agent. To assess this suggestion we need to examine the specific rationales

[71] EW III, 146; T 111.
[72] EW III, 41; T 39.

Hobbes offers for each of the Laws of Nature. If each law is given a rationale in terms of the agent's self-interest, then the fact that not all agents stand to benefit from peace will not be sufficient to show that the Laws of Nature are not essentially directives of personal prudence.[73]

But if it is implausible to suppose of some Law of Nature that violating it would pose any particular threat to the agent's preservation or other personal interest, then this fact should speak against the individualistic view. And if in that case it *is* plausible to think that violating the specified law would nonetheless threaten peace, and thus humanity's interests in peaceable, sociable, and comfortable living, that fact should count as evidence in favor of the common good view.

Consider first a Law of Nature that seems to fit comfortably within the individualistic model, namely, the law against contempt of others. Hobbes writes: "And because all signs of hatred, or contempt, provoke to fight; insomuch as most men choose rather to hazard their life, than not to be revenged; we may...for a law of nature, set down this precept... [against] *contumely*".[74] This rationale for the law fits nicely with the individual preservation model, because it is not difficult to see how insulting another might provoke him to attack *oneself.* Here, we can easily understand how one's own preservation could be at risk. (Of course, it fits as well with the common good account.)

But the rationale for many other Laws of Nature is not at all like this. The eleventh Law of Nature, requiring equity in judging, is not justified by a claim that if one judges partially, one's fellows are likely to harm *him* (an uncertain claim at best), but rather by the consideration that one who is partial in his judgment "doth what in him lies, to deter men from the use of judges, and arbitrators; and consequently, against the fundamental Law of Nature, is the cause of war".[75] The fault of the biased judge is that she is the cause of war, not that she puts her self-interest at risk.

[73] To show that would require a further argument to the effect that the peace and prudence rationales for the Laws of Nature are so ordered that the former never outweighs the latter, for if it did, an agent might find that his personal interest in undermining peace (by violating the Law of Nature) trumps whatever lesser personal gain it might bring him to follow the Law of Nature. In such a case, following the Laws of Nature would not be justifiable as the best course for securing each agent's self-interest.

[74] EW III, 140; T 107.

[75] EW III, 142; T 108.

The fourth Law of Nature, against ingratitude, condemns ingratitude not as making it less likely that the ungrateful agent will get the essentials for his survival; he might well be able to charm any number of new benefactors into lavishing gifts and kindnesses on him, despite leaving his disappointed benefactors soured on helping others in the future. Hobbes instead condemns ingratitude on the ground that unless people are grateful for gifts, "there will be no beginning of benevolence, or trust; nor consequently of mutual help; nor of reconciliation of one man to another...contrary to the first and fundamental law of nature, which commandeth men to *seek peace*".[76] Even when no ill consequence arrives to the ingrate, it nonetheless serves to undermine mutual aid among humanity generally. Because we are vulnerable and interdependent creatures who need settled society, it is essential to the common good that we encourage mutual aid, trust, and reconciliation.

Similarly, Hobbes does not justify his fifteenth Law of Nature, requiring that mediators be allowed safe conduct, by arguing that one is likely to be killed or otherwise personally harmed if one waylays a mediator (nor would that be a particularly plausible contention), but rather by the fact that mediators are a necessary means to peace. Again, the sixth Law of Nature, requiring that one pardon repentant offenders, is not urged on the ground that if one refuses them pardon, they will threaten or harm oneself (presumably they are locked up and incapable of inflicting harm), but rather because to refuse to pardon them "is sign of an aversion to peace; and therefore contrary to the law of nature".[77] Hobbes offers a similar rationale for the seventh Law of Nature, requiring that punishments look only to a future good. It is harms to humanity generally that corrode peace, and it is as such that violations of the Laws of Nature matter. Hobbes shows little interest in the specific effect of violating a Law of Nature on the particular individual agent who violates it. Yet if the Laws of Nature were fundamentally dictates of individual prudence, he ought to be taking great care to establish such connections in his rationales for those laws.

76 EW III, 138; T 106.
77 EW III, 139; T 106.

Sovereigns and the Laws of Nature

Do the Laws of Nature impose duties on sovereigns? If so, are those duties justified in terms of the sovereign's narrow self-interest, or rather on grounds of the good of men generally?

There is some precedent in Hobbes studies for understanding the sovereign as not bound by the Laws of Nature, but rather as one who can lay down their content, through his interpretations of their meanings. Hobbes's text clearly rules out that suggestion. Equity in judging is the eleventh Law of Nature, yet "[T]here is no judge subordinate, *nor sovereign,* but may err in a judgment of equity".[78] If sovereigns can err in their judgments of equity, it strictly follows that they do not define equity by their judgments. Sovereigns don't determine the content of the Laws of Nature.[79]

As we saw in Chapter 1, sovereigns are bound like the rest of us by the Laws of Nature, for instance, by equity "to which, as being a precept of the law of nature, a sovereign is as much subject, as any of the meanest of his people".[80] "It is true, that sovereigns are all subject to the laws of nature; because such laws be divine, and cannot by any man, or commonwealth be abrogated";[81] the sovereign "is the subject of God, and bound thereby to observe the laws of nature";[82] "only children, and madmen are excused from offences against the law natural", Hobbes plainly states.[83]

Recall that Hobbes also insists that "[t]he office of the sovereign... consisteth in... the procuration of *the safety of the people;* to which he

78 EW III, 263; T 192, emphasis added.

79 Of course, sovereigns do have the right to lay down "authoritative" judgments. The sovereign's pronouncements are to be respected as authoritative (finally determinative) even if they are "cosmically" incorrect. In this respect, sovereigns are like umpires, or Supreme Court justices; their judgment is to be deferred to, even when it is wrong. Hobbes holds what I have elsewhere described as a hierarchical view of responsibility: that God requires subjects to obey the directives of their civil sovereigns, but he holds sovereigns accountable to himself for their directives to their subjects. I document this system and assess its plausibility in "Coercion, Ideology, and Education in Hobbes's *Leviathan*", in Andrews Reath, Barbara Herman, and Christine Korsgaard, eds., *Reclaiming the History of Ethics* (Cambridge, 1997), 36–65. I will discuss Hobbes's hierarchy of responsibility in Chapter 6 below.

80 EW III, 332; T 238.

81 EW III, 312; T 224.

82 EW III, 200; T 148.

83 EW III, 288; T 208.

is obliged by the law of nature, and to render an account thereof to God",[84] and that sovereigns have a "duty" to instruct their subjects in "the essential rights which are the natural and fundamental laws of sovereignty",[85] because these conduce to the maintenance of peace and the welfare of the general population. But recall that sovereigns have no *contractual* obligations toward their subjects; the social contract is among subjects authorizing the sovereign, who is not party to the deal.[86] Sovereigns have no naturally given contractual obligations at all, and are bound only by the Laws of Nature. So whatever duties sovereigns *qua* sovereigns have can only be natural duties. Thus their duty to procure the safety of the people and to instruct subjects in the necessities of peace must be a requirement of the Laws of Nature.

What particularly interests us is the *rationale* Hobbes offers for why sovereigns should instruct subjects as the Laws of Nature require in the essential rights of sovereignty. Hobbes's rationale is telling, because it drives a wedge between narrow self-interest and the requirements of duty, and then insists that the sovereign has reasons for enforcing the Laws of Nature from both of these, but with self-interest in second place. Hobbes writes: "in the instruction of the people in the essential rights which are the natural and fundamental laws of sovereignty... it is his *duty,* to cause them to be so instructed; and *not only his duty,* but his benefit also, and security against the danger that may arrive to himself in his natural person from rebellion".[87]

The sovereign should do as the Laws of Nature require because it is his duty, and, if he needs further incentive, he should note that it is not only his duty but also in his personal interest, assuming he wants to be safe from rebellion. This passage is obviously incompatible with the self-interest account's attempt to *reduce* the Laws of Nature to mere precepts of personal prudence. If the Laws of Nature were just directives to pursue narrow self-interest, what would be the point of

[84] EW III, 322; T 231.

[85] EW III, 326; T 233.

[86] What to say about sovereigns by acquisition is a vexing question. In my view the only consistent position for Hobbes to have held is that although sovereigns have granted subjects their lives on condition of obedience and so are morally obligated to adhere to those terms, their being sovereigns entails that they enjoy sole authority to judge disputes concerning whether the terms have been honored, and so enjoy authority every bit as extensive as sovereigns by institution.

[87] EW III, 326; T 233, emphasis added.

so redundantly insisting that they are "in one's interest, and not only in one's interest, but to one's benefit also"? In contrast, the common good account makes natural sense of this passage.

One might concede the sovereign has a natural duty to procure the good of others than himself, but contend that this duty is somehow unique to him, that the sovereign "is required by a *special* law of nature to procure the safety and well-being of his people".[88] Although I can find no textual evidence at all for that contention, Hobbes does indicate some natural duties that would naturally be understood as being office-specific, for instance, the laws requiring impartiality in judging will apply only to judges.[89] But although it may be true that only judges are in a position to carry out impartial judging (even though nonjudges may contribute to equitable judging, through provision of honest testimony and the like), it is clearly not true that *only* sovereigns are in a position to contribute to the safety of the people. Each subject can contribute to the safety of the people by observing the laws, both natural and civil; or at least each can contribute to destroying its safety by refusing to observe those laws.[90] The task of securing the common good is *not* office-specific.

Furthermore, there is some direct evidence for the conjecture that Hobbes intended the Laws of Nature as directives to secure the good of humans at large, irrespective of the social position of the directee. It is not just the sovereign whom Hobbes requires to respect the good of others. Even the *least* privileged are to be held to the Laws of Nature's norms requiring reasonable accommodation of the interests of others: "The multitude of poor, and yet strong people still increasing, they are to be transplanted into countries not sufficiently inhabited: where nevertheless, *they are not to exterminate those they find there;* but constrain them to inhabit closer together, and... to court each little plot with art and labour, to give them their sustenance in due season".[91]

88 Kavka, *Hobbesian Moral and Political Theory*, 356, emphasis added.

89 The only example of office-specific duties Hobbes explicitly mentions is of public ministers (EW III, 258; T 188).

90 "For as in the midst of the sea, though a man perceive no sound of that part of the water next him, yet he is well assured, that part contributes as much to the roaring of the sea, as any other part of the same quantity; so also, though we perceive no great unquietness in one or two men, yet we may be well assured, that their singular passions, are parts of the seditious roaring of a troubled nation" (EW III, 63; T 54).

91 EW III, 335; T 239, emphasis added.

Even the poor must respect the needs of indigenous populations whom they have conquered (and who thus pose no threat to their self-preservation), and not simply exterminate them, despite the obvious fact that, once exterminated ('exterminate' being a success term), a native population can pose no threat at all to their narrow self-interests. Here the Law of Nature evidently forbids harming others even when doing so cannot redound to one's personal disadvantage. It is unclear how the self-interest account can accommodate this requirement, for although the self-interest account can say that we are not to exterminate others unless our preservation is at stake, it cannot explain why we are still not allowed to exterminate others even when there is no downside to us and our self-interest would be better served by doing so, if, as it maintains, the ultimate aim of the Laws of Nature is to secure our self-interest.

The Sum of the Laws of Nature and a Telling Illustration

Hobbes repeatedly insists that the Laws of Nature can all be captured in the dictum "*Do not that to another, which thou wouldest not have done to thyself*".[92] We can make stark the contrast between our competing interpretations of the function that ultimately unifies the Laws of Nature by stating their respective answers to the question "Why shouldn't I treat others in ways I would not want to be treated?" Hobbes's official answer is, as we've seen, that right reason forbids it. But if we asked what is it that right reason forbids, the self-interest interpretation answers, "doing what will hurt you personally". The common good account answers "doing what is generally harmful".

Hobbes recognized that the Laws of Nature will seem to agents to actually run contrary to their personal interests. It is telling that he responds to this concern, not by arguing that in fact the Laws of Nature *do* best promote the agent's rational self-interest, but rather by instructing us in how to so situate ourselves that we can nonetheless recognize the Laws of Nature as *reasonable.* He writes:

> [T]hough this may seem too subtle a deduction of the laws of nature, to be taken notice of by all men... yet to leave all men inexcusable, they have

[92] EW III, 144; T 109. Cf. III, 258; T 188; II, 263–264; and IV 113.

been contracted into one easy sum, intelligible even to the meanest capacity; and that is, *Do not that to another, which thou wouldest not have done to thyself;* which sheweth him, that he has no more to do in learning the laws of nature, but, when weighing the actions of other men with his own, they seem too heavy, to put them into the other part of the balance, and his own into their place, that his own passions, and self-love, may add nothing to the weight; and then there is none of these laws of nature that will not appear unto him very reasonable.[93]

We will recognize how reasonable the Laws of Nature are if we adopt a stance that does not make exceptions in our favor of rules that we want others to keep in relation to ourselves. This is impartiality of a specific sort. To do this is to take the interests of everyman – of humanity – as our vantage point. If, as Hobbes here indicates, the Laws of Nature are to be justified to individuals from that vantage point – from consideration of what is reasonable – then it seems likely that the Laws of Nature are essential rules to secure the interests of humanity.

Further textual evidence that Hobbes understood the Laws of Nature to be rules of impartial attention to the interests of humanity appears in earlier versions of his political philosophy. In the *Elements of Law,* Hobbes wrote that "the sum [of the Laws of Nature] ... consisteth in forbidding us to be our own judges",[94] that is, the sum of the Laws of Nature forbids self-partiality. And in *Philosophical Rudiments,* Hobbes wrote that the commandment "*Thou shalt love thy neighbor as thyself*...was given...even before Moses; *for it is the natural law, having its beginning with rational nature itself*".[95] It would seem awfully strained to admit that Hobbes conceives the Law of Nature as this principle of *impartial* love while insisting that Hobbes justifies the Law of Nature by reference to the narrow self-interest of each agent.

An extremely telling illustration of how Hobbes's Laws of Nature require agents to identify with the interests of other men is provided by the example Hobbes offers of an application of the Law of Nature

[93] EW III, 144–145; T 110.
[94] EW IV, 107–108.
[95] EW II, 263–264, second emphasis added.

to an action-type not explicitly proscribed by any law. Hobbes insists that ignorance of the Law of Nature "excuseth no man" because

> every man that hath attained to the use of reason, is supposed to know, he ought not to do to another, what he would not have done to himself. Therefore into what place soever a man shall come, if he do anything contrary to that law, it is a crime. If a man come from the Indies hither, and persuade men here to receive a new religion, . . . he commits a crime, . . . because he does that which he would not approve in another, namely, that coming from hence, he should endeavour to alter the religion there.[96]

There is no suggestion in this passage or elsewhere that the would-be missionary is acting against his self-interest or in any way threatening to his preservation in attempting to convert Englishmen to his religion – no suggestion that he will provoke or offend others to react in a way that threatens him. But he is violating the Law of Nature.

Of course, it is possible that his efforts at conversion may eventually destabilize the peace in England (as Hobbes urges that changes of religion, or disagreement over it, almost invariably do), and so there is no difficulty is seeing why the Law of Nature would condemn them. They destabilize peace, which is against the interests of humans generally. But what makes this case so telling is that here a defender of the individualistic view cannot plausibly suggest that the value of maintaining peace is reducible to the agent's self-preservation – that it is valuable only *qua* necessary condition for the self-preservation or other personal interest of the agent. In this example Hobbes stipulates that the offender is foreign to the society his actions destabilize, and so not only may he have long since returned to the safety of his native land before the destabilizing effects on England of his actions are felt, but his security within his own nation may actually *increase* as a result of England's instability. Hobbes asserts that his actions violate the Laws of Nature, but they do not compromise his personal prospects; therefore, the Laws of Nature cannot essentially aim to secure the agent's personal prospects.

96 EW III, 279–280; T 202.

An Intriguing Omission: The Puzzling Case of the Missing Virtues

According to the self-interest account, Hobbes's Laws of Nature direct, are picked out by, and aim at their contribution to the narrow self-interest of the agent. We should thus expect Hobbes to include among the Laws of Nature all virtues that importantly contribute to promoting or securing the agent's narrow self-interest. Yet the Laws of Nature omit a number of obvious personally profitable virtues, including fortitude and the cardinal virtues of prudence, courage, and temperance. If, as the self-interest account contends, the Laws of Nature are essentially rules for personal preservation or profit, why did Hobbes exclude rules directing the exercise of these virtues?

It is not that Hobbes failed to notice that these virtues contribute to the good of the person who possesses them. He did acknowledge all four of these as virtues, indeed, as "precepts of rational nature", which "are virtues of citizens... *as men*" because "these virtues are useful... to those individual men who have them" and tend to their "own private good". But Hobbes does not number rules directing them among his Laws of Nature because those virtues do not contribute to the "public good"; "[n]or, in truth, should one demand that the courage and prudence of the private man, if useful only to himself, be praised or held as a virtue... by any other men whatsoever to whom these same are not useful".[97]

These virtues of primarily personal profit, while rational excellences, are not *moral* virtues, because moral virtues are the qualities that are useful to others as well as to oneself; they are generally beneficial qualities. "For moral philosophy is nothing else but the science of what is *good,* and *evil,* in the conversation, and society of mankind"; and the "laws of nature, are... *moral virtues;*... and therefore the true doctrine of the laws of nature, is the true moral philosophy", which reveals that these virtues are valued "as the means of peaceable, sociable, and comfortable living".[98] Hobbes's Laws of Nature are rules for the good of humanity collectively and "are called not only *natural,*

97 Gert, *Man and Citizen,* 70.
98 EW III, 146–147; T 111.

but also *moral* laws; consisting in the moral virtues, as justice, equity, and all habits of the mind that conduce to peace, and charity".[99] In *De Homine,* Hobbes insists that "all moral virtue is contained in these two": justice and charity. He continues:

> However, the other three virtues...that are called cardinal – *courage, prudence,* and *temperance* – are not virtues of citizens as citizens, but as men, for these virtues are useful not so much to the state as they are to those individual men who have them. For just as the state is not preserved save by the courage, prudence, and temperance of good citizens, so is it not destroyed save by the courage, prudence, and temperance of its enemies. For courage, like prudence, is more a strength of mind than a goodness of manners; and temperance is more a privation of those vices that arise from the greedy dispositions of those that harm not the state, but themselves, than it is a moral virtue.... [G]ood dispositions are those which are suitable for entering into civil society; and good manners (that is, moral virtues) are those whereby what was entered upon can be best preserved.[100]

The Laws of Nature articulate moral virtues, and moral virtues are the dispositions that create and sustain civil society, that is, the commonwealth-based form of life requisite for peaceable, sociable, and comfortable living. Rational excellences that contribute to the interests of the agent but not reliably to the interests of the collective – of "men in multitudes" – are neither moral virtues nor among "the" Laws of Nature Hobbes enumerates. All of those Laws of Nature can be captured in the precept that we are not to treat others in ways we would object to being treated; and all moral virtues "are contained in justice and charity... [and] vices are all contained in injustice and in a mind insensible to another's evils, that is, in a lack of charity".[101]

Serendipitiously, here in Hobbes's discussion appears that rare case of the exception that actually does prove the rule. Across his writings, Hobbes seems to equivocate about temperance (especially about drunkenness). In *Leviathan* he remarks that "There be other

[99] EW III, 271; T 197. More strongly, Hobbes suggests equivalence between the Laws of Nature and the moral law: "All writers do agree, that the natural law is the same with the moral" (EW II, 47). "The laws of nature...are the sum of *moral* philosophy" (EW II, 49).

[100] Gert, *Man and Citizen,* 69–70.

[101] Ibid., 70.

things tending to the destruction of particular men; as drunkenness, and all other parts of intemperance; which may therefore also be reckoned amongst those things which the law of nature hath forbidden; but are not necessary to be mentioned, nor are pertinent enough to this place".[102] This passage would appear to conflict with his earlier assertion that temperance is not a moral virtue and so not among the Laws of Nature, although it is a "[precept] of *rational* nature... because intemperance tends to sickness and death".[103] Can a virtue justified solely by reference to the narrow self-interest of the agent count as one of the Laws of Nature?

In fact, no. The reason why the Law of Nature forbids drunkenness and other intemperance is that such intemperance impairs our exercise of the rational powers we must use to follow the Laws of Nature. That is why the Law of Nature "hath forbidden it".[104] In what is, to my knowledge, Hobbes's only explicit account of the wrongness of drunkenness he writes:

> [F]orasmuch as the laws of nature are nought else but the dictates of reason; so as, unless a man endeavour to preserve the faculty of right reasoning, he cannot observe the laws of nature; it is manifest, that he who knowingly or willingly doth aught whereby the rational faculty may be destroyed or weakened, he knowingly and willingly breaks the law of nature. For there is no difference between a man who performs not his duty, and him who does such things willingly as make it impossible for him to do it. But they destroy and weaken the reasoning faculty, who do that which disturbs the mind from its natural state; that which most manifestly happens to drunkards, and gluttons. We therefore sin... against the law of nature by drunkenness.[105]

Intemperance can be understood as forbidden by the Laws of Nature insofar as it compromises people's ability to observe those laws. *Not* because it harms the agent personally; rather *only* because it may

[102] EW III, 144; T 109.
[103] EW II, 49.
[104] Note, in addition to the present argument, that Hobbes's language here in asserting that the Law of Nature has forbidden intemperance need not imply that there is any Law of Nature against it, but only that the Laws of Nature there are *imply* that intemperance is not permissible, as disabling their observation.
[105] EW II, 44.

contribute to actions by individual agents that do damage to the common good, in violation of the Laws of Nature.

Thus the self-interest account runs afoul of Hobbes's explanation of our puzzling case of the missing virtues, while the common good account squares fully with that explanation.

A Conceptual Argument for the Common Good Account

I now offer a simple argument – a *reductio ad absurdum* – against the self-interest account's claim that function ultimately served by the Laws of Nature is to secure the individual agent's preservation. (An analogous argument can be run against the claim that the Laws of Nature are directives of other sorts of narrow self-interest; for clarity I focus here on a most basic sort of self-interest, the interest in self-preservation. Almost everyone who has seen it hates this argument, and it is certainly itchy. I don't hold that against it.)

1. Suppose the Laws of Nature *are* essentially rules for securing the self-preservation of the agent.
2. Then, obviously, no rule could count as a Law of Nature if following it reliably caused the immediate death of those who followed it – nothing could be a rule of self-preservation that reliably brought about self-destruction.
3. But the sovereign can *make* following *any* rule reliably cause the immediate death of those who follow it, simply by attaching a death penalty to it (to be summarily executed). (For instance, the sovereign could pronounce that judges who judge impartially, not giving presumption of right to litigants belonging to the king's party, are to be immediately executed; or that subjects who allow safe conduct to foreign mediators are to be hanged on the spot.)
4. It follows that the sovereign can cause it to be the case that following a rule identical in content to a Law of Nature reliably causes the death of those who follow it.
5. But by our earlier assumption, no rule the following of which reliably brought self-destruction could be a rule of self-preservation, and the Laws of Nature were assumed to be rules of self-preservation.

6. Therefore, by annexing the death penalty to behaviors sanctioned by a Law of Nature, the sovereign can either
   a. cause the rule sanctioning those behaviors to cease to be a Law of Nature (thereby *changing* the Laws of Nature); or else
   b. cause that rule to be simultaneously both a Law of Nature and not a Law of Nature.
7. But the sovereign cannot change the Laws of Nature. Hobbes is emphatic on this point, writing that "the laws of nature are immutable and eternal" such that

> Princes succeed one another; and one judge passeth, another commeth; nay, heaven and earth shall pass; but not one tittle of the law of nature shall pass; for it is the eternal law of God,[106]

and

> [S]overeigns are all subject to the laws of nature; because such laws be divine, and cannot by any man, or commonwealth be abrogated.[107]

8. Thus, (a) is false.
9. But then (b), that the sovereign can make a rule simultaneously a Law of Nature and not a Law of Nature, must be true.
10. But (b) cannot be true, because it is the statement of a contradiction.
11. Therefore, the Laws of Nature are not essentially rules of individual self-preservation. QED

In short, because which behaviors actually conduce to one's preservation or other self-interest is dependent on the sovereign's will in annexing punishments to behaviors, and because the Laws of Nature are not dependent on the sovereign's will, the Laws of Nature cannot be essentially about which behaviors conduce to one's preservation or other self-interest. The self-interest account cannot be right.

I recognize that this annoying argument may invite the objection that it is only the sovereign's *interference* in the "natural order" of consequences that forces a "distortion" of the content of the Laws of Nature (thus invalidating the argument's conclusion). But how can we say that

[106] EW III, 264; T 192.
[107] EW III, 312; T 244.

the Laws of Nature must be those that would be good only for a man who faced no interference – a man in a social vacuum? After all, the problem of coordinating people's actions is obviously a central concern of Hobbes's political theory. We cannot characterize the Laws of Nature as rules about "what *would* preserve individuals *unless* others act in ways that interfere", because humanity's problem is precisely that the actions of each are bound to interfere with the actions of others; the very *raison d'être* of the Laws of Nature is to address this problem. In the world as it is, the course that profits anyone will be at least partially dictated by the actions of others, including, perhaps especially, the actions of "the powers that be". Thus, Hobbes gives us no grounds for claiming that the Laws of Nature should abstract from consideration of what sovereigns do.

A further, more important, objection to the *reductio* offered would note that while sovereigns can *locally* affect whether adherence to the Laws of Nature promotes the narrow self-interest of agents, they cannot do so universally, or in the "long run". This observation is almost certainly correct, but it functions as an objection only to the self-preservation account of the Laws of Nature, and not as an objection to the common good account. Because the common good account looks to the interests of mankind generally, it can adopt the perspective of the long run; losses imposed on existing persons by respecting the requirements of the Laws of Nature may plausibly be more than compensated by gains to humankind in the long run. Hence whatever local harms an antisocial sovereign might do now may turn out to be nothing more than salutary lessons to future generations. In contrast, the self-interest account cannot make good use of this sort of appeal to the long run. It insists that the measure of value must be contained in the space of an individual life; and it is very much less likely that personally harmful adherences to the Law of Nature now will ever be eclipsed by compensating advantages to that very same particular agent in the short span of her life (life spans are too short, and times don't change that fast). One misstep in an individual life is frequently fatal. So arguments by appeal to long-run interests fare best for subjects that have a lengthy life history. Humanity is such a subject. Any named individual is not. So the fact that serious violations of the Law of Nature are possible locally but not universally because of their harmful long-run effects is an indictment of the self-interest account, but not, it seems, of the common good account.[108]

The Final Law of Nature

All Hobbes scholars have noticed that Hobbes stressed the importance of a further Law of Nature, one not enumerated in his initial discussion, but few have commented on its implications for the self-interest interpretation of the Laws of Nature. Hobbes states this law twice: once in a negative fashion, and later in a positive fashion. He writes, "it is a dictate of natural reason, and consequently an evident law of nature, that no man ought to weaken that power, the protection whereof he hath himself demanded, or wittingly received against others"[109] and later, in his Review and Conclusion, "To the Laws of Nature, declared in Chapter XV. I would have this added, that every man is bound by nature, as much as in him lieth, to protect in war the authority, by which he is himself protected in time of peace".[110]

Let us focus on the latter formulation. Here Hobbes asserts that the Laws of Nature require everyone to do all they can to defend the sovereign in wartime: "when the defense of the commonwealth, requireth at once the help of all that are able to bear arms, every one is obliged", even though, in less extreme cases, allowance is to be made "for natural timorousness; not only to women... but also to men of feminine courage".[111] This Law of Nature does not say that people are obliged to defend their sovereign in wartime only if they expect to gain personally from doing so, nor does it excuse them from this duty when they stand to fare worse by honoring it. People are to do all that is within their power, no matter what their personal interest, to defend in war the state that has formerly protected them. They

[108] It should also be noticed that the *reductio* does not claim that the sovereign can make it a duty for a man to do what threatens his own life: Hobbes's suspension condition ensures that men are never duty bound to deadly *in foro externo* observation of the Laws of Nature. The claim is rather that if the Laws of Nature were necessarily precepts for self-preservation, a sovereign could *alter* their content. But this is just what Hobbes denies. When a sovereign penalizes conformity to the Laws of Nature, it is he who sins against the Laws of Nature.

[109] EW III, 260; T 190.

[110] EW III, 703; T 485.

[111] EW III, 205; T 151.

are even required to risk death in defending the sovereign, to just the extent they are psychologically able to bring themselves to do so.[112]

It is difficult to see how this requirement of the Law of Nature could possibly be understood as a dictate of personal prudence. War is dangerous. Once war is underway and one's state is under siege, it seems that narrow self-interest must direct one to apply his efforts in whichever direction seems most likely to profit himself. If one judges that the enemy is likely to win, the individually rational strategy may be to collaborate. If the outcome is uncertain and the fighting fierce, the best personal strategy may be to lie low and await a resolution. Or to flee, as Hobbes did, may be the safest option. But it is hard to imagine any remotely plausible argument to the conclusion that every individual in every case stands to profit by participating in war to defend his besieged sovereign. If the Laws of Nature were rules for securing the agent's self-interest or self-preservation, this last Law of Nature would have to be an outright error.

In contrast, the common good account makes good sense of Hobbes's final Law of Nature. We can admit that defending one's existing sovereign may not conduce to the particular agent's self-interest or self-preservation while recognizing that such a strategy may indeed best promote humanity's interest in peace. Our actions to resist aggression may act as a deterrent to future would-be aggressors. (Certainly many defenders of lost causes have told themselves just this.) If people pursue a general policy of resisting invasions and internal usurpations of power, it stands to reason that would-be aggressors will think twice before indulging their ambitions. Obeying the directive of this Law of Nature will almost certainly compromise the particular interests of many of the individuals who obey it, but it is nonetheless quite plausibly a rule that it benefits humanity to have generally followed.[113]

[112] Once they have been captured, are within the guards and garrisons of the enemy, then they are permitted (although not required) to save their lives by promising allegiance to their captor. But until that happens, the final Law of Nature requires them to fight for their sovereign to the utmost of their power.

[113] Kinch Hoekstra has pointed out to me that this argument may appear to prove too much, because why should we not by this same logic argue that it is best for humanity to refuse *any allegiance* to successful usurpers or conquerors? Hobbes clearly holds (all agree) that we may permissibly submit to successful usurpers or conquerors, yet the common good interpretation would seem to imply that the Laws of Nature must forbid submission to successful usurpers or conquerors,

I conclude, on the basis of this and all our previously considered arguments, that Hobbes's Laws of Nature are most faithfully understood as ultimately serving the function of securing the common good, or the good of humanity in general.

CONSTRUCTIVE RECIPROCITY AND TEMPTATION

As the common good account understands them, the Laws of Nature are dictates of what might be called "constructive reciprocity". They require people to act in ways that, when reciprocated, advance the interest of humanity generally. To think of Laws of Nature this way makes sense if we recognize that rules are most useful when they counteract our natural tendencies to contrary behavior. Hobbes's Laws of Nature counteract our temptations to ingratitude, arrogance, partiality, and vengefulness, and (the last Law of Nature) to pursue our own safety at humanity's expense. We do not need to be instructed to seek our personal advantage (that comes easily), but we do need to be reminded to resist our urges to act in ways inimical to the preservation of decent human society and civil life. The Laws of Nature hold us to our "consciences", to doing what we dispassionately judge that reason requires of everyone, but nonetheless don't want to do because of our particular interests. The Laws of Nature address human frailty, calling us to do what humankind needs. That seems a natural role for moral injunctions.

because such submission only encourages disruptive attempts at usurpation and conquest. However, the humanity argument is sustained by noting that the difference between defending one's own besieged sovereign and resisting a successful conqueror or usurper is that what was when fighting for one's sovereign a duty to *risk death* in a condition in which *all options were risky* becomes, once a usurper or conqueror has obtained sovereign power, a duty to *suffer death* (as the price of nonsubmission) at the hands of one's new could-be sovereign protector. Because it is not *credible* that men will reliably fulfill this duty to suffer death rather than submit, no would-be usurper or conqueror can reasonably expect that they will. So the idea that they will cannot deter any would-be usurper. This being so, there is absolutely no point in extending the Laws of Nature to forbid submission to successful conquerors and usurpers, because it will not enhance deterrence against actions that are bad for humanity generally. But it remains true that Hobbes's Law of Nature requiring resistance to would-be usurpers and conquerors is a deterrent to usurpation and conquest, and thus does advance the interests of humanity generally.

Still, even the reader who acknowledges the force of the case for taking Hobbes's laws to necessarily promote only the common good of humanity generally will rightly worry that, so understood, the Laws of Nature cannot be motivationally efficacious for Hobbesian agents, who may very well not care at all for humanity's good. I grant that Hobbes does not believe that many men care for humanity in general, but, because I do not think that the normativity or motivational efficacy of Hobbes's Laws of Nature depends on any such assumption, I do not share their worry. I shall offer my own arguments addressing these further questions, the third and fourth questions distinguished at the beginning, in Chapter 5. But let me summarize the conclusions of the present investigation of the questions of the definition of a Law of Nature and of the function that ultimately unifies the particular Laws of Nature Hobbes enumerates in the context of his moral philosophy. Hobbes *defines* a Law of Nature simply as a rule of reason. And those Laws of Nature concerning our mutual interactions (i.e., moral laws) – which all *do* promote peace (and so universally *are called good and praised,* and are also *called* divine laws) – ultimately function to secure the common good of mankind understood as the maintenance of human society and civil life. Further, these are argued to be rules *by which* the average agent can hope to secure her personal good – her individual preservation and profit. This account, the elements of which appear in various combinations across Hobbes's several formulations of a definition, is a neat package of definitional essence, primary function, explanation of how we talk about the thing defined, and linkage to one important potential motivation for compliance with them. It reflects a well-crafted dialectical strategy, aimed both intellectually to persuade and emotionally to sway compliance with the norms that will ground Hobbes's argument for submission to political authority. But, despite appearances, *the Law of Nature is not defined as those rules that secure, or tend to secure, or whatever he thinks will secure, the individual agent's preservation or profit, nor is doing so its ultimate function.* Nor, despite our prejudices, is it plausible that the function that ultimately unifies the Laws of Nature is that of securing the self-interest, whether preservation or profit, of the individual agent who follows them. *The ultimate function of the Laws of Nature is to secure the common good,* the good of humankind generally, the same good earlier natural law theorists had understood natural law to secure, and to which Hobbes alluded by his use of natural law talk. Once this is seen, it becomes possible to entertain an entirely different way of understanding the normativity, motivational efficacy, and metaphysical status of Hobbes's Laws of Nature.

4

A Critical Examination of Derivations of the Laws of Nature

Reasoning is simply the joining together and linking of names.
(Third Set of Objections to Descartes's *Meditations*)[1]

Having now surveyed Hobbesian psychology and the casuistry, definition, and function of the Laws of Nature, we are well situated to consider various interpretive proposals as to how Hobbes derives these Laws of Nature as "theorems of reason". An adequate account of their derivation will plausibly explain how the specific norms Hobbes identifies as Laws of Nature can be understood to be requirements of reason having the requisite normativity for complex Hobbesian agents, and how they can serve the role Hobbes assigns them in his political philosophy. Separating out these desiderata, an adequate interpretation will do the following:

1. Rely only on psychological assumptions that are true of complex Hobbesian agents (*psychological fit*)
2. Yield norms with the particular content Hobbes identifies in his own Laws of Nature, as well as all of the conclusions, or "cases in the Law of Nature" that Hobbes identifies as required or prohibited by the Laws of Nature (*content*)
3. Show how those norms are normative in the right way, that is, how they make potentially motivationally efficacious ought-claims that

[1] In *The Philosophical Writings of Descartes*, vol. 2, trans. J. Cottingham, R. Stoothoff, and D. Murdoch (Cambridge, 1984), 125.

are universal and inescapable for Hobbesian agents (weakness of will notwithstanding) (*normativity*)

4. Be philosophically and practically plausible – that is, the account will not be irredeemably elliptical, extremely dubious, obviously false, or outlandish (*plausibility*) and importantly
5. Show that the Law of Nature requires submission to political authority not just from the few who initiate commonwealths by institution or by acquisition in a state of nature, but from the vast majority who are born into ongoing societies whose sovereigns they have not themselves established (*political function*). The place of Hobbes's Laws of Nature in his political philosophy is to lay down a normative requirement of submission to sovereign authority, so any adequate account of those laws will have to show how they do so for the most usual and practically pressing case of subjects within ongoing commonwealths.

Each reasonable in themselves, these criteria collectively recommend rejection of many familiar accounts of Hobbes's Laws of Nature. While some defenders of these accounts cheerfully admit that Hobbes's derivation is, as they interpret it, implausible or reliant on a false psychology, or inadequately normative, I want to insist that the best interpretation of Hobbes's derivation of his Laws of Nature will be the one that most fully meets these desiderata. In this chapter I survey some of the most significant attempts to derive Hobbes's Laws of Nature, sorting them in three derivational paradigms – desire-based derivations, duty-based derivations, and definitional derivations. I consolidate under the criteria just articulated some of the difficulties with these attempts that I or others have noted. The particular derivation of the Laws of Nature I develop in the next chapter reflects my understanding of the strengths as well as the vulnerabilities and deficiencies of these approaches.

DESIRE-BASED DERIVATIONS

Traditional Desire-Based Derivations

Traditional desire-based derivations of Hobbes's Laws of Nature owe their continuing popularity, I speculate, to their easy fit with the tone of Hobbes's texts and the simplicity of their structure. Such derivations come in two flavors: those that derive the Laws of Nature as necessary means for the satisfaction of the agent's self-interest (however conceived), and those that derive the Laws of Nature as necessary means for the satisfaction of the agent's desire for self-preservation. Both versions embody a picture of reason as instrumentally related to the satisfaction of desire. Their normativity is supposed to be ensured by their connection to that desire, which is said in each case to be necessary and paramount.

The two sorts of traditional desire-based derivations hold respectively:

1. The Laws of Nature articulate necessary means to maximize the satisfaction of any agent's desires, that is, what he deems his "good" (no matter its content).
2. The Laws of Nature articulate necessary means to avoid violent bodily death.

Accounts of both sorts seek to derive the Laws of Nature from the designated desire (for self-interest or self-preservation) in conjunction with the 'Right of Nature' (i.e., the right to do whatever one sincerely judges necessary for one's self-interest or self-preservation). From this right it is said that there necessarily arises a state of war that causes everyone to desire peace, and so to embrace the Laws of Nature as necessary conditions for establishing and maintaining peace. So, schematically, traditional desire-based accounts offer a derivation of the following sort:

Desire for self-interest or self-preservation + Right of Nature => war of all against all => desire for peace => desire for necessary means for peace + necessary means for peace = Laws of Nature => submission to civil authority.[2]

[2] This scheme indicates the rough movement of arguments advocated by Gauthier, Watkins, Nagel, Kavka, Hampton, and Curley, among many others. See David Gauthier, *The Logic of 'Leviathan': The Moral and Political Theory of Thomas Hobbes* (Oxford, 1969); J. W. N. Watkins, *Hobbes's System of Ideas* (London, 1965); Thomas Nagel, "Hobbes's Concept of Obligation", *Philosophical Review* 68 (1959): 68–83; Gregory Kavka, *Hobbesian Moral and Political Theory* (Princeton, NJ, 1986); Jean Hampton, *Hobbes and the Social Contract Tradition* (Cambridge, 1986); Edwin Curley, "Introduction to Hobbes's *Leviathan*" (Indianapolis, 1994). Related to desire-based derivations but importantly different from them are Darwall's projectivist interpretation and Gert's rationally required end interpretation (which I categorize as

Whether in a self-interest form or a self-preservation form, variants of desire-based derivations are importantly distinguished by the account they give of the Right of Nature, so we begin with discussion of how that starting assumption is settled.

Step 1: Settling a Starting Assumption

Several ways of grounding the crucial Right of Nature from which desire-based derivations proceed have been proposed. The first takes Hobbes's Right of Nature as *primitive*, the most basic normative claim in Hobbes's political philosophy, which itself stands in no need of justification. One might interpret the Right of Nature as purely *descriptive* – as just positing an "absence of external impediments" to doing what one judges needful for one's preservation or one's self-interest – rather than as a normative axiom. But I shall set aside that possibility. Were it correct, and people living under the Right of Nature in fact suffer no external resistance to their actions in pursuit of self-preservation or self-interest, the state of nature would not be a state of war; hence neither Laws of Nature nor commonwealth would be needed. Further, as frequently noted by perplexed Hobbes scholars, it is not clear that Hobbes can explain liberty and obligation in a way that leaves liberty a purely descriptive notion.[3] So let us consider the variant that sees Hobbes's view as fundamentally rights-based, and irreducibly normative. We just do, by nature, have a moral right to do what we judge necessary for our preservation or our self-interest (the Right of Nature), and everything else flows from this free-standing, primitive moral fact.

A natural philosophical worry about any such view is how nature can be normative in the requisite sense, but let us set this worry aside. More specific to Hobbes interpretation is the worry as to how taking the Right of Nature as the foundation of the theory can be reconciled

a duty-based derivation), both of which retain the instrumentalism of desire-based interpretations while denying that the concern for self-preservation that ultimately grounds the Laws of Nature is properly characterized as a desire. See Stephen Darwall, "Normativity and Projection in Hobbes's *Leviathan*", *Philosophical Review* 109, no. 3 (2000): 313–347; Bernard Gert, "Hobbes's Psychology", in Tom Sorell, ed., *The Cambridge Companion to Hobbes* (Cambridge, 1996), 157–174.

[3] We take up the relation between liberty, obligation, and law in Chapter 6.

with Hobbes's stated method of beginning only from uncontroversial premises, those that experience having found true, or passion not distrusting, will not seek to displace. For understood as allowing as morally permissible any action one thinks necessary for self-preservation or self-interest, the Right of Nature denies the convictions of the many readers who believe that duty constrains our pursuit of self-preservation or self-interest – that one may not justifiably betray king and country, dishonor parents, abandon children, or deny true religion in the name of self-preservation or self-interest. Sometimes martyrdom is obligatory; desertion is condemnable, etc. For Hobbes to offer the Right of Nature as the normative basis of his theory would have been to beg the question against his opponents, for whom selfish exemptions from duty require the moral permissions of true religion, natural law, or constituted authority. He needs to prove, rather than to assume, that duty permits us to put ourselves first.

For these reasons, versions of traditional desire-based accounts that seek to provide grounding for the normative Right of Nature in more basic descriptive premises may prove preferable. Indeed these variants (or rather those relying on the desire for self-preservation, as there is no textual support for a self-interest interpretation of the Right of Nature) enjoy some textual support in Hobbes's insistence that men "shun death by a certain impulsion of nature".[4] An account that begins from men's desire for self-preservation makes use of remarks like these in an attempt to justify the otherwise arbitrary and controversial normative Right of Nature.[5] The Right of Nature might be grounded in the desire for self-preservation in either of a

4 And "to every man remaineth, from the natural and necessary appetite of his own conservation, the right of protecting himself by his private strength" (EW III, 165–166; T 125).

5 Leo Strauss holds a view of this sort, attributing to Hobbes the "attempt to deduce the natural law or the moral law from the natural right of self-preservation or from the inescapable power of the fear of violent death" ("The Spirit of Hobbes's Political Philosophy", in K. C. Brown, ed., *Hobbes Studies* [Cambridge, MA, 1965], 1–29, 17). In Hobbes's thought, says Strauss, "the fear of violent death expresses most forcefully the most powerful and the most fundamental of natural desires, the initial desire, the desire for self-preservation.

"If, then, natural law must be deduced from the desire for self-preservation, if, in other words, the desire for self-preservation is the sole root of all justice and morality, the fundamental moral fact is not a duty but a right; all duties are derivative from the fundamental and inalienable right of self-preservation.... [T]he fundamental

couple of ways. It could be derived from that desire via the premise *that one has a right to pursue whatever one desires:* We have a right to pursue self-preservation because we have a right to pursue whatever we desire, and we desire self-preservation. Unfortunately, this is a highly implausible premise, never proposed by Hobbes, that his political theory requires him to reject in any case. Hobbes does argue that in some circumstances, one has a right to do that which he sincerely and in good conscience judges to be necessary for defense of his own life, but that is as far as he is willing to go.

A more promising alternative is to argue *that all men necessarily desire self-preservation,* and that because they cannot but desire it, we must grant, by the principle "ought implies can" that it is not the case that they ought to refrain from pursuing this desire. If we then add the premise that *one has a right to do what one cannot refrain from doing,* we may conclude the normative Right of Nature from which the rest of the traditional account proceeds. Something like this "ought implies can" variant of the traditional account is perhaps the most widely accepted interpretation of Hobbes's argument, which is surprising considering the serious difficulties with this position.

A minor difficulty is that, as it stands, the argument is elliptical; even if ought implies can and people cannot but desire self-preservation, it will not follow that they have a right to act on that desire for self-preservation unless we add the further premise that people cannot but act on their desires – a premise that is not particularly attractive, indeed is likely false, and certainly fails to meet Hobbes's "no controversy" requirement for basic assumptions. (The supposition that people cannot but act on their *strongest* desire may seem more plausible, perhaps even analytically true, but the needed companion premise, that people cannot but most desire their self-preservation runs afoul of the psychological fit and plausibility criteria for interpretation.) Nor does the general principle that *one has a right to do what one cannot refrain from doing* comport with our ordinary understanding of rights, implying as it does that, for instance, when blown by a strong wind onto your trespass-protected property, I have a right to be standing upon it. (I may be held blameless for landing on it, although blameworthy

and absolute moral fact is a right and not a duty.... Hobbes... squarely made an unconditional natural right the basis of all natural duties" (13–14).

if I continue to stand on it; but to excuse my forced presence is not, in our ordinary understanding, to grant me a "right" to be there.) Or that I have a right to commit a crime of passion. This is a perversion of ordinary rights talk. More generally, the acknowledgment of impossibility it taps fails to track our notions of distinctively *moral* permissibility, yielding strange results. For instance, it implies that, because it is impossible for the past to be other than it is, and so one must (by *ought implies can*) have a right that the past be as it is, it follows that the murderer has today a right that he yesterday murdered his victim. He has today a right to have done in the past what he had in the past no right to do. Were we to accept this, it would be difficult to make sense of our practices of punishment. This indicates the conceptual gap between acknowledging impossibility and granting the moral license entailed by rights ascriptions.

Worse still for the *ought implies can* variant of the traditional account, Hobbes's political theory requires him to reject its underlying assumption that people have a right to do what they cannot help doing. Hobbes's strict determinism commits him to the view that men's voluntary actions are all causally necessitated by prior causes and that whatever one does one could not but have done, given those prior causes.[6] If we then attribute to Hobbes the traditional account's premise that people have a right to do what they could not but have done, it will follow that for everyone, *one has a right to do whatever one in fact does!* No conclusion could be further from either the spirit or letter of Hobbes's philosophy.

We thus cannot attribute to Hobbes the general principle that one has a "right" to do whatever one cannot but do. Nor can we ascribe

[6] Hobbes famously wrote: "*Liberty*, and *necessity* are consistent: as in the water, that hath not only *liberty*, but *a necessity* of descending by the channel; so likewise in the actions which men voluntarily do: which, because they proceed from their will, proceed from *liberty;* and yet, because every act of man's will, and every desire, and inclination proceedeth from some cause, and that from another cause, in a continual chain, whose first link is in the hand of God the first of all causes, proceed from *necessity*.... [T]he liberty of man in doing what he will, is accompanied with the *necessity* of doing that which God will, and no more, nor less.... [Men] can have no passion, nor appetite to anything, of which appetite God's will is not the cause. And did not his will assure the *necessity* of man's will, and consequently of all that on man's will dependeth, the *liberty* of men would be a contradiction, and impediment to the omnipotence and *liberty* of God" (EW III, 197–198; T 146).

to him the weaker principle that one cannot be "blamed" for doing whatever one cannot help doing. The fact that our actions are causally determined by prior causes does not undermine (he assumed) our ordinary practices of praise, blame, and punishment. In the discussion in chapter 27 of *Leviathan* of "crimes, excuses, and extenuations", Hobbes argues that some actions against the law must be punished, while others may be excused, despite the fact that all are equally the result of necessitation by prior causes:

> [A]ll crimes are not, as the Stoics of old time maintained, of the same allay. There is place, not only for EXCUSE, by which that which seemed a crime, is proved to be none at all; but also for EXTENUATION, by which the crime, that seemed great, is made less. For though all crimes do equally deserve the name of injustice, as all deviation from a straight line is equally crookedness, which the Stoics rightly observed: yet it does not follow that all crimes are equally unjust, no more than that all crooked lines are equally crooked.[7]

Interestingly, Hobbes insists that although some fears, for instance bodily fear of imminent death or injury, excuse the unlawful actions they produce, other fears, for instance, superstitious fears of suffering the wrath of "spirits", do not excuse, and unlawful actions issuing from them ought to be punished. Yet the actions in each case are equally causally necessitated, and equally the product of the passion fear.

We must conclude that while Hobbes acknowledges that the necessity of attempting self-preservation may excuse certain actions, he does not *derive* the permissibility of attempting self-preservation from the *general principle* that *one cannot be blamed for doing what one cannot but do*, nor from the stronger principle that *one has a right to do what one cannot but do*. The blamelessness of trying to preserve oneself comes from some source other than those implausible general principles. Later I shall offer an alternative explanation. It is worth noting too that Hobbes never indicates that one is blameless in pursing one's self-interest generally.

The first difficulty then with traditional desire-based accounts is that they fail to establish their initial premise. The Right of Nature is not plausible as a primitive assumption of Hobbes's political

7 EW III, 287; T 208.

philosophy because of its extreme controversiality and mysterious normativity; and when we back up to the more plausible starting point of a descriptive assumption of a universal desire for self-preservation, we find this must be supplemented by either of two implausible general principles to yield the Right of Nature. We must assume either that people have a right to whatever they desire, or that people have a right to do (or cannot be blamed for doing) whatever they cannot refrain from doing. Neither of these assumptions is plausible. So on these traditional desire-based derivations, the plausibility criterion for interpretation is already violated.

Also worth mentioning is that the descriptive assumption of a universal dominant desire for self-preservation is itself problematic: It is not true. As we saw in Chapter 2, while most people desire the preservation of their bodies, some do not. Some are so burdened or miserable that they prefer not to continue to live; some while valuing their survival nonetheless prefer to sacrifice their lives for a greater good, or risk it in defending loved ones or caring for the sick. Some people do commit suicide,[8] to escape grief or pain, or for reasons as fantastical as the harm of a soiled reputation, and from causes as mechanical as light deprivation or drug-induced paranoia. And although some people do most value their temporal bodily preservation, very many people do not, particularly those, like Hobbes's contemporary readers, who care more for the safety of their souls in the next life than for their bodies in this one. Reliance on the assumption, which Hobbes denies, that all people most value bodily self-preservation disables these accounts from satisfying the psychological fit criterion on interpretation. Perhaps a traditional account can make do with the weaker assumption that most people desire self-preservation enough to put it first in many cases, although this weakened assumption degrades the normativity of the Laws of Nature from universal and inescapable to statistically probable although uncertain, thus offsetting a gain in view of the psychological fit criterion for interpretation with a loss in view of the normativity criterion. And even if some empirically acceptable version of the self-preservation assumption could be found, the failures we have noted in attempted arguments from that

[8] Or risk death in dueling, as Hobbes remarks.

premise to the Right of Nature raise serious doubts about the viability of traditional derivations of the Laws of Nature.

I found these three considerations – the controversiality of the Right of Nature as a normative primitive, the implausibility and textual indefensibility of a universal and overriding desire for self-preservation from which attempted derivations of the Right of Nature proceed, and the philosophical unacceptability of either of the connecting principles needed to make such a derivation – motivation enough to search for an alternative account of the Laws of Nature. But glaring gaps in later stages of those attempted derivations settled my conviction that the traditional account cannot be what Hobbes intended. Some of these we have already noted in the earlier discussion of the essential function of the Laws of Nature, but it may be useful to review them in the present context.

Steps 2, 3, and 4: Traditional Desire-Based Accounts

Traditional desire-based derivations infer from the Right of Nature along with their favored desire the necessity of a "war of all against all". Even proponents of these accounts have expressed doubts about this step in the argument they attribute to Hobbes. Won't the results of the Right of Nature depend on the content of people's various desires, and on their contingent beliefs? Won't outcomes depend as well on the availability of resources, the density of population, happenstance alliances, brute luck, and much else?[9] Locke wasn't doing rocket science

[9] The best recent game-theoretic efforts to model Hobbes's state of nature reveal how highly artificial and unrealistic are the assumptions required to demonstrate that the state of nature must necessarily be a war of all against all. Specific assumptions about the numerical proportions of those inclined to observe or to violate the Laws of Nature, the transmissibility of characteristics, communication of information, elimination of extrinsic contingencies, and many more such idealized assumptions are indispensable to that project. For outstanding recent work in this genre of Hobbes interpretation, see Peter Vanderschraaf, "War and Peace: A Dynamical Analysis of Anarchy", *Economics and Philosophy* 5 (2006): 321–351. Although this may not be the intent of Vanderschraaf and others engaged in game-theoretic modeling of Hobbes's arguments, I take this work to show decisively that on traditional desire-based interpretations, the requisite assumptions for demonstrating the necessity that the state of nature must be a war of all against all are straightforwardly incompatible with the complex Hobbesian psychology, accordance with which forms one constraint on adequate interpretation. Because they are psychologically untenable,

when he observed that under remotely realistic assumptions, a state of nature cannot as a matter of necessity be a literal war of all against all. This step of traditional interpretations violates the plausibility criterion on interpretation. Alternatively, if the condition constituted by a Universal Right of Nature is understood to be merely *defined* as a state of war, what then guarantees that people will find such a condition sufficiently inhospitable as to warrant submission to an absolutist government? Unless it is that inhospitable, the political function criterion for adequate interpretation threatens to go unsatisfied.

Furthermore, that the war of all against all must give rise to a universal desire for peace is another questionable step in the argument attributed to Hobbes. Remember those needy and hardy men who may reasonably stand to gain by stirring up war, or those of superior power to impose a preferable settlement against others. Surely the desire for peace, acknowledged even by traditional interpreters to be instrumental only, depends on one's other ends, one's relative power, and one's self-conception. Might not some people care more for obtaining glory through conquest, as Hobbes admits,[10] extracting what they claim as due respect from others, or converting others to their religion, forcibly if necessary, than they do for peace or any end to be served by peace? Might not some people believe (even if falsely) that their superior situation, perhaps as a result of lucky circumstance, excellent alliances, or superior skill, makes victory so likely that settling for peace would be suboptimal? In the last chapter we surveyed reasons for thinking that it is not true, and that Hobbes recognized that it is not true, that everyone's desire to secure self-preservation or self-interest is best satisfied by a condition of peace, particularly if peace is understood to require submission to an absolute sovereign, as Hobbes wishes to argue. This stage of traditional derivations thus runs afoul of the psychological fit and plausibility criteria for interpretation.

In their fourth step, traditional accounts infer from men's desire for peace that each man embraces the Laws of Nature as his rules

these unrealistic posits also run afoul of the normativity and plausibility constraints on interpretation.

[10] As Hobbes explicitly maintains. See *Leviathan,* chapter 13, EW III, 86–87; T 71, 110; T 87 ff.

for action, *qua* necessary means to peace. This step has then two segments: a claim that peace can be had only if each and every person observes each and every one of the specific Laws of Nature, and a claim that seeing this, each man will observe, or will insofar as he is rational observe, all of these Laws of Nature. Unless this is so, the normativity of the Laws of Nature is compromised, with them making various claims of varying strength on different persons, but no universal inescapable claim on every rational person. The difficulty is, of course, that it would be ridiculous to assert that peace can be had only if each and every individual adheres to all of the Laws of Nature. Every known society even in its peaceful periods has always had numerous members who violated some, perhaps all, of the Laws of Nature without thereby transforming it into a war of all against all. Societies count as peaceful even in Hobbes's theory despite the fact of crime, that some of their members lie, cheat, steal, murder. Indeed, the peaceful stability of some societies may have actually depended upon some performing such actions, for instance, treacherous waylaying of mediators offering tempting but dangerous terms for peace. As we saw in the previous chapter, it is very likely that for societies to enjoy domestic peace, most of their people most of the time must adhere to most of the norms Hobbes identifies as Laws of Nature, and that such behavior secures the good of humanity generally. But that is a far cry from the much stronger categorical assertion required to carry through traditional desire-based interpretations of the Laws of Nature, and even the substituted relatively feeble probabilistic claim is in any case disallowed for purposes of deriving Hobbes's Laws of Nature by his stated philosophical method of analytic demonstration, as I will explain at greater length when we come to survey definitional derivations. Interpretations that attribute to Hobbes the view that peace can be had only if each and every individual always adheres to all of the Laws of Nature will be patently false, in gross violation of the philosophical and practical plausibility criterion for adequate interpretation.

An alternative way of construing Hobbes's argument would be as claiming not that peace collapses unless every person follows the Laws of Nature, but that any individual who does not follow the Laws of Nature will be excluded from the peaceful society. Others will make war on lawbreakers, depriving them of the benefits of peace.

It is sometimes supposed that Hobbes's reply to the Foole offers an argument of this form.[11] The difficulty with this alternative is that lawbreakers will be excluded from peace only if their violations are detected, and they are unable to avoid punishment. But not all violations are detected, and some lawbreakers succeed in avoiding punishment, by deceit, bribery, force, flight, and other means. Hobbes grants that wickedness is sometimes successful. It is unrealistic to assume that no one can ever reasonably expect his lawbreaking to be profitable, so the most that could be concluded on this construal of Hobbes's argument is that breaking the Laws of Nature may result in hostility toward oneself. That conclusion does not secure the kind of universal inescapable normativity Hobbes ascribes to the Laws of Nature.

The strengths of traditional desire-based interpretations are that they appear to secure the motivational efficacy of the Laws of Nature by instrumentally linking them to some necessary and overriding desire, that they are simple and straightforward in construction, and enjoy an easy fit with the tone of many of Hobbes's remarks. These interpretations are, at least for today's post-Humean reader, the most natural construal of Hobbes's theory. Their disadvantages are that they rely on assumptions and arguments that conflict with complex Hobbesian psychology and so are of dubious normativity, they do not reliably track the particular content of the Laws of Nature, and they ascribe to Hobbes arguments so philosophically and practically implausible as to raise doubts about Hobbes's competence. Considered in the proper context of Hobbes's political project, these interpretations are almost comically perverse. They have Hobbes showing that if men want to preserve their lives, they should submit to government rather than take up arms against it. It cannot have been news to his readers that war may be hazardous to one's health. Hobbes's project is to dissuade people from armed insurrection. Those willing to fight the state are clearly willing to risk death in pursuit of their ends, so how could Hobbes have intended to dissuade them by proffering a demonstration that war threatens their preservation? It makes no sense.

[11] We offer a different interpretation of Hobbes's reply to the Foole in Chapter 7.

Rule-Utility Versions of Desire-Based Derivations

In contrast to traditional desire-based interpretations, which urge that in every instance actions in conformity with the Laws of Nature are necessary for securing the agent's preservation or profit, rule-utility versions of desire-based derivations make only the weaker claim that the best *strategy* for securing self-interest or preservation is always to conform to, or at least to accept and try to conform to, the Laws of Nature, even in those specific cases in which violating the laws can be seen to be in one's interest. For each Law of Nature, accepting it as the correct norm and either conforming or trying to conform to it enables Hobbesian agents to fare better, no matter their ends or circumstances, than would acceptance of any other non–Law of Nature maxim of action, including the maxim that agents are to seek to maximize the satisfaction of their interests on a case-by-case basis. Gregory Kavka's seminal presentation of such a view is probably the best-known and most widely embraced version of this approach. He calls the theory of morality he attributes to Hobbes "rule egoism".

Kavka's attempted improvement on traditional desire-based interpretation reproduces in Hobbes studies the familiar modern debate within utilitarianism between act utilitarians and various varieties of "indirect" utilitarianism.[12] Kavka's view holds out the prospect of remedying the main defects of standard "act-egoist" interpretations of the Laws of Nature by weakening the causal claims they make, substituting for the implausible claim that in every instance, action in accordance with the Laws of Nature is necessary to procure survival or self-interest the somewhat less implausible claim that a general strategy of adhering unfailingly to the Laws of Nature is better for achieving self-preservation or self-interest overall than any other possible strategy. Kavka's approach allows us to concede that in some instances the agent may actually do best by violating the Laws of Nature, while maintaining nonetheless that the general strategy most in our overall self-interest is to pursue a policy of always unthinkingly adhering to them. This is a considerable benefit, but we need to inquire about the costs of providing it.

[12] It is not surprising that as a young man, Kavka had a serious interest in that utilitarian debate.

Kavka is fully committed to a self-interest interpretation of the Laws of Nature, but differs from more traditional act-egoist views in the way self-interest is understood to come into their derivation. Like traditionalists, Kavka maintains that "the laws of nature are grounded in self-interest and may be considered rules of rational prudence"; the Laws of Nature "prescribe... modes of behavior as means to, or parts of, peace"; and the Laws of Nature are "common necessary means to the satisfaction of each person's basic desire to survive".[13] However, he insists that the Laws of Nature are exceptionless moral norms which are to be followed even in those specific instances in which doing so is suboptimal for self-interest or self-preservation. Let us try to construct out of Kavka's discussion an argument in support of his rule-egoist interpretation of the Laws of Nature, beginning from his Rule Egoist Principle.[14]

A Rule-Egoist Derivation of the Laws of Nature

1. The Rule Egoist Principle: Each agent should attempt always to follow that set of general rules of conduct whose acceptance (and sincere attempt to follow) by him on all occasions would produce the best expected outcomes for him.[15]
2. For each agent, seeking peace produces the best expected outcomes for him.
3. The Laws of Nature articulate the necessary means to peace.[16]

Therefore, each agent should attempt always to follow the Laws of Nature.

The second and third premises of this argument are common to the traditional arguments already examined, and subject to the same objections already noted, that peace is not in the greatest interest of

[13] Kavka, *Hobbesian Moral and Political Theory*, 310.

[14] Kavka adopts the term "Rule Egoism" from Stanley Moore. Moore's articles appeared in *Journal of the History of Philosophy*, beginning in 1971.

[15] Kavka, *Hobbesian Moral and Political Theory*, 358–359.

[16] "[F]or *everyone*, seeking peace (when it can be obtained) is the best long-run strategy for promoting one's interests, and the behaviors described in the laws of nature are means to peace" (ibid., 363). "[All mortals] will generally best promote their interests by pursuing peace – and the specific means to it enunciated in the laws of nature – when peace is obtainable" (364).

some, and that peace does not require that all people follow all (or even any one) of the Laws of Nature. The first premise is what distinguishes Kavka's argument from others, so we must ask what justifies assuming the Rule Egoist Principle?

Kavka grants that Hobbes never explicitly states the Rule Egoist Principle itself, nor any similar principle: "This specific principle... is not to be attributed to Hobbes in all its particulars. The claim is that a rule-egoistic grounding of some such sort is what he intends"[17] and "viewing Hobbes as a rule-egoist is surely necessary to enable us to understand what he is up to in his moral philosophy".[18] Kavka's informal argument for assuming the Rule Egoist Principle, which he insists would suffice to establish his interpretation were it not for the competition of divine command theories, begins from his assertion that "it is obvious" from Hobbes's various remarks that the Laws of Nature are general prescriptive rules of conduct, and that Hobbes's definitions of natural law "make it evident" that these laws are fundamentally rules of prudence. Since the "main aim of his moral theory is to reveal the consequentialist grounding or justification of traditional morality and its requirements",[19] Hobbes must have intended something like the Rule Egoist Principle.

Setting aside Kavka's unargued claim about the main aim of Hobbes's moral theory, one difficulty with this informal justification of the Rule Egoist Principle is that Kavka's own analysis of the Laws of Nature is incompatible with the claim that they are "fundamentally" rules of prudence. He writes:

> The conduct recommended in the main clauses of the laws of nature...is the sort of conduct that promotes the well-being of others and society, as well as that of the agent. Nor is this overlap between Hobbes's egoistic rules and utilitarian rules accidental.... [T]he main clauses of natural law are supposed to pick out precisely those kinds of conduct that tend to promote one's own interests, *because* they promote peace by also respecting and advancing the interests of others.[20]

[17] Ibid., 358n39.

[18] Ibid., 383.

[19] Ibid., 360.

[20] Ibid., 371. Kavka goes on to concede that some of Hobbes's justifications for his particular Laws of Nature are utilitarian rather than rule egoistic, but says this is "not too surprising" given the nonaccidental overlap he has just identified.

If the Laws of Nature pick out from all conduct that promotes self-interest only the subset of such conduct that does so by advancing the interests of others and society (humanity's interests), what justifies the claim that they are "fundamentally" about self-interest rather than collective interest? If a theory were designed to pick out only those rules for advancing self-interest that do so by increasing firm productivity (assuming individual welfare depends upon firm productivity – what's good for GM is good for us, a rising tide lifts all boats, etc.), we would not say this theory were fundamentally about self-interest. Such a theory is fundamentally about the requirements of firm profitability, in which we have a self-interested stake. Similarly, a theory that picks out only those practices that advance self-interest by creating a rich public intellectual and artistic culture is better described as fundamentally about the enrichment of public culture than as fundamentally about self-interest. It is a theory about enriching public culture, in which we have a self-interested stake. And a theory that picks out only those rules for advancing self-interest that do so by constituting the game of baseball (in which we have a self-interested entertainment stake) are surely more correctly described as rules of baseball than as "fundamentally" rules of self-interest. Kavka's own, quite proper, insistence on the nonaccidental convergence of the Laws of Nature with the subset of self-interested norms that secure humanity's common-interest collapses one pillar of his informal justification of the Rule Egoist Principle, for he is not entitled to his premise that the Laws of Nature are fundamentally rules of prudence. On the Rule Egoist Principle, the Laws of Nature are general prescriptive rules of prudence, justified consequentially. This is a problem for Kavka's justification of the Rule Egoist Principle, although not necessarily for the Rule Egoist Principle, or for Hobbes should he have intended the Rule Egoist Principle on other grounds.

A further difficulty with Kavka's informal justification of the Rule Egoist Principle that does create a problem for Hobbes as well as for Kavka is that nothing in it rules out the possibility that the Laws of Nature are mere rules of thumb for prudent action, rather than the iron-clad exceptionless moral principles the Rule Egoist Principle turns them into, which Hobbes says they are, and which it is desirable for them to be according to the normativity criterion for interpretation. To note that they are general prescriptive rules of conduct does not suffice to settle the question in favor of the iron-clad principle as against the rule of thumb construal. For this reason, the Rule Egoist Principle requires explicit justification. Kavka sketches two possible lines of support, which I collect and present below.

Argument One

1. Each person desires what he deems best for himself.
2. Rationality requires that one take the most effective means for procuring whatever he deems best for himself.
3. Any person procures what he deems best for himself better by strictly adhering to the Rule Egoist Principle than by acting in any other way. (Because, as against deciding on a case-by-case basis how to act, rule-determined "[d]ecision-making is easier, less costly, and less time consuming.... There is less room for self-deceptive shortsightedness... [and] [i]nterpersonal co-ordination, reliance, and cooperation, which promote mutual benefit, are facilitated".)[21]

Therefore, the Rule Egoist Principle.

Objections to Argument One

Kavka's argument joins the standard dispute between act and rule consequentialisms, inviting the objection that it involves irrational rule worship, requiring actions contrary to self-interest. For instance, Hampton objects that

> the rule egoist is prepared to follow a cooperative rule contained in a law of nature, the performance of which is generally justified as conducive to one's self-preservation, even in those particular cases in which it is not.... Would Hobbes counsel a person to follow the law of nature anyway? I do not see that he would, or could, given his psychology.... If a medicine that normally cures me of a disease will actually make me sicker when I take it in certain circumstances, I should not take it. And if a cooperative action that normally advances my long-term self-interest will actually hurt that self-interest on a particular occasion, then, as a person concerned above all else with advancing that self-interest, I should not perform it. Nowhere in *Leviathan* does Hobbes, given his psychological views, endorse the rationality or even the possibility of an individual described by that psychology performing

[21] Ibid., 365.

the cooperative action in the law anyway. Such behavior would strike him as inexplicable rule worship.[22]

As it stands, Hampton's objection is loosely cast as denying that Hobbes did, could, or would accept the implications of rule-egoism. But the underlying objection can be elaborated, again by analogy with a famous objection to rule-utilitarianism, as presenting a dilemma: either rule-egoism requires the agent, who cares most about her self-interest, to act irrationally on some occasions, or else it so specifies the rules that they guarantee that the agent is never required to act against her own best-interest, in which case it collapses into act-egoism.

This form of objection does not pose an intractable problem for rule-utilitarianism, which can deflect the charge of irrationality by pointing out that the aim of the theory is not to maximize utility but rather to identify those among universalizable principles that have the best consequences of all such formally equitable principles.[23] In such equity-based views, what matters most is that we hold ourselves to standards that all could be held to without ill effect. Consequences do matter, but only in a limited way, as reasons for selecting one set of universalizable rules over others, and thus there is no inconsistency in selecting standards that may sometimes actually produce suboptimal outcomes.

But this sort of reply cannot be made in defense of Kavka's rule-egoism. To count as an egoist, self-interest must trump or at least usually dominate all one's other ends. While it is true that those whom Kavka terms "predominant egoists" may sometimes, or in particular

[22] Hampton, *Hobbes and the Social Contract Tradition*, 93. Gauthier objects that a psychological egoist will not be able to adopt the best rules (which will require sometimes acting against her interest at the time of action), because she is incapable of being motivated to act on them; while "the second-best set of rules that she can adopt will, I suppose, not govern her behavior in a way that would make a society of such individuals stable"; "Taming Leviathan", *Philosophy and Public Affairs* 16 (1987): 280–298, 287. But one could address this problem by giving up psychological egoism, which there can be no reason not to do once we understand Hobbes's full conception of human nature.

[23] On this interpretation, which I favor, rule-utilitarian theories are forms of deontological theory that take consequences into account in a particular way, as the criterion for selecting among legitimate principles, where the criterion for the legitimacy of principles is their universalizability.

cases, be motivated to act against perceived self-interest, it would be untrue to say even of them that they do not care most about self-interest. So one cannot evade the charge that it is irrational for those who care most about self-interest to follow rules when doing so is against their self-interest by replying that egoists do not care most about self-interest. Were we conveniently to stipulate that predominant egoists care most for self-interest only when its pursuit does not require violations of the Laws of Nature, we would in effect have posited some systematically trumping nonegoistic motive of Hobbesian men, which motive is necessary for the Laws of Nature to enjoy the kind of overriding normativity Kavka (and Hobbes) ascribe to them. But this calls into doubt Kavka's claim to have shown that the Laws of Nature enjoy their normativity for Hobbesian agents *qua* rules of self-interest. Nor, clearly, could we give up the claim that egoists care most about their self-interest, while still propounding a rule-egoist account of the Laws of Nature.

It might further be objected to Kavka's first argument for the Rule Egoist Principle that because the Rule Egoist Principle rules out specific action-descriptions particularized to the circumstances and features of the agent, the laws it picks out cannot adequately provide for the self-interest of the agent. That is, the Rule Egoist Principle stipulates that the rules we ought to follow must be characterizable in perfectly general terms, using no "time-specific or person-specific descriptions" of acts.[24] But, considering what a blunt instrument this constraint renders the Laws of Nature for purposes of securing self-interest, what justifies this insistence that we turn a blind eye to features of our specific circumstance that suggest more finely tuned value judgments? It may be perfectly obvious in some circumstance that the best strategy is to follow the Laws of Nature except in this particular case. If so, the Laws of Nature become mere rules of thumb for securing self-interest, and Kavka has no way to rule out this possibility. What justifies forbidding the adoption of rules that are not general in Kavka's specified sense? An egoist account presumably must answer that self-interest is best secured when agents are compelled to act on general rules. Yet as the previous objection suggests, this answer may be doubted. What is at issue between the act-egoist

[24] Kavka, *Hobbesian Moral and Political Theory*, 359.

and the rule-egoist is precisely whether the most effective maxim of rational action must make specific reference to the agent and his particular situation.

Argument Two

A second argument is suggested by Kavka's remark that "[t]he first and fundamental law of nature [to seek peace] ... is a moral *requirement* because its status as such is necessary if it is to enable agents to rely sufficiently on one another so as to obtain peace".[25]

Seeking to develop this claim into an argument for the Rule Egoist Principle, let's try the following:

1. Only the Rule Egoist Principle gives the Law of Nature the status of a moral requirement (always binding).*
2. Unless the Law of Nature has the status of a moral requirement, it will not serve to enable agents to obtain peace.

   Therefore, the Rule Egoist Principle is a justified assumption.

   *This assumption would make sense of Kavka's remark that his rule egoistic interpretation would be established were it not for the divine command theory; the latter also confers on the Law of Nature the status of a moral requirement, so this assumption will be true only if the divine command interpretation (and any other that makes the Laws of Nature exceptionless, overriding requirements) is defeated.

This second argument might be understood in a couple of different ways. The narrowly textual interpretation of the second argument understands Kavka's claim to be that because Hobbes thinks the Law of Nature secures peace, and because it could not do so unless everyone regarded it as an overriding, exceptionless, nonoptional moral requirement, Hobbes thought (or should have thought) that it is a moral requirement, which it could be only if the Rule Egoist Principle is true; therefore Hobbes assumed (or should have assumed) the Rule Egoist Principle. The Rule Egoist Principle is justified for purposes of interpreting Hobbes because Hobbes is committed to the Rule Egoist Principle. This could of course be true even if the Rule

[25] Ibid., 348.

Egoist Principle is false, and in fact an unjustifiable assumption of any plausible moral theory.

Objections to Argument Two on Its Narrowly Textual Interpretation

If successful, this argument establishes only that (1′) Hobbes believed or was committed to believing the Rule Egoist Principle. The first problem with this interpretation is that if we substitute (1′) for (1) in Kavka's justification for the Laws of Nature, its conclusion no longer follows. That each of us ought always to attempt to follow the Laws of Nature cannot be derived from the argument Kavka attributes to Hobbes, if its major premise depends upon considerations of what Hobbes, given his aims, thought or should have thought.

A further difficulty for this first interpretation of Kavka's second argument is that Kavka's stated project is to scour Hobbes's own theory to devise a more defensible theory that builds on what is true or suggestively useful in Hobbes's own theory. So if Kavka ascribes the Rule Egoist Principle to Hobbesian theory, as he does, he must judge it acceptable on its own merits as a normative principle. Hence there must be some justification for it other than that Hobbes is committed to it. Kavka, while respectful of what he understands to be Hobbes's authentic position, is merciless in expunging those elements of it he believes are errors. He thus would not have retained in his own Hobbesian theory so crucial an element as the Rule Egoist Principle in spite of all its difficulties without other justification than that the historical Hobbes needed to hold it. This is a further consideration against the first interpretation.

There is however a second and much more interesting possible interpretation of Kavka's second argument. He may be intending to offer what we might term an optative justification for the Rule Egoist Principle: only the Rule Egoist Principle gives the Law of Nature the status it would need in order to do what we want it to do; therefore the Rule Egoist Principle is true. Here the force of our desire to achieve peace is communicated backward into an optative justification of the prerequisites for satisfying that desire, of the sort "let the Rule Egoist Principle be so". We want the self-preservation that comes from peace; the Laws of Nature could not secure peace unless they had the status of binding moral principles; for them to have that status, the Rule Egoist Principle would have to be true; therefore, the Rule Egoist Principle. The Rule Egoist Principle is justified as a necessary requirement for our having the Laws of Nature do what we want them to do.

Objection to Argument Two on Its Optative Interpretation

This is an intriguing suggestion. But it immediately appears open to the objection that optative justification is not generally acceptable because it will justify our embracing falsehoods when doing so is necessary for satisfying our desires. Optative justification would justify, for instance, the stalker's belief that the movie star will love him when she meets him, because his actions in pursuit of her couldn't have their desired effect unless this were true. The form of optative justification is: A because only if A may desired effect x be obtained. This invites wishful thinking, an acknowledged species of cognitive defect. Thus, the stalker reasons: because I desire that she love me, and to love me she must meet me, and for her to meet me I must take certain instrumentally related steps, but my taking those steps could not effect her loving me unless it were true that she'll love me when she meets me; therefore, she'll love me when she meets me. This stalker logic does not differ at all in form from that of positing the Rule Egoist Principle as securing self-interest (this is the force of Kavka's "one ought") because unless the Rule Egoist Principle were true, following the Laws of Nature, which are needed for peace, which is needed for securing self-interest, would not secure peace and thus self-interest.

Of course, it is true that to embrace fictions for pragmatic purposes is not necessarily objectionable, but neither can pragmatic necessity serve as a general justification. It is objectionable to embrace, without further justification, the fundamental premise of astrology, on the ground that such acceptance is needed if the principles of astrology are to function as guides to our conduct in pursuit of our happiness, as they undeniably do for many people. What distinguishes Kavka's own argument for the Rule Egoist Principle from the astrology case, or the stalker case? Until we can assure ourselves that something does, this optative interpretation of the second argument for the Rule Egoist Principle is highly problematic.

Rule-Egoism within Hobbes's Theory

Objection That Hobbesian Men Are Not Transparent

So far we have reviewed objections to the soundness of Kavka's derivation of the Laws of Nature based on objections to each of its three component premises – to the Rule Egoist Principle, to the necessary connection between self-interest and peace, and to the necessary connection between strict adherence to the Laws of Nature and peace. But in these last two Kavka's quoted remarks overstate the case he actually wishes to make; all he really requires to make out his rule-egoist interpretation is that unfailing pursuit of peace be the best strategy for securing self-interest, and that strict, exceptionless, adherence to the particular Laws of Nature be the best strategy for securing peace. That is to say, Kavka need only show that there is no better strategy for securing self-interest than always, as critics would say, slavishly, following all of Hobbes's Laws of Nature. So we should consider how he might hope to show this. Because common sense tells us that we may perceive in our very particular circumstances features of our situation that would make the general rule given by the Laws of Nature suboptimal for securing our best outcome, the burden of argument lies in showing that such common sense beliefs should nonetheless be discounted. We are not to trust our common sense beliefs, because these will lead us to act counterproductively.

In appealing to Hobbes's reply to the Foole to support this contention, Kavka attributes to Hobbes the argument that we must adopt the policy of always seeking to conform to the requirements of the Laws of Nature because otherwise our fellow men will discern our inclination to deviate from those laws at their expense when we think it suits our interest, and will retaliate by excluding us from social "cooperation". This position is sustainable only if one believes that the agent's intentions are easily, or at least ordinarily or often, discerned by others, so that we cannot reasonably hope to deceive others about our rule of action. That is, Kavka attributes to Hobbes the view that men are sufficiently *transparent* that they cannot reasonably hope to deceive others, and thus must actually internalize the policy of slavish conformity to the Laws of Nature in order to maintain the needed cooperation with others.[26] But Hobbes's texts strongly support the opposite conclusion. Hobbes insists that men's intentions are easily hidden, and that men are in general so gullible that they may be made to believe almost anything, as, for instance, in this passage:

> [T]he *objects* of the passions, which are the things *desired, feared, hoped,* &c;... the constitution individual, and particular education, do so vary, and *they are so easy to be kept from our knowledge, that the characters of man's heart, blotted and confounded as they are with dissembling, lying, counterfeiting, and erroneous doctrines, are legible only to him that searcheth hearts.* And though by men's actions we do discover their design *sometimes;* yet to do it [as we ordinarily do] ... is to decypher without a key, *and be for the most part deceived, by too much trust, or by too much diffidence;* as he that reads, is himself a good or evil man.[27]

And

> So easy are men to be drawn to believe any thing, from such men as have gotten credit with them;[28]
>
> For such is the ignorance and aptitude to error generally of all men... as by innumerable and easy tricks to be abused.[29]

Not only are Hobbesian men not transparent to one another in the way that Kavka's argument requires, they are so opaque to one another that it is "easy" for them to deceive one another. Thus, Kavka is not entitled to the assumption he needs in order to make plausible his otherwise implausible claim that slavish adherence to the Laws of Nature is each man's personally best strategy for securing self-interest.

26 Gauthier is required to posit a similar assumption of "transluscency" in order to demonstrate the rationality of internalizing "moral" norms of conduct in his *Morals by Agreement* (Oxford, 1969), 174–178. It is interesting that David Boonin-Vail's interpretation of Hobbes as a virtue ethicist (*Thomas Hobbes and the Science of Moral Virtue* [Cambridge, 1994]), which inverts the relation of action to disposition given by traditional accounts, also relies on a transparency assumption to support its claim that Hobbesian men must internalize the Laws of Nature by becoming virtuous persons "because one's disposition is revealed to others through one's behavior" (145), and the disposition of the man who, like the Foole, has not internalized the Laws of Nature, "exposes him to the unacceptable risk of being found out" (150). Presumably his actions risk exposing his disposition only on the assumption that men are transparent.

27 EW III, xi–xii; T 11, final emphases added.

28 EW III, 103; T 82.

29 EW III, 434; T 305.

Objection That Hobbes's Right of Nature Becomes Otiose

It will also be relevant to assessing the acceptability of Kavka's rule-egoistic derivation of the Laws of Nature to consider how well it fits within the broader scheme of Hobbes's normative theory. One very striking feature of Kavka's derivation is that it makes no use whatsoever of Hobbes's Right of Nature. In particular, the Laws of Nature are not derived from the Right of Nature. In this, Kavka's argument departs from all traditional variants of desire-based accounts. Because the Rule Egoist Principle, an "ought" principle, does not depend on the Right of Nature, a postulated "genuine moral permission" principle, and the Laws of Nature follow from the Rule Egoist Principle combined with purely descriptive (non-normative) premises, the Right of Nature has no role to play in their derivation.

This feature of Kavka's account is especially surprising because he asserts that for Hobbes, the Right of Nature "is the foundational postulate of his moral theory".[30] According to Kavka, it is also a normative primitive, not derived from facts about human nature or human desires: "No argument is ever offered for ascribing this natural right to us, and all other rights are derived, by Hobbes, from it. Hence, it functions as a normative *postulate* of Hobbes's moral theory".[31] We have already considered reasons for thinking Hobbes should not have offered the Right of Nature as a primitive assumption. But if it does not figure into the derivation of the Laws of Nature, from which flow the civil obligations Hobbes is concerned to establish, it is difficult to understand how it could be the foundational postulate of Hobbes's moral theory, the Laws of Nature being, as Hobbes insists, the true moral philosophy. On the view Kavka offers, the Laws of Nature are not derived from the Right of Nature, nor is it derived from them. How then are these concepts understood to be related, and what if any necessary work in the theory does the Right of Nature do?

Perhaps the Right of Nature could play some indirect role within Hobbes's theory. The Right of Nature might be thought important because without it the state of nature would not generate sufficient conflict to motivate Hobbesian men to desire peace. This, of course, implies that Hobbesian men will act only if they believe they have the

[30] Kavka, *Hobbesian Moral and Political Theory*, 316.
[31] Ibid., 315.

right to so act, a controversial claim to be sure, and one that appears to fit poorly with Kavka's emphasis on Hobbesian man's drive to satisfy the demands of desire. But if it were true that Hobbesian men will not usually act on their interests or desires unless they believe they have a right to do so, something like the Right of Nature would have to be posited in order to generate the war of all against all. I am not certain what Kavka would say about assigning this role to the Right of Nature, but it is not, in any case, a possibility he can embrace consistently with his explicitly stated methodological approach, according to which the account of conflict in the state of nature, and of how it is rational to act, belongs to descriptive theory, and not to the distinct realm of normative theory in which the Right of Nature appears as a postulate.[32]

An alternative possibility is that although it plays no role in Kavka's derivation of the Laws of Nature, the Right of Nature must be posited in order to carry out Hobbes's later account of submission to government. We submit to authority by laying down or transferring rights, which, if all particular rights flow from the Right of Nature, we could not do unless we had the Right of Nature. But this argument positing rights solely for the purpose of having something to lay down assigns us unnecessary busywork. It is not compelling once we recognize that submission could just as well be effected by simply promising to substitute the sovereign's judgment of justified action for our own; so long as we can assume binding obligations by promising, rights are superfluous.[33] If all the Right of Nature does is license Hobbes's particular language in describing the mechanism of submission to government, it will be an idle gear in the moral theory.

The last possibility I'll consider is that Kavka sees the Right of Nature as *indirectly* involved in Hobbes's moral theory because he

[32] Gert criticizes Kavka for putting the account of how it is rational to act into the descriptive, rather than normative part of the theory on pages 160 and 162 of his review of Kavka's *Hobbesian Moral and Political Theory* in *Political Theory* 16 (1988): 159–163. He says this leads Kavka incorrectly to treat the Right of Nature as a normative postulate because he does not see that it is established by an argument about right reason, that is, rationality.

[33] Indeed, the language of promising serves better than the language of rights, because it allows for the mobster's promise to cease extracting protection money to create a binding obligation, even though he could not have done so by laying down the right (which he never had) to collect it.

believes the *content* of Hobbes's Laws of Nature cannot be captured without reference to it or to particular rights that can be understood only as having been derived from it. Kavka claims that each of the Laws of Nature has a two-part structure consisting of a directive about how the agent is to act so long as others are also doing the same, and a permission to refrain from that action when others are not performing it or other morally desirable actions. He writes of the "logical form" of the Laws of Nature: "They possess a common two-part structure. First, there is a main clause which requires behavior of a traditionally moral kind. Second, there is a qualifying clause which indicates that the agent is released from the requirement of the main clause if others are not satisfying that requirement (or other requirements of the laws of nature)".[34]

He concedes that, excepting the first two of Hobbes's twenty Laws of Nature, Hobbes does not formulate these laws as having a qualifying clause, but Kavka insists that they nonetheless implicitly contain such a clause. As evidence for this he interprets Hobbes's remark that the Laws of Nature apply *in foro externo* only when in following them one would not "procure his own certain ruin", as meaning that "an agent is required to act as the main clauses of these laws require (i.e., is obliged *in foro externo*) when and only when others are doing the same".[35] By "the same" here, Kavka means to require that others be observing the very same particular requirement toward the agent, or at least toward others, and/or be observing "other requirements of the laws of nature", again either toward the agent or toward others, or both.

I do not see how such an interpretation can be defended. On Kavka's analysis, we should read, for instance, the fourth Law of Nature dictating gratitude as requiring that one be grateful to those who benefit him unless others are not being grateful to their benefactors, and/or are violating other Laws of Nature, by being, for instance, immodest, unaccommodating, unmerciful, inequitable, or unjust either to others or to oneself. Such a position does not track common moral sense. Why should my duty of gratitude to my parents hinge on whether my students are properly grateful to me, or on whether other children

[34] Kavka, *Hobbesian Moral and Political Theory*, 344.
[35] Ibid., 346.

are grateful to their parents, let alone on whether others are treating their captives mercilessly, are keeping their gardening contracts with me or their house-painting contracts with others who are strangers to me? This is a kind of Wonderland ethics, where Mad Hatters define moral duties for the rest of us. We can agree with Hobbes's common-sense claim that in such time as "no man else" should observe moral norms, those who would unilaterally observe them "procure their own certain ruin", and that no plausible moral theory requires such self-destruction. The proper inference is that in those times we are bound only to the intention (*in foro interno*) and not to strict performance (*in foro externo*) of the moral law. But nothing in this implies that each and every moral injunction is contingent upon everyone else's doing all that they ought, as Kavka's two-part analysis stipulates.

A. P. Martinich offers the following further argument against Kavka's claim that the Laws of Nature have a two-part structure that includes a permission clause: First, Hobbes insists that all of the laws of bature can be derived from the Golden Rule (*Do unto others as you would have them do unto you*); yet the two-part structure of the Laws of Nature cannot be derived from the Golden Rule, as Kavka concedes. For instance, one may want others not to retaliate for one's own mean actions, and so by the Golden Rule be required not to retaliate for their mean actions, but this will not imply, as Kavka's interpretation maintains, that one is required to refrain from retaliation only if others are also refraining from retaliation. Here Martinich calls attention to the fact that while Hobbes identifies his Laws of Nature with the Golden Rule, Kavka's interpretation of those rules requires demoting them to the status of dictates of what, as we have seen, Kavka calls "the Copper Rule", *Treat others as they treat you*, or *act as others act*. This reverse alchemy involves a momentous change in meaning, which threatens to pick out an entirely different set of action-rules than those which Hobbes *explicitly* dictates, and so should be accepted only if there is compelling textual and philosophical reason for making the change.[36]

[36] Martinich argues further that permissions, that is, rights, cannot be parts of Hobbes's Laws of Nature because Hobbes insisted that laws state requirements, while rights delineate permissions, and that law and right "differ as contraries", just like obligation and liberty. "[L]aw, and right, differ as much, as obligation, and

I conclude that although Kavka may have seen the Right of Nature as a moving part of Hobbes's moral theory, because he assigned it a role in grounding what he said were qualifying clauses of the Laws of Nature, it does not properly serve this role because there is no such role to be served. The Laws of Nature do not contain qualifying clauses, so the Right of Nature is not needed to account for the content of those laws. With the failure of this possible explanation of the role of the Right of Nature in Hobbes's moral philosophy, we should grant that the cost of accepting Kavka's derivation of the Laws of Nature is that it makes idle Hobbes's Right of Nature. If the Right of Nature does not matter, this is no great cost. If it does, this provides further reason to reject Kavka's rule-egoistic account of the Laws of Nature.

The Problem of Subjectivism

The last of the difficulties I will address with Kavka's account of how the Laws of Nature are derived raises a thorny interpretive tangle that we will not be able fully to unknot until the next chapter. Kavka asserts that in order for the rule-egoistic derivation of the Laws of Nature to prove adequate, we must reject any subjectivist reading of the Laws of Nature. Such readings declare that one ought to do what *one judges best* for achieving one's purposes, avoiding harms to oneself, or securing one's good. Kavka notes, correctly, that if we were to read the Laws of Nature as directing us to do what *we merely think or believe* best for ourselves, then given the variability of men's beliefs, they would not reliably yield the universal set of specific norms of conduct Hobbes lays down in his Laws of Nature. Because we may be wrong about what best conduces to our self-interest, or even to self-preservation, lighting on norms that differ from Hobbes's specific Laws of Nature, subjectivist readings cannot ensure that what I have called the content criterion for adequate interpretation will be met. The same will be true of any traditional desire-based interpretation that adopts a subjectivist reading of the Laws of Nature. Kavka notes the ambiguity in what he takes to be Hobbes's definition of the Law of Nature: it forbids both acts destructive to one's life, and commands

liberty; which in one and the same matter are inconsistent" (EW III, 117; T 92). See A. P. Martinich, *Thomas Hobbes* (Routledge, 2005), chapter 3.

one's doing that "by which he *thinketh* it may be best preserved". But, Kavka maintains, the "'subjective' interpretation of the content of the laws of nature must be rejected, because it is incompatible with the claim that the laws of nature are general prescriptions having the specific content that Hobbes says they have".[37] We thus must understand the Laws of Nature to command actions in accordance with our objective interest, rather than commanding efforts to secure what we believe to be in our interest.

The difficulty is that Hobbes will not give up the subjective language he adopted in *Leviathan*. Indeed, Hobbes in the Latin *Leviathan* of 1668 intensifies Kavka's problem, for there, as we saw in the previous chapter, he expunges all nonsubjective language from his definition of the Law of Nature. There he alters the definition to read that a Law of Nature is a rational precept "by which a man is forbidden to do, that, which seems to him to tend to his own loss". This definition, which he either newly introduced or else elected to let stand in 1668, is purely subjective (and appears to favor self-interest readings over self-preservation readings). So Kavka's interpretation forces its proponents to choose between rejecting Hobbes's explicit textual formulations, with the further disadvantage of rendering mysterious how men who believe their self-interest lies elsewhere can be motivated to adhere to the Laws of Nature, or instead ascribing to him a view upon which the specific content of Hobbes's universal Laws of Nature is not derivable and their status as universal norms undermined. This is an unhappy choice.

To summarize, I have argued against Kavka's rule-egoistic improvement on traditional desire-based interpretations that it makes idle Hobbes's right of nature, and requires that we deny the subjectivism that Hobbes so unrelentingly insisted upon, or else give up the specific content and normativity of those laws. These problems of "fit" within the larger theory are worrisome. Adding to these the further considerations that Hobbes's texts give no statement of the Rule Egoist Principle or a similar principle, that we are not able to construct any philosophically plausible argument in support of the Rule Egoist Principle, and that Kavka's rule-egoist interpretation imports the standard deficiencies of the later steps of standard desire-based

[37] Kavka, *Hobbesian Moral and Political Theory*, 341.

interpretations, we see that Kavka's popular attempted improvement on traditional desire-based interpretations is not satisfactory.

Duty-Based Derivations of the Laws of Nature

Duty-based derivations seek to derive the Laws of Nature from claims that we have certain duties, or natural obligations. By positing a normatively primitive duty incumbent on all standard human beings, these interpretations promise to meet the content and normativity criteria on interpretations. I view both the family of *divine command* interpretations and Bernard Gert's *rationally required end* view as belonging to this category.

DIVINE COMMAND DERIVATIONS

A. E. Taylor, Howard Warrender, F. C. Hood, and most recently A. P. Martinich have defended interpretations that, despite their substantial differences, have been jointly classified as divine command interpretations.[38] These views agree in understanding the normativity of Hobbes's Laws of Nature to be a function of their having been commanded for our observance by God.[39] Some of these views adopt a traditional instrumental account of the derivation of the Laws of Nature, but append to it an argument from the nature of law to ensure the normativity of the derived laws, *qua* God's commands. Others suggest that knowledge of the Laws of Nature is innate, written in the heart. Taylor argued as against traditional desire-based derivations that Hobbes's moral theory is independent of his psychological theory and

[38] See A. E. Taylor, "The Ethical Doctrine of Hobbes", in K. C. Brown, ed., *Hobbes Studies* (1965), 35–55; Howard Warrender, *The Political Philosophy of Hobbes: His Theory of Obligation* (Oxford, 1957); Francis C. Hood, *The Divine Politics of Thomas Hobbes* (Oxford, 1964); and A. P. Martinich, *The Two Gods of Leviathan: Thomas Hobbes on Religion and Politics* (Cambridge, 1992). These views hold that the Laws of Nature are literally laws because commanded by God, and that the laws' normativity (although not necessarily men's actual motive for obeying them) depends upon that fact.

[39] Warrender thinks God's command makes the Laws of Nature obligatory, but is willing to allow that one might just as well think of the Laws of Nature as free-standing moral imperatives bearing their own authority. However, they are not to be thought of as contingently obligatory depending upon their instrumental relation to the satisfaction of any desire.

is a strict deontology. Warrender, too, took Hobbes's psychological theory to formulate empirical postulates employed in the application of his moral theory (his theory of obligation), although no part of that theory. While Martinich does not press their logical independence thesis, he does agree with Taylor and Warrender that God's command grounds the obligatory nature of the Laws of Nature.

Let me begin by schematizing a generic derivation congenial to the divine command school of interpretation, before discussing various ways of continuing the derivation of the Laws of Nature. Divine command interpretations deploy wrongly neglected passages in Hobbes's writings, emphasizing his well-documented assertions that the only law that obligates in the state of nature is the law of nature. Law is command, not counsel, directed toward one formerly obligated to obey. The only source of natural obligation in the state of nature is God's irresistible power. Therefore, the Law of Nature obligates in virtue of its being commanded by God toward those formerly obligated by God's irresistible power to obey.[40]

On this basis they insist that the Laws of Nature are literally laws, binding as such, and in this way they account for the normativity of the Laws of Nature. And, of course, they are unquestionably right that Hobbes maintains consistently throughout his political writings that the Laws of Nature track God's laws as revealed through prophesy, and that considered as God's commands in his natural kingdom, the Laws of Nature are literally laws. This does not suffice to prove that their normativity consists in their being God's laws, but it would be silly to deny that Hobbes viewed them as God's laws. The main question, however (setting aside familiar worries about how mere power, even God's, could create genuinely moral obligation), is how to continue from here to derive the specific Laws of Nature Hobbes enumerates. To say with Martinich that "Hobbes takes it as beyond question that what is deducible as the best means to self-preservation must be the command of God"[41] is to lay one's interpretation open to most

40 Martinich offers this variation on the argument: Justice and injustice require a law. Law requires a common power. The only law in the state of nature is the Law of Nature. The only common power in the state of nature is God. Therefore, justice and injustice exist in the state of nature because God establishes the Law of Nature. See his chapter 4 in his *The Two Gods of Leviathan.*

41 Ibid., 335.

of the failings of traditional desire-based views while heaping on top the further problem of explaining how those not graced by prophetic knowledge can learn what God has commanded, a serious epistemological problem, which unless resolved will undermine the normativity of divine command derivations. The alternative of assuming this knowledge to be innate sits poorly with Hobbes's texts and general method, and with his unwavering insistence that the Laws of Nature are *theorems* of reason, rules *found out by reasoning.* As Kavka put this point, "In the end, we must infer the content of God's commands from our knowledge of the contents of the laws of nature, not vice versa".[42]

Martinich has recently suggested an indirect proof of the first Law of Nature, "seek peace", as follows:

> To prove: A person endeavors peace. (1) A person does not do what is destructive of his life. (Content of the definition of the law of nature). (2) A person does not endeavour peace (Supposition). (3) If a person does not endeavor peace, then a person does what is destructive of his life. (From the definition of 'not endeavoring peace'.) (4) A person does what is destructive of his life. (From 3 and 2 by *modus ponens.*) (5) A person does what is destructive of his life and a person does not do what is destructive of his life. (From 4 and 1 by conjunction.) (6) Therefore, a person endeavors peace. (From 5 by *reduction ad absurdum.*) QED".[43]

Martinich acknowledges that the premises and conclusions of his demonstration are propositions rather than the imperatives Hobbes used and sought to establish, but maintains that a proper reconstruction of Hobbes's argument requires separating the force of an imperative from the proposition attached to it, a position that echoes that of John Deigh's definitional derivation (which we will analyze shortly). I do not see how Martinich's propositions adequately capture Hobbes's meaning or preserve the sense of Hobbes's argument. To prove that a person does endeavor peace is no more to prove that she ought to endeavor peace than is a demonstration that she endeavors to sing karaoke a proof that she ought to do so. Even if she wants peace, or to sing karaoke, there may be other things she values more, such as preserving her dignity. To distinguish the cases by saying that peace is

[42] Kavka, *Hobbesian Moral and Political Theory*, 362.

[43] Martinich, *Thomas Hobbes*, chapter 3.

desired most of all and for its own sake contradicts Hobbes's treatment of peace as an instrumental good.

But in any case, the main difficulty I find in Martinich's proof is that his assumption (3) assumes precisely what is in need of proving. On traditional desire-based views and those divine command views that subsume their traditional derivations, the goal of the argument is to demonstrate that pursuit of peace is instrumentally necessary to self-preservation. Assumption (3) assumes this conclusion.

Some divine command interpretations (I am thinking of Taylor's particularly) also run afoul of the political function criterion for adequate interpretation. Taylor holds that the reason one should obey the government is that he has promised to do so, and that the reason he ought to keep his promises is that by the Law of Nature God has commanded him to do so. But none of that suffices to settle any duty to obey government. What is needed is an argument that God requires us under the Law of Nature to make a promise to obey government. This Taylor does not offer, and the two possible ways of doing so just surveyed – the traditional desire-based way and the innate knowledge way – won't serve.

GERT'S "RATIONALLY REQUIRED END" DUTY-BASED DERIVATION

Bernard Gert has made a strong case in a number of important works over many years that Hobbes actually took reason to have an end of its own, imposing on us a duty of self-preservation, which duty in turn grounds the Laws of Nature. Gert collects substantial textual support for his interpretation, and it shares the advantage with other duty-based interpretations of offering to give a firm normative support for the Laws of Nature. One textual difficulty for any view of this sort is that it will conflict with Hobbes's definition of the Right of Nature as a liberty to use, or *not use*, whatever means one deems needful for preservation. Because for Hobbes a right is a liberty to do or forebear an action, one has a right only if one has no obligation either to do or to forbear the action over which one has a right. Thus, Gert's interpretation invites the worry that Hobbes cannot reconcile the Right of Nature – our liberty to do or not do what we deem necessary for our defense – with the foundational duty of self-defense upon which his theory is said to be grounded. But this consideration should not be treated as decisive.

Gert's view departs from traditional desire-based interpretation in its insistence that natural reason is not merely instrumental, but has its own end or goal, namely self-preservation. Although it may not be the case that all men do in fact desire self-preservation, reason imposes upon them a requirement to pursue this end, and insists that they rationally ought to desire it.[44] Gert suggests increasingly that self-preservation, while the most important of the rationally required desires, is not the only such desire; desires for one's own long-term benefit – for health, for security, to avoid pain and disability – are also rationally required. Some natural desires are not rationally required, but all rationally required desires are natural, Gert maintains, which allows Hobbes to use them as a universal basis for his moral and political conclusions. Gert's argument for the Laws of Nature proceeds as follows:

1. The desire for (temporal bodily) self-preservation is rationally required.
2. Seeking peace is necessary for satisfaction of the desire for (temporal bodily) self-preservation.

   C1. Therefore, men should seek peace (as being rationally required).
3. The Laws of Nature are a necessary means to peace.

   C2. Therefore, reason requires men to follow the Laws of Nature.

This argument adopts the instrumental form of traditional desire-based derivations, but would if successful evade their failure to meet

[44] David Johnston, in *The Rhetoric of 'Leviathan': Thomas Hobbes and the Politics of Cultural Transformation* (Princeton, NJ, 1986), suggests something similar when he claims that Hobbes's political project is to transform men from superstitious self-sacrificers into the rational egoists Johnston thinks they would need to be in order for the sovereign's threatened punishments to be effective in securing political obedience. In his preface Johnston explains his thesis that Hobbes hoped to induce people to abandon the theological and metaphysical opinions that had undermined a rational political equilibrium (xx). Johnston agrees with Gert that real Hobbesian agents do not always most value self-preservation, but that Hobbes thought they ought to do so, and grounded his derivation of the Laws of Nature on the needs of self-preservation. I believe Johnston's position is subject as well to the criticisms I raise against Gert's below. For criticism of Johnston's view on this point, see *IAI*, 326n18, 367n4, 374–375n3.

the psychological fit criterion. By now the gripe against premise (2) of the argument is a familiar refrain; seeking peace is not always and for everyone either necessary or most conducive to self-preservation (let alone self-interest more broadly defined). The difficulty unique to Gert's sort of view comes with premise (1). First, there is scant textual evidence that Hobbes believed reason imposes upon us a duty, obligation, or demand to desire any particular ends. Gert offers in favor of it the passage from *De Cive* in which Hobbes says that the rational part of human nature "teaches every man to fly a contranatural dissolution as the greatest mischief that can arrive to nature". Gert takes this as showing that Hobbes thinks reason lays down the end of avoiding violent death, but it is just as naturally read as saying that given that men by nature actually most desire to avoid a violent death, their rational part teaches them to run from or resist violent death. Nothing in the language of this passage requires interpreting it as taking reason to impose ends rather than as taking reason to impose means to satisfying given ends, as traditional desire-based interpretations maintain. Gert also produces as evidence the correct observation that Hobbes conceived of madness as passions run amok, overvehement by our ordinary standards, and unguided by reason. But it is not obvious how this could be supposed evidence that reason dictates ends. For to take Gert's own example, asserting that "someone who uses all of his experience, instrumental reasoning, verbal reasoning, and science in order to kill himself in the most painful possible way, [is] not only... mad, but [is] acting irrationally",[45] his madness (i.e., overvehemence of passion) does not suffice to make his action irrational unless we assume that he does not, for example, most desire to achieve salvation, and believe that choosing a painful death of self-induced martyrdom will best achieve his end. But, of course, we can assume no such thing. Even in Gert's imagined extreme case, there is no difficulty in understanding how the behavior might be both mad and rational by Hobbes's analysis. So Hobbes's view that madness exists cannot show that he rejected an instrumental conception of rationality.

[45] Bernard Gert, "Hobbes on Reason", *Pacific Philosophical Quarterly* 82 (2001): 243–257, 248.

More importantly, Hobbes explicitly acknowledges that reason may *require* self-sacrifice or risking death when the survival of the commonwealth is at stake – this is the content of his final Law of Nature – as Gert himself acknowledges. It makes no sense to hold that reason necessarily requires acting to secure self-preservation and also forbids it on some occasions.

Third, we count actions as against reason only when they are blameworthy, according to Hobbes; what is wrong with actions against reason is that they cannot be justified to others. But the failure to desire one's own preservation is not itself blameworthy in this sense. (We might well justify our suicide to others in terms of the pain, shame, comparative dispensability or pointlessness of our life.) Of course, we may blame a person for her suicide or recklessness when her death precludes her fulfilling her obligations to dependent others, say, but the fault in such cases lies in her failure to honor her obligations and not in her failure to desire or to act to secure self-preservation.

Fourth, and crucially, in relying on premise (1), Gert's argument fails to account for the normativity of the Laws of Nature, even though this ought to have been its great advantage. Not only may some people lack any motivation at all to follow those laws, should they not actually desire self-preservation, but by deriving the duty to seek peace from the assertion that one ought to desire self-preservation, the "oughtness" of that fundamental Law of Nature receives no satisfying explanation. What is the normative force of Hobbes's oughts on Gert's interpretation? We ought to seek peace because we ought to desire self-preservation, but we still have no explanation of how the demand that one desire or take self-preservation as one's paramount end is supposed to be normative for actual people just by saying that not to do so is irrational. What, exactly, is the problem Gert sees with irrationality? Is it that irrationality angers God, as divine command interpretations suggest? Is the problem that irrationality gets us less of what we want, as traditional desire-based interpretations maintain? Or is irrationality supposed to be simply bad *per se*, for no reason? Notice too that the third and fourth of these problems become intensified when Gert expands his list of rationally required desires, because it is only more doubtful that we will see it as proper to blame men for failing to desire each of those things – health, security, avoidance of disability or pain, no matter their other desires, in all or even most cases, and that actual men will desire all the things they "ought" to on this view.

Finally, and to my mind most significantly, Gert's account cannot accommodate men's *transcendent interests* in any way that is compatible with its suggested derivation of the Laws of Nature, and is for that reason sharply incompatible with Hobbes's complex psychology. Gert holds that self-preservation is rationally required. Is this temporal self-preservation, preservation of our natural bodily life, or is it cosmic self-preservation of the Christian person beyond bodily death? Because Gert holds that all rationally required desires are *natural*, but expectations for life eternal cannot be natural and must instead depend upon supernatural revelation, he cannot take as rationally required anything other than preservation of one's present bodily life. Consideration for the preservation of our current bodily selves is thus supposed to dictate the ultimate requirements of reason. Not only does such a view of reason render it motivationally inefficacious for most of Hobbes's immediate readership, as our fourth objection notes, but Hobbes himself clearly rejects it in his many statements proclaiming the rationality of our concern for our eternal over our merely temporal prospects; for instance:

> That the fear of God's wrath doth expel corporeal fear, is well said,... and proveth strongly, that fear of the greater evil may necessitate in a man a courage to endure the lesser evil;[46]
>
> [I]f the command be such as cannot be obeyed, without being damned to eternal death; then it were madness to obey it;[47]
>
> [*E*]*ternal life* is a greater reward than the *life present;* and *eternal torment* a greater punishment than the *death of nature*.[48]

Gert recognizes that the text is not his friend in these cases, but steadfastly maintains that there is a difference between what people irrationally believe then pursue, and what they ought rationally to believe and pursue. I certainly do not want to deny that. All I would say is that Hobbes's texts show that securing bodily temporal self-preservation is not only not always in fact normatively determinative, but generally should not be normative for rational agents who value their greater

[46] EW V, 289.
[47] EW III, 585; T 403.
[48] EW III, 437; T 307.

good. He could not then have sought to derive his eternal and immutable Laws of Nature from such a slender duty.

DEFINITIONAL DERIVATIONS OF THE LAWS OF NATURE

The last school of interpretation I will discuss is the definitional derivation pioneered by F. S. McNeilly and recently revitalized by John Deigh. These definitional accounts seek to derive the various Laws of Nature from Hobbes's definition of a Law of Nature in conjunction with other premises analytic to the theory. These accounts do not rely on the contingent or rationally mandated desires of Hobbesian men, nor on normative postulates of duty, but aim to take seriously Hobbes's methodological commitments to what he calls the "geometrical method" in framing their account of the derivation of Hobbes's Laws of Nature.

Recent Hobbes scholarship has seen a resurgence of interest in definitional derivations of Hobbes's Laws of Nature of the sort pioneered by F. S. McNeilly in his powerful book *The Anatomy of Leviathan.*[49] Definitional-derivations of Hobbes's Laws of Nature enjoy some important interpretive advantages over desire- and duty-based derivations, for which reason they merit careful consideration. After distinguishing definitional derivation from its main rivals, and mentioning some of its advantages, I shall consider the particular definitional derivation of the Laws of Nature recently offered by John Deigh,[50] and the quite different definitional derivation developed by his predecessor McNeilly. Although I do think each of these interpretations advances our understanding of Hobbes's moral philosophy, I do not believe that either actually succeeds in deriving Hobbes's Laws of Nature as required by the content criterion for interpretation. In the next chapter I will offer a quite different definitional derivation of my own.

49 F. S. McNeilly, *The Anatomy of Leviathan* (New York, 1968).

50 John Deigh, "Reason and Ethics in Hobbes's *Leviathan*", *Journal of the History of Philosophy* 34 (1996): 33–60. Deigh calls his view "definitivist"; I prefer the term "definitional", as does Kinch Hoekstra in his "Hobbes on Law, Nature, and Reason", *Journal of the History of Philosophy* 41 (2003): 111–120.

Distinguishing Definitional Derivations

Definitional derivations are distinguished from more familiar desire-based interpretations by their refusal to allow any synthetic[51] premises into Hobbes's derivation of his Laws of Nature. Their reasons for doing so are primarily methodological: Because Hobbes viewed moral philosophy as a science – to be precise, as the science of the Laws of Nature – and insisted that science is a system of demonstrated truths deduced from universal propositions true by virtue of the definitions of their component terms, no synthetic empirical premises could properly appear in the derivation of the precepts that are the theorems of this science. This methodological constraint would appear to rule out as impermissible the two sorts of empirical claims upon which desire-based derivations typically depend: the psychological claim that men desire self-preservation above all else, and the causal claims that peace is the only (or the best) means for achieving self-preservation, and that the actions and prohibitions demanded or prohibited by the second through twentieth Laws of Nature are the only (or the best) means for achieving peace. Hobbes is articulating a conventionalist view of science as a purely formal system modeled on Euclidean geometry, and is committed to the view that moral philosophy, *qua* science (as well as the political philosophy it is intended to ground), must conform to these methodological constraints.[52] The superior fit of definitional derivations of the Laws of Nature with the

[51] The intended contrast is between premises that are true by definition (analytic) and those that are "referring to a statement (sentence, proposition, judgment) which asserts something about the real world (and not about how words are used or about the meaning of words)". See Peter A. Angeles, *Dictionary of Philosophy* (New York, 1981), 287 (under definition of 'synthetic'). Hobbes argues from premises supposed to be true by definition, or in virtue of the way words are used, without dependence on verification in experience (except, of course, our experience with language use).

[52] See Hobbes's *Elements of Philosophy*, EW I, chapters 1–6. Notice that Hobbes's classificatory chart of the sciences in chapter 9 of *Leviathan* merely sorts sciences by subject, but does not tell us anything about scientific method. Ethics can be about the consequences of the passions of men and still be a science so long as reasoning proceeds from definitions only, without reliance on mere empirical generalizations. Although civil philosophy can proceed from the definition of a commonwealth, independently of moral philosophy (the science of the Laws of Nature), I'll offer in the next chapter a derivation of Laws of Nature that shows them to impose a duty

philosophical method Hobbes explicitly insists he is using constitutes their primary advantage over desire-based derivations as interpretations of Hobbes's intended theory.[53]

Although definitional derivations refuse to countenance empirical generalizations about our desires as elements of Hobbes's derivation of his Laws of Nature, they need not exclude *analytic* claims about what we necessarily desire, supposing any such claims are plausible, and that Hobbes made them.[54] Thus, if, as I'll argue, it is analytic that rational agents must desire that their actions enjoy rational warrant, and that the conditions for the effective exercise of their agency obtain, such premises are happily admitted into a definitional derivation of Hobbes's Laws of Nature. And had it been true that Hobbes took it to be a matter of *definition* that to be human is to desire self-preservation, such a premise would also be admissible in Hobbes's demonstration of the Laws of Nature.

Few, if any, commentators see evidence that Hobbes held it to be true that it is *true by definition* that men desire self-preservation, let alone that it is logically necessary because analytic that men *must* desire self-preservation *above all else*, implying that no one who failed to care most about his own personal present physical survival could count as a man.[55]

(and motive) to submit to commonwealth, providing in this way a ground for the political philosophy.

53 It may be that divine command interpretations of the Laws of Nature are best understood as offering a thesis about the source of the normativity of those laws, rather than a distinctive approach to deriving them. Some of the interpretations, such as Taylor's and Warrender's, agree with Deigh that Hobbes's moral philosophy is independent of his moral psychology, whereas Martinich parts company with the other divine command interpreters in denying that they enjoy this independence. Insofar as divine command interpretations confine themselves to making claims about the source of the normativity and motivational efficacy of the Laws of Nature, without entering the fray over how to derive the Laws of Nature, they appear to be technically compatible with both desire-based and definitional derivations. Thought of in that way, they are not a pole in a triangulated dispute, but rather a neutral meta-thesis about the normative and motivational founts of the Laws of Nature.

54 For this reason, Deigh's claim about the independence of Hobbes's ethical theory from his moral psychology is no essential part of the definitional interpretation.

55 Gert does appear to hold that it is analytic that to be a rational man is to adopt self-preservation as one's end. But because he does not take the conclusions of reason to be desires (but rather normative requirements potentially counterposed to desires), his view does not support the claim that it is true by definition that men

Nor do commentators claim that it is even empirically true that all men do in fact most care about saving their skins, irrespective of the fates of their children, kinfolk, tribe, nation, just cause, or their own immortal souls in the hereafter. Such a claim strikes us as so manifestly false that it would be uncharitable to saddle Hobbes with it, even had he not said (as he often and explicitly did) that men often do and may rightly care more for their honor, their salvation, and their loved ones than they do for their own continuation of natural life. Clearly we do not believe that the clinically depressed or suicidal person who now has no desire to preserve his life is no longer human, as is entailed by the analytic claim; nor that the person whose desire to live is overridden by his interest in being freed from unremitting pain or a desire not to lose his dignity fails for that reason to be human. Even less do we believe that the person who cares more for other ends than he does to preserve his own life has necessarily ceased to be a man. On the contrary, in many cases we take men's willingness to risk or to sacrifice their preservation in pursuit of their transcendent interests in securing the good of their children, their religion, their country, or their ideals as markers of a more expansive and honorable humanity, rather than of its absence or degradation.[56] More to the point, Hobbes acknowledged all this, noting that most men prefer revenge to safety,[57] that it would be madness to sacrifice one's eternal prospects for temporal security,[58] that men's desire for honor often trumps their desire for self-preservation,[59] and very many more such instances of that complexity of men's psychology that precludes ascribing to them a single uniform overriding desire.

So while definitional derivations permissibly allow analytic premises about men's desires, the premise that to be a man is to desire self-preservation above all else will certainly not be one of these, as not

desire self-preservation; it rather claims that insofar as a man is rational he ought to take self-preservation as one of his ends, absent any stronger reason not to.

56 For discussion of transcendent interests in Hobbes, see Pasquale Pasquino, "Hobbes, Religion, and Rational Choice: Hobbes's Two Leviathans and the Fool", *Pacific Philosophical Quarterly* 82 (2001): 406–419, and Garrath Williams, "Normatively Demanding Creatures: Hobbes, the Fall and Individual Responsibility", *Res Publica* 6, no. 3 (2000): 301–319.

57 EW III, 140; T 107.

58 EW III, 585; T 403; cf. EW III, 584; T 403.

59 EW II, 38.

being properly analytic. But notice that because the very considerations that speak against positing an overriding desire for self-preservation as true of men *by definition* speak equally against positing it as universally true of men even as a synthetic, empirical matter, these same considerations undermine the soundness of traditional desire-based derivations of the Laws of Nature. The difference is that although definitional derivations *can* proceed without assuming the desire for self-preservation, the traditional desire-based views under consideration cannot, and this appears to offer a second advantage of definitional over desire-based approaches.

There is some textual evidence that Hobbes intends to preclude positing the necessity of desiring *any* particular object or end when he writes in the introduction to *Leviathan* that although introspection may reveal to us the form of the operation of the human mind in general, it cannot tell us anything about the particular *objects* of that operation.[60] Hobbes appears to be making the plausible point that we cannot generalize from our own introspective experience what must be the particular objects of desire for anyone else. Although, Hobbes asserts, introspection of our own mental operations in thinking, opining, hoping, or desiring can inform us of what goes on in anyone who carries out those mental operations, we cannot thereby know what are the *particular objects* of others' thoughts, opinions, hopes, or desires. These will vary according to the particular experience, education, and bodily constitution of each individual to such a degree that we cannot infer from the fact that we desire some end, that anyone else, let alone everyone else, desires that same end.[61] This provides good reason for the definitionalists' claim that Hobbes's derivation of his Laws of Nature cannot depend on observational generalizations about the objects of men's desires.

Still, the question of the degree to which definitional derivations enjoy methodological advantage is more complicated than the preceding account suggests, because Hobbes is quite willing to admit into scientific derivations facts about what men take terms to mean in

60 EW III, xi; T 11.

61 Hobbes's position here provides another reason for doubting traditional interpretations' claim that Hobbes intends his argument for the Laws of Nature to depend upon the assumption that all men primarily desire self-preservation. This premise cannot be established, according to Hobbes.

their ordinary discourse, and, as I shall argue in the next chapter, may even provisionally accept into reasoned argument certain nonanalytic introspectables, that "passion not mistrusting", may serve as universally acceptable premises.

Deigh's Definitional Derivation of the Laws of Nature

Although John Deigh's contemporary definitional derivation of the Laws of Nature is an instance of the definitional approach, his specific concerns lead him to formulate his view in ways that definitionalism as such is not committed to. He is specifically concerned to establish the *logical independence* of Hobbes's ethics from his moral psychology, and thus aims to show that none of Hobbes's derivations of his Laws of Nature need depend on *any human desires* at all, nor on the assumption of any end that those to whom the law is addressed have; facts about human desires have no role in determining the truth or falsity of the theorems of ethics. This displays the contrast with desire-based interpretations, which depend essentially upon men's moral psychology.[62] He argues that in Hobbes's ethics, which is captured in his Laws of Nature, reason does not follow the lead of desire in its deductions of the Laws of Nature, but rather proceeds independently of desire. Deigh believes that the Laws of Nature can be derived from the very *definition of a Law of Nature*, entirely analytically, without reliance on any of the synthetic propositions that comprise Hobbes's moral psychology; in particular, without reference to men's desires.

Deigh concedes that Hobbes's actual derivation of the Laws of Nature in chapters 14 and 15 of *Leviathan*[63] does not remotely adhere to the analytic template dictated by Hobbes's official method, and conjectures that this departure was simply Hobbes's effort to "avoid the tedium of first presenting these [Laws of Nature] and then applying them to statements of fact so as to obtain the conclusions about

62 Also views like Gert's, which take rationality to dictate certain mandatory ends to any sane person. But a definitional view that does not insist on the independence thesis might well be compatible with Gert's view.

63 Deigh makes a point of saying that his argument is restricted to *Leviathan;* however, his argument depends on the text of the English *Leviathan* only, and he does not take into account crucial differences in Hobbes's Latin version that importantly affect his proposed derivation of the Laws of Nature.

obedience he wanted to propagate".[64] In an effort not to bore his readers, and thus as an expedient to his project of persuading them to obey their sovereign, Hobbes "meant to be at once presenting the science of the laws of nature and applying it to the facts of the human condition".[65] Deigh insists that the synthetic empirical propositions Hobbes admits into his derivation of the Laws of Nature for the sake of economy "*would drop out if the science were presented as pure science, [and] are thus eliminable*".[66]

Although one imagines that Hobbes would have been loath to compromise the philosophical rigor of his demonstration of the central component of his argument for submission to government, it is true that he did care greatly for the palatability of his presentation, so perhaps Deigh's explanation is not so implausible. And Deigh mounts a strong case that Hobbes was committed to the method here said to be invisibly underlying Hobbes's actual exposition. Reason must operate as an independent faculty,[67] not merely as an instrumental aid in seeking means to satisfy desire's ends, if Hobbes is to preserve consistency between what Deigh identifies as his definition of reason as nothing but reckoning of appellations[68] and his definition of Laws of Nature as theorems of reason. Hobbes defines the Laws of Nature as theorems; a theorem is a proposition that follows by deduction from those definitions that ground the science of which it is a theorem. Reason begins only with speech and involves first linking names into definitions (which is done properly when each component term of the definition enjoys settled, unambiguous signification that raises in the listener's mind the same thought entertained in the speaker's, and all things collected under the subject are included among the things collected under the predicate), finally proceeding through a succession of definitions, analytically, from one proposition to another. To view reason as instrumental, or as applying a material criterion

64 Deigh, "Reason and Ethics in Hobbes's *Leviathan*", 43.

65 Ibid.

66 Ibid., emphasis added.

67 Hobbes does not usually speak of reason as a faculty, but he does so speak of it in the section of chapter 5 of *Leviathan* in which Deigh locates the conception of reason he thinks central to Hobbes's theory: "we may define...what that is, which is meant by this word *reason*, when we reckon it amongst the faculties of the mind" (EW III, 30; T 32).

68 Deigh, "Reason and Ethics in Hobbes's *Leviathan*", 40.

(such as Gert's rationally required end of self-preservation), would be inconsistent, Deigh argues, with both Hobbes's official definition of reason as reckoning and, more importantly, his characterization of the Laws of Nature as theorems of a science, or of "philosophy", both of which proceed in a strictly demonstrative fashion, after the model of geometry. So there is reason to believe Hobbes must intend his official derivation of the Laws of Nature to be purely formal.

But notice that these same considerations of method that preclude nonanalytic premises about men's desires also preclude any *other* nonanalytic premises about anything else, including premises about causal relations and the probable consequences of actions and states of affairs, upon which, I'll argue momentarily, Deigh's own argument would appear to depend. Conversely, these same considerations of method do *not* disallow premises about human desires or ends, *so long as these are analytic*, that is, true by definition under Hobbes's analysis. So *if* Hobbes's ethics is logically independent of Hobbes's moral psychology, its independence will not be secured, *pace* Deigh, by Hobbes's methodological constraints, but rather by the fact (supposing it is a fact) that the derivation of the Laws of Nature does not depend upon any permissible analytic assumptions about human ends and desires.[69] (The definitional argument I will offer in the following chapter deploys premises ascribing necessary ends or desires to agents, and so agrees with Deigh about proper Hobbesian method while rejecting his thesis of logical independence.) Because my interest is to assess Deigh's definitional derivation of the Laws of Nature, I'll set aside further consideration of his arguments for his logical independence thesis.

As Deigh himself notes, his definitional interpretation has the peculiarity that it disables Hobbes from deducing the imperatives we traditionally take the Laws of Nature to be, that is, from deducing normative, prescriptive rules of the form "do x". If the major premise of the derivation has the form "a Law of Nature is such and such", it will, of course, be possible to derive only descriptive conclusions

[69] Or at least does not depend on analytic assumptions about human desires that are about such desires in a way that requires the dependence of ethics on psychology. Perhaps the premise that "to be a living human is to have desires" is about desires, but in a way that does not secure dependence.

of the form "so-and-so is a Law of Nature". This threatens to fail to meet our first desideratum for interpretations, that of capturing the laws Hobbes actually articulates. But Deigh is not worried about this implication of his interpretation, arguing that the derivation of an observation that some imperative is a Law of Nature is just as good as deriving the imperative itself, in the way that deriving the conclusion that "'F is x' is true" is just as good as deriving "F is x". Deigh maintains that just as to say "P is true" commits us to believing P, so to say "that men do A is a Law of Nature" commits us to doing A, or at least to agreeing that we ought to do A. This had better be true, for if Deigh's interpretation does not permit the derivation of Hobbes's actual Laws of Nature, it will have failed to meet the content criterion for interpretative adequacy. One question, then, is whether "'that men do A' is a Law of Nature" is relevantly like "'F is x' is true", or rather like the propositions "'that men do A' is a norm of etiquette", and "'that men do A' is a rule of baseball", which, absent special further assumptions, do not in the least commit us to doing A, or even to thinking that we ought to do A.

This raises a worry about whether and how the Laws of Nature are properly normative, on Deigh's interpretation. Some critics have alleged (mistakenly, in my view) that an interpretation that makes the Laws of Nature purely descriptive assertions that "to do such and such is a Law of Nature" cannot explain how it is that these assertions are normative for Hobbesian men, making ought claims on them, and potentially moving them to action.[70] Deigh, who believes that Hobbes thought men's predominant desire is for self-preservation,[71] offers what is on the basis of that belief the plausible position that because "Hobbes embeds the ultimate end of right action [i.e. self-preservation] in a definition, and it then serves as a criterion for qualifying principles of action as laws of nature",[72] descriptive conclusions about what precepts are Laws of Nature will naturally be taken as normative by Hobbesian men. Just as those who want to play baseball will take the fact that something is a rule of baseball as

[70] Mark Murphy makes a claim of this sort in his "Desire and Ethics in Hobbes's *Leviathan:* A Response to Professor Deigh", *Journal of the History of Philosophy* 38 (2000): 259–268.

[71] Deigh, "Reason and Ethics in Hobbes's *Leviathan*", 60.

[72] Ibid., 59.

action-guiding, and those who care about being polite will regard as normative facts about what actions are norms of etiquette, so those who desire to preserve themselves will take to heart reason's conclusions as to which precepts are Laws of Nature. Deigh does not explain what he means by "predominant", but if he means that the desire for self-preservation is universal and overriding, he can conclude that everyone will in fact regard the conclusions of reason about what is a Law of Nature as normative, thus accounting for Hobbes's insistence that the Laws of Nature are eternal and immutable, and always binding *in foro interno*. With this explanation, Deigh would seek simultaneously to answer the objection that his view does not actually yield the prescriptive norms Hobbes offers as Laws of Nature, and that it cannot account for the normativity of the Laws of Nature (our third desideratum for interpretations).

However, the solution just attributed to Deigh does crucially depend on construing his term "predominant" as grounding the assumption that all men most desire to preserve themselves, which assumption, as I earlier argued, is false and was rejected by Hobbes himself. So while, on this interpretation, Deigh may be able to offer a derivation of the Laws of Nature that is exceptionless, the normativity of those laws will remain dependent on men's having a certain desire of a certain status, which some in fact fail to have – rendering Deigh's victory over the desire-based interpreter Pyrrhic. Like his desire-based foes, Deigh would purchase a normativity for Hobbes's Laws of Nature conferred by assuming a universal overriding desire for self-preservation at the expense of violating the reasonable requirement that interpretations respect the complex psychology of Hobbesian men.

Alternatively, Deigh might mean by a predominant desire for self-preservation something more like what Kavka meant by "predominant egoism", namely, that in most human beings the desire for self-preservation is usually stronger than other desires, but is not necessarily always the strongest desire, or always occurrent and motivating. But this weakened claim, while less implausible than the stronger claim, will not suffice to establish the *inescapable* normativity of "eternal and immutable" Laws of Nature that always and ever bind *in foro interno*. To say that the Laws of Nature *always* bind in conscience is to deny that they can *ever* fail to make a claim on us. But if their claim on us depended upon our possessing a particular desire, of a particular status or strength, which some of us are conceded (as the "predominant" formulation does concede) not to have, then those laws could not make an inescapable claim on each and every one of us, as Hobbes insists they do. Thus if, as Deigh maintains, predominant self-preservation is the relevant desire, the Laws of Nature would not bind – even *in foro interno* – those who lack this desire, or those who do usually have it on any occasion in which they temporarily lack it. Those laws would not bind everywhere and always, *pace* Hobbes. (And, of course, although they might make *some* claim on those whose desire for self-preservation is weaker than their other desires, they could not make an all-things-considered claim, even on the conscience only.) It is not Hobbes's view that the requirements of the Laws of Nature are optional for those who lack certain desires, or who care more for other ends than for those the Laws of Nature serve. If they are always to bind everyone *in foro interno*, their claim on us must either depend on no desires, or on a desire that no human can fail at any time to have.

A further textual difficulty for Deigh's interpretation is that he takes Hobbes's definition of a Law of Nature as a premise in the imagined derivations of Hobbes's Laws of Nature. Deigh takes "Law of Nature" to be defined as "a precept that forbids one from doing something destructive of one's life, and is discoverable by reason". Kinch Hoekstra has argued that "a curious consequence of Deigh's definitional account of Hobbes, according to which the natural laws are deductions from well-defined terms, is that he makes "natural law" neither natural nor law according to Hobbes's definitions thereof. This is a conspicuous weakness given that Hobbes tells us that "when men make a name of two Names" we must understand that signification by discovering the signification of each of the component names".[73] Hoekstra concludes that this reveals an underlying difficulty with the definitional approach, which relies, in Deigh's case, on what seems to Hoekstra to be a faulty definition of a Law of Nature. But not every definitional approach must derive the Laws of Nature from Hobbes's

[73] Hoekstra, "Hobbes on Law, Nature, and Reason", 113. Of course, it is available to Deigh to reply that the name "Law of Nature" is not a compound name composed of two names, but is a simple name defined in another manner (akin perhaps to, e.g., "king of spades" or "French toast"); however, Hoekstra does explicitly assess its definition as independent of the definition of its component words.

definition of a Law of Nature, as will become clear when considering my own version of a definitional derivation.

My concerns about Deigh's inclusion of the definition of a Law of Nature as a premise in his derivation are different. First, Hobbes's insistence that the definition of geometry is *no* premise in derivations of the theorems of geometry suggests that Hobbes would have viewed Deigh's reliance on the definition of a Law of Nature in his derivation of the particular Laws of Nature as similarly improper. Hobbes writes that we may appeal to the definition of geometry in deciding who is or is not a geometer, "though the definition of geometry serve not for proof, *nor enter into any geometrical demonstration*".[74] It does seem peculiar that the definition of a science should enter as a premise in the derivation of the theorems of that science. Indeed, this would appear to involve a category mistake, because the definition of a science will belong to first philosophy, while the theorems of that science will belong to science itself. It is this consideration, and not a failure of normativity, that makes the meta-prescriptive form of Deigh's conclusions so problematic. We see that concluding that we should do something is very different from concluding that it is a theorem of some science that we should do that thing. Definitional interpretations must rely on definitions, but they need not rely on any definition of a Law of Nature itself.

The category mistake here described may be what Deigh referred to as the problem of impredicative definition to which his interpretation commits Hobbes. Deigh presented the choice between his interpretation and others as a choice between attributing to Hobbes's argument a vicious circularity (as Deigh's does), or attributing to Hobbes an inconsistency in his understanding of reason (as Deigh argues that other interpretations do). But this is a false dilemma if there is a possible definitional derivation that does not take any definition of a Law of Nature as a premise. The definitional derivation I shall offer below does not include a definition of a law, and so avoids circularity. Further, that derivation does not rely on a conception of reason at odds with the definition from chapter 5 of *Leviathan* that Deigh insists we should privilege.

74 EW VII, 191, emphasis added.

Second, and significantly, the particular definition of a Law of Nature upon which Deigh supposed the derivation must depend is not only different from every one of Hobbes's earlier formulations of the concept Law of Nature, but Hobbes *radically revises* the content of that definition in his 1668 Latin version of *Leviathan*, according to which a Law of Nature is a precept found out by reason "by which a man is forbidden to do, that, *which seems to him to tend to his own loss*" (emphasis added).[75] There is no mention here of self-preservation at all, undermining altogether Deigh's stated source of normativity for the Laws of Nature. That is a serious difficulty for Deigh's particular interpretation. Considering that the revised definition appears to depend heavily on subjective perception, and on what counts as a personal loss – both of which are highly variable across persons – it is even more doubtful that any Laws of Nature whose derivation depended on this definition would enjoy the exceptionless normativity Hobbes discerns in his own Laws of Nature, for a man's judgments of, say, whether the Law of Nature prohibiting ingratitude, or partial judging, does or does not tend to his own harm may radically diverge from the fact of the matter, objectively assessed. Harm being an even fuzzier notion than preservation, Hobbes's reformulation of the definition of a Law of Nature may seem to introduce an even greater gap between the laws, which are objectively stated behavioral requirements – for example, "that men perform their covenants made" – and a man's own judgment.

It is difficult to state with any confidence how Deigh's derivation would fare were we to use Hobbes's corrected definition of "Law of Nature" as a premise, not least because Deigh *never offers any actual derivations of any of the Laws of Nature.* He suggests, in a schematic sort of way, how an argument for some particular Laws of Nature might go (he thinks the fourth and the eighth may fit this sketch), but even

[75] As we noted in the previous chapter, the surprising fact is that there is no feature that every one of Hobbes's apparent definitions of a Law of Nature shares except the claim that a Law of Nature is a rule of reason. I believe that we should take Hobbes seriously when he writes that "the laws of nature are nought else but the dictates of reason" (EW II, 44) and understand the various other specifications of what goods they secure, how they are spoken of, and what motives of ours they may engage that Hobbes typically lumps in along with the definition as extrinsic to the proper formal definition of a Law of Nature.

these rough suggestions rely on contraband "factual" (although he conjectures strictly eliminable) premises expressing causal relations. Further, the arguments sketched depend upon already having demonstrated the fundamental Law of Nature requiring the seeking of peace; and this he does not attempt. Yet some such demonstration is needed for any of these subsequent arguments to get off the ground.

Because Deigh thinks it *important that the definition of a Law of Nature incorporate a prohibition on doing what is destructive of one's life*, one may reasonably suppose him to hold that any derivation of the Laws of Nature will depend upon that incorporated end. This invites an instrumental sequel in the argument, perhaps arguing, parallel to traditional desire-based interpretations, that war is destructive to one's life because war tends to increase the probability of death, and that the sorts of action-types prohibited by subsequent Laws of Nature are so prohibited because they increase the probability of war. Whether these claims are empirically plausible is not the issue. The question posed by Hobbes's definitional method is, are they *strictly analytic?*

Clearly they are not. This is easy to demonstrate by counterexample, because all that is required to refute a claim of necessity is a single showing of contrary possibility. And we have any number of these, both possible and actual. It is not true *by definition* that war is destructive of one's life, and the existence of veterans falsifies this even as a merely empirical claim. The "savages of America", writes Hobbes, live in a state of nature; if the state of nature is a state of war, but that state has not rendered those savages extinct, we must presume that the lives of at least critical numbers of savages have *not* been destroyed by war, hence it cannot be true *by definition* that war is destructive of one's life, nor could Hobbes have thought it was. Further, we can imagine cases in the state of nature in which war is the only way to avoid certain death, and so tends more toward self-preservation than does any alternative course of action or inaction (as indeed Hobbes seems to recognize).

More important is to consider Hobbes's own definition of war. Hobbes defines war as a tract of time wherein the will to contend by battle is sufficiently known. His definition of war is consistent with a condition in which no fighting of any sort occurs, nor any deaths at all, should the will to contend by battle happen to encounter no cause for contention. We ourselves acknowledge the point that "war" need not involve any actual fighting nor any deaths at all in our concept of "cold war". And we can certainly at least imagine cases in which, although people not only will to but actually do contend by battle, their methods are so ineffective or misguided that they do not actually manage to kill anyone (perhaps they wage war by putting hexes on one another, or by abducting one another's daughters into domestic servitude). In such cases the proposition that our end of self-preservation necessitates aversion to war would not be true, let alone analytically true. These difficulties attend any claim that it is true by definitions alone that action to preserve oneself *is* action to avoid any "tract of time wherein the will to contend by battle is sufficiently known".

A further textually significant consideration against taking Hobbes's derivation of his laws of nature to depend upon any claim that it is analytic that the Laws of Nature forbid risking death, is that Hobbes's own final Law of Nature *requires* risking death. That law, stated in *Leviathan*'s "Review and Conclusion", adds to the laws previously derived this one, "*that every man is bound by nature, as much as in him lieth, to protect in war the authority, by which he is himself protected in time of peace*".[76] There is no plausible interpretation of this law as recommending the course of action least risky to one's own preservation. While fleeing abroad in wartime (as Hobbes did), defecting to the other side, or "lying low" (to use Kavka's famous term) may often better secure self-preservation, Hobbes nonetheless here insists that reason requires that each do all he can possibly force himself to do to fight for his sovereign, undertaking not just the risk of death, but, if he is sufficiently hardy or generous, even the certainty of death in defense of his sovereign's authority. This is a remarkable Law of Nature, not only for its content, but also for how little remarked upon is the fact that it is remarkable. It seems to me to pose a very serious challenge to the views of desire-based interpreters every bit as worrisome for their view as it is for Deigh's. When Hobbes writes that "it can never be that war shall preserve life",[77] he should be understood as claiming, not that it is either analytically or empirically true that for any agent, war kills himself; but rather, as I argued in the previous

[76] EW III, 703; T 485.
[77] EW III, 145; T 110.

chapter, that perpetual warfare destroys human life generally, that is, "with war joins the *destruction of mankind*".[78] On plausible assumptions about deterrence and human nature, there is no inconsistency in supposing that Hobbes's Laws of Nature function to avert the destruction of mankind while nonetheless requiring individual agents to risk death in defense of their sovereigns in accordance with Hobbes's final Law of Nature. For these reasons, Deigh cannot suppose that it is analytic that the Laws of Nature forbid risking death.

What then of the claim that it is analytic – true by virtue of the concepts alone – that to violate any of Hobbes's specific Laws of Nature is to bring about war (which is to secure death,[79] or at least devastation)? Or even the weaker claim that it is true *by definition* that violating Hobbes's Laws of Nature *significantly increases the probability of* war, and thus of death or devastation? It is simply not believable that all such violations necessarily bring about war, or that people may *never* improve their prospects by violating the Laws of Nature. Consider, for instance, the third Law of Nature against breaking covenants, and suppose that two tiny African nations have covenanted with each other not to extradite citizens of the other. Now imagine that the United States (in 2006) accuses one of these nations of harboring a terrorist, and lays down an ultimatum that unless it extradites that person post haste, it will face the economic and military wrath of the United States. To stand by the covenant assures war; and because the United States will deter any retaliation by the disappointed covenant partner, no war will result from breach of the Law of Nature. Nor in this case is it plausible to insist that the prospects of this nation are not enhanced by violating the Law of Nature that requires the keeping of this particular covenant. Is it even plausible to suppose, in this case, that a Kavka-like argument for adopting the *general policy* of never violating one's covenants better conduces to the avoidance of death or destruction than does any other policy more sensitive to the *de facto* power relations among nations? Evidently not; and if this is correct, then we have sufficient proof against the analyticity of

78 EW II, 207, emphasis added.

79 Hobbes allows an exemption from the requirement of adherence to the Laws of Nature when such adherence would "procure [one's own] certain ruin", but this does not support the claim that violation of the Laws of Nature necessarily leads to war, or that war necessarily leads to death or devastation.

the claim that to violate any of the Laws of Nature is necessarily to suffer war, or necessarily to bring death or destruction upon oneself. Indeed, here the best way to avoid these burdens is to violate the Law of Nature.[80]

McNeilly's Definitional Derivation of the Laws of Nature

F. S. McNeilly conducted a close comparison of *Leviathan* with Hobbes's earlier versions of his moral philosophy, and argued that in *Leviathan* Hobbes largely managed finally to bring his philosophy into line with his stated demonstrative method. He believes, as does Deigh, that "in *Leviathan* Hobbes attempts to construct a formal science which leaves no place for descriptions of psychological tendencies".[81] I would extend this injunction to include description of mere tendencies of any sort, whether psychological or nonpsychological. Like Deigh, McNeilly recognizes that Hobbes's actual presentation of his derivation of the Laws of Nature in *Leviathan* occasionally includes illicit nonanalytic premises, but takes this to be the effect of Hobbes's simultaneously articulating his formal theory and applying it to what he takes to be men's actual material circumstances. Accordingly, McNeilly sifts out the contraband premises and reformulates Hobbes's argument in conformity, as he thinks, with Hobbes's official scientific method.

McNeilly's central claim is that "the form of the argument is to show that peace is a necessary value for any rational being who has contingent values" and is in relation to other such beings.[82] Because

[80] Examples can be multiplied by imagining quite possible empirical circumstances in which adhering to the law would not best avoid war (for instance, cases in which an iniquitous judicial judgment would placate a prejudiced mob, while an equitable judgment would incite violent riots). Kavka's effort to argue that any man may rationally expect to do best in avoiding disaster for himself if he adopts the policy of always adhering to the Laws of Nature over any other policy is not, in my view, successful, even as articulating a merely empirical claim. But regardless of one's view on that question, all that matters for present purposes is to observe that Kavka's claim is not a necessary proposition within Hobbes's system, nor does Kavka himself believe it to be true in virtue of the definitions of terms.

[81] McNeilly, *The Anatomy of Leviathan*, 203.

[82] Ibid., 205.

he believes that Hobbes thought men are averse to death because they see it as frustrating all their desires, McNeilly interprets the English *Leviathan*'s definition of a Law of Nature as "saying, formally, that a law of nature is a rational precept forbidding a man to do that which would lead to the frustration of all his desires (values) or would prevent him from realising them, and to omit that which would lead to their realization".[83] A state of nature is a state in which all have a right to all, but "so long as natural right continues no man can reasonably expect anything but the frustration of his desires – that is, has grounds for despair".[84] Peace, McNeilly notes, is defined by Hobbes as "simply that state of affairs in which there is not war", while war is defined as a tract of time in which there is a "known disposition [to fighting]", fighting being defined by McNeilly for Hobbes as actively exercising power over another "in such a way as to prevent [that other] from exercising his own power as he wills".[85] Therefore, McNeilly concludes in this first leg of his derivation, war "threatens the realisation of one's objectives", no matter what those objectives may be.[86]

Here McNeilly makes the same sort of methodologically impermissible move I earlier criticized in Deigh's argument, by admitting a nonanalytic generalization about the tendencies or likelihood of war to have certain consequences. Unless it is true by definition that war voids effective agency, no premise asserting that war may or sometimes does or is likely to diminish effective agency will be appropriately included in a definitional derivation. However, McNeilly might be satisfied to accept this stronger version of his subconclusion, and so I shall assume it as a premise in his subsequent argument.

If war undermines the realization of one's objectives, "[p]eace then, is a situation in which there exist sufficient restrictions on the general exercise of the Right of Nature to give a man a reasonable hope of success in the pursuit of his objectives".[87] But "when there is no 'common power' there is a state of war",[88] a common power being defined

[83] Ibid., 184–185.
[84] Ibid., 185.
[85] Ibid., 185–186.
[86] Ibid., 186.
[87] Ibid.
[88] Ibid.

as "a guarantee that (on the whole) the law will not be broken with impunity".[89]

Here again, I suspect that McNeilly's phrase "on the whole" signals the illicit importation of an empirical generalization to the effect that if there is a common power then *usually* the law will not be broken with impunity. This may be true, but it does not appear to be true as a matter of definition. But supposing we also grant this premise, McNeilly goes on to assert that no society so homogeneous in values that no common power is necessary for peace would be a *human* society. This will need to be understood as an analytic proposition, and to do that would entail taking it as true by definition that humans *must* disagree with one another in values. I do not find this plausible, particularly in light of the fact that within some human communities, men do agree in values.

McNeilly concludes from the argument just reconstructed that "it is unreasonable for any man not to seek peace, whatever his values, so long as he has *some* values, because only in a situation of peace, guaranteed by a 'common power', can a man have good reason not to despair".[90] This is meant to prove the first and fundamental Law of Nature, that a man be willing to seek peace when others are also willing. Not to seek peace with willing others would be to act in a way that will frustrate all of one's desires, and so to seek peace is a Law of Nature.

McNeilly sees peace as what he terms a "necessary" value, because, like power, it is something a person who wants anything must also want. But he distinguishes sharply between the reasonableness of seeking peace and the reasonableness of entering a peace. Obtaining peace on just any terms is not reasonable, for "[p]eace is not to be promoted at the cost of all the values which it is intended to serve.... How this cost is calculated will depend on the particular values of each particular person".[91] So while the fundamental Law of Nature requires us to think of peace as desirable and to investigate whether it makes sense for us to do what we'd need to do to secure it, *that law does not actually require us to make peace.*

89 Ibid., 189.
90 Ibid., 191.
91 Ibid., 195.

This is the real Trojan horse in McNeilly's attempted derivation of the Laws of Nature, for it understands the first and fundamental Law of Nature to say that we should do what it takes to settle a peace *only if we believe our ends are best promoted by doing so.* Whether and on what terms to settle a peace is entirely up to the individual, according to his own particular values, beliefs, sense of his relative power and bargaining position, and the like. And so long as enough others do seek peace that a general social environment is created that will allow the agent some hope of success in pursuing his ends, there is no need at all for the agent himself to do anything other than perhaps appear to go along with the norms others have obligated themselves to observe, or fly below their radar in pursuing his own ends. Because it is not true at all, least of all true by definition, that others will settle a peace only if *every individual* participates, or that others will settle a peace only if *I*, the agent do so as well, McNeilly's account will not yield Hobbes's intended Law of Nature, which directs each and every agent to settle a peace with willing others. Even allowing McNeilly his definitionally suspect premises, it appears that he cannot get the first Law of Nature.

This problem is reproduced in his effort to derive the second Law of Nature requiring that a man be willing when others are also willing to lay down his right to all things and be contented with as much liberty as he is willing to allow to others. Although it is true that so long as everyone retains his or her right to all things there can be no peace, it does not automatically follow that each must give up this right, or that all who do so must do so equally.[92] It is enough to undo the terrible effects of a universal unlimited right that not everyone retains a right to all things. And because, again, it is neither empirically plausible nor true by definition that no one will lay down his right unless each and every person does so equally, McNeilly's considerations will not yield Hobbes's second Law of Nature. It should be obvious that this problem is not confined to McNeilly's definitional interpretation, but is endemic to desire-based derivations as well. All of these equally elide the argument from the desirability of peace to the conclusion that any rational agent must do his fair share in securing peace.

[92] Martinich argues that it may be rational to settle peace on subequal terms in *Thomas Hobbes*, chapter 3.

What is needed is an analytically defended premise that shows that *reason dictates reciprocity*. The effort to derive by strict definitional method such a premise is what primarily distinguishes my own definitional derivation of the Laws of Nature from the arguments of other definitional interpreters. To this derivation we now turn.

5

The Reciprocity Interpretation of Hobbes's Moral Philosophy

> [N]ot being circumscribed within reasonable bounds, their reason becomes invisible.
>
> (*A Discourse of Laws*, p. 106)

> *Thou shalt love thy neighbor as thyself*...is the natural law, having its beginning with rational nature itself.
>
> (EW II, 263–264)

We have seen that neither Hobbes's definition of a Law of Nature nor the function reliably served by the Laws of Nature lends particular support to traditional desire-based derivations of those laws. We have also surveyed some of the problems that attend familiar versions of desire-based, duty-based, and definitional derivations. In this chapter I offer a derivation of Hobbes's Laws of Nature that I believe avoids the problems of alternative derivations, fits well with Hobbes's positions on the definition and function of the Laws of Nature, comports with his declared method, and enjoys substantial textual support.[1]

[1] Hobbes's contemporaries, particularly his opponents, recognized that Hobbes's attempted method was definitional, but whined about the proposed definitions from which he preceded. John Wallis wrote in sympathy to Robert Boyle: "Mr Hobs is very dexterous in confuting others by putting a new sense on their words rehearsed by himself: different from what the word signifie with other men. And therefore if you shall have the occasion to speak of chalk, he'll tell you that by chalk he means cheese: and then if he can prove that what you say of chalk is not of true cheese, he reckons himself to have gotten a great victory"; quoted in Steven Shapin and Simon

OVERVIEW OF THE INTUITIVE ARGUMENT

Hobbes has a conception of correct philosophical method that requires him to argue from commonly agreed definitions by a series of linked syllogisms designed to reveal the logical connections among terms. Ideally, philosophical argument should proceed entirely analytically, and so nonanalytic premises (including probabilistic causal claims) are generally inappropriate to Hobbes's project of demonstrating his Laws of Nature.

However, it makes sense to distinguish between those improperly synthetic premises that are harmful to Hobbes's project and those that while improperly synthetic are nonetheless benign. Hobbes is engaged in the practical project of showing his countrymen that they have a good and sufficient reason to submit to the authority of their existing government. The great virtue of adopting scientific method in the service of this project is the greater degree of confidence in one's conclusion conferred by this method. Hobbes wants his political conclusions to be not doubted, and not contestable, at least by all those prepared to be both reasonable and reasonably attentive to his arguments. So the best strategy is to proceed entirely definitionally. But Hobbes may be able to achieve his goal just as well by admitting into his argument those few nonanalytic premises that each man can assure himself of by direct introspection. These will not be premises about "what all men desire", because the objects of other men's desires are not available to oneself by introspection. But there will be some, let us call them *indubitable introspectables*, that "passion not mistrusting, will not seek to displace";[2] and an argument based on these as well as definitional premises will not compromise confidence in its conclusions. These indubitable introspectables will be premises that the reader will see as undoubtedly true in his or her own case. They are not true by definition, and so we cannot know them to be true of

Schaffer, *Leviathan and the Air Pump* (Princeton, NJ, 1985), cited in Philip Pettit *Made with Words* (Princeton, NJ, 2008).

[2] Hobbes writes, "To reduce this doctrine [of justice and policy in general] to the rules and infallibility of reason, there is no way, but, first put such principles down for a foundation, as passion, not mistrusting, may not seek to displace; and afterwards to build thereon the truth of cases in the law of nature (which hitherto have been built in the air) by degrees, till the whole have been inexpugnable" (Epistle to William, Earl of Newcastle, *Human Nature*, EW IV, xii).

everyone. But because each of us does not doubt them, they may be admitted into Hobbes's derivation without any cost to the degree of confidence in his conclusions. Their inclusion will compromise the scientific status of his derivation, but not achievement of the end for which he elected to use a scientific model. The derivation I describe does rely on indubitable introspectables at two points, premises 17 and 22, but otherwise proceeds entirely analytically.

Hobbes's method, properly executed, tends to produce lengthy, tedious arguments. Moreover, our tendency to project our own modern meanings onto the terms Hobbes employs makes understanding more difficult, for although Hobbes maintains that he is operating with the meanings his contemporary readers commonly give to the terms that appear in his argument, that argument crucially depends on the specific meanings he attaches (as he thinks properly) to those terms. For instance, as we'll see, his term 'contrary to reason' has a broader meaning than we generally give it, and comprehends unreasonable actions as well as those we would characterize as irrational. Because defending his argument requires exhibiting the conceptual links he is relying upon, I will momentarily lay out his argument in the cumbersome way his method necessitates. But it may be helpful first to sketch, in an intuitive way, the general movement of his intended argument.

In brief, starting from our common definition of man as rational, the argument is that we won't count a person as rational unless he is willing to offer what he regards as justifying considerations for his actions. But to offer a consideration as justifying one's action commits one to accepting that same consideration as justifying the like actions of others, *ceteris paribus*. (Nothing counts as a reason for doing a particular action unless it counts as a reason for doing actions of the type of which the particular action is an instance, other things equal.) But we do not count an act as contrary to reason unless we are prepared to fault the agent for performing it. So when one does what one is prepared to fault others for doing, one acts contrary to reason.

From this "reciprocity theorem of rational agency" Hobbes argues that a rational person is required to submit herself to government. If we would judge it unreasonable of others to whom we have no special obligations to condemn us for directing our actions by our own private judgment, the reciprocity theorem requires us to grant a universal right of private judgment. Yet, considering our ineliminable diversity in judgment, universal self-government by private judgment is bound to lead to perpetual irresoluble contention, which, by pitting the power of others against our own, interferes with our effective pursuit of our ends (whatever those ends may be) and is, for this reason, something any rational agent must be concerned to avoid. The only reasonable alternative to universal private judgment is joint submission to authoritative arbitration of disputes, all asymmetrical alternatives having been ruled out by the reciprocity theorem. Because such submission makes possible an environment in which agency may be effectively exercised, it accords with reason that we submit to the same authoritative arbitration we would fault others for failing to submit to. A sovereign is nothing more that an authoritative arbitrator of disputes, with the associated rights necessary if arbitration is to eliminate contention.

So the reciprocity theorem, conjoined with the requirements of effective agency (no matter the agent's ends), dictates that we submit to sovereign authority. Furthermore, because reason requires that one conform her behavior to the standards she would accept as reasonable were she on the receiving end of such behavior, *sovereigns themselves* will be subject to strict equity constraints on the kinds of laws they may justifiably make, and those they must not omit to make. This constraint creates a strong pressure on legislation toward substantive equity.

HOBBES'S AIM, METHOD, AND THE SUBSTANTIVE ASSUMPTIONS THEY DICTATE

Let us begin by considering briefly the substantive assumptions Hobbes's aim and method require him to make. Hobbes held that the end or scope of all philosophy is human benefit.[3] The end of civil philosophy is the benefit we receive by avoiding civil war, civil war resulting, Hobbes thinks, from our ignorance of the scope and limits of political obligation. Thus the object of civil philosophy is knowledge of the duties and rights of subjects and rulers.

Civil philosophy seeks to determine the rights and duties of men *qua* subjects and sovereigns from consideration of the component

[3] EW I, 7–8.

notions that together comprise the *definition of a commonwealth*. This definition must, according to Hobbes, include the method of generating the thing defined.[4] In order to determine the generation of anything, we must consider how it could have come into being from a state in which it was not. So we must begin civil philosophy by considering a condition in which no commonwealth exists, and hence in which no one bears the relation of subject or sovereign to anyone else, for those relations obtain only within a commonwealth. Because to be a subject is to have a duty to submit to the judgment of another over how one is to behave, and to be a ruler is to have a right to such submission from others, civil philosophy must begin from consideration of a condition in which no such duties or rights exist. Hobbes calls this condition "the condition of mere nature", the most extreme sort of state of nature. In this way Hobbes's conception of sound philosophical method requires consideration of a state of nature.

As we noted in Chapter 2, the most desirable conception of this state of nature for purposes of securing the normativity and motivational efficacy of the conclusions of civil philosophy will be the one that departs as little as possible from actual men's circumstances and characteristics, although some important differences are entailed by the methodologically necessitated assumption that no one has any obligation of obedience toward any other person. Apart from these obligations, we are to imagine persons in the state of nature as in all other ways just like us – as interacting, cooperating, and socializing in all sorts of familiar ways – and then to consider whether reason dictates to such men that they undertake political obligations.

To suppose that men have no political relations of duty to obey and right to rule necessitates the further supposition that men are to be regarded as roughly equal in the capacities that could matter to political relations. Hobbes holds that were some people sufficiently superior in strength or wit to compel others to obey them, those others would be under a "natural obligation" to obey their commands. He illustrates this sort of bond by the limiting case of God: God's power

4 As, indeed, Hobbes's does: He defines a commonwealth as "*one person, of whose acts a great multitude, by mutual covenants one with another, have made themselves every one the author, to the end he may use the strength and means of them all, as he shall think expedient, for their peace and common defence*" (EW III, 158; T 121).

is irresistible, and his will incontrovertible. So we are under a "natural obligation" of obedience to God, for "Whether men will or not, they must be subject always to the divine power", and even those who deny the existence or providence of God "may shake off their ease, but not their yoke".[5] Were there to be any man of irresistible power, "there had been no reason, why he should not by that power have ruled.... To those therefore whose power is irresistible, the dominion of all men adhereth naturally by their excellence of power".[6] Indeed, any imbalance of power sufficient to enable some to save or destroy others at will is incompatible with a condition of mere nature, because "every man is supposed [i.e., presumed] to promise obedience, to him, in whose power it is to save, or destroy him".[7] On Hobbes's understanding of the condition of mere nature, traditional interpretations will have put the relationship between equality and mutual obligation exactly backwards. It is not that because men *are* equals they have no obligations of obedience. Rather, it is that because we are considering a condition in which men have no obligations of obedience, we must posit their rough equality in possession of those qualities that would allow some to dominate others and thus to emerge as natural rulers.[8]

The condition of mere nature permits the undertaking of obligations to perform specific actions (assuming the actions are both possible and permissible under the Law of Nature). This undertaking is accomplished simply by vowing, pledging, promising, or contracting to do those actions. One can, for instance, obligate oneself to obey the divine positive law alleged by someone who claims to be divinely inspired, even though he cannot know that law to be true: "For if the law declared, be not against the law of nature, which is undoubtedly God's law, and he undertake to obey it, he is bound by his own act; bound I say to obey it".[9] The only obligations ruled out by the framing

[5] EW III, 344; T 245.
[6] EW III, 346; T 246.
[7] EW III, 188; T 141.
[8] Jean Hampton exemplifies this inverted view, but finds it puzzling: "Hobbes derives individuals' freedom from political subjugation in the state of nature from the assumption of their rough equality with one another. This derivation strikes twentieth-century readers as very odd"; Jean Hampton, *Hobbes and the Social Contract Tradition* (Cambridge, 1986), 25.
[9] EW III, 273; T 198.

assumption of a state of nature are obligations of obedience to one's fellows. However, Hobbes makes clear that in discussing the Laws of Nature, he is assuming that no one has undertaken any special obligations to others, writing of a law concerning property distribution that this law "is to be understood, *as all the rest of the laws of nature, without any other covenant antecedent:* for a man may have given away his right... and so the case be altered".[10] So we are to assume that there exist no "covenant antecedent", that is, no prior obligation (as distinct from natural duty) owed by anyone to anyone else.

It is the necessity of disallowing political obligations that justifies Hobbes's suggestion, which we discussed in Chapter 2, that in thinking of a state of nature we should "consider men as if but even now sprung out of the earth, and suddenly, like mushrooms, come to full maturity, without all kind of engagement to each other".[11] As earlier noted, if one took this passage in isolation, one might easily suppose that "without all kind of engagement to each other" is intended to track the notion "without any social interaction of any sort". But when Hobbes spoke of "engagement" he meant specifically the undertaking of obligations of obedience, and not some generic idea of unspecified interaction, an interpretation we confirmed by analyzing his remarks about the relation of children to parents. Recall Hobbes's insistence that sons and daughters (although grown children of living parents) *are not and never have been* in a state of nature, precisely because they are under obligations of obedience to their parents. Hence, to consider a condition in which no one has any obligation of obedience toward anyone else, we must counterfactually assume that men did not begin as helpless infants preserved by parents, but rather consider them as if they had been "sprung out of the earth, and suddenly, as mushrooms come to full maturity, without all kinds of engagement". Only such entities could possibly be supposed *not* to have undertaken obligations of obedience.

If we interpret Hobbes's state of nature as eliminating from consideration only those features of our circumstance that presuppose or imply relations of political obligation, it becomes easy to understand why Hobbes persistently characterizes the state of nature as a state of

[10] EW IV, 104–105, emphasis added.
[11] EW II, 109.

private judgment. In *Leviathan* he writes, "And therefore so long a man is in the condition of mere nature, which is a condition of war, as private appetite is the measure of good, and evil".[12] This passage does not say that so long as people are in the condition of mere nature, their private appetites are the measure of good and evil. Rather, it says that so long as private appetite is the measure of good and evil, people are in the condition of mere nature (which is a state of war). But individual government by private judgment obtains only when people have no obligations of obedience to others; or at least it is legitimate only then. Hobbes explicitly argues in every version of his political theory that in the condition of mere nature men are justified in following their own private judgment, which, of course, entails that they have no prior obligation of obedience to others. Yet he also argues that when men who do have obligations to obey others refuse to do so, insisting instead on exercising private judgment, the resulting condition of *de facto* "masterless men" will share all of the incommodities and disadvantages of the condition of mere nature, differing from it only with respect to the justifiability of men's actions in it.[13] The undesirability of what results from universal self-government according to private judgment does not depend upon whether that exercise is legitimate or illegitimate. So, if what one thinks salient about the state of nature is its consequences, one might choose to define a state of nature simply as a condition of universal private judgment.[14] But Hobbes's required methodological assumption that men have no obligations of obedience to others guarantees that in the condition of mere nature, the exercise of private judgment is legitimate. Hence, we may elect to define the state of nature as a condition of justified or rightful exercise of universal private judgment, keeping in mind that were we to do so, or to define it simply as a condition without

[12] EW III, 146; T 111.

[13] Indeed it is our experience with civil wars – conditions in which men act on their own private judgment as to whether their former sovereign is to be obeyed or not, or his opponents obeyed or not – that helps us to imagine what the effects of totally unbridled private judgment in a condition of mere nature would be like. See, e.g., EW III, 114–15; T 90: "it may be perceived what manner of life there would be, where there were no common power to fear, by the manner of life, which men that have formerly lived under a peaceful government, use to degenerate into, in a civil war".

[14] This is the definition I formerly offered in *IAI,* chapter 7, 260–263.

political obligations, no civil war that had not yet resulted in such complete insecurity that man's civil obligations were entirely extinguished would count as a state of nature.

THE STATE OF NATURE DERIVATION OF THE DUTY TO SUBMIT TO GOVERNMENT

Phase 1: Derivation of the Law of Nature (the Reciprocity Theorem)

With these background assumptions in place, and keeping in mind that Hobbes means to be exposing the logical connections among terms as he takes them to be commonly understood, Hobbes argues that rational nature imposes upon us a *reciprocity requirement* that we not act in ways we would judge to be unjustified in the case of others:

1. Man is rational.[15]
2. Insofar as a man is rational, his action is not contrary to reason.
3. That which is not contrary to reason is judged to be done with right.[16] But because what is judged to be done without right is not judged to be done with right, it follows (by contraposition) that whatever one judges to be done without right is contrary to reason; and so that
4. To do what one judges to be done without right is to act contrary to reason.

[15] This is a definition. EW III, 21; T 26: "The names *man* and *rational,* are of equal extent, comprehending mutually one another". Cf. EW I, 24; EW IV, 2: "Man's *nature* is the *sum of his natural faculties and powers*...contained in the definition of man, under these words, *animal* and *rational*"; and EW I, 4: "compounded into this one name, *body-animated-rational,* or *man*".

[16] "[T]hat which is not contrary to right reason, that all men account to be done justly, and with right" (EW II, 8–9). "[S]ince all do grant, that is done by *right,* which is not done against reason, we ought to judge those actions only *wrong,* which are repugnant to right reason" (EW II, 15). Hobbes is here offering to analytically unfold the concept of being done with right. It would be beside the point to complain that some people don't always speak as precisely. Hobbes does not understand his assertion as an empirical generalization, as the claim that every individual invariably judges as "done with right" every action "not contrary to reason". Rather, Hobbes holds that applied to actions, "not contrary to reason" = "judged to be done with right" = blameless. Mistaken individual judgments do not threaten conceptual connections.

5. If one judges another's doing of an action to be without right, one judges the action done to be done without right.
6. Therefore, *If one judges another's doing of an action to be without right, and yet does that action oneself, one acts contrary to reason* (from 4 & 5). That is, *to do what one condemns in another is contrary to reason.*

Call statement 6 the reciprocity theorem of reason. *The reciprocity theorem articulates the primary constraint in Hobbes's moral and civil philosophy on the justifiability in reason of actions.* No action that fails to satisfy the reciprocity theorem accords with reason, no matter how well it serves the particular ends of the agent who performs it. Rational justifiability requires conformity with a principle of normative consistency over a description, which I characterize as a reciprocity constraint because it requires that the considerations one offers to others as justifying one's own actions be considerations one is willing to accept reciprocally from them as justifying their like actions.[17]

[17] Henry E. Allison, in the very different context of developing a Kantian argument to bridge the gap between being maxim-governed to being subject to an unconditional practical law, in one segment of his argument appears to endorse as plausible something akin to Hobbes's argument. He writes, "in claiming that one's reason for acting in a certain way is a 'good' in the sense of justifying reason, one is, implicitly, at least, assuming its appropriateness for all rational beings. The intuition behind this is simply that if reason R justifies my X-ing in circumstances C, then it must also justify the X-ing of any other agent in such circumstances. As Marcus Singer, paraphrasing Sidgwick, remarks, 'A reason in one case is a reason in all cases – or else it is not a reason at all'...the universalizability of one's intention, maxim or plan of action, seems to be presupposed as a condition of the possibility of justifying one's action, even when this justification does not take an explicitly moral form"; Henry E. Allison, "Morality and Freedom: Kant's Reciprocity Thesis", in Paul Guyer, ed., *Kant's Groundwork of the Metaphysics of Morals: Critical Essays* (Lanham, MD, 1998, 273–302, 283). Also resembling this portion of Hobbes's argument, he continues, "a rational agent cannot simply refuse to play the justification game...an agent for whom the whole question of justification is irrelevant, who never weighs the reason for his action, who acts without at least believing at the same time that his reasons are 'good' reasons, would not be regarded as rational" (284). Hobbes insists on this latter point. However, Hobbes puts these intuitions to use in a much different way than does the Kantian argument Allison develops. For Hobbes, this "universalizability" requirement – a term Hobbes does not use, and "reciprocity" better suits his meaning – demands only that the particular agent be willing to accept from others the justifications she offers them, or to accept fault when she acts on the reasons she faults them for acting on, and not that those reasons be acceptable from any more objective point of view than her own consistent, if idiosyncratic, perspective. I discuss this comparison further below.

As we noted in Chapter 1, the various notions Hobbes uses in the effort to call our attention to the core requirement of natural law – disapproving, judging unreasonable, iniquitous, or unacceptable, being unwilling to allow – are not strictly equivalent. But they do all convey our judgment of the *unjustifiability* or *blameworthiness* of the actions they characterize, and this is the judgment Hobbes sees as salient. (This is the judgment men express in their ascriptions of fault or blame.) Reason imposes a consistency constraint on justifiable actions – quite weak and sensitive to subjective differences, but nonetheless a constraint – that one render judgments of justifiability over action-types without regard to considerations that do not differentiate action-types. I defer discussion of how Hobbes thinks of the faculty of reason until we come to discuss motivation to conform to reason's dictates, but note here that the argument for the reciprocity theorem spells out the connection to reason Hobbes alludes to when he writes that "God himself, *because He hath made men rational,* hath enjoined the following law on them, and hath inscribed it in all hearts: that no one should do to another that which he would consider inequitable for the other to do unto him".[18] Should this leg of the argument succeed, the reciprocity theorem must have a normative claim on all humans who have attained the use of reason, no matter what their particular desires or ends.

Hobbes regards steps 1 through 5 as straightforward, uncontroversial analyses of our common use of terms. While the third premise and the fourth step which is derived from it may jar our contemporary ear, these should be understood as simply unfolding the conception of reason Hobbes takes to be the common understanding of his time, and the conception underlying the natural law tradition that he insists he is illuminating.[19] It is worth noticing that it is premise 3, which takes rightfulness or justifiability to belong to the concept of conformity with reason, that is doing the heavy lifting in Hobbes's argument for

[18] Bernard Gert, ed., *Man and Citizen: Thomas Hobbes* (Indianapolis, 1991), 73, emphasis added.

[19] On this interpretation, Hobbes's claim to be operating within the familiar natural law tradition, which did not strongly distinguish what we term the reasonable from the rational, is more credible than on alternative interpretations that see Hobbes as viewing the Laws of Nature as mere recommendations for securing the narrow self-interest of the agent who follows them.

the reciprocity theorem. Premises 1 and 2 come into play only later in the argument, when Hobbes seeks to motivate compliance with the reciprocity theorem, and with the conclusions he derives using it. I elaborate these points further on.

It is the fifth premise that seems to me to raise the most interesting questions. To assert that in judging another's action (under a description) to be against reason we are committed to judging *any* action under that description to be against reason, we are maintaining that the identity of the agent performing an action is irrelevant to assessments of the action's conformity to reason, and this may be doubted. Can the layman not consistently fault the priest for acting in violation of the clergy's vow of celibacy without concluding that the layman should be condemned for his own lack of celibacy?

Certainly he can, on Hobbes's view, because his *reason* for faulting the priest's noncelibacy is that it violates the priest's vow, whereas the layman, having made no such vow, cannot be faulted for violating it by his lack of celibacy. His condemnation is not for lack of celibacy simply, as it might be for cruelty simply; it is for lack of celibacy in a person who is vowed to celibacy and holds himself out as a moral example to others. So Hobbes's argument is always to be understood as agreeing with common sense that the differing positions, obligations, and circumstances of agents are properly relevant to our judgments of blame or fault by entering into the description of the action at hand. What premise 5 asserts is that when we condemn the action of another insofar as it falls under a particular action-type, for example, the breaking of a vow, it is contrary to reason for us to do any action falling under that very same action-type.[20]

If there is a problem here, it is not with the use of indexicals, understanding these as placeholders for such general notions as "the agent", "the speaker", or generically, "the occupant of such and such a position". Thus, if "It is wrong for Anthony to do A in circumstance

[20] Allison makes the same point. "To be sure", he writes, "there is a perfectly legitimate sense in which I might claim that something is 'right for me' and not for others; but this must be construed as an elliptical way of stating that there is something peculiar about my circumstances (which can include, among other things, my desires and capacities)....What I may not do is to claim that the possession of these attributes justifies my action but not that of other similarly inclined and endowed agents" ("Morality and Freedom: Kant's Reciprocity Thesis", 283).

C" is understood to mean "It is wrong for the agent to do A in C", then Hobbes's premise 5 is unproblematic. It will follow from our judgment that it is wrong for Anthony to do A in C, that the doing of A in C is wrong, and so that it is wrong for Cleopatra to do A in C, and also wrong for me, should I find myself in C, to do A. To gain traction, the objector must rather insist either that who does an action can (at least sometimes) be what accounts for its wrongness, or else that the description that picks out the action depends essentially on the identity of the agent, identified by a proper name or definite description.

In the former case, our reason for holding that Anthony's action (under a fixed description of its internal properties, incitements and effects, and circumstances) is wrong, while the indistinguishable action (under that same fixed description) done by Cleopatra is not wrong is that we take the fact of Anthony's doing an action to be the very thing that makes that action wrong. Such a position would make sense only if *every* action done by Anthony is a wrong action just in virtue of that fact. Otherwise, there is no way to distinguish Anthony's *indistinguishable from ours but wrong* actions from his *indistinguishable from ours but not wrong* actions. This position threatens incoherence by committing us to judging wrong both *Anthony's doing A in C* and *Anthony's refraining from doing A in C.* For this reason we should reject the suggestion that the wrong-making property of wrong actions is who does them.

In the latter case, the worry that we cannot infer from the wrongness of one person's action the wrongness of the like actions of others urges that particular actions otherwise identical but done by different agents belong to different *action-types.* So A-when-done-by-Anthony is a different *action-type* than A-when-done-by-Cleopatra, even holding fixed all other features of the action and its circumstances than who does it. Thus, judgments that hold for the one need not hold for the other.

The peculiarity of this sort of reasoning becomes apparent when we analogize this position about action-types to the same form of reasoning for object-types. To do so would commit us to arguing, for instance, that we cannot infer from what is true of the triangle Anthony considers anything at all about what is true of the triangle Cleopatra considers, for these are different objects in virtue of who is thinking of them. To be sure, they can be otherwise described in just the same way, as three-sided closed figures; and granted, Anthony's demonstration that the sum of the angles of his triangle equals two right angles does not depend on any particular features of his triangle – not on its size, nor the color of ink in which he drew the drawing that represented it, nor on the time of day he considered it. Nonetheless, by this objection, we can infer nothing about what is true of Cleopatra's triangle from what is true of Anthony's, because they are considering *different objects*. He is considering an Anangle, while she is considering a Cleangle, and no inference from one to the other is possible given that difference. No matter what properties they share, goes the objection, the difference in provenance defeats any effort to draw common conclusions about all objects of that type, just as differences in who performs an action defeat any effort to draw conclusions about the justifiability of actions of that type. We might say, if action-types are to be distinguished by doers, and object-types to be distinguished by perceivers or cognizers, there can be no common normative standards for either, if this objection is sound.

Whatever we may wish to say in our own voices in answer to this objection, it is answered within Hobbes's system by his constraint on the demonstrative method of syllogistic inference from definitions.[21] The Laws of Nature, of which the reciprocity theorem is the main one, are *theorems* of reason. A theorem is, by definition, a conclusion reached by *demonstration*. Demonstration is, by definition, the method of establishing conclusions by syllogistic inference from *definitions*. A definition is, by definition, a determination of the meaning of a word by equating it with other names of *settled and determinate meaning*. A term enjoys settled and determinate meaning only if it is unequivocal, that is, has a meaning *from our consent and agreement about the appellations of things* (is part of a public language rather than an idiosyncratic private language) and is unambiguous (raises the same idea all of the time in all listeners and in all speakers). This constraint on terms implies that no aberrant, private language definitions of terms may appear in the derivation, nor may terms that are of *systematically inconstant signification*. For any person to insist that the term 'action' (or any of the particular actions falling under that term, e.g., "breaking a covenant") means one thing in the case that others perform it,

[21] This is laid out in Hobbes's *Elements of Philosophy*, EW I, chapters 1–6.

but something quite different when she does a qualitatively identical thing, is to employ an aberrant private language disallowed by the requirement that our terms be settled by consent and agreement. Thus, premise 5 holds.

Conflict over Action Description

A further question may arise about how we are to determine the appropriate action-description to be assessed by the reciprocity theorem in cases where the appropriate action-description is contested. The reciprocity theorem itself gives guidance in answering this question. Suppose, for example, that Anthony and Cleopatra both want to impose uniform practice according to the true religion on the empire, but they disagree about which of their religions is the true religion, and so are unwilling to characterize each other's actions as falling under the description "imposing the true religion". He condemns her action as an effort to impose false religion, and she likewise condemns his; but he approves the imposition of his true religion, as does she her true religion. Thus each claims a right to impose his or her religion because it is true, while denying the other any right to impose his or her religion because it is false.

In such a case we must step back a pace from the primary dispute and ask whether each is content to allow the other to deliberate on the basis of that other's preferred action-description. If so, and they are content to disagree, the reciprocity theorem allows that each acts in accordance with reason in seeking to impose his or her own (as they see it, true) religion while condemning the other's attempt to impose their different religion. If not, and each would fault the other for arrogantly insisting upon his or her own action-description in this important contested case, then the reciprocity theorem is brought again into play. Because it disallows as against reason doing what one would fault another for doing, it will not permit those who fault others for insisting on a contested action-description to insist on their own contested action-description. Thus if Anthony is prepared to fault Cleopatra for insisting that he accept her description of what she is doing as imposing true religion, neither may he insist that she accept his competing description.

In many cases of conflict, the reciprocity theorem will require that we evaluate actions using *the most specific, noncontested description* of our action. In the example at hand, the reciprocity theorem would require describing the action as "imposing one's own religion", or as "imposing the religion one believes to be true", and will allow Anthony to do actions falling under those descriptions only if he is willing to allow that Cleopatra is justified in doing so as well. Because Hobbes thinks disagreement in judgment is at the root of all social disorder, the reciprocity theorem provides him with an extraordinarily useful tool for working out his solution. The reciprocity theorem requires that every disagreement in which we are not content to agree to disagree be settled by considering what course of action we would judge justifiable under a mutually acceptable action-description.[22]

Because the general problem of maxim description looms large for many contemporary philosophers, this move by Hobbes may seem more bold than it actually is, and so I want to offer a couple of remarks by way of clarification. Within Hobbes's view, the reciprocity theorem won't require *anything at all* until we plug in the particular agent's judgment that he would blame others were they to do some specified action. These judgments of fault are fixed by individual introspection, and may vary from person to person. Anthony may fault Cleopatra for trying to impose her own religion on others, while Octavian does not, and in such a case Anthony acts against reason in trying to impose his own religion on others, while Octavian does not act against reason in trying to impose his own religion on others. Because men differ to some degree in their ascriptions of blame, there is no reason to expect that the application of the reciprocity theorem will yield an extensive single set of universal norms, or convergence among all competent reasoners on all questions.[23]

[22] A captivating illustration of how reciprocity requires adopting the most specific, noncontested action description occurs in chapter 27 of *Leviathan*. Hobbes argues that if a man comes from the Indies to England and persuades Englishmen to change religion, he may justly be punished "because he does that which he would not approve in another, namely, that coming from hence, he should endeavour to alter the religion there" (EW III, 279–280; T 202).

[23] Despite some measure of affinity with T. M. Scanlon's view, Hobbes is not seeking to identify principles that could not be reasonably rejected by anyone moved to find principles for the general regulation of everyone's behavior that no one similarly motivated could reasonably reject. Nor is he offering, anticipating Kant, to show that only those principles accord with reason that can consistently be willed by *all* rational agents. Nonetheless, the view he pioneers shares with these later views an insistence on the irreducibility of (what we now call) the reasonable

Hobbes does *not* hold that because other people's reasons for wanting things are of the same kind as mine, their reasons are reasons *for me*.[24] The only reasons for me are my reasons; Hobbes's point is merely that I have nothing that counts as a reason at all, unless it is a justifying consideration I would be willing not just to give to others, but also to accept from them as justifying their like conduct. It is never the case for Hobbes that, just because someone else wants something, I have a reason to provide it. I have reason to do so only if I would fault others in circumstances relevantly similar to mine for failing to provide it to him. To illustrate, suppose both you and I want to send our respective children to college in order to help them succeed. I will have reason to help you send your child to college only if I would fault others in circumstances relevantly similar to mine for failing to help you, or would fault those others or you (supposing your circumstances are relevantly like mine) for failing to help me send my child to college. Your wants (or even needs) become reasons for me only if I am prepared to fault those who do not take such wants (or needs) as reasons for acting. The crucial point is that for Hobbes, only one's own *judgments of blameworthiness* can provide one with reasons. Even my own wants will not provide me with reasons to act, unless I am prepared to fault others for failing to act on wants of that sort in relevantly similar circumstances. Justifying action by appeal to reasons is an exercise of the faculty of judgment, not of desire; desires do not provide reasons for action, although they do motivate and, concomitant with judgment, cause actions.

It is an implication of this view that we may often permissibly do what we have no reason to do, as when we do something just because we want to, and would not fault others for doing the same. A further implication of Hobbes's view would seem to be that animals that lack

to the rational. For Scanlon's view, see his *What We Owe to Each Other* (Cambridge, MA, 1999).

[24] Hobbes is not proposing anything so bold as the position of Alan Gewirth, criticized this way by Brian Barry: "I have reasons for wanting things and other people have reasons for wanting things. My allowing that their reasons for wanting things are of the same kind and the same validity as mine does not, on the face of it, entail that I must, on pain of self-contradiction, concede that their reasons are also reasons for me. The reasons apparently come irreducibly attached to particular people"; Brian Barry, *A Treatise on Social Justice, Volume 1: Theories of Justice* (Berkeley, 1989), 286–287.

general concepts do not have any reasons. ("There is no reason in earthly creatures, but human reason".)[25] Most striking, perhaps, is the implication that atheists and rebels against God have no reason to obey even an omnipotent and vengeful God, because they are not willing to fault others for disobedience. (Here we ignore the possibility that agnostics might, on grounds suggested by Pascal, fault the disobedient for their narrow irrationality given the consequences of wagering wrongly, and in light of our epistemological limitations.) The position Hobbes articulates does not aspire to establish the universality or full generality of moral norms. It provides an intermediate point between that position on the one hand and egoism on the other – a kind of *moral minimum* that is nonetheless recognizably moral, at least for those views that do not dictate a set of substantive considerations that must be taken as reasons for action in order for an outlook to count as moral. This is part of what I find so fascinating about Hobbes's view, and also the feature that makes it particularly appealing in times like ours when robust moral consensus seems to be unreachable. And this is one of the features of Hobbes's view that lends support to John Rawls's suspicion that Hobbes was the first "political liberal".

Returning to the case in which the correct action-description of the action being judged is contested, we must ask whether we would, in that case, blame another for insisting that her own action-description trump our competing one in practical deliberation. If we *would* blame her for insisting on her own contested action-description, then, by the reciprocity theorem, neither must we insist on our preferred but contested description. In such a case, the only alternative to giving up altogether on the possibility of practical judgment and mutually justifying our actions is to proceed to some noncontested action-description, and, because of the importance we afford conflict-resolution and mutual justification, we may well fault her for refusing to settle with us on a noncontested action-description. But because the more general the action-description, the less fine-grained the practical judgments we can make, it behooves us to settle on the least abstract noncontested action-description available. Although there may be no

[25] EW VI, 5.

unique action-description that is both sufficiently abstract and uncontested by all parties, pressure to abstract for the sake of agreement will be counterbalanced by pressure toward specificity to preserve the salient features of the action to be judged. The Archimedean point these countervailing pressures fix is the least abstract, noncontested description available, or any of these, should there turn out to be more than one.[26] Thus when we would judge others unreasonable for refusing to fix with us on a mutually acceptable action-description for purposes of practical assessment of our actions, reason requires that we adopt the least abstract noncontested description available.

Suppose, on the other hand, that we would *not* blame another for insisting, in this case, on her own contested action-description, that we find it not unreasonable that she should insist upon it in that particular case: then reason does not require us to refrain from using our own. Hobbes thinks this sort of liberal largesse seldom attends those cases in which we regard the question at hand as one that importantly affects our own important interests. But it is plausible that over actions that harm *only* the agent (or others only in very insignificant ways, or only with their willing consent and participation), we tend not to blame others for insisting on their own description of what they are doing. (For instance, I describe my viewing of reality television shows as entertaining myself while you describe it as wasting my time, but you nonetheless don't fault me for sticking to my own description of what I am doing.) Hobbes thought this true not only in matters of little importance, as are questions of "small morals, as how to pick one's teeth in company", but also in the most profoundly serious question of determining what actions are necessary to avoid one's own damnation, in which we could hardly blame a man for insisting on his own judgment, "For who is there, that knowing there is so great danger in an error, whom the natural care of himself, compelleth not to hazard his soul upon his own judgment, rather than that of any other man that is unconcerned in his damnation"?[27]

[26] For cases in which there is disagreement as to which of several equally abstract noncontested descriptions to use, a further application of the reciprocity theorem may serve to settle on one of them, if, for instance, each would fault the other for refusing to determine the choice by the use of some random decision procedure like flipping a coin, or drawing straws.

[27] EW III, 684; T 471.

But over acts that engage our own significant interests as well as the agent's, we are apt to blame her for insisting on an action-description of what she is doing that we find faulty. We blame her for her arrogance, insensitivity, or recklessness in insisting against us upon her own action-description when our important interests are at stake. Here Hobbes's position anticipates J. S. Mill's "liberty principle".[28]

The Reasonable and the Rational

To forestall misunderstanding then, we should keep in mind these subjective and empirical features of Hobbes's analysis of his idea of accordance with reason. What Hobbes is describing is a *consistency requirement of an individual's evaluative attitude toward an action under a description.* To violate this requirement of reason is, says Hobbes, a form of absurdity. While Hobbes's consistency requirement falls short of the robust reciprocity that a theory like Scanlon's demands, nonetheless it is appropriate to characterize it as requiring reciprocity, because Hobbes insists that the reciprocity theorem requires that we grant to others all rights, permissions, and privileges we demand be granted to ourselves. In this sense consistency in the evaluation of actions across persons is a kind of reciprocity. And while his theory falls short of demanding Kantian universality, its requirement of consistency in judgment universally across all actions falling under a description does invoke a requirement appropriately described as a weak universality requirement. These limited requirements of reciprocity and universality must be observed if an action is to accord with reason, for men's courses "not being circumscribed within reasonable bounds, their reason becomes invisible".[29]

So while our Hobbes is neither Kant nor Scanlon, he is nonetheless not your father's Hobbes, for whom accordance with reason was

[28] J. S. Mill, Introduction to *On Liberty,* in John Gray, ed., *John Stuart Mill: On Liberty and Other Essays* (Oxford, 1991).

[29] From "A Discourse of Laws", in Noel B. Reynolds and Arlene W. Saxonhouse, eds., *Thomas Hobbes: Three Discourses* (Chicago, 1995), 106. The behavior Hobbes is here describing as not being circumscribed within reasonable bounds is the measuring of one's actions, not "by the rule of Aequum and Justum, but by the square of their own benefit, and affections: *and so not being circumscribed within reasonable bounds, their reason becomes invisible*" (emphasis added). This work, initially published anonymously in 1620, is now believed by some, on the basis of word-printing analysis by computer, to have been authored by the young Hobbes.

solely a matter of instrumental fit to whatever ends the agent happens to have, with these ends immune from reasoned scrutiny except in terms of their coherence with the agent's other equally contingent ends.[30] Reason requires that if I fault another for his action under a description, it is against reason for me to do actions falling under the same description. But there is more than one ground upon which one may fault another for his action: One may condemn it because of its effects on the agent himself – as irrational, imprudent, rash, short-sighted, counterproductive, and the like – or one may condemn it because of the effects it has or the attitudes it expresses toward others (possibly including oneself). When we fault others for choosing what they perceive to be the lesser good over the greater good, or for adopting an end while refusing to adopt what they recognize to be the necessary means, we act against reason to do so ourselves just as much as we act against reason in performing actions we condemn as iniquitous, unjust, or uncharitable in others. Hobbes's notion of "accordance with reason" thus encompasses, without differentiation, both what we would call the reasonable and the rational. The rational is not primary, nor is the reasonable reducible to it or derivable from it. It is not, in general, against reason to refrain from acting on one's desires, even on one's greatest desire, since some such actions may be unreasonable. What the argument establishing the reciprocity theorem tells us is that it is against reason to do what one faults others for doing, even if doing so would best advance the ends one happens to have. Hobbes goes so far as explicitly to *deny* that for men "those actions are most reasonable that conduce most to their ends".[31]

[30] As we noted in the previous chapter, Bernard Gert has argued that Hobbes thinks reason has an end of its own, namely, self-preservation, which is to be used as a standard for assessing the accordance of actions with reason, and thus embraces the instrumentalism of traditional desire-based interpretations while rejecting their claim that the coherence of contingent ends suffices to ground conformity with reason. But because Gert, who understands this claim as just the claim that it is irrational not to avoid death unless you have an adequate reason for not doing so, recognizes that for Hobbes there can be adequate reasons not to avoid death, and does not see Hobbes as offering a general account of the adequacy of reasons, I do not see his position as significantly different in its practical interpretative implications from traditional instrumentalist interpretations.

[31] EW III, 133; T 102, in Hobbes's reply to the Foole, where Hobbes condemns the reasoning relying on this claim as "specious" but "false". The Foole passage, because it takes on the challenge posed by the person who rejects all moral norms or

For Hobbes, an action can effectively serve a desired end and still be contrary to reason. But it is also true that on Hobbes's conception of reason, it may accord with reason to pursue ends that not all men can agree upon, and to act in ways that not all men can approve.

Like the textbook Hobbes, this Hobbes remains the turning point between premodern and modern moral philosophy, but not because he marks a polar shift to individualism, subjectivism, or skepticism, or toward one hemisphere across the rational/reasonable divide. Our Hobbes informs Kant[32] just as much as he inspires Gauthier.[33] Hobbes's conception of reason takes over the natural law tradition that was his inheritance, according to which reason condemns both immoral and imprudent action, and shows how its claims are true, albeit in a more limited way than earlier natural law theorists had supposed. Unreasonable action is against reason, but this is so because it involves a kind of absurdity or inconsistency of shifting standards in disapproving an action in another while approving it in ourselves. Similarly, irrationality is against reason, but not because our judgments fail to serve our prior contingent ends effectively. Rather, irrationality involves (as I'll argue shortly) the adoption of particular ends and means that cannot be squared with the requirements of effective agency (which requirements are necessary and noncontingent), as well as reliance on the sorts of faulty principles of inference the Foole employs, failures in means-ends reasoning, and short-sighted self-indulgence. From our modern, bifurcated perspective, Hobbes may appear to be pulling a rabbit out of a hat, deriving the reasonable from the rational. It would be more accurate to say that he is pulling a rabbit out of a hat with a rabbit in it already (as the science of illusionists teaches), showing us

requirements of the reasonable, tries to show that even from the vantage point of the merely rational, it is not true that those actions are most reasonable that most conduce to the agent's ends. This principle has already been ruled out as against reason by the reciprocity theorem.

32 As was correctly noted and convincingly argued by Taylor and Warrender, though, in my view, they were mistaken in supposing Hobbes to have held a divine command theory. See Howard Warrender, *The Political Philosophy of Hobbes: His Theory of Obligation* (Oxford, 1957), and A. E. Taylor, "The Ethical Doctrine of Hobbes", in K. C. Brown, ed., *Hobbes Studies* (Cambridge, MA, 1965).

33 I say inspires, rather than anticipates, because I argue in Chapter 8 that Gauthier's use of Hobbes relies on a misreading of Hobbes's basic project, and that Hobbes is not properly viewed as an ancestor of either Gauthier's own Moral Contractarianism or Rawls's Political Liberalism.

that the reasonable is built into our conception of man as a rational animal from the very beginning. Perhaps the best way to approach his argument is to consider the merits of his notion of accordance with reason, which does a surprising amount of the work we want done, and in a much less polarizing way than our own, while offering hope of a reconciliation of the requirements of reason.

But how does this conception of reason fare under Deigh's challenge that no proper derivation of Hobbes's Laws of Nature may attribute to Hobbes a notion of reason inconsistent with the notion of "reason as reckoning" in chapter 5 of *Leviathan?* Although premise 5 does not articulate a conception of reason as reckoning, it is nonetheless fully consistent with that conception, as we can see by tracing the way Hobbes links the ideas of reason, wisdom, philosophy, and impartiality. Reason, understood as "*reckoning*...of the consequences of general names agreed upon",[34] is the means by which "we travel from the contemplation of particular things to the inference or result of universal actions".[35] Wisdom, which is "*the perfect knowledge of the truth in all matters whatsoever*", is "the work...of a well-balanced reason; which by the compendium of a word, we call *philosophy*".[36] Like other branches of philosophy, moral philosophy thus depends on reason as reckoning. But reason is inconsistent with partiality, as Hobbes makes plain in his remark that it is ironic that Cato should have such a reputation for wisdom, considering that with him "animosity should so prevail instead of judgment, and *partiality instead of reason, that the very same thing which he thought just* in his popular state, *he should censure as unjust* in a monarchical".[37] Had earlier moral philosophers performed their proper task of facilitating wisdom, men would have learned already that it is contrary to reason to evaluate one's own actions differently than one evaluates the like actions of others: "that the very same man should...esteem his own actions far otherwise in himself than he does in others...[is one of] so many signs, so many manifest arguments, that what hath hitherto been written by moral philosophers, hath not made any progress in the knowledge of

[34] EW III, 30; T 32.
[35] EW II, iii.
[36] Ibid.
[37] EW II, ii, emphases added.

the truth".[38] Thus Hobbes's conceptual linkages show that reason as reckoning *commits* rational men to impartiality and to consistency in their evaluative judgments across settled descriptions of actions, the requirement articulated in premise 5. That requirement does not run afoul of Deigh's desideratum of consistency with Hobbes's notion of reason as reckoning.

The Reciprocity Theorem in the Context of Hobbes's Overall Political Argument

To return to the main line of argument, it is striking that Hobbes, once granted the reciprocity theorem, can argue quite directly for the requirement of civil obedience and its particular elements. Using the reciprocity theorem, Hobbes can, for example, derive a requirement of reason that we be willing to submit our disputes with others to binding arbitration, just so long as it is the case that we would blame others for refusing to submit to such arbitration. He can show that our unwillingness to permit others to exempt themselves from laws they judge wrong entails that we must not exempt ourselves from laws we disapprove. He can even support his absolutist stance, by arguing that (although we may be willing to permit others to seek to overthrow our common government whenever *we* judge the government to be illegitimate, or evil) if we are not willing to allow as legitimate others' acting to overthrow our common government whenever *they* judge it (however wrongly in our view) to be illegitimate or evil, then we must also refrain from seeking to overthrow our government on the basis of our own judgment of its demerits.

Moreover, the reciprocity theorem allows Hobbes to ground the Right of Nature (as we are about to see in phase two of Hobbes's argument) and its successor rights, the true liberties of subjects, and to delimit their scope nonarbitrarily. For our human drives and frailties limit what we will think may be reasonably expected of us, while necessitating that we make certain demands on others. It is our judgments of what it would be unreasonable to blame us for doing, balanced against our judgments of what harms to us others should be faulted for inflicting, that set the limits of justifiable liberty in a principled, determinate way. For example, Hobbes's position that so long as the

[38] EW II, v.

state can execute offenders we are to be allowed the liberty to disobey orders to execute ourselves can be viewed as balancing our readiness to fault others for refusing the state that obedience without which it cannot effectively protect us, against our judgment that it would be wrong of others to fault us for failing to do what we may be unable to bring ourselves to do, especially when others can do it in our stead. Similar balancing between the actions we are prepared to fault in others and those actions of our own for which we are unwilling to be faulted explains Hobbes's positions on the liberties to refuse military service if providing a substitute and against self-incrimination.

Once Hobbes has the reciprocity theorem, he need not be concerned about free-rider problems, or "fooles", for that theorem licenses only *symmetrical* worlds in which (from the individual's point of view) everyone is justified in doing/forbearing certain types of action in the circumstances, or no one is justified in doing/forbearing those types of action in the circumstances, but never asymmetrical worlds in which reason approves our doing what cannot be approved in others.[39] And it enables him to avoid the ridiculous claims of causal dependence desire-based interpretations saddle him with. These include claims that unless you keep your promises, no one else will keep his, or that unless each and every person keeps all her promises, social order will

[39] In contrast, the problem of free-riders and fools looms large on more traditional interpretations according to which Hobbes is trying to show that reason approves whatever course of action is expected to best achieve the satisfaction of our desire for self-preservation (or more generally for our own good) in the long run. For it may well be true that undetected unilateral defection from beneficial cooperative schemes not infrequently *does* best advance our ends, and that men can often reasonably count upon being able to unilaterally defect without detection. As we will see in Chapter 7, those who offer such interpretations generally fault Hobbes's reply to the Foole as woefully inadequate as a proof of the irrationality of free-riding, and I would agree with them in that assessment. But because, on the interpretation we've been investigating, Hobbes has already proved that reason dictates a reciprocity constraint on action that rules out free-riding, his reply to the Foole is better understood as a (successful) rebuttal to the claim that if an action turns out well, it cannot have been against reason to do it. This inference is obviously faulty (e.g., the fact that the holder of a winning lottery ticket chose his winning number by compiling the birthdates of his family members does not allow us to infer that his betting those numbers [or any numbers, for that matter] was rational) and explains why the person who defends it is a fool. Hobbes's thin, deflationary reply is perfectly adequate to answer defenses of immoral behavior defended by appeal to the Foole's principle that "those actions are most reasonable that conduce most to [one's] ends" (EW III, 133; T 102).

collapse into a war of all against all. Without the reciprocity theorem, the arguments for *each* of the second through nineteenth Laws of Nature (which are said to articulate necessary conditions for peace) will depend upon the patently false assumption that unless the agent himself does as the law requires, a war of all against all will ensue. True it is that unless people generally behave gratefully, justly, mercifully, etc., war may ensue; but it is clearly not true that all must behave in these ways if war is to be avoided. Indeed, without the reciprocity theorem it is not clear that Hobbes can validly derive even the first Law of Nature to "seek peace". Even if all value peace, we have no reason to think that peace will obtain only if each and every person seeks it. By limiting the choice of reasonable principles to those that require everyone to seek peace, keep promises, etc., or those that require no one to seek peace, keep promises, etc., the reciprocity theorem makes it clear that if we value peace, we must prefer principles requiring all to behave sociably to principles requiring sociable behavior of no one. All principles recommending unilateral self-exemption have been proved contrary to reason.

With a principle as powerful as the reciprocity theorem, Hobbes can derive a requirement of reason to perform any action or forbear from it should the universal neglect of that action or forbearance undermine peace, *provided he can demonstrate that any rational agent must desire peace.* That is what the remainder of his state of nature argument is designed to show. Let us continue laying out that argument.

THE STATE OF NATURE DERIVATION OF THE DUTY TO SUBMIT TO GOVERNMENT

Phase 2: From the Reciprocity Theorem to the Universal Right of Nature

6. It is against reason to do what one would judge it unreasonable for others to do. (the reciprocity theorem)
7. One would judge it unreasonable for others to fault one for defending one's own life.[40]

[40] Notice that although this premise is not analytic, neither is it an empirical generalization. It is an "indubitable introspectable", a premise whose truth each person

Therefore, it is against reason to fault others for defending their lives.[41]

8. Whatever is not reasonable to fault men for doing is not contrary to reason.[42]
9. Whatever it is unreasonable to fault men for doing, is said to be done with right. (from 3 and 8)

(S1) Thus, any man has a right to defend his life.[43]

10. "[W]hatsoever is vain, is against reason".[44]
11. Men's right to defend their lives is vain without the right to do and use that without which they cannot defend their lives.

can confirm for himself by introspection, and thus one consistent with Hobbes's exclusive reliance on premises that "passion not mistrusting" will not seek to displace. Against the background state of nature assumption that we owe no special obligations to others, and considering that one has a natural impulse to defend one's life (also an indubitable introspectable), which may prove irresistible, premise 7 seems acceptable.

41 It would be ridiculously anachronistic to attempt to render the argument in first order logic because Hobbes is working within Aristotelian syllogistic logic. Furthermore, formalization often turns a beautiful intuitively obvious argument into an ugly thing. Nevertheless, I'll do it just this once to satisfy J.G.

Let φ range over actions, x, y, z over agents.
Let "Do(y,φ)" mean "y does φ", that is, "agent y performs the action φ".
Let "xJNR[P]" mean "x judges it unreasonable that P".
Let "R[P]" mean "it is in accordance with reason that P".
Let "Faults(y,[P])" refer to the action faulting y for P, and let the constant d refer to the action of defending oneself.
Step 6 (the Reciprocity Theorem) states
$\forall x\, \forall y\, (xJNR[Do(y,\varphi)] \rightarrow \neg R[Do(x,\varphi)])$
Notice this implies the denial of the conjunction "$xJNR[Do(y,\varphi)]\ \&\ R[Do(x,\varphi)]$", namely, x judging it unreasonable for y to do φ while it being in accordance with reason for x to do φ himself.
Then we have
$\forall y\, (\forall x\, xJNR[Do(y,\varphi)] \rightarrow \forall x\, \neg R[Do(x,\varphi)])$
Let $\varphi = Faults(z,Do(z,d))$, that is, "faulting z for defending himself".
As an indubitable introspectable, step 7 states,
$\forall x\, xJNR[Do(y, \varphi)]$
Therefore,
$\forall x\, \neg R[Do(x,Fault(y,Do(y,d)))]$,
that is, "It is against reason to fault others for defending their lives".
QED.

42 This is analytic.

43 "It is therefore neither absurd nor reprehensible, neither against the dictates of true reason, for a man to use all his endeavours to preserve and defend his body and the members thereof from death and sorrows" (EW II, 8). Cf. EW II, 9.

44 EW IV, 101.

(S2) Thus, men have a right to what is necessary for defending their lives.[45]

12. Because somebody or other must have the right to judge what is necessary to defend one's life if the right to what is necessary for self-defense is not to be vain, either (A) it accords with reason that one be judge of what concerns one's self-defense, or (not A) it does not accord with reason that one be judge of what concerns one's self-defense, but rather someone not oneself (another) be judge of what concerns one's self-defense.[46]
13. If (A) then it accords with reason that every man has the right to judge what is necessary to defend his own life.
14. If one has both the right to defend one's own life and the right to judge what is necessary to defend one's own life, then one has the right to what one judges necessary to defend one's own life.[47]
15. If (A) then it accords with reason that *every man has the right to what he judges necessary to defend his own life.* Call this the *Universal Right of Nature.*
16. If (not A), then by the reciprocity theorem it accords with reason that each may judge what concerns another, including that other's judgments and their correctness, and so it accords with reason that one judge the correctness of the judgments of others, including the correctness of their judgments of what is necessary to one's own preservation.[48]

[45] EW II, 9: "since every man hath a right to preserve himself, he must also be allowed a right *to use all the means, and do all the actions, without which he cannot preserve himself*". Hobbes's point is that we are properly said to refuse to fault a person for defending herself (that is, to grant her an unqualified right to self-defense) only if we are prepared not to fault her for using any means necessary. For to fault her for doing the action without which she cannot save herself, is to fault her for saving herself by doing that action (which, because the action was necessary, is to fault her for saving herself).

[46] Another seeming possibility is that both oneself and others be judge of (every) one's right. But that would result in either a stalemate that would make the right vain, or else will collapse into a right to judge oneself by the same reasoning (quoted in the next note) Hobbes uses to establish our subconclusion (S3) below.

[47] This is analytic.

[48] "For if it be contrary to right reason that I should judge of mine own peril, say, that another man is judge. Why now, because he judgeth of what concerns me, by the same reason, because we are equal by nature, will I judge also of things which do belong to him. Therefore it agrees with right reason, that is, it is the right of nature

17. But to judge the correctness of a judgment of x is to judge x.

    (S3) Thus, if (not A), it accords with reason that *every man has the right to what he judges necessary to defend his own life* (the Universal Right of Nature). (from S2, 15–17)

    (S4) Thus, whether A or not A, *every man has the right to what he judges necessary to defend his own life.* (the Universal Right of Nature)

18. Therefore, *every man has the right to what he judges necessary to defend his own life.* (the Universal Right of Nature)

Notice the limited supporting role that aversion to death is playing in this leg of Hobbes's argument. Combined with the reciprocity theorem, it establishes the Universal Right of Nature (which on our interpretation is derived, rather than primitive). *Pace* other interpretations, aversion to death does not fix an end that all must pursue, and to the achievement of which all subsequent Laws of Nature are instrumental. As we saw in Chapter 2, Hobbes does not assume that all or any men do or must care *most* about avoiding their own bodily death. Premise 7 is much weaker, claiming only that in a situation in which we have no special obligations to anyone else, we would judge it unreasonable of others to blame us for defending our lives (in part because we have a natural aversion to death that we may find ourselves unable to refrain from acting on.) That seems correct, but not the sort of observation that could bear the weight placed on it by desire-based derivations of the Laws of Nature.

Considering its susceptibility to cultural modification, its defeasibility by passions or prior planning (as we earlier noted, while you cannot suffocate yourself by holding your breath, you can accomplish the same end by putting heavy rocks in your pockets before you jump in the river), and our ability to subordinate our natural aversion to death in the service of transcendent interests such as the preservation of our children, or our liberty, or in pursuit of justice or human rights, or in avenging perceived slights (as Hobbes saw in dueling), it is clear that our natural aversion to death cannot be expected to determine our conduct. Although that assumption does little work in predicting or explaining human behavior, it does work here in Hobbes's proof

that I judge of his opinion, that is, whether it conduce to my preservation or not" (EW II, 9).

in supporting the claim that people would judge a moral theory that systematically required them not to defend their lives to be unreasonable. People are not to be required to behave as if their survival meant nothing to them, or to be subject to blame and moral censure for wanting to resist death. That is too much to ask of men, who, although rational animals, are nonetheless animals, subject to the demands of their animal nature, who cannot be sure that they would, in the face of a mortal threat, even be capable of squelching their impulse to defend themselves. The impulse to self-preservation figures into Hobbes's derivation of his Laws of Nature, but not in the way desire-based derivations suppose.

THE STATE OF NATURE DERIVATION OF THE DUTY TO SUBMIT TO GOVERNMENT

Phase 3: From the Universal Right of Nature to the Right of All to All

18. Everyone has the right to what he judges necessary to defend his life.[49] (the Universal Right of Nature)
19. For any action, one may judge that action necessary to defend one's life.[50]
20. Therefore, in principle, *all have a right to all.*

Hobbes puts this conclusion in the most dramatic way possible, to emphasize the potential for conflict a universal right of private judgment introduces. But we should keep in mind that this right is limited by conscience to what one sincerely believes needful for self-defense. It does not justify claims to inessential objects of desire – mere superfluities, other men's wives, luxury real estate. Hobbes's point is that there is nothing to which any or all of us may not lay a legitimate claim, should we conscientiously judge it needful for our defense. Clearly the Right of All to All introduces the potential for conflict, as we each go about judging what we "need". This right to all things is a right to exercise private judgment as to what we need.

49 Or, "the right of protecting ourselves according to our own wills" (EW II, 13).
50 Confirmed by introspection.

THE STATE OF NATURE DERIVATION OF THE DUTY TO SUBMIT TO GOVERNMENT

Phase 4: From the Right of All to All to the Fundamental Law of Nature

Stage 1: From the Right of All to All to Perpetual War

20. All have a right to all.
21. Private judgment is the rule of all actions. (from 20)
22. Men's private judgments are variable and sometimes conflicting.[51]
23. Therefore, the right of all to all will generate contention, which, because men are by supposition sufficiently equal to preclude natural obligation, must be irresoluble, and so perpetual.[52]

Stage 2: From Perpetual War to the Fundamental Law of Nature

24. Men desire what appears to them to be good.[53]
25. A man's power is his present means to obtain some future apparent good.[54]
26. Power is a necessary condition of the exercise of effective agency. (from 25)
27. In a state in which the continued possession from moment to moment of means, and of conditions that would make those means useful for achieving one's ends are wholly unpredictable, men have, for practical purposes, no power. (from 25)
28. A state of perpetual irresoluble contention ("war") is such a state.
29. Any man (*qua* rational agent) must want, no matter what else he wants, that the necessary conditions of his effective agency obtain.

[51] This premise is not analytic. It is established as an *indubitable introspectable* by noticing that one's own judgments are inconsistent over time, varying as it seems with the concatenation of numerous external and internal influences. Even were we to imagine that other people's judgments are wholly fixed, our recognition of the inconstancy of our own judgments threatens to create contention with others. However, Hobbes assumes that observation, both ordinary and historical, will confirm the variability of judgments across persons.

[52] EW II, 12.

[53] Hobbes regards this as analytic.

[54] Hobbes takes this to be true by definition.

30. Because all men must want power (as being a necessary condition for their exercise of effective agency), no man desires a state of perpetual contention (war).
31. Therefore, no man can consistently desire that the Right of All to All be sustained.[55]
32. The absence of perpetual irresoluble contention is peace. (def)
33. Therefore, men desire peace.
34. It is against reason to seek peace when it cannot be had. (from irrationality of vain undertakings)
35. Therefore, it accords with reason to seek peace when, but only when, it may be had.

QED *The Fundamental Law of Nature, "that every man ought to endeavour peace, as far as he has hope of obtaining it".*[56]

Because what makes the condition of mere nature a state of perpetual irresoluble contention is that all have a right to all, and because this is the effect of our universal right of private judgment in defending our lives authorized by the reciprocity theorem, this right must be abridged if we are to avoid a condition that undermines our effective pursuit of our ends, whatever ends we may have. The reciprocity theorem insists that this abridgment must be reciprocal and universal across the social space we want to make available for effective exercise of our agency. Hence, the argument so far impels us to move from the Fundamental Law of Nature to the rational requirement that we cede our right to all things, and submit mutually to a constraint on that right, as Hobbes's second Law of Nature requiring submission to government requires. But before we examine this last step in Hobbes's derivation of a duty to submit to government, a critical examination of the previous segment of his argument is in order.

Desire, Good, Will, and Power

As we discussed in Chapter 2, there is a long tradition of interpreting Hobbes as a psychological egoist who held that the only motive of voluntary human action is the desire for good for oneself. We earlier

55 "Whosoever therefore holds, that it had been best to have continued in that state in which all things were lawful for all men, he contradicts himself" (EW II, 12).

56 EW III, 117; T 92.

considered why the mechanistic materialism usually cited in support of this view fails to establish it. We also acknowledged that, although Hobbes does not espouse psychological egoism, his language invites that misunderstanding. Hobbes's insistence that men call good what they desire, and necessarily will the good does not tell us anything about what things Hobbes thought actually *are* good, nor about what Hobbes takes the meaning of 'good' to be.

In Chapter 2 I offered an argument that Hobbes has improperly been thought to be a value subjectivist. I argued that those of his remarks generally interpreted as endorsing subjectivism are nothing more or less than an observation about our actual tendency to use evaluative language to signal personal desires, and certainly not any endorsement of that tendency. Hobbes insists that the meaning of a word depends upon agreement in the community of speakers. And while people may call the things they desire 'good', they do not think that 'good' means 'what I desire', nor even 'desired by the speaker'.

I argued that Hobbes viewed men's tendency to use evaluative terms subjectively as *highly problematic*.[57] It makes terms like 'good' and 'evil' of *inconstant signification*, and this inconstancy hinders mutual understanding. Recall Hobbes's argument that this tendency encourages the use of private judgment, which creates serious conflict. It misleads men into thinking that the proper measure of good and evil is their own liking or disliking, rather than the Law of Nature, or their sovereign's judgment. We noted that nothing in Hobbes's linguistic theory precludes the possibility that we use words that mean one thing to communicate something else, and so it is perfectly possible that Hobbes affirmed an objective conception of goodness, while highlighting men's improper and harmful tendency to take their own desires as the measure of goodness.

I argued that we should believe Hobbes when he says that men call the things they desire good, and take this seriously as a mere observation about how people use 'good', rather than an endorsement of it. This interpretation makes sense of Hobbes's claims that (1) men will

[57] Hobbes remarks "[h]ow fallacious it is to judge of the nature of things by the ordinary and inconstant use of words" (EW III, 240; T 175), and illustrates this sort of problematic inconstancy by noting the way men use words like 'counsel' and 'command' to conflate concepts that ought to be distinguished.

their (apparent) good, (2) men call good what they desire, and (3) the will is just the appetite or aversion a man acted on in acting as he did, and thus (4) his conclusion that "whatsoever a man would, it therefore seems good to him because he wills it".[58]

The question, then, is how all this normative judgment is implemented. According to Hobbes, the implementation of our final desire – that is, our will – crucially depends upon our *power.* Power is any person's "present means to obtain some future apparent good". Things that may count as present means for effecting one's ends include possession of friends, reputation, beauty, wealth, eloquence, prudence, arms, popularity, good luck – anything that serves to secure some future desired end. But the possession of any particular quality will count as the possession of power only if possession of that power propels its possessor into a position of *relative dominance.* Because other people's ends may conflict with our own and their actions may cross and thwart our efforts, effecting our ends will require sufficient superiority of means to outdo our competitors. Thus one has power only if she can impose what she wants against what her fellows want. This makes power strictly a matter of *relative advantage,* and thus *essentially comparative.* Buying power at an auction provides a simple illustration. My financial resources will not provide me buying power if the greater financial resources of others enable them to outbid me for the object we both desire. This is why Hobbes defines natural power as "the *eminence* of the faculties of body, or mind: as *extraordinary* strength, form, prudence, arts, eloquence, liberality, nobility".[59]

The intrinsically competitive nature of power comes out strikingly in Hobbes's famous analogy of life to a race. He writes, "But this *race* we must suppose to have no other *goal,* nor other *garland,* but being foremost, and in it:... Continually to be out-gone, is *misery.* Continually to out-go the next before, is *felicity*".[60] When we remember that Hobbes defines felicity as "[*c*]*ontinual success* in obtaining those things which a man from time to time desireth",[61] says men deem good whatever they desire,[62] and defines power as "present means; to obtain some future

58 EW II, 10.
59 EW III, 74; T 62, emphasis added.
60 EW IV, 53.
61 EW III, 51; T 46.
62 EW III, 41; T 40.

apparent good",[63] Hobbes's comparison of life with a race confirms that he believes that *whether* one has power – and *how much* power one has – depends essentially on what *others* have. If the goal of life is to meet continual success in achieving one's ends, we must strive to amass greater powers than others, and must regard our collected assets – no matter what they consist in (friends, eloquence, wealth, reputation, etc.) or how great they are by absolute measures – as conferring no power on us unless they are significantly greater than the assets of our competitors. He writes, "And because the power of one man resisteth and hindereth the effects of the power of another, *power* simply is no more, but the *excess* of the power of one above that of another: for equal powers opposed, destroy one another; and such their opposition is called contention".[64]

Power is thus *inherently comparative,* which implies that equality of capacity voids power. When brought into conflict, persons with equal abilities have *no* power, no matter how great in absolute terms are their resources. Like those parallel universe Star Trek heroes and villains whose deployment of symmetrical matter and antimatter lock them in futile combat eternally, with neither able to accomplish their ends, so does our agency depend upon either our greater relative power or, alternatively, a social organization that coordinates our respective exercises of power, so that they do not impede each other.

An interesting feature of the argument recounted earlier is that it is perfectly general. It purports to show that because the state of perpetual contention among relative equals, all of whom are acknowledged to be justified in acting on their own private judgment, is one in which no one can reliably tell what means will be needed to achieve his ends, let alone be assured of being able to hang on to those means, men must see themselves as lacking the power needed to exercise effective agency, *no matter what their particular ends.* There is *no* plan that a man can have confidence in being able to carry out in that state; not a plan to organize a religion, lead an army, build a business, earn a comfortable living, paint a fresco, make a scientific discovery, bring up his children to adulthood, complete a novel, succor the needy, or preserve his own life. A man cannot even rely on having the power to

[63] EW III, 74; T 62.
[64] EW IV, 38.

carry out a nefarious plot of mass murder of his enemies, or a simple plan to commit suicide when the pain becomes too great, because he cannot count on the relative resources needed to prevent him from being in the meantime captured, controlled, or killed by another, or deprived of the external resources his plan requires. The unpredictable free-for-all that may ensue when all may do whatever they judge needful sufficiently compromises effective agency that it is against reason for men to accept such a condition, if there is any better alternative. The generality of the argument increases its attractiveness, for although men disagree with one another about the value of pursuing particular ends, none can deny the value of securing conditions for the possibility of pursuing any ends whatsoever.[65]

Having noted this fact, we can see how one might simplify Hobbes's argument by importing into it any end one thinks to be sufficiently uncontroversial to illustrate the general point. So one might alternatively argue (as Hobbes does in some works):

*Stage Two**

24′. Men desire self-preservation.
25′. War threatens man's preservation.
26′. Perpetual war perpetually threatens man's preservation, because it can never settle a victory.[66]
27′. No man desires a perpetual war.
28′. Therefore, no man can consistently desire that the Right of All to All be sustained.
etc.

Because Hobbes has assumed, as a supporting consideration in his derivation of the Right of Nature that men do, at least by nature, desire self-preservation, that desire serves as a good example and sound application of his general argumentative strategy. Most of us can identify with it, and even if we don't, we acknowledge the force of Hobbes's prior argument that we should allow as reasonable that others act on that desire. But Hobbes could just as well have run his argument from any of the other myriad things men value. This fact

65 EW III, 88; T 72.
66 EW II, 12.

explains why Hobbes persistently describes the deprivations of the state of nature by a *long list*. It is not just that a perpetual war among approximate equals undermines our power to preserve our lives; it also undermines our efforts to achieve comfort, freedom from fear, prosperity, elegancy, science, arts, control over the natural world, and sociable living itself.[67] Hobbes's argument is plausible no matter which of these widely valued ends we consider. It is thus important that we recognize how limited is Hobbes's assumption that men naturally desire to preserve their lives. The only work it does is to explain why we would judge it unreasonable of others to whom we owe no special obligations to fault us for defending our lives, which judgment requires us, by the reciprocity theorem, to grant the Universal Right of Nature; it is not needed for anything else in the theory. It is a point that may reasonably serve as a provisional lowest common denominator for getting Hobbes's argument against universal private judgment off the ground, despite the fact that natural preservation does not top the list of what accounts for the behavior of socialized men as known by experience (either our own or Hobbes's).

THE STATE OF NATURE DERIVATION OF THE DUTY TO SUBMIT TO GOVERNMENT

Phase 5: From the Fundamental Law of Nature to the Obligation to Submit to Government (OSG)

Once Hobbes derives the necessary unacceptability to any rational agent of the Right of All to All, the duty to quit the condition of universal private judgment (the state of nature) by submitting to political authority follows straightforwardly. If the Universal Right of Nature entails the Right of All to All, rational agents must will the abridgment of the Universal Right of Nature. To abridge a universal right to act according to private judgment is to take some questions out of the purview of private judgment and submit them to arbitration (public judgment).[68] A sovereign/government/political authority is

[67] Recall the contrast between savage and civic life depicted in Figure 1 (Chapter 3).

[68] An alternative way of defeating the Universal Right of Nature would be to leave all questions within the purview of private judgment, but take some people's

nothing more than the repository of public judgment, empowered to make that judgment effective. Thus, reason requires submission to government. In particular, it requires that one be willing, at least when others are also, to give up that portion of private judgment one thinks necessary for peace and defense, and be content with the remaining liberty of private judgment one is willing to allow to others. Thus is derived Hobbes's second Law of Nature.

Still, if we renege on our authorization to a public arbitrator of the right to judge controversies whenever we dislike the outcome of that arbitration, or reserve a right to act on our own private judgment when its decision goes against our interests or values, we void our prior transfer of the right of judgment. To act in this way sustains a condition of universal private judgment which just continues contention. And so Hobbes writes that "From that law of nature, by which we are obliged to transfer to another, such rights, as being retained, hinder the peace of mankind, there followeth a third [law of nature]; which is this, *that men perform their covenants made:* without which, covenants are in vain".[69] Thus is derived the third Law of Nature. Derivation of the rest of Hobbes's many Laws of Nature follows the same pattern.

Law, Reason, and the Desire for Self-Justification

The definitional derivation of Hobbes's Laws of Nature I have just laid out begins from the definition of man as a rational agent and aims to proceed analytically by unfolding the meanings of Hobbes's key concepts – reason, right, good, will, and power – supplemented by a couple of indubitable introspectables. It purports to show that any agent whose actions are to accord with reason must regulate his own actions by the standards of judgment he applies to the actions of others. From this reciprocity theorem, Hobbes is able to show that effective agency is undermined by ascribing a universal right of private judgment, and thus that rational agents must be willing to join into a scheme of reciprocal universal restriction on the scope of private judgment.

judgments out of consideration; but the reciprocity theorem rules out this asymmetric possibility.

69 EW III, 130; T 100.

What accounts for the normativity of Hobbes's conclusion, on this interpretation of his derivation? And is it realistic to suppose that people can be motivated to do what this conclusion shows they ought? Hobbes points to our shared conception of ourselves as rational agents, beings who pursue ends for justifying reasons, in premises one and two of the derivation. Unlike lesser elements of God's creation, we humans direct our actions according to the reasons we take ourselves to have. Supposing Hobbes's substantive argument is sound, it follows that *if* we are *rational agents,* we ought to be willing to join into a scheme of reciprocal universal restriction of the scope of private judgment. Unless others join such a scheme, our agency will be thwarted, thus as agents, we must insist that they join; and reason forbids us to fault them for not joining unless we will join ourselves, thus as rational, we must join. Thus we ought to participate in limiting the scope of private judgment because rational agency requires it, and we view ourselves as rational agents. On this account, the normativity of the Laws of Nature depends neither upon their having been commanded by God, as divine command interpretations maintain, nor upon their instrumentality to preserving the agent's life or promoting his narrow self-interest, as desire-based interpretations would have it. In locating normativity where it does, it avoids the epistemological problems of the divine command view as well as the implausibly impoverished psychological theory of traditional views.

What then can motivate us to follow the Laws of Nature as we ought to do? There is an obvious source of motivation, introduced in Chapter 2, widespread among people and very powerful. This is the desire to justify oneself – to be in the right, to show that one is reasonable, to command from others the respect due a person of wisdom, a sense of pride in one's own judgment – and the desire to be admired or approved of by others. To be seen as unreasonable or as acting unjustifiably is felt as shameful if true, insulting and degrading if not. *Leviathan*'s theme of the pervasiveness of pride as a basic human motivation and source of contention makes it sensible to interpret Hobbes's derivation of the Laws of Nature as depending for its motivational force on our pride in being a special creation whose rationality both makes possible and demands that we offer justifying reasons for what we do. Hobbes's insistence that "pretence of right", or the sense that we are morally or religiously justified in our cause, is a *necessary* condition for rebellion shows how seriously Hobbes took this motive. Any desire to justify one's actions capable of holding in check rebellion among even those who are discontented and believe they might be able to win, just because they do not see a way to justify their actions, must be an enormously powerful motive. It is abundantly clear that Hobbes believed it to be so.

Has Hobbes identified a plausible motive? Good Hobbesian method should invite us to introspect – each to ask ourselves, am I concerned that others should think me a reasonable, right-thinking person, acting on good reasons? Would I find it shameful to be systematically wrong-thinking or unreasonable? Would it anger me or offend my sense of dignity to see adversaries with no good reasons – dogmatists, hypocrites, bullies, blowhards, idiots – held in higher esteem than am I? Would I feel diminished were others to discount every reason or justification I might offer in support of my judgments and actions?

As I registered in Chapter 2, the desire to be justified may appear fanciful until we consider what is the significance to us of our status as reasoning creatures. Many lesser animals share with us the capacity to fit means to desired ends, but unlike us, they seem not able to judge whether they have good reasons to act on the various inclinations that assail them. Without judgment, our doings would be, like theirs, entirely determined by our instincts, drives, and desires, in conjunction with external environmental conditions. Our voluntary actions would be more properly described as happenings than as doings. Again, the relevant contrast is not between philosophical voluntarism and determinism of the will; it is rather a contrast between being a distinctively *human* being, whose actions, although strictly determined, are nonetheless determined by the exercise of human judgment as well as one's animal passions, and being a creature whose doings are driven by instincts or desires alone.

Whatever the exact connection Hobbes had in mind, it is clear that Hobbes identified natural law with reason, and reason with distinctively human nature. It is with this connection in mind that Hobbes writes approvingly (supposing him to be author of the *Discourse of Laws*) that "Plato affirms the necessity of Laws to be so great and absolute that men otherwise could not be distinguished from unreasonable creatures".[70] Hobbes strongly identifies reason with law, and the absence of both with bestiality, in his remark that

> Law and Reason are twins, the absence of one, is the deformity of the other; being in a kind *convertibilia,* and inseparable.... And thus the reverence, and duty we owe to Laws, is nothing else but obedience to reason, which is the begetter, corrector, and preserver, of the very Laws themselves: those therefore who will not obey them, do come more near the nature of Brutes and Savages, than men endowed with reason.[71]

On this picture, it seems plausible that those who see themselves as fundamentally rational, that is, reason-bearing agents (especially if they think of themselves as having been divinely created with that nature), should recognize as normative for them a derivation of duty beginning from the requirements of rational agency. And it is also natural to suppose that such people would strongly desire to justify themselves to others and in the sight of God, and would thus be motivated to act as Hobbes's derivation proves they ought.

With this account of Hobbes's moral psychology in hand, we can perhaps better understand why Hobbes identified so strongly with Plato's philosophy. Not only did their conceptual approaches to knowledge have an affinity, but Plato's identification of *thumos* as the spirited part of the soul that seeks admiration and esteem has much in common with the notion of pride we find in Hobbes.[72] When *thumos* has been trained and subordinated to values set by reason, it contributes to the orderly state of the soul that constitutes justice, that is, to the psychic health and virtue of the person. The desire for esteem and self-esteem, properly trained, enables one to hold in check the "many headed protean monster" of desire, as required by the conclusions of reason. This sense of self-esteem may enable one to make sacrifices and face dangers in the service of reason's judgments. The properly grounded pride of a Hobbesian "generous nature" enables

70 Hobbes, "A Discourse of Laws", 106.

71 Ibid., 115.

72 In the following discussion, I draw heavily on the analyses of the role of *thumos* in Plato's account of the soul offered by John M. Cooper in his "Plato on Human Motivation" in *Reason and Emotion: Essays on Ancient Moral Psychology and Ethical Theory* (Princeton, NJ, 1999), and by Julia Annas in *An Introduction to Plato's Republic* (Oxford, 1981).

him to risk or embrace sacrifice in defense of the commonwealth, as the final Law of Nature requires. Of course, the timocratic person, whose *thumos* motivations have not been disciplined to service but rather fix his goals, is a haughty person who seeks public recognition irrespective of his desert – he is the sort of ambitious, prideful, and vainglorious person whom Hobbes detests. He is also dangerous, for his high-spirited, warring demand for esteem may lead him to act in ways that threaten the stability or existence of the commonwealth. John Cooper suggests that "the motivations that Plato classifies under the heading of spirit are to be understood as having their root in competitiveness and the desire for self-esteem and (as a normal presupposition of this) esteem by others".[73] I suggest that the motivations Hobbes appeals to as the primary forces to either support or to destroy a commonwealth (depending upon whether they are subordinated to reason's requirements) tap a similar root. Hobbes's is not an innovative conception of human psychology, but one with ancient pedigree, and contemporary resonance.

Hobbes in the Social Contract Tradition

In the next chapter, we will ask how, precisely, Hobbes uses his reciprocity theorem to derive a duty to undertake political obligation. We will want to consider how these very general Laws of Nature could be plausibly understood as requiring submission to an absolute sovereign, who may or may not be incorporating the requirements of natural law into his or her positive laws. What exactly is supposed to be the relation between natural and positive law in Hobbes's system?

But before closing this chapter it may be interesting to take a short detour to consider Hobbes's legacy. Because Hobbes has traditionally been regarded as a founding father of social contract theory, it may be of interest to those who see him in that way to consider how he fares, on the interpretation under consideration, as a social contract theorist. I would argue that he appears in a more attractive light on the interpretation proposed than on desire-based interpretations.

Contractarian justifications of political authority and of legitimate law are well known to be vulnerable to two sorts of potentially serious

[73] Cooper, "Plato on Human Motivation", 133–134.

objection. Hobbes's theory, as it is traditionally understood, exhibits these theoretical defects to an extreme degree. Seventeenth-century social contract theories typically sought to justify systems of political authority by showing that from a suitably characterized initial situation, suitably characterized persons expecting to have to live under those systems would agree to them. Further, particular laws were supposed to derive their justification from the fact that they flowed by correct procedures from, and conformed to the constraints imposed by, the basic political system that properly situated and characterized agents would choose. Although the aims of contemporary contractarian theories may be somewhat wider than these – for instance, Rawls extends this general approach to consider what principles of justice are best suited to order the entire basic structure of a certain sort of society, and Gauthier offers a contractarian basis for all of morality – what I am taking to be characteristic of social contract theories is their attempt to justify whatever it is they seek to justify by appeal to the decisions, conclusions, or agreements competent, properly motivated, and situated rational agents would reach for the purpose of ordering their common life.

Because we cannot suppose that the mere fact that people agree on an arrangement suffices to justify that arrangement, contractarian theories do not ask simply what the readers to whom they are addressed will actually agree to from their current circumstances. Coercion, manipulation, irrationality, ignorance, compulsion, differences in need, differences in power, bad choices, bad options, and bad luck may all in their different ways deprive certain *de facto* agreements of moral legitimacy. Not only would such a project fail to legitimate arrangements, it is also highly doubtful that any determinate answer to the question as to what, if any, agreement would be reached could be found, for actual people's interests, temperaments, values, and circumstances may vary so widely, and be sufficiently unstable over time, that the answer is practically incalculable.

For both these reasons, contractarian theories must to some degree *idealize both contractors and their circumstances.* Locke, for instance, characterizes his contractors as equally free from prior political obligations, as rational, sociable, and cognizant of certain divinely dictated moral laws that they generally observe as well as of God-given rights that they seek to defend, living together cooperatively in a situation favorable to such cooperation. Gauthier assumes that his contractors are self-owning, property-owning, independent Robinson Crusoes, rational and interested in maximizing the satisfaction of their interests in the long run, capable of seeing through others to discern the real intentions of those others but reciprocally translucent to them, mutually disinterested, and operating in conditions in which cooperation is both possible and potentially profitable. And Rawls assumes that his rational contractors, fairly situated and behind a veil of ignorance as to many features of the persons they represent and particulars of the society for which principles of justice are being selected, will seek to ensure for those citizens a sufficient share of the liberties, opportunities, and resources they need in order to satisfy their higher order interests in exercising their moral powers and in pursuing their determinate permissible conception of the good.

These sorts of idealizations are crucial to social contract theories, but as is often noted, they are also highly problematic. The first problem is that we are importantly different from those ideal contractors, and our circumstances are really not at all like theirs. How, then, can the imagined decisions of people like them in circumstances like theirs be normative for us, let alone motivationally efficacious?

One way to address this difficulty would be to show that a theory relies only on values and conceptions we share, and ideals to which we aspire. In this vein Rawls took pains to explain his view that the constraints on reasoners and on reasoning in the original position reflect our own present moral convictions and our shared conceptions of citizen and society, what "we, here and now" accept as correct moral constraints on deliberations of this sort.

But his critics have continued to ask the question "Who are you calling 'we'?" To the extent that we do not agree on the prior moral constraints on the appropriate characterization of contractors and their deliberative circumstances and options, the claims to justification of social contract theories are undermined. Without some such constraints, they are bound to be indeterminate and implausible; with them, they become controversial, and perhaps objectionably parochial.

The second problem with social contract theories is that the social decision procedures they legitimate may churn out particular laws that would be deemed substantively unjust by intuitive considerations of equity or by the best moral theory we have. Social contract theories particularly invite this danger because their need to idealize, generalize, and abstract from the particular compels them to settle on general decision-procedures rather than on specific substantive norms. But because social contract theories are plausibly authoritative and practical only when they idealize, the best they can hope to settle is an overarching general normative structure, together with a set of procedures designed to realize the ends of that structure. The cost of idealization is loss of the ability to micromanage to ensure that particular laws licensed by legitimate political authority do not turn out to be substantively unjust.

To illustrate, Locke's system justifies enslaving criminals, enforcing contracts tantamount to indentured servitude, including inequitable marriage contracts, and upholding enormous differentials in property holdings (as well as notoriously licensing limitation of the franchise to propertied males). And Rawls has been criticized for a contract theory that endorses principles of justice that permit oppressive family forms that impose inegalitarian distributions of authority and unjust divisions of labor upon their female members.[74] Hence social contract theories threaten to legitimize substantively unjust particular laws, or legally enforceable or permissible arrangements. I offer no proof that this slippage is a necessary consequence of social contract theory's requirement of idealization, but such slippage is a serious danger that counts against the overall appeal of contractarianisms.

These then are two fairly obvious problems with social contract theory: it demands idealizations that undermine its normativity, and its idealizations determine largely procedural conceptions of law that allow or invite substantively unjust laws to lay claim on us. Finding these defects in contractarianism's founding father Hobbes's social contract theory is, on standard interpretations, the easiest thing in the world. On those interpretations of his view, the conception of human nature Hobbes wishes to offer us as capturing what is morally relevant in our own natures is as likely to insult us as to give us grounds for identifying with his reasoning. He invites us to imagine

[74] For instance, see Susan Moller Okin, "*Political Liberalism,* Justice, and Gender", *Ethics* 105 (1994): 23–43. For an argument that Rawls's theory does not suffer this defect, see S. A. Lloyd, "Family Justice and Social Justice", *Pacific Philosophical Quarterly* 75 (1994): 353–371.

men devoid of all social ties, "sprung up like mushrooms", reacting to external forces according only to how they affect themselves. Hobbes does posit the equality of humankind, but this is understood to be an equality of vulnerability to being murdered or, somewhat more optimistically, equality in the capacity to kill or otherwise harm others in pursuit of one's own perceived good. Each measures value only by his own particular appetites. In view of men's short-sightedness and the variability of appetites across persons and over time, this propensity causes dissension and conflict over values, as well as conflict when individual judgments overlap on scarce resources or zero-sum goods. Men are vain and easily offended, willing to extract recognition from others by force. Pushed and pulled by their passions, but driven by fear to preemptively attack others, our Hobbesian representatives inhabit a miserable world of universal warfare. This is the description of those aspects of our nature and circumstances that we are supposed to accept as properly reflecting the morally relevant features of our lives for purposes of settling the terms of our political obligations.

And it gets worse. On the usual understanding of Hobbes's theory, from the condition just described, our state of nature counterparts will find it rational to grant that arrangements extracted by overt coercion or entered into for lack of any nondisastrous options should be counted as morally binding. Hobbes's infamous position that we are morally required to keep our promise to the highway robber follows just as naturally as his conclusion that we are bound to submit to the laws, whatever their content, of an absolute sovereign. Serious times require serious measures. If absolute sovereignty is, as Hobbes argues, the only stable solution to the decision problem his description of the state of nature poses, then his social contract theory will justify political absolutism. And since the very nature of political absolutism is to claim authority to impose laws whose legitimacy depends not on their content but entirely on their provenance, we should expect that the laws deemed legitimate by Hobbesian social contract theory will often be substantively unjust. This of all theories would seem to be disabled from providing any guarantee of the substantive justice of the laws it legitimates.

But consider now the reciprocity interpretation of Hobbes's moral philosophy as just discussed in his definitional derivation of the Laws of Nature. On this interpretation, Hobbes's theory seems not to be vulnerable to the two problems I've described, or at least looks much less vulnerable to them than is the traditional Hobbes, and probably than are the contractarianisms of Locke and Gauthier. Hobbes means to derive the obligation to submit to political authority from a conception of ourselves as rational agents, without reliance on any controversial suppositions about our actual ends. In the course of his argument he shows that reason commits us to an independent constraint on interpersonal action that operates against substantively unjust legislation.

By arguing that our conception of ourselves as rational agents commits us to undertaking political obligations, Hobbes engages interests that none of us can fail to have. Thereby he avoids the first objection that the determinations of parties to the social contract may make no normative claim on us. By arguing that rationality commits every rational agent, including the sovereign, to a particular reciprocity constraint on justifiable interpersonal action, the possibility of legitimating substantively unjust legislation is minimized. Thus he largely averts the second objection.

Having established the reciprocity theorem as a requirement of reason, Hobbes can use it, as we saw in Chapter 1, to delimit the justifiable actions of governments. The Law of Nature requires sovereigns to advance, to the best of their abilities, the welfare of the people who have reposed trust in them. This theorem unequivocally requires that any sovereign pursue the good of his subject people: "Now all the duties of rulers are contained in this one sentence, *the safety of the people is the supreme law*... it is their duty in all things, as much as possibly they can, to yield obedience unto right reason, which is natural, moral and divine law".

Having established this end of sovereignty, Hobbes uses the reciprocity theorem to constrain the legitimate legislation of any government. For instance, *no sovereign may impose a law on his subjects he would not be content should be imposed on him were he a subject.* The first implication of this constraint is that governments must not unduly limit citizens' liberty. The government may make no law that is not necessary for keeping subjects safe and able to pursue their ends without mutual obstruction, and so may not restrict their liberty without good public justification.[75] In particular, "to leave man as much liberty as may

[75] EW II, 179.

be, &c. is the duty of a sovereign by the law of nature".[76] Unless reason itself prohibits some action-type, the civil law should not prohibit it because otherwise people would be prone to accidentally violating the laws through ignorance, as if "to entrap their harmless liberty; which supreme commanders are bound to preserve for their subjects by the laws of nature".[77]

How funds may be raised and the uses to which they must be put also fall, on Hobbes's view, under the constraints of the Law of Nature. The government must impose fair tax policies that equitably burden subjects, which, by Hobbes's careful argument, requires a consumption tax rather than an income tax,[78] and which must be kept as low as is compatible with the sovereign's fulfilling his public function.[79] Public policy must encourage "labour and thrift" by supporting the useful arts and sciences, and perhaps by imposing luxury taxes (increasing wealth by preying on other nations "is not to be brought into rule and fashion").[80] And the government must institute a social safety net that provides work for those who are able to work, and support for those who are not able to work; to leave men to the hazard of uncertain private charity is contrary to the duty of a sovereign.[81]

Sovereigns must root out judicial corruption, and provide for mechanisms of appeal against suspect judges.[82] Settled punishments must be prescribed by the laws, established with an eye to the public benefit, and not departed from arbitrarily; and "natural equity commands that equal transgressors be equally punished".[83]

In foreign policy, if population pressures compel them to colonize foreign territories, sovereigns must, under the Law of Nature, restrain colonial settlements so that they do not extinguish native populations or deprive them of means of preservation.[84] The reciprocity theorem dictates that the sovereign may not go to war unless that war is necessary

76 EW IV, 215, marginal summary; Cf. EW III, 335; T 240.
77 EW II, 179.
78 EW II, 173–174; EW IV, 216.
79 EW IV, 201.
80 EW II, 176–177.
81 EW III, 334; T 239.
82 EW II, 181.
83 EW II, 179–180.
84 EW III, 335; T 239.

for the preservation of its subjects.[85] But since sovereigns "are, by the law of nature, bound to use their whole endeavour in procuring the welfare of their subjects: it follows, that it is not only lawful for them to send out spies, to maintain soldiers, [etc.]; but also that not to do thus is unlawful.... For rulers are bound according to their power to prevent the evils they suspect".[86]

Finally, a sovereign "is bound by the *law of nature... of not returning evil for good,* prudently to provide that by his death the city suffer not a dissolution",[87] by establishing an effective mechanism for the seamless transfer of power from government to government.

I conjecture that building on these examples of how Hobbes used his reciprocity theorem to reach plausible principles of legislation and policy, and taking those principles as bases for further reasoning, we would find the resulting system of legal norms conforms reasonably well with our considered convictions of equity. Hobbes's method of building cases in the law of nature creates pressures against inequitable legislation.

Of course, this fact provides no practical *guarantee* that actual sovereigns would never legislate iniquitously. No theory guarantees conformity with its own requirements, nor precludes corrupt, illegitimate departures from is requirements. (We might say, bad things happen to good theories, sometimes.) What I've suggested is that on this construction of Hobbes's view, it legitimates only legislation that we would (arguably) agree is equitable.[88]

[85] EW IV, 219–220.

[86] EW II, 171.

[87] EW II, 103.

[88] In contrast, Locke's theory seems to legitimate morally dubious policies like enslavement of criminals, indentured servitude, and unequal marital rights, not as *corruptions* of the theory, but as *correct* applications of the theory. Perhaps there is some way of reinterpreting Locke's theory that will allow it to preclude these results. But since Locke himself acknowledges these as conclusions of his view, and since his sympathetic interpreters either acknowledge these as belonging to Locke's view (as A. John Simmons does), or try to rationalize these views (as Joshua Cohen does for restricted suffrage), or else try to excuse them (as Jeremy Waldron does in some but not all cases), it would seem that Locke suffers from this defect of contractarian theory in a way that our reconstructed Hobbes does not. For an ultimately critical interpretation of Locke's view, see A. John Simmons, *On the Edge of Anarchy* (Princeton, NJ, 1993). For somewhat more sympathetic interpretations of Locke, see Joshua Cohen, "Structure, Choice, and Legitimacy: Locke's Theory

If so, Hobbes's social contract theory is much less vulnerable than is usually supposed to the objections that it cannot be normative for us, and that it may license unacceptable legislation. The two worries about social contract theories we before noted were that having to abstract from our actual interests and ends, they may yield requirements that are not normative for us, and that they legitimate general procedures that may license substantively unjust particular laws. The only assumptions Hobbes makes about our essential interests are that we are concerned to conform to the requirements of rationality, and of effective exercise of our agency. Because he thinks we accept a conception of ourselves as rational agents, he believes this argument should have normative purchase on all of us, no matter our other idiosyncratic particular interests and ends. He does assume that we would judge it unreasonable of others toward whom we have no special obligations to condemn us for doing what we judge necessary to defend our own lives (a judgment each can introspectively confirm as true in his or her own case). But this assumption stops well short of an assumption that we all care most about our own lives, as would be needed to ground political obligation on considerations of narrow self-interest. Thus on the reciprocity interpretation, Hobbes proves to be a more impressive forefather than has been generally appreciated.

of the State", *Philosophy and Public Affairs* 15 (1986): 301–324; and Jeremy Waldron, *God, Locke, and Equality* (Cambridge, 2002).

PART THREE

FROM MORAL PHILOSOPHY TO CIVIL PHILOSOPHY

6

Self-Effacing Natural Law and the Duty to Submit to Government

> King: Methinks I could not die anywhere so contented as in the king's company, his cause being just and his quarrel honorable.
>
> Williams: That's more than we know.
>
> Bates: Ay, or more than we should seek after, for we know enough if we know we are the king's subjects. If his cause be wrong, our obedience to the king wipes the crime of it out of us.
>
> (Shakespeare, *Henry V*, Act IV, Scene 1)

> [I]f I wage war at the commandment of my prince, conceiving the war to be unjustly undertaken, I do not therefore do unjustly; but rather if I refuse to do it, arrogating to myself the knowledge of what is just and unjust, which pertains only to my prince.
>
> (EW II, 152)

In order to understand how Hobbes thought the Law of Nature dictates submission to an absolute sovereign, we need to consider his view of the relation between natural law and civil law, and how his notion of what I shall call a hierarchy of responsibility harmonizes that relation. We will also need to sort out some puzzles about how liberty, law, and obligation are to be reconciled within Hobbes's system. Those are the tasks of the current chapter, and they must be successfully completed if the reciprocity interpretation is to satisfy the desideratum laid down in Chapter 4, that an adequate interpretation of Hobbes's moral philosophy must explain precisely, and in a plausible way, how the Law of Nature directs us to submit to the rule of an unlimited sovereign power. There may seem to be a serious barrier to any interpretation's meeting that standard, for it is difficult to understand how the requirements of a set of substantive moral laws, as are the Laws of Nature, could possibly be squared with the requirements of an arbitrary, possibly immoral, set of civil laws instituted by sovereign authority. My solution to this problem is to show how on the reciprocity interpretation Hobbes can be seen to have developed a self-effacing natural law theory, rather than a legal positivism at odds with his Laws of Nature.

Strictly speaking, it is, of course, anachronistic to speak of Hobbes as a legal positivist. The earliest of positivism's central theoretical writings postdates *Leviathan* by more than a century. Nonetheless, many philosophers have been struck by the evident affinities between Hobbes's views on civil law and those of Austin and Bentham, Kelsen and Hart. It has seemed to them that Hobbes endorses something very like Legal Positivism's "social" and "separability" theses.[1] Indeed, Hobbes does seem to have held that what the civil law *is* depends solely upon its pedigree – on its having been commanded or otherwise propounded by the sovereign – without regard to the morality of its content. Or, to frame the similarity in terms closer to what Hobbes actually cares about, he seems to have believed that subjects' obligation to obey the sovereign's commands was not contingent upon any determination of the moral permissibility of the actions commanded.[2]

That Hobbes appears to have held something very like a positivist conception of civil law is startling in light of the fact that Hobbes insisted that he was offering a theory of political obligation grounded in the requirements of "eternal and immutable laws of nature", timeless and unalterable normative requirements, accessible by unaided

[1] See, for example, M. M. Goldsmith, "Hobbes on Law", in Tom Sorell, ed., *The Cambridge Companion to Hobbes* (Cambridge, 1996). Jules Coleman and Brian Leiter characterize the social thesis as holding that "what counts as law in any particular society is fundamentally a matter of social fact or convention", and the separability thesis as holding that "there is no necessary connection between law and morality". See their "Legal Positivism", in Dennis Patterson, ed., *A Companion to Philosophy of Law and Legal Theory* (Malden, 1999), 241–260; 241.

[2] Put in this way, his view's relation to positivism is murkier, because positivists may disagree over whether their social and separability theses have any implications for the requirement of obedience to law.

natural reason, to all mature persons in possession of that faculty. Hobbes presents his normative theory under the rubric of natural law. We understand what it is to espouse legal positivism as an *alternative* to natural law theory, but the prospect of a legal positivism *grounded in* natural law is puzzling, to say the least. On traditional understandings of natural law, natural law imposes moral constraints on the content of positive law, and may under certain conditions justify disobedience to civil laws that fail to respect those moral constraints. Yet Hobbes elects to employ this language of "natural law" to build his case for virtually absolute obedience to the civil law, no matter its content. What I shall argue in this chapter is that Hobbes successfully did what he seems to have so improbably intended to do, namely, to ground a *practical* "as if" legal positivism in a theory that gives ultimate normative authority to Laws of Nature conceived as independent of any human legislation. I am not here concerned to address the more familiar question of whether the Laws of Nature are "literally law".[3] My aim is to display the structure of Hobbes's normative theory by defending an attractive account of the relationship between civil laws and the norms he terms "the Laws of Nature". Because the account I shall offer does not depend upon answering the question of the literalness of these laws one way rather than another, there is no reason in principle why adversaries in debates about those issues might not accept the account I develop of the normative theory's structure.

I shall argue that the core commitment of natural law – the reciprocity theorem – imposes upon subjects a genuine and virtually indefeasible duty to comply with the sovereign's civil laws, even when the behaviors commanded violate the requirements of discrete particular Laws of Nature. Because we would *not* think it reasonable of everyone else to exercise their own *private judgment* as to which, if any, civil laws to obey (for such license is likely to undermine the arrangements that make it possible for us effectively to pursue our ends), the reciprocity theorem requires us also to refrain from holding those

[3] My argument will not suffice to show that Hobbes has a "genuine" natural law theory if that claim entails that the Laws of Nature are "literally laws" on Hobbes's account. I conclude that his Laws of Nature play a foundational role in his general theory that does not depend on their being literally laws, say, as commanded by a divine sovereign. Perhaps they are (at least in relation to some people), but nothing I say presupposes that.

laws hostage to our own private judgment of their merits. In short, a commitment to being *reasonable*, as is needed if we are to justify our actions to others, requires that we subordinate our *private* judgments to an agreed upon *public* judgment in all matters of common concern, and so defer to the laws even when we correctly believe them to command immoral actions. This is so because our paramount duty under the Law of Nature is to hold ourselves to the standards we think it reasonable to impose on others, and our shared basic interests preclude our allowing as reasonable that people should insist on their private judgments in contested matters of common concern. The natural law imposes a duty to treat positive law as authoritative, no matter its substantive merits.[4] Such a theory turns out to be in practical terms indistinguishable from legal positivism. Yet at the level of theory it runs afoul of a defining positivist commitment to the separation of law and morals, insisting as it does that no command it would be immoral to obey could count as a law. For lack of a better term (and because I rather like this one), I call this position a *self-effacing natural law theory*. So far as I know, this theory is original to Hobbes.

WHAT LAW IS

Hobbes is remarkably consistent across his writings in defining law. Law is the command to us of one whose commands we are under an obligation to obey. "[L]aw in general, is not counsel, but command; nor a command of any man to any man; but only of him, whose command is addressed to one formerly obliged to obey him",[5] and "the *civil laws* (that we may define them) are nothing else but *the commands of him who hath the chief authority in the city, for direction of the future actions of his citizens*".[6] Hobbes thinks of these commands as commands that one use particular rules to order one's actions. A rule is a law to a

4 This remains true despite the fact that there are some authoritative civil laws disobedience to which, while properly subjecting us to civil punishment, does not subject us to moral censure. These laws touch on the true liberties of subjects, and although Hobbes expresses doubt that a sovereign would make any such law (requiring, for instance, executing one's parent), if it did make such a law, that law would have authority, violations of it being criminal, though not shameful.

5 EW III, 251; T 184.

6 EW II, 77.

person only if that person has been commanded to use that rule for distinguishing right from wrong by someone whom he or she is already obligated to obey. Thus, "our obligation to civil obedience, by virtue whereof the civil laws are valid, is before all civil law".[7] The first thing to notice in this definition of a law is that the existence of law *presupposes* a prior obligation to treat someone's pronouncements as authoritative (as requiring obedience). This means that the question whether we ought to obey the law is idle, for only the command of one whom we ought to obey is a candidate for law. It also means that for Hobbes there can be no such deep separation of law and morals as marks the later positivist position.[8]

Laws do not only create specific obligations; they presuppose an important general obligation. If law depends upon a prior obligation to take someone's commands as authoritative, understanding the normativity of law will require understanding how that prior obligation is created. For Hobbes, all obligations-proper are self-imposed; they are in practical fact optional undertakings by an agent. Covenanting and contracting are paradigmatic modes of undertaking obligations; one can acquire an obligation to do something by promising others one will do that thing, or by consenting to do it, against appropriate background conditions. Thus one may acquire an obligation to take someone's commands as authoritative by agreeing to do so, provided one is under no prior obligation to obey someone else in the same matter (in which case the latter agreement is void).[9]

This is not to say that every duty is self-imposed, for not all duties are obligations. In particular, the Laws of Nature articulate a set of natural duties, whose claim on us does not depend on our having undertaken or covenanted to obey them. Natural duties, such as of gratitude, equity, and abstention from cruelty, are not self-imposed, and are thus not obligations. A careful reading of Hobbes's remark in chapter 14 of *Leviathan* allows us to see this distinction between obligations and duties. When a man has renounced or transferred his right to something, say, a house, he is obligated not to interfere

7 EW II, 200.

8 David Gauthier makes the same observation in his "Thomas Hobbes and Contractarian Theory of Law", *Canadian Journal of Philosophy*, Supp. 16 (1990): 5–34.

9 EW III, 127; T 98.

with others' enjoyment of the house. It is his duty not to renege on his transfer of right, that is, not "voluntarily to undo that, which from the beginning he had voluntarily done".[10] His duty, a natural duty articulated by the third Law of Nature, is to keep his covenant, and this duty does not depend for its normativity on his having covenanted (or otherwise voluntarily agreed) not to break his covenants. His obligation is to stand out of the way of others using the house, and the moral claim on him to do that does depend on his prior covenant or consent. Thus Hobbes can consistently maintain that there is no obligation on any man that does not arise from his own consent, while holding that the Laws of Nature bind us independent of our consent, are eternal and immutable, and always bind *in foro interno*. Hobbes's term 'obliged' covers both obligations and natural duties, as well as what objects, inanimate and animate both, are compelled by external forces to do.

Hobbes's position that law requires a prior obligation to take the law-giver's commands as authoritative entails that positive law depends on prior submission to political authority.[11] The first question, then, is: How is submission to political authority normatively dictated in Hobbes's system? How does Hobbes generate a universal (nonoptional) duty to undertake those political obligations that ground positive civil law? The second question is: How can that duty be so stringent as to require us to obey civil law even when it conflicts with the Laws of Nature themselves?

HOW NATURAL LAW DICTATES THAT SUBMISSION TO POLITICAL AUTHORITY THAT GROUNDS POSITIVE LAW

Hobbes blithely asserts throughout his writings that the Law of Nature dictates our submission to political authority, despite the fact that it is

[10] EW III, 119; T 93.

[11] This is true even in the case of God's laws, *qua* laws. Although all persons, animals, plants, and inanimate objects are subject to God's power, only those that acknowledge his existence and providence and have covenanted to have God for their sovereign are subjects in the kingdom of God, which began, Hobbes supposes, with Adam's submission to God's government, and was later "constituted by the votes of the people of Israel in peculiar manner; wherein they chose God for their king by covenant made with him" (EW III, 397; T 280).

not at all clear at any point in those writings how, exactly, he understands it to do so (or when it seems clear, that understanding is challenged by other passages). Let us consider several possible routes.

The Third Law of Nature

Fragments of text suggest that the third Law of Nature requiring the keeping of faith – that men perform their covenants made – is what directs us to obey all of the sovereign's commands, even when they conflict with other Laws of Nature. There is no doubt that Hobbes takes consent by covenant or promise to be a mode of undertaking a political obligation. But we are searching not for a *mode* of undertaking political obligations, but rather a Law of Nature that *requires us to undertake* political obligations, by whatever mode. The Law of Nature requiring that covenants be kept won't bind us to obey a state unless and until we have covenanted to do so, and our question is one of how the Law of Nature requires us to make that covenant. The third Law of Nature is of no help here.

Of course, *once* people have, for whatever reason, promised their obedience to a sovereign, the third Law of Nature will enjoy a privileged position among the Laws of Nature, as providing the clearest and most direct account of why those laws forbid disobedience. Hobbes elevates it in just such circumstances, as we can see in his answer to the question "What commandments are those that God hath given us?": "The laws of God therefore are none but the Laws of Nature, whereof the principal is, that we should not violate our faith, that is, a commandment to obey our civil sovereigns, which we constituted over us by mutual pact one with another".[12]

Once we've promised obedience, the third Law of Nature normatively underwrites our obligation of obedience. So if we could suppose that everyone living within any political society actually had previously consented to be obedient to its government, the third Law of Nature would, it seems, suffice to make political obligation mandatory. But such a supposition will be clearly incorrect unless we count mere nonemigration, nonresistance, acceptance of benefits, or other such behaviors as forms of tacit consent understood as binding consent, a

[12] EW III, 587; T 404. This remark does not appear in his Latin *Leviathan*.

liberalization of the notion of consent that threatens to undermine whatever normative appeal consent has as a justification for political obligation. While it appears that Hobbes was willing to count subjects' failure to refuse explicitly the benefit of protection provided by the sovereign as their having given consent, the problems that attend such a view[13] make it desirable not to ascribe to Hobbes an account of political obligation that depends upon that sort of unwitting "consent". This is particularly so because Hobbes is offering an absolutist theory, which gives the sovereign a blank check on which the citizenry may not stop payment. To assume that by their mere inaction subjects have consented to such an extreme subjection strains credibility.[14] Nonetheless, although Hobbes cannot ground the duty to submit to government on the Law of Nature requiring that covenants be kept, that law will reinforce the obligations of those who have taken oaths, and it is for this reason that Hobbes maintains that there is some security for subjects in the oaths that princes take to secure the good of the people.

The Fundamental Law of Nature

Perhaps it is not surprising that the third Law of Nature turns out not to enjoy any sort of normative priority within the Laws of Nature, for why would one think that keeping covenants matters more, morally speaking, than avoiding cruelty, treating others fairly, submitting disputes to impartial arbitration, or accommodating the essential needs of others, as further Laws of Nature require? These other norms seem just as important to establishing and maintaining decent human communities, or, as Hobbes puts it, "human society and the civil life of the present world".[15] However, the "first and fundamental" Law of

[13] See, for example, David Hume, 'Of the Original Contract' (1748), and A. John Simmons, *On the Edge of Anarchy* (Princeton, NJ, 1993).

[14] On the flip side of the coin, if we attribute to Hobbes the position that only those who have consented to obey are politically obligated, those who unreasonably refuse their consent (say, holding out for better than equal terms) will be morally blameless, contrary to the plausible judgment that people ought to do their part in establishing or maintaining fair and mutually beneficial social arrangements. For instance, Rawls maintains that there is a natural duty of justice to cooperate in establishing just institutions. See his *A Theory of Justice* (1971), sections 19 and 52.

[15] EW II, 152.

Nature, which is to seek peace when it can be had, and confederates in war when it cannot, may seem privileged.[16] Hobbes often notes that other Laws of Nature spell out the means of seeking peace, and can in this sense be derived from the first and fundamental Law of Nature. It is plausible that subjection to government might be instrumental to achieving peace. So the first Law of Nature is the natural source to tap for a duty to undertake an obligation of civil obedience. We are to submit to political authority because that is what peace requires, and the fundamental Law of Nature directs us to do what peace requires.

Unfortunately for this suggestion, it is not clear, at least under desire- or duty-based interpretations, that the first Law of Nature does unequivocally direct us to do what peace requires. Hobbes surmises that there is not "any that esteems a war of all against all... to be good for him. And so it happens, that through fear of each other we think it fit to rid ourselves of this condition, and to get some fellows; that if there needs must be war, it may not yet be against all men, or without some helps".[17]

The impetus here is to pursue self-defense, one way or another. That does not yet direct us to seek peace, or even to prefer peace-seeking to other strategies for gaining the confederates we need to defend ourselves. Some confederates come naturally, for instance, one's family members, friends, and like-thinking neighbors.[18] Even supposing it could be shown that *if* peace could be had it would be preferable to building defensive coalitions, it is we who are to judge whether peace can be had, and if so, to pursue it. Because confederates may be acquired by force in conquest or vanquishing of an aggressor, by charm or deception (which Hobbes terms "wiles"), and

[16] *De Cive*: "*that peace is to be sought after, where it may be found; and where not, there to provide ourselves for helps of war*" (EW II, 16); *Elements:* "to seek after peace, as far forth as there is hope to attain the same; and strengthen himself with all the help he can procure, for his own defence against those, from whom such peace cannot be obtained" (EW IV, 86); *Leviathan:* "*that every man, ought to endeavour peace, as far as he has hope of obtaining it; and when he cannot obtain it, that he may seek, and use, all helps, and advantages of war*" (EW III, 117; T 91); *Elements:* "[N]ever to give *peace*... is against the general definition of the law of nature" (EW IV, 100).

[17] EW II, 12.

[18] In chapter 12 of *Leviathan*, Hobbes makes clear that the seeds of natural religion will, even in the state of nature, lead to the development of groups of like-thinking followers of persons who present themselves as spiritual leaders.

even by just breeding and rearing children,[19] it is plausible that many persons in a state of nature will find it easiest, most natural, and most rational to seek confederates rather than breech the vicissitudes and vulnerabilities of peace-making.[20] If that is true, then one has no reason to be confident that peace *can* be had. How shall we think peace can be had when we see that others find it most rational to build war coalitions? And that still others prefer the glory they expect to enjoy from their conquests to whatever comforts peace might bring? The first clause of the first Law of Nature requires only that we seek peace when we believe it can be had. If we don't believe it can be had, we will faithfully follow the first and fundamental Law of Nature by building coalitions for war, in accordance with its second clause. The difficulty, then, is that the first Law of Nature cannot ground any requirement to submit to government and civil laws unless and until we can establish that one ought to seek peace *rather than* confederates in war. It is a well-known and long-standing worry among commentators that nothing Hobbes says about the rational pursuit of self-defense conclusively establishes this. Notice too that most of the further Laws of Nature, for example, the third requiring keeping of faith, will further *both* peace efforts and the building of war-time confederacies, and so are compatible with either clause of the first and fundamental Law of Nature. Just as there must be honor even among thieves if they are to

[19] In *De Cive* Hobbes notes that "a son cannot be understood to be at any time in the state of nature, as being under the power and command of them to whom he owes his protection as soon as ever he is born, namely, either his father's or his mother's, or him that nourished him" (EW II, 10n). This suggests that the state of nature will contain families, clans, and extended households, as well as confederations of religious believers (see chapter 12 of *Leviathan*), whose numbers may be augmented by force or wiles into formidable confederations.

[20] I am reminded of an early scene in *Braveheart*, a fictional recounting of the life of William Wallace, in which a meeting organized ostensibly for the purpose of settling a peace between the Scots and the English provides the occasion for an efficient slaughter of the Scottish resistance. We may suppose that Hobbes knew enough Machiavelli to have appreciated this possibility. In *Leviathan* he writes, "there is no way for any man to secure himself, so reasonable, as anticipation; that is, by force, or wiles, to master the persons of all men he can, so long, till he see no other power great enough to endanger him: and this is no more than his own conservation requireth, and is generally allowed" (EW III, 111; T 87). Some commentators, including Gregory Kavka, have discussed the rationality of building defensive coalitions, and wondered whether these couldn't suffice for our security without subjecting ourselves to a state. See Kavka, *Hobbesian Moral and Political Theory* (Princeton, NJ, 1986), especially chapter 4.

work as a group,[21] so must war-time confederates keep their mutual covenants, be tractable, fair, modest, and the rest if they are to hold their confederacy together. These are as much virtues for those bent on conquest or defense as those seeking to make peace.

None of this is meant to suggest that Hobbes doesn't intend us to see submission to political authority as entailed by the requirement to seek peace; undoubtedly he does. What is not clear is how the fundamental Law of Nature can successfully entail submission to political authority, for it does not categorically require peace-seeking. I'll propose a solution to this difficulty shortly.

The Summary Formulation of the Laws of Nature

Another possible way of forging the needed connection, is by appealing to the "sum of the Laws of Nature", to wit, "*Do not that to another, which thou wouldest not have done to thyself* ".[22] "The laws of nature therefore need not any publishing, nor proclamation", Hobbes tells us, "as being contained in this one sentence, approved by all the world, *Do not that to another, which thou thinkest unreasonable to be done by another to thyself*".[23] This summary formulation of the Laws of Nature is familiar to us as the reciprocity theorem. We could appeal to the reciprocity theorem to argue that if we want others to submit themselves to political authority (as we must, if we are to avoid the incommodities of a state of nature), we must do so as well. This sort of reasoning could ground a natural law duty to submit to political authority.[24]

Further, it could ground a duty to treat positive law as having final authority. If we want others to defer to the judgment of an authoritative arbiter in the matter of how the Laws of Nature are to be understood and applied (as we will, if we value the maintenance of peace), then the Law of Nature directs us to ourselves accept that arbiter's judgment

[21] I am reminded of the strict rules of fidelity and gratitude within Mafia families as depicted in Mario Puzo's *The Godfather.*

[22] EW III, 144; T 109.

[23] EW III, 258; T 188.

[24] This sort of reasoning was entirely familiar to both Hobbes and his readers from canonical works in the natural law tradition. George Shelton takes care to trace the history within natural law theorizing of the "negative" formulation of the Golden Rule as the primary content of natural law in his *Morality and Sovereignty in the Philosophy of Hobbes* (1992).

as authoritative. Put more strongly, because we cannot rationally want others in our society to use their own *private judgment* in interpreting and judging what the Laws of Nature require, we ought not to do so either.

One interesting feature of the reciprocity theorem or summary formulation of the Laws of Nature is that it introduces a distinction between levels of description of our actions. Although some particular Law of Nature might actually conflict with our sovereign's command, the reciprocity theorem directs us not to concern ourselves with that, but rather to attend to the question of whose judgment in such matters we would think it reasonable to be bound to take as authoritative, and to conform to the dictates of that judgment ourselves. We are to do x, not under the description of "doing x", but rather under the description of "deferring to A's judgment as to whether or not x is to be done". Compelling this shift in which level of description of our actions is to be given priority is the unique contribution of the reciprocity theorem. There is reason to think this recasting of the question is what submission to civil authority requires, and that the reciprocity theorem is the only Law of Nature that can impose a duty to adopt that standpoint.

We have some indirect evidence that Hobbes gives the reciprocity theorem priority over other more specific Laws of Nature. For instance, he argues for many of his discrete Laws of Nature by tying them to the summary formulation, whereas he does not use any other of the particular Laws of Nature to provide a unified rationale, excepting the portion of the fundamental law that tells us to seek peace when it may be had. Hobbes explicitly *identifies* the reciprocity theorem with the second Law of Nature's requirement that a man "*be contented with so much liberty against other men, as he would allow other men against himself*", saying that this is "that law of all men, *quod tibi fieri non vis, alteri ne feceris*".[25] The reciprocity theorem is closely related to Hobbes's ninth and tenth laws. Hobbes stipulates as his tenth law that "*at the entrance into conditions of peace, no man require to reserve to himself any right, which he is not content should be reserved to every one of the rest*",[26] and this certainly implies that if we are not willing that others should reserve their right of private judgment concerning interpretation of the Laws of Nature,

[25] EW III, 118; T 92; i.e., do not do to others what you do not want done to yourself.
[26] EW III, 141; T 107.

then we may not do so either. The reason for this law is that if, as Hobbes writes, "men require for themselves, that which they would not have to be granted to others, they do contrary to the precedent law, that commandeth the acknowledgment of natural equality, and therefore also against the law of nature".[27] The precedent law, against pride, stipulates "*that every man acknowledge another for his equal by nature*".[28] This implies that we must admit the judgment of others as having as great a claim on the common reason as our own, and it is precisely this admission of natural equality that makes it imperative that we submit to arbitration, covenanting, as the sixteenth Law of Nature directs us to, "mutually to stand to the sentence of another".[29] The reciprocity theorem is thus clearly linked to the sixteenth law as well, and to the other laws involving adjudication, including the seventeenth, eighteenth, and nineteenth. We can easily see then how RT captures a *core notion* uniting many discrete Laws of Nature.

By way of more direct evidence, Hobbes seems content to have this summary formulation given preference over any of the more particular laws. In distinguishing the Laws of Nature from the civil law, Hobbes writes that the Laws of Nature

> need not any publishing nor proclamation; as being contained in this one sentence, approved by all the world, *Do not that to another, which thou thinkest unreasonable to be done by another to thyself.*[30]

No man can plead ignorance of the Laws of Nature because

> they have been contracted into one easy sum, intelligible even to the meanest capacity; and that is, *Do not that to another, which thou wouldest not have done to thyself;*[31]

and

> [i]gnorance of the law of nature excuseth no man; because every man that hath attained to the use of reason, is supposed to know, he ought not to do to another, what he would not have done to himself.[32]

[27] Ibid.
[28] Ibid.
[29] EW III, 143; T 109.
[30] EW III, 258; T 188.
[31] EW III, 144; T 109.
[32] EW III, 279; T 202. As I earlier mentioned, Hobbes goes on to illustrate this point in a very interesting way, arguing that if a person goes to a foreign land and attempts

Hobbes offers the reciprocity theorem as the essence of the Law of Nature, and suggests as a means of operationalizing its requirements that we imaginatively change places with those who would be on the receiving end of the actions we are proposing.[33] If one need know only the reciprocity theorem in order to count as knowing the Laws of Nature, while Hobbes never asserts this of any other of the discrete Laws of Nature, then we may reasonably conclude that Hobbes is willing for this summary formulation to have priority over any other.

So privileged is the reciprocity theorem that Hobbes at times identifies it with reason itself, presumably because it can be directly derived, as we saw in the previous chapter, from Hobbes's definition of man as rational. Recall his remark in *De Homine* that "God himself, *because He hath made men rational*, hath enjoined the following law on them, and inscribed it in all hearts: that no one should do unto another that which he would consider inequitable for the other to do unto him".[34] And observe how Hobbes goes on to use the reciprocity theorem to argue directly for a duty of political obedience. He continues:

> In this precept are contained both universal justice and civil obedience. For who would not judge it inequitable, if he were constituted by the people with the highest sovereignty in the state, in order to rule and to issue laws, for his laws to be spurned, or his authority overlooked, not to mention disputed, by any subject whatsoever? Therefore, if, when you were a king, you judged this

to persuade the people he finds there to receive a new religion, "he commits a crime, and may be justly punished for the same,...because he does that which he would not approve in another, namely, that coming from hence, he should endeavour to alter the religion there" (EW III, 280). Notice that the wrongness of his action does not depend upon its violating any covenant. Such action might undermine peace, and would thus violate the first Law of Nature as well as the reciprocity theorem, which makes it all the more striking that Hobbes chooses to argue in terms of reciprocity rather than the first Law of Nature.

33 This is sometimes called the "shoehorn maneuver" – putting oneself in the place of the other. Hobbes writes that for a person to learn how to apply the LAW OF NATURE "he has no more to do...but, when weighing the actions of other men with his own, they seem too heavy, to put them into the other part of the balance, and his own into their place, that his own passions, and self-love, may add nothing to the weight; and then there is none of these laws of nature that will not appear unto him very reasonable" (EW III, 144–145; T 110).

34 Bernard Gert, ed., *Man and Citizen: Thomas Hobbes* (Indianapolis, 1991), 73, emphasis added.

to be inequitable, would you not have, in law, a most certain rule for your actions?[35]

His willingness in this (unappealing) argument to apply the reciprocity theorem directly, without the mediation of other Laws of Nature, such as those requiring covenant-keeping or peace-seeking, shows that he regarded that theorem as sufficient for establishing political obligation. It also suggests that he was thinking about political obligation in terms of reciprocity. Indeed, he plainly states that "in this precept" (the reciprocity theorem) is "contained…civil obedience". The argument is interesting in another way as well; it draws our attention to the moralized or normative nature of the judgment being made when applying the reciprocity theorem. We are not to consider our own mere preferences – how we would not "want" or "like" to be treated – but rather what sort of treatment we would judge "inequitable", or in his earlier rendering of the reciprocity theorem, "unreasonable", or generally blameworthy. This suggests a greater compatibility between the reciprocity theorem and the common good interpretation of the unifying function of the Laws of Nature for which I argued in Chapter 3, than between the reciprocity theorem and the self-interest interpretation of the function of those laws.

A further advantage of the reciprocity theorem is that by using it we can make the first Law of Nature's requirement that we seek confederates in war only when peace cannot be had *operate as a stringent requirement* to seek peace with willing others. We would think it quite unreasonable of others to persist in providing themselves for war with us when we are willing to make peace with them – their doing so imposes an unnecessary harm on us in pursuit of an end of theirs that (because we are willing to make peace) they can satisfy just as well or better by other less damaging means. Because the reciprocity theorem dictates that we not treat others in ways we would think it unreasonable for them to treat us, it strictly follows that we are to be willing to make peace on equal terms when others are willing. The reciprocity theorem thus singles out pursuing peace as the favored clause of the first Law of Nature, by importing a reciprocity constraint on which of the rational strategies we are to pursue. Once

[35] Ibid.

that is done, the other laws can be seen as unified by their relation to peace as well as to the reciprocity theorem's own requirement of not acting in ways one would fault others for acting. In this way the reciprocity theorem creates *coherence* among all of Hobbes's Laws of Nature, which explains why Hobbes calls it their "core" or "sum".

An even greater advantage of the reciprocity theorem, noted in Chapter 1, is that it makes sense of Hobbes's repeated insistence that the Law of Nature imposes on sovereigns a duty to pursue *salus populi*, the good of their subjects. This requirement must be quite mysterious by the account offered by the third Law of Nature, because sovereigns have *not* covenanted with subjects to promote the public good;[36] the second Law of Nature, understood as a command to lay down one's right to all things, fares no better, because the sovereign lays down none of his initial rights, but retains them all intact. One might torture out of the first Law of Nature a roundabout argument that unless he pursues the public good the sovereign is failing to seek peace by tempting his subjects to rebel. But this argument is normatively weak because it depends upon assuming that subjects will do what the Laws of Nature give them no right to do, and Hobbes has explicitly argued that "pretense of right" is a necessary condition for rebellion, even the discontented being unwilling to rebel unless they see themselves as having just cause. The reciprocity theorem accounts for the sovereign's duty by pointing out that were he in the subjects' place, he would think it unreasonable for his sovereign to indulge himself without care for the end subjects had in submitting to his rule in the first place. Were the sovereign a subject, he would find such behavior blameworthy as being inequitable, ungrateful, and the like. Because he would not approve it in another, the reciprocity theorem condemns it. This argument is just the symmetric variant of what I earlier called the unappealing argument: Because subjects would judge disobedience blameworthy were they in the sovereign's place, they must obey; and conversely, because sovereigns would judge rule that is publicly harmful to be blameworthy were they in the subjects' place, they must rule for the public good. The reciprocity theorem provides the most

[36] Even in the case of sovereignty by acquisition (conquest), the sovereign has covenanted no farther than to grant the vanquished their lives on condition of their submission.

plausible account of how the Law of Nature requires that sovereigns pursue the good of their subjects, as Hobbes insisted it does.

How does the reciprocity theorem direct us to submit, not just to some sort of political authority, but to an absolute sovereign, a sovereign whose civil laws trump the requirements of natural law? What is striking about the reciprocity theorem is that it calls us to submit to impartial and equitable arbitration of disputes. We would think it unreasonable of others to refuse to agree to impartial arbitration of their dispute with us when we are willing to do so (considering the horrible consequences for all of us and the effective exercise of our agency of failing to resolve our disputes), so we must likewise be willing to submit to such arbitration when they are willing. Hobbes explicitly emphasizes this core idea of the Law of Nature when he speaks of the "laws of nature, the sum whereof consisteth in forbidding us to be our own judges".[37] Willingness to submit to arbitration of disputes is closely tied to the willingness not to engage in special pleading for ourselves required by the reciprocity theorem. If we must allow our adversaries the same status we accord ourselves, conflicts between us sufficiently serious that we see the need to resolve them will demand that we submit to authoritative arbitration. Such submission is thus an implication of the reciprocity theorem. Because the sovereign is defined by Hobbes to be the authoritative arbiter of disputes (with the associated powers required for arbitration to effectively settle disputes), submission to the sovereign is also an implication of the reciprocity theorem, on Hobbes's view.

SOVEREIGN AS UNIVERSAL AUTHORITATIVE ARBITER

Now, if this is to be the route by which our duty to submit to political authority is established by the Law of Nature, our conception of the essential nature of that authority needs revising. Traditionally, the Hobbesian sovereign has been thought of as a mechanism for making and enforcing laws. But on our account, the sovereign's essential function is as supreme judge. That is to say, the essential function of sovereignty is authoritative adjudication of disputes, rather than legislation or execution of existing laws; it is to replace the cacophony

[37] EW II, 107–108.

of clashing private judgments with a uniform public judgment. Of course, Hobbes held that this supremacy in judging carries all of the other essential functions of government with it (for otherwise it would be vain), so the *practical* effect of our account is indistinguishable from standard accounts. But our understanding of political obligation remains quite different. If we understand the sovereign to be the authoritative arbiter of *all* disputes, it follows that she may legitimately settle disputes as to *what the law – including natural law – is*, how it is properly interpreted, whether a particular question falls under any existing law, whether she has or has not rightly judged the question at hand, whether she has or has not exceeded its legitimate authority, and the like. Absolutism falls out of this grant of authority to judge *all* disputes.

Once we see this, the *self-effacing* character of Hobbes's natural law theory is guaranteed. There is no sense to be given to the idea that we should disobey the sovereign's declarations of positive law on the ground that in our judgment they conflict with the natural law. Natural law commits us to regarding the judgment of the sovereign as authoritatively and properly adjudicating *all* disputes, including those over what does or does not conflict with natural law. If this is what the Law of Nature requires, there is no legitimate position or perspective from which we can criticize or resist the sovereign's decisions (a fact that also straightforwardly yields the sovereign's absolute authority). It would thus seem that Hobbes's position contains a strongly positivistic element. Natural law has supreme authority; but it directs us, first and foremost, to act as if legal positivism were true. Natural law is thus self-effacing.[38]

[38] Having granted that natural law is self-effacing, we might wonder whether its self-effacing character could have been established more directly by noting Hobbes's insistence that "[t]he law of nature, and the civil law, contain each other, and are of equal extent" (EW III, 253; T 185). Hobbes assumes that the Law of Nature "is a part of the civil law in all commonwealths of the world", and again asserts that "reciprocally also, the civil law is a part of the dictates of nature". I find these remarks to raise more questions than they answer. How are we to understand the idea that these types of law are of "equal extent"? That cannot mean that the Law of Nature and the civil law are *identical*, for then Hobbes's insistence that the Law of Nature is part of all systems of civil law would imply that all systems of civil law are identical, a patent falsehood. Nor can Hobbes have meant to be saying that the elements of natural and civil law are *equinumerous*, because as part to whole, the Law of Nature has many fewer elements than any commonwealth's civil law; the dictates

TEXTUAL SUPPORT FOR THE SELF-EFFACING INTERPRETATION OF HOBBES'S NATURAL LAWS

Hobbes's text offers strong indirect evidence that he intended to advocate the sort of self-effacing natural law theory I have been describing. From the point of view of conscientious agents, a precondition of buying into such a theory is adequate assurance that one will not fail in executing one's responsibilities by deferring to the sovereign's judgment as to how one should behave. For if we were properly accountable for the fulfilling of the particular requirements of some norms other than civil law, we would risk failing to fulfill those responsibilities when abiding by the requirements of civil law. Because people do generally care about fulfilling their responsibilities – presumably Hobbes's religious audience cared very much about that – Hobbes's ordering of legal imperatives may not suffice to motivate compliance with civil law unless there is a corresponding *hierarchy of responsibility*, or moral liability, as it were. Hobbes argues explicitly for just such a hierarchy of responsibility, and that hierarchy reveals that the Law of Nature is self-effacing. Hobbes establishes this hierarchy in the first instance for civil law in relation to divine positive law, but then indicates that this hierarchy

of the two could be equinumerous only if both were conceived as *infinite* in number (which would indeed allow a one-one mapping of the Law of Nature onto the civil laws), but this is a conception of these laws both highly implausible in itself and unsupported by Hobbes's texts. If the Law of Nature and the civil law are neither identical nor equinumerous, in what sense are they of "equal extent"?

Hobbes's remark can be sensibly interpreted as asserting that the civil law contains the natural law as an element, and that *natural law requires submission to civil law.* But this is bare assertion; far from counting as an argument for the self-effacing character of natural law, it stands in need of an argument for support. Civil law may provide the authoritative interpretation of natural law, but that would show natural law to be self-effacing only if it is natural law that requires us to submit to civil law. How then is it that natural law requires submission to civil law? That is the question we have been addressing, and I've offered the reciprocity theorem as the most attractive answer to that question. If this answer is correct, natural law turns out, perhaps quite unexpectedly, to be self-effacing because *it* directs submission to a civil law that will authoritatively interpret it. Until we have some such answer, we cannot know the relation of natural to civil law and so cannot establish the self-effacing character of natural law. Arguably, the best explanation of Hobbes's elliptical remark in chapter 26 of *Leviathan* is that he believes himself already to have demonstrated in chapters 14 and 15 that the natural law is self-effacing because it requires submission to an authoritative arbiter of what norms are laws and of what those laws require. Thus, Hobbes's later assertion presupposes, and cannot replace, the explanation of that relation we have been investigating.

holds for natural law as well. I will lay out his argument with respect to divine positive law, then show how he extends it to cover the case of interest to us, namely natural law.

Consider Hobbes's insistence that

> [A] Christian, holding firmly in his heart the faith of Christ, hath the same liberty which the prophet Elisha allowed to Naaman the Syrian ... that whatsoever a subject, as Naaman was, is compelled to do in obedience to his sovereign, and doth it not in order to his own mind, but in order to the laws of his country, that action is not his, but his sovereign's; nor is it he that in this case denieth Christ before men, but his governor, and the law of his country.[39]

Here Hobbes asserts that subjects are not to be held responsible for the sovereign's commands or their actions in obedience to them. Presumably God, who desires the preservation and flourishing of his human creation, directs men (via his Laws of Nature and revealed positive laws) to submit themselves to a sovereign; once they have chosen a sovereign, their first duty to God is to obey that sovereign in all that he should command. God lays down this system because it better conduces to men's well-being than one in which they exercise their private judgments about how to act. So subjects are accountable to God for their obedience to the sovereign. Sovereigns, in contrast, are accountable to God for the content of their commands, and should they command subjects to do something wrong, God will hold them responsible for the resulting actions.

We find textual evidence that Hobbes intends a hierarchy of responsibility in this passage:

> [A Christian king] cannot oblige men to believe; though as a civil sovereign he may make laws suitable to his doctrine, which may oblige men to certain actions, and sometimes to such as they would not otherwise do, and which he ought not to command; and yet when they are commanded, they are laws; and the external actions done in obedience to them, without the inward approbation, are the actions of the sovereign, and not of the subject, which is in that case but as an instrument, without any motion of his own at all; because God hath commanded to obey them.[40]

[39] EW III, 493–494; T 344.
[40] EW III, 564; T 389.

Once subjects bind themselves to obey a sovereign, the sovereign becomes the author of its commands, and the obedient (if unwilling) subject a mere actor. Reading 'subject' for 'actor' and 'sovereign' for 'author', we see a categorical statement of Hobbes's hierarchical picture of responsibility in his systematic discussion of authorization in chapter 16 of *Leviathan:*

> When the [subject] doth anything against the law of nature by command of the [sovereign], if he be obliged by former covenant to obey him, not he, but the [sovereign] breaketh the law of nature; for though the action be against the law of nature; yet it is not his: but contrarily, to refuse to do it, is against the law of nature, that forbiddeth breach of covenant.[41]

The substitution of 'subject' for 'actor' and 'sovereign' for 'author' is licensed not only by Hobbes's text,[42] but also by the logic of this passage: because sovereigns have made no covenant to obey anyone, the referent of "he" (which stands in for "actor") in "if he be obliged by former covenant to obey him" can only be the subject. And since only sovereigns command, "by the command of the author" cannot mean by command of the subject.[43] This squares with Hobbes's position in *De Homine* that "If someone sins at another's command, both sin, since neither did right; *unless*, by chance, the *state* commanded it to be done, *so that the actor ought not to refuse*".[44]

[41] EW III, 149; T 113.

[42] In chapter 27 of *Leviathan*, Hobbes identifies the sovereign as the author of actions done in obedience to his commands: "when that man, or assembly, that hath the sovereign power, commandeth a man to do that which is contrary to a former law, the doing of it is totally excused: for he ought not to condemn it himself, because he is the author; and what cannot be justly condemned by the sovereign, cannot justly be punished by any other". Hobbes is relying on the principle that "no man ought to accuse his own fact in another, that is but his instrument" (EW III, 289; T 209).

[43] The way Hobbes revises the quoted passage in his Latin *Leviathan* makes it even clearer that the subject must be the actor in this case. Hobbes eliminates the end of the quote, "not his; but contrarily, to refuse to do it is against the law of nature that forbiddeth breach of covenant" and replaces it with "not the actor's but the author's; because the actor would have violated the law if he had not done it, since he had covenanted to do it". Because sovereigns are no party to any covenant, whereas subjects establish the sovereign by covenant with one another, only the subject could be the author who "had covenanted to do it"; Curley, "Introduction to Hobbes's *Leviathan*", *Leviathan* with selected variants from the Latin edition of 1668, ed. E. Curley (Indianapolis, 1994), 102.

[44] Gert, *Man and Citizen*, 84, emphasis added.

That the subject is not author of actions commanded by his sovereign in violation of natural law is clearly Hobbes's position, but we might wonder how this can be consistent with his view in chapters 17 and 18 of *Leviathan* that subjects "own and authorize" the actions of their sovereigns. Authorization must be *transitive:* if subjects authorize their sovereign to defend them, and their sovereign commands an action as a means to their defense that is unjust, iniquitous, or otherwise contrary to the Laws of Nature, then surely the subjects must have authorized that unjust or iniquitous action.[45] So if Hobbes wishes also to hold, as we have shown him to, that iniquitous actions are the sole responsibility of the sovereign, his theory will be internally inconsistent.

This inconsistency turns out to be merely apparent for the simple reason that subjects *cannot* authorize the sovereign to violate the Laws of Nature because *they have themselves no right* to violate the Laws of Nature: "they that vow anything contrary to any law of nature, vow in vain; as being a thing unjust to pay such vow".[46] Subjects cannot authorize the sovereign to act iniquitously, "[f]or unless he that is the author hath the right of acting himself, the actor hath no authority to act".[47] Thus when the sovereign requires actions that violate natural law, those violations are his own because they *could not have been* authorized by subjects. The transitivity of authorization thus in no way impugns Hobbes's hierarchy of responsibility.

The precise sense then in which the sovereign's command is to be thought of as the subjects' own lies in Hobbes's distinction between public and private conscience:

For the conscience being nothing else but a man's settled judgment and opinion, when he hath once transferred his right of judging to another, that which shall be commanded, is no less his judgment, than [it is] the judgment of that other. So that in obedience to laws, a man doth still according to his own conscience, *but not his private conscience.* And whatsoever is done contrary

45 This clearly correct formulation of the problem belongs to A. P. Martinich, who called my attention to the difficulty posed by the transitivity of authorization. My discussion here elaborates that offered in my "Coercion, Ideology, and Education in Hobbes's *Leviathan*", in Andrews Reath, Barbara Herman, and Christine Korsgaard, eds., *Reclaiming the History of Ethics* (Cambridge, 1997).

46 EW III, 126; T 97.

47 Gert, *Man and Citizen*, 84.

to private conscience, is then a sin, when the laws have left him to his own liberty, *and never else*.[48]

Action against one's private conscience is blameworthy only when one's authorized public conscience (the sovereign) has issued no command concerning that action. To follow a sovereign command I believe to be wrong is no sin, because of the hierarchy of responsibility just explained; to do what I believe wrong absent any sovereign command to do so is indeed wrong, and my own responsibility. Thus it makes sense to say that my sovereign's wrongful command both is and isn't mine, as it both accords with my public conscience and fails to accord with my private conscience. Hobbes's view here is no more inconsistent than our own view that the will of the majority is (in one sense) our will even though we willed (in another sense, by our vote for the minority position) a defeated course. Hobbes holds this position even when it comes to erroneous commands about how to worship God, "For though this kind of commands may be sometimes contrary to right reason, and therefore sins in them who command them; yet are they not against right reason, nor sins in subjects; whose right reason, in points of controversy, is that which submits itself to the reason of the city".[49]

We see then that Hobbes establishes a hierarchical structure of responsibility.[50] We can think of such a system on the model of parents' directives to their young children. Parents, who recognize that their children's own judgment will be inadequate to keep them from harming themselves and each other, direct them first and foremost to obey a responsible (although, of course, fallible) adult, their babysitter, for example. The children are responsible for obeying the babysitter, and are to be faulted for failing to do so; but the babysitter is responsible

[48] EW IV, 186–187, emphasis added. This invites fear that Hobbes was advocating the "I-was-only-following-orders defense", one that we have come to find morally repugnant. Hobbes might try to defend against this charge by noting that given the importance for peace of submission to authoritative arbitration, and considering the fact that no one has a right to violate natural law (and that God will settle accounts in the end), his hierarchy of moral liability is approved by the best theory of how to secure the interests of mankind. This worry, raised by Martinich, is a serious one that merits a more detailed response than the one I've just sketched on Hobbes's behalf.

[49] EW II, 224.

[50] Further evidence is provided in EW V, 177–178.

for the content of his directives and is to be faulted for issuing a wrongful directive. The alternative of letting the children decide whether the babysitter is to be obeyed (and hence how to act) is rejected as more dangerous than subjecting them to his authority, even though he is fallible.[51]

This textual evidence, along with Hobbes's extensive *Leviathan* discussion of the Scriptural evidence that God requires men first and foremost to obey their princes,[52] shows that Hobbes treated divine positive law (i.e., Scriptural law) as self-effacing, directing subjects to obey their sovereign's commands even when those commands run contrary to the doctrines or practices laid down by divine positive law. He justifies and motivates the required obedience to wrongful commands by developing the idea of a hierarchy of responsibility, or of moral liability; this is necessary if people are to be able to accept a self-effacing theory of divine positive law.

This evidence does not by itself establish that Hobbes thought natural law works in the same way as divine positive law, and so does not by itself establish that natural law is likewise self-effacing. Still, three considerations make it much more likely than not that Hobbes intended to be offering a similarly self-effacing natural law theory. First, Hobbes insisted on the compatibility of natural with divine positive laws, that "there is no law of natural reason, that can be against the law divine",[53] and so that "[a]s the law of nature is all of it divine, so the law of Christ by conversion... is all of it also... the

[51] Here the babysitting analogy can even support Hobbes's insistence that subjects retain the right to resist force used against them, since parents will of course not require that children passively submit to life-threatening abuse by their babysitter. There is textual evidence that Hobbes does think even adult persons need such paternalistic intervention, for example, "For the use of laws...is not to bind the people from all voluntary actions; but to direct and keep them in such a motion, as not to hurt themselves by their own impetuous desires, rashness or indiscretion; as hedges are set, not to stop travellers, but to keep them in their way" (EW III, 335; T 239–240). That people need guidance in avoiding harm justifies God's adoption of the hierarchical authority structure Hobbes describes. But we need not assume this paternalistic stance in order to make sense of Hobbes's position that we ought to submit to authoritative impartial arbitration of disputes; that is a requirement of reciprocity or fairness in the face of disagreement and does not depend on any attribution of childlike incompetence.

[52] For example, EW III, 586–587; T 404.

[53] EW IV, 116.

doctrine of nature".[54] Second, he consistently seeks to "confirm" the Laws of Nature out of laws in Scripture by mapping them one for one onto each other.[55] And third, there is the wealth of direct textual evidence we have already surveyed that Hobbes approved a hierarchy of responsibility in the case of natural law.

Interestingly, the fact that Hobbes insists upon mapping divine positive law onto natural law further enhances the case for taking the reciprocity theorem as the privileged route by which the Law of Nature directs submission to a civil law that will then be authoritative in deciding controversies about the interpretation of natural law. Divine positive law directs submission to civil law. Hobbes maps the core principles of divine positive law onto the reciprocity theorem. So the reciprocity theorem must direct submission to civil law. This answers our initial question of how exactly it is that the Law of Nature requires us to submit to government.

Hobbes's identification of the core of divine positive law with the reciprocity theorem comes out clearly in this passage from *De Cive* where he writes:

> that law of nature, which commands every man to allow the same rights to others they would be allowed themselves, and which contains in it all the other laws besides, is the same which Moses sets down (Levit. xix. 18): *Thou shalt love thy neighbour as thyself.* And our Saviour calls it *the sum of the moral law:* Matth. xxii. 36–40. ... But to love our neighbour as ourselves, is nothing else but to grant him all we desire to have granted to ourselves.[56]

[54] EW II, 62.

[55] See *De Cive,* chapter 4, "That the Law of nature Is a Divine Law", EW II, 59ff.; also *Elements of Law,* chapter V, "A Confirmation out of Holy Scripture of the principal points mentioned in the last two Chapters concerning the Law of Nature" (EW IV, 111). Hobbes consistently speaks of the Law of Nature as God's law – see, for instance, EW III, 273; T 198; EW III, 312; T 224; EW III, 347; T 248; EW III, 494; T 344; EW III, 580; T 400; and EW III, 600; T 413. It would be peculiar for one part of God's law to authorize a hierarchy of responsibility while the other part did not.

[56] EW II, 57. The *Elements of Law* also contains a similar passage: "That men content themselves with equality, *as it is the foundation of natural law,* so also is it of the second table of the divine law, Matth. xxii. 39, 40: *Thou shalt love thy neighbour as thyself...* [which is to be understood as requiring that] he should esteem his neighbour worthy [of] all rights and privileges that he himself enjoyeth; and attribute unto him, whatsoever he looketh should be attributed unto himself" (EW IV, 113, first emphasis added).

And here in *Leviathan:*

> [he who] alloweth to himself that which he denieth to another, [acts] contrary to the words of our Saviour [Luke vi. 31], *Whatsoever you would that men should do unto you, that do ye unto them;* and contrary to the law of nature, which is the indubitable everlasting law of God, *Do not to another, that which thou wouldest not he should do unto thee.*[57]

If divine positive law directs deference to civil law, and the core command of divine positive law for our treatment of our fellows is just the reciprocity theorem, then it is not unreasonable to conclude that the reciprocity theorem similarly directs deference to civil law.[58]

Hobbes's self-effacing natural law theory seems to me to be quite ingenious, and sensible, even if somewhat frightening. Hobbes is not posing a question of calculating expected utilities. He is, rather, showing that if we can see that in the face of disagreement with others, fairness requires us to submit to authoritative adjudication of our disputes by submitting to a common civil sovereign and a set of positive laws, the moral choice to be made should be seen as one between accepting the risk in committing to adjudication that civil judgment will go against us, or going to war in an attempt to secure by force the rule of our private judgment over and against the judgment of our opponents. Hobbes argues that the reasonable course of submission to adjudication most accords with reason, even should we fare worse under it. His view turns out to be, perhaps surprisingly, liberal, if liberals are those who take seriously the claims of their opponents and seek to resolve disputes in a way that can be justified to all willing reciprocally to take seriously the claims of their opponents. In just this way Hobbes's Law of Nature (the reciprocity theorem) requires

57 EW III, 494 T 344.

58 Hobbes does not discuss what subjects should do were their sovereign to command them to disobey his positive laws according to their private judgments of the requirements of natural law. Then should they obey natural law, which commands them to obey positive law, or positive law, which commands them to ignore itself in favor of conscientious judgment of the requirements of natural law? Nor does Hobbes discuss the similar question I posed in *IAI* of what should be our response to a sovereign who declares what God's law is, and then commands us to disobey it, considering that it is God's positive laws in Scripture that command us to take our sovereign's interpretation of Scripture as authoritative. These questions must be too farfetched for Hobbes to have thought it necessary to discuss them.

men to submit mutually to authoritative arbitration with all willing others. According to Hobbes, disagreeing with others, but affording them the consideration we claim due to ourselves as the reciprocity theorem requires, we must submit to fair arbitration. Whether the arbitration is or isn't fair must be judged – as must be any other disputed issue – not by the disputing parties, but by a fair arbitrator. To avoid an interminable regress, all parties must agree to let the buck stop somewhere. That somewhere, Hobbes termed a sovereign. And when they really cannot live with the decisions of that authoritative judge, they will defy the requirements of reason and wage war to reshuffle the deck, as Hobbes recognizes. Sometimes, when the provocation is extreme, we will find ourselves unwilling to fault them for doing so. But they won't be able to settle a new peace, unless and until they and their adversaries are willing once again to be guided by reason in its demand to submit to authoritative adjudication of contested questions. This is the way in which reason dictates reciprocity, and reciprocity lays the foundation for peace. Hobbes recognized that there are fates worse than death, that some things are worth dying for, and that peace at any price is a price too high for many, perhaps most, people. What he hoped to demonstrate, however, is that even if we are moved by such transcendent interests, when they are properly conceived according to a sound moral philosophy and a sound Christian religion, we will find that they are best served by conforming to the requirements of reason as embodied in the reciprocity theorem.

LIBERTY, OBLIGATION, AND LAW

Few topics in Hobbes studies have created more confusion and consternation in commentators than his discussions of liberty, obligation, and law. Hobbes affirms several basic premises, each important for his various arguments, which seem nonetheless to be mutually incompatible. For instance,

> The civil laws do not limit liberty.
> Obligations do limit liberty.
> Law is an obligation.

And

Obligations limit liberty.
Liberty is the absence of external impediments.
Internal determinants of the will do not limit liberty.
Obligations operate as internal determinants of the will, and thus do not limit liberty.

And

People obey the civil law for fear of punishment.
Fear does not limit liberty.
Civil law takes away the liberty the Law of Nature gave us.

Each of these various premises has a good claim to being ineliminable from Hobbes's theory. Hobbes needs to maintain that actions done from fear are actions the actor had liberty not to do in order to maintain that such actions are voluntary, and so capable of creating obligations upon the agent. Because the covenant of political submission is often entered into for fear, either of one's fellows or of a conqueror, Hobbes must maintain that covenants entered into from fear are nonetheless valid and binding. But a condition on binding agreement is that it be voluntary, that is, that it be one the agent was at liberty to refuse, had he a will to refuse. It is also necessary to his project that Hobbes hold that obligations limit liberty, for if they did not, the obligation created by our covenant of submission to government would effect no change from the state of nature. Unless civil law deprived us of liberties we enjoyed under natural law, it would do no better in facilitating peaceful cooperation than the natural law alone. Hobbes needs to insist that liberty, properly understood, is nothing more than the absence of impediments to doing what one wills to do if he is to defend his compatibilist position that while all our actions are causally necessitated, we nonetheless act freely. His is a deflationary claim that although no one is "free" to will one thing rather than another, to be free is to find no stop in doing what one was necessitated to will to do.[59] Hobbes insists upon the position that

59 Hobbes writes, "he is *free* to do a thing, that may do it if he have the will to do it, and may forbear, if he have the will to forbear" (EW IV, 240). "[I]t cannot be conceived that there is any liberty greater, than for a man to do what he will.... [H]e that can

civil laws do not limit liberty, because he needs to show that no subject can legitimately complain of his government that it is to be resisted because it deprives subjects of liberties they would enjoy under other regimes. The most effective way to do this is to say, as Hobbes does, that civil liberty is the same under all regimes, and the firmest foundation for this claim is the one he makes, namely, that civil laws do not limit liberty at all. Yet these various positions do not seem to make for a happy marriage.

Our account, drawing upon the interpretation of authorization just described, renders these seemingly inconsistent elements compatible. Obligations do limit liberty, civil laws do not limit liberty, and subjects do have an obligation to obey civil laws. Here is the explanation. Civil laws do not affect what it is that a subject wills to do, in the same way that fear does, by entering into deliberation.[60] In Hobbes's account, civil laws *express* the subject's *own* will, because he has "owned and authorized" the sovereign's will as his will, and the laws express the sovereign's will. Thus, Hobbes writes, that in obeying his sovereign, a man does "according to his conscience and judgment, as having deposited his judgment in all controversies in the hands of the sovereign power".[61] Because liberty is limited only by impediments that impede action on the will, civil laws do not limit subjects' liberty, for the civil laws express the subject's will.

But obligations do limit liberty. Obligations are owed to other people and are not "contained in the nature and intrinsical qualities of the agent". Sensation, thoughts, and train of thoughts, desire, fear, and hope are the only "intrinsical" qualities of agents, on Hobbes's account. These intrinsic qualities explain why we undertake obligations, but the resulting obligations themselves are not contained in the nature and intrinsic qualities of the agent. (They result from the interaction of the independent requirements of reason with those of our intrinsic qualities that contribute to our judgments.) While it is true that both natural duties and "obligations proper" make normative claims on us only because we naturally think, desire, and fear

do what he will, hath all liberty possible, and he that cannot, hath none at all" (EW IV, 263).

[60] Here I correct a mistake I made in *IAI* in arguing that law affects behavior by affecting what it is that the agent wills to do.

[61] EW IV, 204.

certain things, it is not true that those obligations are "contained in the nature and intrinsical qualities" of men. To offer an analogy, like children, who originate in their parents' pursuit of their appetites and willful acts, so do obligations impose claims independent of the continuing wills of those who brought them into being. The fact that the existence of such things as children and obligations depends upon our actions – which are conceded to be a function of our beliefs and appetites – in no way serves to show that the requirements for sustaining those things, or the normative pressure to do so, depends on our present beliefs or appetites. Obligations (like children) are, in Hobbes's sense, *external* impediments to our doing what we have the will and power to do. Subjects, by their covenant of obedience to government, which they were duty-bound under the Law of Nature to undertake, do have an obligation to obey the government that does limit their natural liberty to act on their private wills; but each particular civil law, as an expression of their considered will, cannot limit their liberty, because it poses no impediment to their doing what they will to do, their will now being expressed by those civil laws.

To bring further evidence to bear in support of this account, it is worth noting that Hobbes stipulates that the will is "the last appetite in deliberation". I understand this to mean that what we call an agent's "will" is the appetite she acted on in acting as she did.[62] "Her will" is thus a term that is applied with confidence only *ex post facto.* Although we cannot in this stage of our science, at least, accurately predict anyone's will from a description of known facts about her prior deliberations, our ordinary language licenses us to say with certainty, that her will was to act in the way she actually acted. Given Hobbes's account of the will, we can show all subjects of a commonwealth may rightly be understood to have acted freely in relation to the civil law.

To adapt a set of distinctions made famous by Aristotle to the present case, Hobbes's *virtuous* subject, who because of his prior covenant of obedience to government accepts the sovereign's will as his own will, will regard the civil laws as articulating *his own authentic will.*

[62] Hobbes insists that our appetites "proceed *not from, but are the will;* and the will is not voluntary" (EW IV, 69).

If a particular civil law commands him to do "x", his will in following that law is correctly described as the will to do "x". Hence, he enjoys liberty in its full and proper sense, of finding no external impediment to his doing what he wills to do.

The *continent* subject, who recognizes that she is morally committed to taking the sovereign's will as expressed in the civil laws as her own will, but finds herself unable to "feel it", follows the laws, but does so from fear of the punishment that would attend her violation of the laws; not from her recognition of obligation, but solely from fear. Nonetheless, on Hobbes's account, she is free. She may, by fear, suffer some diminishment of power, but she is just as much at liberty when she obeys as the virtuous subject is when he obeys.

Furthermore, the *criminal* is also, on Hobbes's analysis, free, since for anyone who breaks the laws, the laws clearly failed to pose an external obstacle to his doing what he willed to do. Of course, if we assume that the criminal's real will is to both break the law and evade punishment, the state crosses his will whenever the criminal is caught and punished; and so in that limited sense, effective punishment does limit liberty. But effective punishment should not be confused with civil laws, or their force. Hobbes is still correct to maintain that civil law does not limit liberty.

In this way our interpretation allows us to accept all of Hobbes's core claims, while forging a coherent picture of his view of liberty and obligation to law. That interpretation will show itself more natural when we think plainly about what Hobbes is trying to say about laws and obligations. These intellectual notions cannot *make* anyone do anything. Whatever force they have for us is not *that* kind of brute physical force. If obligations have force, it is because their force doesn't depend upon how we happen to *feel* about what they tell us. If they have force, it is because they take away our *right* to act in some of the ways that we are, and cannot but be, at *liberty* to act. As Hobbes writes of the process of acquiring obligations, "because it is impossible for any man really to transfer his own strength to another, or for that other to receive it; it is to be understood, that to transfer a man's power and strength, is no more but to lay by, or relinquish his own right of resisting him to whom he so transferreth it".[63] One might say,

[63] EW IV, 123.

we impose obligations on ourselves only when we *cannot* materially constrain liberty: If we could make it impossible for people to do certain things, there'd be no point in forbidding them to do those things. Obligations, then, track what we want to condemn as *wrongful exercises of liberty*.

7

Fools, Hypocrites, Zealots, and Dupes: Civic Character and Social Stability

> Every great city is as a standing army, which if it be not under the sovereigns command, the people are miserable; if they be, they may be taught their duties in the Universities safely and easily, and be happy.
>
> (EW IV, 439)

> But if the people see once any ambition in their teachers, they will sooner learn that, than any other doctrine; and from ambition proceeds rebellion.
>
> (EW IV, 346)

It is one thing to see that reason requires submission to political authority, and to appreciate the goods achieved by such submission; it is quite another to possess the sort of character that will enable one reliably to act on these perceptions. What sorts of people are they whose characters prevent them from acting in the ways that a stable social peace requires? Who are they that either do not grasp what reason requires or, grasping it, do nonetheless systematically act contrary to those requirements?

In answering these questions, I shall not consider the sorts of ordinary failures of reason that do not importantly affect the stability of political society. Children not yet arrived at the age of reason, persons with dementia and those severely mentally disabled, ordinary criminals, disloyal friends and cheating spouses, those who practice poor health habits or are weak of will within the normal range, and all other politically insignificant violators of the requirements of reason need not be considered in order to assess the viability of Hobbes's political theory. Of the potentially politically disruptive sorts of characters, I shall follow Hobbes in paying special attention to four types: fools, hypocrites, dupes, and zealots. Each of these may actively contribute to social disorder.

I'll begin by describing each of the problematic character-types, explaining how persons of that type contribute to social disorder. I'll then discuss the mechanisms Hobbes proposes for preventing the formation of such characters. Finally, I'll critically assess Hobbes's proposals with respect to both how effective they can be expected to be, and their moral acceptability from our contemporary point of view.

THE FOOLE

One of the most discussed passages in all of *Leviathan* is Hobbes's discussion in chapter 15 of "the Foole".[1] This passage has usually been interpreted as an attempt to demonstrate the narrow rationality of morality. Some commentators have supposed that Hobbes is arguing that it is never in one's self-interest to violate the third Law of Nature prohibiting breaking covenants, or for that matter, to violate any others of the Laws of Nature. Thus understood, the Foole passage is presumed to count as evidence in favor of a self-interest interpretation of the Laws of Nature, for unless the Laws of Nature are themselves rules for securing the self-interest of the agent, how could it be crucial to showing that those laws are in accord with reason (hence Laws of Nature) to show that they cannot require actions not approved by self-interest? However, as David van Mill has correctly argued, because the only thing the Foole cares about is his self-interest, and not his religious or moral duties, and perhaps not even the good of others, it can be but weak evidence indeed for the self-interest interpretation of the Laws of Nature that Hobbes does not reply to the Foole by insisting that injustice is contrary to duty or bad for humanity generally.[2] The interpretation I shall offer, while enabling Hobbes to answer the Foole in the Foole's own terms, is nonetheless fully compatible with the

[1] EW III, 132–135; T 102–103.

[2] David van Mill, *Liberty, Rationality, and Agency in Hobbes's Leviathan* (Albany, NY, 2001), 132.

common good account of the Laws of Nature, as well as with Hobbes's definitional method. If this interpretation is plausible, traditional self-interest accounts of the Laws of Nature will have been deprived of one of their main props in Hobbes's discussion of the Foole.

In the Latin *Leviathan* Hobbes made unusually extensive revisions to his earlier reply to the Foole, and we will be making use of the Latin as well as English versions.[3] We can present the Foole's position as this:

> [T]here is no such thing as justice;...every man's conservation and contentment being committed to his own care, there could be no reason why every man might not do what he thought conduced thereunto, and therefore also to make or not make, keep or not keep, covenants was not against reason, when it conduced to one's benefit....The kingdom of God is gotten by violence; but what if it could be gotten by unjust violence? were it against {right} reason so to get it, when it is impossible to receive hurt by it {but only the supreme good}? and if it be not against reason, it is not against justice; or else justice is not to be approved for good.... [Y]ou may call [regicide by an heir] injustice, or by what other name you will, yet it can never be against reason, seeing all the voluntary actions of men tend to the benefit of themselves, and those actions are most reasonable that conduce most to their ends.[4]

Hobbes writes of the Foole that

> he questioneth whether injustice, taking away the fear of God (for the same fool hath said in his heart there is no God), may not sometimes stand with that reason which dictateth to every man his own good; and particularly then, when it conduceth to such a benefit as shall put a man in a condition

[3] Edwin Curley's edition (Indianapolis, 1994) documents these revisions. I am assuming, perhaps controversially, that while it is possible that portions of the Latin version predate the English, Hobbes did include there changes from the English, or was in any case prepared to let stand those Latin passages that diverge from the English. However, the interpretation I shall offer does not require privileging either of these versions. I mention it here because I shall be making use of both versions. Curley follows Molesworth's Latin *Leviathan* in introducing quotation marks to set off what the Foole says from Hobbes's comment on his position, and these are the passages I compile in the following account of the Foole's position. However, it is an open question whether Molesworth's innovation introduces an overly sharp distinction between attribution and commentary that might prove detrimental to interpretation of Hobbes's reply to the Foole. For this reason, I follow this compilation with quotation of those of Hobbes's remarks that seem to me to occupy this disputed territory. I am grateful to Kinch Hoekstra for discussion of this question.

[4] Curley, ed., *Leviathan,* 90–91. The Latin revisions appear in curly braces. Square brackets contain my supplement to preserve the meaning of the quoted remark.

to neglect, not only the dispraise and revilings, but also the power of other men.[5]

Simply put, the Foole maintains that justice cannot be a rule of reason because *profitable* injustice, and particularly, rebellious injustice that *gains one a kingdom,* is not against reason.

Why is the person who maintains this position a fool, according to Hobbes? In what does the Foole's foolishness consist? One possibility, suggested by various traditional interpretations, is that the Foole's folly lies in his failure to see that *injustice never profits the unjust agent.* However, Hobbes himself grants that indeed there *is* such a thing as "successful wickedness",[6] and that the question why evil men *often* prosper "hath shaken the faith, not only of the vulgar, but of philosophers, and which is more, of the Saints, concerning the Divine Providence".[7] Hobbes laments the fact that "men, from having observed how in all places, and in all ages, unjust actions have been authorized, by the force, *and victories* of those who have committed them" have wrongly inferred that "*examples of former times are good arguments of doing the like again*... to the perpetual disturbance of the peace of the commonwealth".[8] He thus insists that injustice disrupts social order and so is harmful to humanity generally, but clearly *rejects* the suggestion that injustice can never profit the unjust agent. Hence the Foole's folly cannot consist in failing to believe *that.*

A second possibility is that the Foole errs in failing to see that *one can never correctly predict that one will profit by injustice.* Although injustice (or violations of other natural laws) may indeed profit the agent, he can never be epistemically warranted in believing that he will so profit. This position is implausible on its face, at least if we ignore the possibility of divine punishment, as the Foole does. When we think of ordinary occasions for injustice, as when the mail-order retailer who intends to declare bankruptcy nonetheless continues to accept paid orders for merchandise he will not send, or the car mechanic charges for unnecessary parts, or the politician breaks his campaign

[5] Ibid., 90.

[6] Hobbes says this explicitly in the first paragraph of the Foole passage (EW III, 132; T 101).

[7] EW III, 346; T 247.

[8] EW III, 281–282; T 204, first emphasis added.

pledge to a small constituency in order to gain the votes of a larger one, we can see that petty injustices may often be profitable. Further, as before, Hobbes's texts will not support this interpretation, Hobbes acknowledging that at least some groups of people *can* accurately predict that their riches and power will immunize them from any negative consequences of their injustice.[9] I'll argue below that there is something to be said for the claim that a particular kind of injustice, namely, rebellion against the state, raises epistemic problems, at least in the long run. But as a general diagnosis of the Foole's foolishness, the claim that what is to be faulted is his prediction that he will profit by injustice is clearly inadequate to both Hobbes's texts and human experience.

A third possibility congenial to the self-interest interpretation of Hobbes's Laws of Nature is that the Foole's folly lies in his failure to see that he should (put in the anachronistic language of Kavka and others who've embraced this view) adopt a "disaster avoidance strategy", which strategy requires *never* acting unjustly, rather than attempt on a case-by-case basis to "maximize his expected utility", which alternative strategy might allow as justified breaking covenants in those instances in which the probability of detection is low and the expected payoff is high. The idea is that although injustice does sometimes pay, and although sometimes we can very well see that it will pay, reason nonetheless dictates that we are to forego those gains in order to adopt the most conservative strategy of seeking to avoid all highly negative outcomes, no matter their improbability.

The advantage of this rule-consequentialist version over other versions of the traditional self-interest interpretation of the Foole passage is that it grants with Hobbes both that we may with good reason expect injustice to pay, and that on some particular occasions it does. Nevertheless, two problems need to be addressed. First, there is the textual difficulty that Hobbes nowhere actually makes this argument. He does worry about discrepancies in short-term and long-run calculations of consequences; but that is not what Kavka's interpretation is tracking. It is ready to grant that both short- and long-run assessments of utility may converge on some act(s) of injustice, but that these are nonetheless prohibited by the "disaster avoidance principle" that we

9 Bernard Gert, ed., *Man and Citizen* (Cambridge, 1991), 49.

must follow the *general rule* that best avoids all disastrous outcomes, no matter the result of any personal expected utility calculation, however forward-looking and comprehensive. So to support this interpretation textually, we would need something other than recognition of a distinction between short- and long-run prudence.[10]

The second difficulty is philosophical. Why suppose that Hobbesean agents should determine the requirements of reason by inquiring about how to avoid the worst outcomes rather than how to acquire the best outcomes, or how to maximize their expected utility overall? Desire-based interpretations typically ascribe to Hobbes the view that the good is just whatever the agent desires. And so on those views, there is no *principled* reason to privilege disutility avoidance over utility acquisition. That will depend on the relative strength of the individual agent's desires, which, as Hobbes consistently maintains, will vary from person to person and over time.

Compare criticisms of Rawls's use of the maximin rule for choice under uncertainty in his "original position". Rawls's critics have argued that the maximin rule, which requires that one select the scheme the worst outcome of which is better than the worst outcome of any available alternative scheme, is irrational, as exhibiting excessive risk avoidance, and so that Rawls should have adopted the maximization of expected

[10] David Boonin argued against Kavka's position (in a way reminiscent of act utilitarian criticisms of rule utilitarianism) that it involves irrational "rule worship". See David Boonin-Vail, *Thomas Hobbes and the Science of Moral Virtue* (Cambridge, 1994), 89. I'm inclined to think his criticism is sound, and also to accept Kinch Hoekstra's observation that Boonin's own virtue theory interpretation is challenged by a similar objection. Hoekstra argues that Boonin's strategy of "justifying an uncompromising disposition in terms of overall or long-term advantage is no more acceptable than justifying a rigid rule [as does Kavka] in these terms" ("Hobbes and the Foole", *Political Theory* 25 (1997): 620–654, 636). I agree with Boonin that character matters to Hobbes because it affects one's motivation to follow moral requirements, and so character is important to Hobbes's overall moral philosophy. However, I do not agree with Boonin that the Laws of Nature address or are about character rather than actions. The Laws of Nature govern actions; good character is properly motivated intention to do good *actions* and is thus parasitic on the independent notion of good action. Unlike genuine virtue-ethical views that deny there can be any rule of good action, but insist rather that we must ostensively define it by reference to the *phronimos,* Hobbes's Laws of Nature pick out "precepts", "theorems of reason", or general rules by which a man is "forbidden to do" some or another action. A good man, then, is one who cares about and tries to do the actions required by those rules.

utility as his criterion for selection among principles of justice in the original position. Rawls argued that several features of the parties and their situation made use of the maximin rule uniquely rational: (1) there was no reliable way to calculate the probability that their representee would occupy one social position rather than another, in part because the schemes themselves determine what social positions there are in the worlds ordered by them; (2) the citizens whom the parties represent care very little for gains above the minimum needed for them to exercise their moral powers; and (3) some outcomes are so bad as to be completely unacceptable. These conditions were particular to Rawls's own project, and made sense in the context of that project.

But it is not true that in the world of Hobbes's contemporary or subsequent readers, conditions analogous to those favoring use of the maximin rule obtain. Not being behind a Rawlsian "veil of ignorance" we have much of the information needed to calculate the odds that we would fare better under one rule than another. We may care plenty for gains above the minimum we could assure ourselves above bare death avoidance, and may be willing to gamble on bad outcomes in the hope of securing better ones, as those who go to war and engage in revolution typically do. Kavka appears to be making use of Rawlsian considerations in proposing his even stronger disaster avoidance principle (which requires adopting the strategy that will avoid *all* disasters, rather than all but the least bad undesirable outcome), but offers no adequate philosophical defense of that approach, nor justification for transposing it from its own context to that of Hobbes interpretation. Kavka does suggest that all three principles – expected utility maximization, maximin, and disaster avoidance – will converge on the strategy of *never* violating a covenant, but this claim is indefensible. The only way the disaster avoidance, maximin, and expected utility principles could be seen *necessarily* to converge would be if there were for all people some uniquely disastrous outcome so bad that no matter how low its probability, it always outweighed the combination of all other values set against it. Temporal death is not such an outcome according to Hobbes,[11] nor does he identify any other. One

[11] I argued this in Chapter 2. For textual evidence that Hobbes did not assume that all people disvalue temporal death most of all, see, for example, *De Homine*, XI, 6;

might argue that eternal damnation is a promising candidate, but the Foole's atheism rules out any reply that appeals to this disvalue. Certainly Kavka, who explicitly grants that Hobbes recognized "fates worse than death", cannot embrace the claim needed to ensure convergence of the three principles.

So although Kavka's suggested interpretation of Hobbes's diagnosis of the Foole as failing to act on the disaster avoidance principle cannot be strictly ruled out on the basis of Hobbes's text, the fact that it receives no support there, along with its general philosophical implausibility as the paramount principle of rational decision-making, leaves our interpretive question unresolved. What is the folly that makes the Foole?

The Foole's Folly

First and foremost, the fault of the fool who denies that justice is a rule of reason is his reliance on a *faulty rule of inference.* In using a strictly speaking absurd rule, he acts contrary to reason. Further, were he to use a correct rule of inference, he would see that seditious covenant breaking is contrary to reason. I argue that Hobbes does not see accordance with reason as a mere matter of promoting the agent's narrow self-interest, and so that he resists reducing reason to prudence. That contention is supported here in his reply to the Foole, where he offers distinct considerations, one from "sapience" and the other from prudence.

First, let us remember that Hobbes distinguishes reason or wisdom from prudence. Reason operates on general truths, right definitions, and correct rules of inference. Only reason can produce certain, infallible knowledge of the sort sought by philosophy. Failures of reason involve conceptual or logical errors. Prudence is conjecture about the future based on past experience, and it is fallible and uncertain. Although far inferior to the wisdom that results from knowledge of correct general principles, prudence is nonetheless superior for obtaining our desired ends to reliance on false principles of the sort exhibited by the unjust fool. Hobbes carefully offers a reply to

EW III, 65; T 56; EW III, 437; T 306–307; EW III, 317; T 227; EW III, 81; T 67; EW III, 140; EW II, 38.

the Foole that exposes both the Foole's failure of reason and his imprudence. He writes in the Latin *Leviathan* that the question posed by the unjust fool is "Whether the one who deceives does so with reason *and* in accordance with his own good. I say he acts against reason *and* imprudently".[12] Hobbes thus explicitly distinguishes the question of accordance with reason from the question of prudence, and proposes to offer a reply to the Foole's challenge on both counts.

It is also important to notice the context in which Hobbes's discussion of the Foole is offered. Hobbes, by showing that the transference of right demanded by the second Law of Nature (which was previously proved to be a rule of reason) would be "vain" (ineffectual) without the third Law of Nature, has *already proved* that the third Law of Nature requiring the keeping of covenants is a rule of reason. This point bears emphasis, because many commentators have failed to notice that Hobbes's discussion of the Foole is *not* intended to constitute a *proof* of the third Law of Nature, but is rather intended only to *answer an objection* to the possibility of any such proof. If the Foole's particular objection fails, Hobbes's argument stands, at least until a more formidable foe presents herself. So it would be a mistake to imagine that Hobbes's reply to the Foole is meant to *establish* covenant keeping as a rule of reason and thus a Law of Nature. All Hobbes need do successfully to answer the Foole is show that the Foole's particular objection is a bad objection. I shall argue that he succeeds, absolutely decisively, in doing that much. It is because I see the aim of Hobbes's reply to the Foole to be much less grand than that of demonstrating the rationality of morality, that I term my interpretation "deflationary". This is not to deny that Hobbes aims to demonstrate that morality accords with reason – for as we saw in Chapter 5 this is exactly what his derivation of the reciprocity theorem and its derivative Laws of Nature shows – but is rather to say that his reply to the Foole does not contain his arguments for that conclusion. And because, as I'll argue, Hobbes's replies to the Foole from both wisdom and prudence observe his stated method of derivation from definitions, my interpretation is aptly described as "definitional". I shall henceforth refer to it as the *deflationary definitional interpretation* of the reply to the Foole.

[12] Curley, ed., *Leviathan,* 91n5, emphasis added.

The fundamental claim of the unjust fool is that covenant keeping is not a rule of reason because covenant breaking is sometimes profitable to those who unjustly engage in it, and "those actions are most reasonable that most conduce to their ends". Pared down to essentials it is that

1. If injustice is ever reasonable, justice cannot be a rule of reason.
2. If an action most conduces to one's ends, then it is reasonable to perform that action.
3. Injustice sometimes (most) conduces to one's ends.
4. Hence, injustice is sometimes reasonable.
5. Therefore, justice cannot be a rule of reason.

Hobbes acknowledges that such reasoning is superficially attractive ("specious"), but offers a simple two-pronged reply, which accepts premise (3), but denies premise (2), and then offers a demonstration that from an indisputably correct principle, rebellious injustice is imprudent. Both prongs of the argument – the first employing wisdom, the second prudence – show that the Foole's position is against right reason understood as correct inference from true principles.

First, and fundamentally, the Foole's principle of inference as contained in premise (2) is false. The Foole thinks that if an action turns out well, it cannot have been against reason to perform it. But the goodness of the outcome does not the reasonableness of the action make, as can be confirmed intuitively by any number of examples. Suppose, for instance, that the holder of the winning lottery ticket explains that he chose his winning number by compiling the birthdates of his family members. We would not be tempted to conclude from the fortuitous outcome that his procedure was rational, nor even perhaps that he was rational to enter the lottery in the first place, considering the odds against winning and how he might otherwise have used his money. Or suppose that he acts to select his mate by randomly selecting a name from the phone book, or by scrambling the letters of his favorite basketball player's name. And suppose that the person thus chosen turns out well for him. Does the fortuitous outcome suffice to vindicate his action as *rational?* Surely not: We are prone to insist that rational actions must employ rational procedures, or at least not irrational ones, and that the goodness of the outcomes should be in some way related to the reliability of those procedures. For this reason, the Foole errs in inferring from the fact that an action turned out well that it was not against reason to do it. Hobbes sees as do we the fault in the Foole's principle that "those actions are most reasonable that most conduce to their ends".

Notice that this first prong alone suffices to defeat the unjust fool's objection. If we substitute Hobbes's negation of the Foole's premise (2), then even granting premise (3), neither his subconclusion (4) nor his conclusion (5) follows. The Foole has failed to provide any argument that covenant keeping is not a rule of reason. His error in affirming (2) is, on Hobbes's analysis, a conceptual error (an absurdity), and thus a failure of scientific reasoning or sapience.[13] Such reasoning depends on general principles whose component terms are correctly related to one another. By wrongly asserting that everything falling under the term "most conduces to one's benefit" also falls under the term "is most reasonable", the Foole has failed to exhibit the proper use of language upon which sapience depends. And because Hobbes holds that "the truth of a conclusion, is no more but the truth of the premises that make it", the Foole's erroneous principle undermines his otherwise valid argument.[14]

Another way of putting Hobbes's point is to say that even if the unjust fool's action happens to turn out well for him, he is foolish because he undertook the action on the basis of an inappropriate consideration. On the subject of corrupt counselors bribed by their own self-interest Hobbes wrote: "For though the counsel they give be never so good; yet he that gives it, is no more a good counsellor,

[13] Hobbes identifies any sort of science as wisdom, but the particular science "from which proceed the true and evident conclusions of what is right and wrong, and what is good and hurtful to the being, and well-being of mankind, the Latins call *sapientia,* and we by the general name of wisdom" (EW IV, 210–211). All science depends upon knowledge of the consequences of words, that is, on correct definitions rightly joined together into syllogisms. In *Leviathan* Hobbes remarks that "[a]s much experience, is *prudence;* so, is much science *sapience.* For though we usually have one name of wisdom for them both, yet the Latins did always distinguish between *prudentia* and *sapientia;* ascribing the former to experience, the latter to science" (EW III, 37; T 36).

[14] EW IV, 95. Cf. EW IV, 72–73. That Hobbes thinks right reasoning conserves truth is evident in his remark that "there is no reason but that if true definitions were premised in all sorts of doctrines, the demonstrations also would be true" (EW I, 87).

than he that giveth a just sentence for a reward, is a just judge".[15] Reasoning analogously, we might say that although, despite his false principle, the Foole lights on an action that in fact profits him, he is not a wise man.

By discrediting the Foole's principle (premise 2), Hobbes may be understood as replying to the Foole like this:

> It is *not* the case that if an action most conduces to one's ends, then it is reasonable to perform that action. So while it is true that injustice sometimes most conduces to one's ends, it does not *follow* that injustice is ever reasonable, nor that justice cannot be (as I have already shown it to be) a rule of reason.

Although this reply adequately answers the Foole's general objection that because injustice is sometimes profitable justice is not a rule of reason, the Foole's specific contention that profitable rebellious injustice is reasonable merits special attention. Hobbes wishes to argue that not only does success not suffice to vindicate an action as rational, when success attaches to an action that should have been expected to be harmful on the basis of all the foresight our experience gives us, but the action is imprudent as well. Hobbes writes, "when a man doth a thing, which notwithstanding any thing can be foreseen, and reckoned on, tendeth to his own destruction, howsoever some accident which he could not expect, arriving may turn it to his benefit; yet such events do not make it reasonably or wisely done".[16] That Hobbes faults one who acts in this manner as *imprudent* is made clear in the Latin revision of this passage, where Hobbes writes: "[A]nyone who does what, as far as can be foreseen and understood by reason, tends to his own destruction, even though something unforeseen happens which makes the outcome fortunate, has nevertheless acted imprudently, *because what happens is unforeseen*".[17] Here it becomes clear that this proper principle is strictly analytic for Hobbes, because true prudence is correct extrapolation from past experience to predict the

[15] EW III, 244; T 178.

[16] EW III, 133; T 102. Hobbes is here assuming the Foole's stated concern to secure his own "conservation and contentment", and to pursue his own benefit. In this way he engages the Foole's interest. However, the general principle need not be stated in terms of that interest.

[17] Curley, ed., *Leviathan*, 91n6, emphasis added.

future,[18] so one whose actions defy the lessons of experience (and succeed only because of some factor that could not have been predicted on the basis of experience) cannot, by definition, be acting prudently.

Using this principle, Hobbes argues that one acts imprudently in acting unjustly, even if (per chance) successfully, because such action depends upon the assumption, contrary to experience, that one can systematically deceive others and so count on them to fail to detect one's injustice. We can put the argument like this:

6. To be prudent is to form one's expectations by correct extrapolation from past experience.
7. If experience shows that an action can be expected to be harmful, then (even should it turn out well due to unforeseeable events) it is imprudent to expect that the action will be profitable.
8. Experience shows that relying on the errors of others for the success of one's actions can be expected to be harmful.
9. Any expectation that unjust action will be profitable requires relying on the errors of others.
10. Therefore, it is imprudent to expect that unjust action will be profitable.

Hobbes argues that because covenant breaking if discovered can be expected to result in one's destruction, it will conduce to one's conservation and contentment only if *others make errors* about one's actions and intentions. But, Hobbes maintains, *one cannot reasonably foresee nor count on others to make those errors.*

Why not? Hobbes is the first to say that people are gullible, that of many proffered miracles, "all the miracle consisteth in this, that the enchanter has deceived a man; which is no miracle, but a very easy matter to do" and that "if we look upon the impostures wrought by confederacy, there is nothing how impossible soever to be done, that is impossible to be believed".[19] So how can Hobbes possibly maintain that it is unreasonable to expect to be able systematically to deceive others?

[18] Or correct explanation on the basis of experience of some past event by observation of its effects.

[19] EW III, 434–435; T 305.

The answer is that while it is true that people are gullible, ourselves no less than others, it is also true that none of us has adequate reason to think ourselves so subtle that we can reliably deceive all those who have an important interest in not being deceived. In almost every case, only a kind of unwarranted and foolish pride could make one believe that one was in a privileged position to deceive without detection. (We will investigate this view presently.) Moreover, because men see their own wit close up, and others' only at a distance, men are systematically prone to *overestimate* their own ingeniousness (subtlety) relative to others. Hobbes writes,

> [A]s to the faculties of the mind...I find yet a greater equality amongst men, than that of strength....That which may perhaps make such equality incredible, is but a vain conceit of one's own wisdom, which almost all men think they have in a greater degree, than...all men but themselves, and a few others, whom by fame, or for concurring with themselves, they approve.... [F]or they see their own wit at hand, and other men's at a distance.[20]

There is no basis in experience for believing we can systematically deceive others, and the cost of failure, at least with respect to the breaking of significant covenants, can be expected to be self-destruction. Therefore, covenant breaking is imprudent. Hobbes writes,

> He therefore that breaketh his covenant, and consequently declareth that he thinks he may with reason do so, cannot be received into any society, that unite themselves for peace and defence, but by the error of them that receive him; nor when he is received, be retained in it, without seeing the danger of their error; which errors a man cannot reasonably reckon upon as the means of his security: and therefore...if he live in society, it is by the errors of other men, which he could not foresee, nor reckon upon; and consequently against the reason of his preservation.[21]

How successful is this second prong of Hobbes's reply, which depends on the claim that experience shows that we cannot expect others to make the errors on which the profitability of our injustice depends? It is wholly *im*plausible that, as a general matter, one

[20] EW III, 110–111; T 87.

[21] EW III, 134; T 102–103. In the Latin version Hobbes writes of the unjust fool, "[w]ho, except by ignorance, will retain him if he has been admitted? So either he will be cast out and perish, or he will owe his not being cast out to the ignorance of the others, which is contrary to right reason" (Curley, ed., *Leviathan*, 92n7).

could never, under any possible circumstances, expect to be able successfully to deceive others, and so reasonably expect to profit by covenant breaking, particularly in ordinary petty matters, such as giving incorrect change, falsely calling in sick, improperly avoiding jury duty, and the like.

However, that is not the particular kind of case that made replying to the Foole seem to Hobbes to be worth doing. In the second prong of his reply Hobbes discusses breaking of the covenants of *mutual assistance that determine whether one is admitted and retained in civil society or rather left or cast into the state of nature.* And elsewhere in the Foole passage Hobbes addresses the Foole's claim that *rebellion* may accord with reason. These cases involve the foundational covenants upon which peace and mutual protection essentially depend.[22] If the particular challenge posed by the unjust fool is to show why it is not true that rebellion is not against reason even though it may prove profitable, Hobbes's reply is quite strong. The Foole's view that rebellion is not against reason when it profits oneself cannot, of course, be supported on the Foole's faulty principle (premise 2), because Hobbes has discredited that principle. And it seems that Hobbes's secondary prudential argument against the Foole is much stronger for this case than for cases of ordinary petty injustice, because experience suggests that to violate one's covenant of submission to government by attempting sedition is highly risky, and generally unlikely to prove profitable. As Hobbes points out, one is unlikely to succeed in taking power, and failure will probably bring the misery of death as a traitor.[23] One's design to overthrow the government is just the sort of covenant breaking we should expect both officials and fellow subjects to be especially vigilant to detect. And even if one should, unexpectedly, succeed, Hobbes argues that one can expect to be challenged by other unjust fools who, supposing the discredited first principle, would take the example of one's own profitable injustice as rational

[22] For the suggestion that Hobbes was primarily concerned not with crime or ordinary lawbreaking, but instead with rebellion or sedition, and that his reply to the Foole is adequate in that context, see my *IAI,* 95–98. It is not inconsistent with this suggestion to note that Hobbes identifies the Foole's faulty principle as one of the causes of crime as well as a premise in (bogus) justifications for rebellion or sedition.

[23] E.g., EW III, 284; T 205.

justification for their own attempt to replace oneself, thus upsetting one's long-term success. This argument specifically against the prudence of rebellion does strike me as more plausible than any more general argument that all injustice must be imprudent.

In light of these considerations, we might reformulate the second prong of Hobbes's reply as follows:

6. To be prudent is to form one's expectations by correct extrapolation from past experience.
7. If experience shows that an action can be expected to be harmful, then (even should it turn out well due to unforeseeable events) it is imprudent to expect that the action will be profitable.

8′. Experience shows that relying on the errors of others for the success of one's *unjust rebellion* can be expected to be harmful.

9′. Any expectation that *unjust rebellion* will be profitable requires relying on the errors of others.

10′. Therefore, it is imprudent to expect that *unjust rebellion* will be profitable.

This does seem to me to be a highly plausible argument as it stands. It would be unassailable, were Hobbes to qualify 9′ and 10′ to read that (9″) *in almost all cases* the expectation that unjust rebellion will be profitable requires relying on the errors of others, and (10″) Therefore, *in almost all cases* it is imprudent to expect that unjust rebellion will be profitable. Indeed, I believe Hobbes is committed to that qualification, because of his stated view, discussed earlier, that the rich and powerful can sometimes rationally predict that their particular circumstance so situates them that they can expect to act unjustly with impugnity. I will not further pursue that point here.

Hoekstra's Explicit Foole

Kinch Hoekstra, who acknowledges both that Hobbes allows for successful wickedness, and so the possibility of profitable covenant breaking, and that Hobbes was primarily concerned to discourage revolution rather than ordinary crime or petty injustices, offers an ingenious and textually plausible suggestion for how best to construe what I have identified as the second prong of the argument.[24] He argues that Hobbes was concerned to answer only the "explicit" Foole who, by loud declaration or flagrant action, advertises his belief that rebellious injustice accords with reason, thereby inciting others to rebel; Hobbes was not attempting to answer the "silent" Foole who affirms the reasonableness of injustice only "in his heart" and by his discrete, undetected actions, for such people are no threat to the stability of the commonwealth. What I find attractive in this interpretation is that it significantly strengthens the second prong of Hobbes's argument, for the odds that the Foole can rely on the errors of others to deceive them about his intentions once he has noisily proclaimed or flagrantly declared them are, obviously, slim indeed, guaranteeing the success of that prong of the argument. Further, Hoekstra adduces substantial textual support for his claim that Hobbes was concerned about fools who are, to at least some degree, explicit.

However, four main considerations speak against Hoekstra's interpretation of the Foole's folly as *depending essentially* on his explicitness. First, Hoekstra argues that the bare language of Hobbes's introduction to the Foole passage indicates that Hobbes has in mind a singular individual rather than a type – that the Foole is one who on some occasions has said with his tongue as well as in his heart that injustice is not against reason.[25] Hoekstra also lays great stress on Hobbes's use in the Foole passage of such phrases as saying "with his tongue", "seriously alleging", "declares", and "consequently declareth". I am inclined to read all this language as showing, not that the Foole is someone who prospectively advertises his intention to act unjustly, thereby inciting rebellion, but rather that he is simply one who, if caught, tries to defend his unjust actions *ex post*. Someone who "breaketh his covenant, and *consequently declareth that he thinks he may with*

[24] Hoekstra, "Hobbes and the Foole"; cf. also his "Nothing to Declare? Hobbes and the Advocate of Injustice", *Political Theory* 27 (1999): 230–235.

[25] I am less sure than Hoekstra about the plain meaning of Hobbes's formulation, because if Hoekstra were right, one would expect Hobbes to have written "The Foole has said in his heart and sometimes also with his tongue: 'there is no such thing as justice'", which he did not. In any case, nothing in this description of the Foole's position licenses Hoekstra's extension of what the Foole says with his tongue to what he does not say with his tongue but that others infer from his actions, so it would at most include loud but not flagrant fools.

reason do so", is one who breaks his covenant and subsequently tries to justify his having done so as reasonable.[26] We can see why Hobbes would have been particularly grieved by such a recalcitrant malefactor without resorting to Hoekstra's Explicit Foole interpretation. Such a person's readiness to defend his prior injustices shows him to be *an unjust man*. Hobbes writes in the Latin *Leviathan* that a man "even if his actions have sometimes been unjust, is still just, provided he loves justice, [and] *himself condemns what he has done unjustly, even if he did it secretly*".[27]

Far from condemning or repenting what he has done, the Foole tries to justify it, and so is an unjust man rather than one who is merely mistaken or weak-willed on particular occasions. Such men are intractable and hardened in their antisocial ways. This is enough to explain why Hobbes should have been especially exercised about fools who try to justify their errors. And tellingly, this passage expresses Hobbes's *indifference* as to whether the injustice was done secretly or publicly, casting doubt on Hoekstra's claim that this is Hobbes's guiding distinction in his characterization of the Foole.

Second, if the account I have so far given is correct, we need not suppose that the Foole is explicit in order to explain his foolishness, for that has already been explained by his embracing a false principle of inference as revealed in the first prong of Hobbes's reply. Whether the Foole is explicit or silent is entirely irrelevant to the success of the first prong. And while the plausibility of the second prong will be *enhanced* by assuming that the Foole is explicit, such an assumption is by no means necessary for the success of that argument.

Third, were Hobbes concerned *only* with explicit Fooles, it would, as others of Hoekstra's critics have noted, be difficult to account for the interest of Hobbes's reply. If all Hobbes can show is that it is foolish to commit injustice in a way that will get you caught and punished, what

[26] Curley, ed., *Leviathan*, 92, emphasis added. That 'consequently' connotes a temporal rather than equivalence notion is indicated by the fact that Hobbes includes no comma after 'consequently'. Compare equivalence – "breaketh his covenant, and in so doing, declareth" – with temporality – "breaketh his covenant, and subsequently declareth": only the latter comports with Hobbes's use of commas. Giving further support to the idea that the Foole tries *ex post* to justify his injustice is Hobbes's use of the term 'alleges'; one standard meaning of 'allege' is (and was in Hobbes's day) to give as an excuse or a defense.

[27] Ibid., 93n10, emphasis added.

may seem the most interesting part of the Foole's challenge remains unmet. What we and the Foole want to know is: How can injustice be foolish if you do it in a way that actually *doesn't* get you caught and punished? By confining Hobbes's reply to the position of the Explicit Foole – the loud or flagrant Foole who practically guarantees his own detection and punishment – Hoekstra seems to have offered Hobbes a reply that either sidesteps the Foole's objection or meets it only because the Explicit Foole is an uninteresting straw man.

This brings us to what I believe to be the main and decisive objection to Hoekstra's interpretation. Hoekstra holds that the problem with the Explicit Foole is that his declaration invites rebellion.[28] What the Foole makes explicit by his loud or flagrant actions is his belief that people should break covenants whenever they see personal profit in doing so, and thus his commitment to breaking his own covenants and to acting unjustly whenever he sees a *personal* advantage in doing so. Hoekstra imagines that such a declaration could incite others to rebel, relying on various passages in which Hobbes notes that rebellions need leaders to blow the trumpet of war. But why should it? First, that the Foole sees personal profit in rebellion is not the sort of reason likely to motivate anyone else, for why should they care about his personal profit? His declaration alone offers them no reason to believe that *they* would profit, nor can we assume that those who are not fools would embrace the Foole's faulty principle of inference in their deliberations even were he to declare it. Of course, *if* others already believe that they also would personally profit from rebellion, the explicit Foole's declaration that rebellion is not against reason may possibly egg them on, supposing they have as weak powers of

[28] The first thing to notice is that it is no answer *to the Foole* to point out to him that his declaration may incite rebellion, for, in the case of the rebellious Foole (the only sort of foole whose injustice potentially incites rebellion), this is just the effect he hopes for. Hobbes nowhere in his reply to the Foole argues that the Foole's personal interests are not best served by the rebellion of *others*. So it may seem strange to adopt an interpretation of the Foole according to which his position is problematic because it incites rebellion, and yet Hobbes's reply to him offers him no reason to see the rebellion he incites as bad for himself. No appeal to potential punishment will solve this problem because punishment may be as well used against the nonrebellious Foole who does not incite rebellion as against the rebellious foole; and to answer the Foole by appeal to his prospective punishment is, again, just to sidestep the interesting challenge posed by the Foole who asks how profitable (that is, unpunished) injustice can be against reason.

reasoning as he. But even this is doubtful, considering that those who express loud and clear for all to hear their intention to overthrow the state if they find it personally advantageous to do so – while admittedly foolish – are not likely to repeat their folly; nor is the example of their fate at the hands of the state likely to inspire imitation. Explicit fools are much less dangerous than Hoekstra seems to imagine.

Furthermore, the Foole's explicit declaration makes clear to all would-be co-conspirators that the Foole intends to *betray his seditious alliance with them* should he see profit in doing so. How would that inspire them to join with him in his injustice? Surely people would be, if anything, much *less* likely to conspire with an explicit Foole, who makes known his treacherous principle, than a silent one. So it cannot be the explicitness of the Foole's declaration that makes for its problematic nature. To be sure, Hobbes wants to discourage others from embracing the Foole's logic and behavior, in part because he sees it as potentially destabilizing, but the Foole's destabilizing potential does *not depend* on his being *explicit.* If enough of the people enough of the time silently withhold their obedience out of the mistaken belief that profitable injustice accords with reason, the state's stability will surely be threatened by those who reason rightly in pursuit of ambition without regard to justice.[29] That the Foole holds this belief makes him vulnerable to recruitment by would-be rebels, explaining why Hobbes should have been concerned to correct his specious, but nevertheless false, reasoning, even if his declarations had absolutely no radicalizing effect on others.

Finally, and most importantly, Hobbes argues that in order to motivate rebellion, people must come to believe that they are *morally justified* in rebelling, justification being one of the three necessary conditions for rebellion. "*The business* ...", Hobbes writes, "[*of*] *the author of rebellion [is] to make men believe that their rebellion is just*".[30] But the Foole does not, either by his declaration or his example, convince others that rebellion is just. To the contrary, he argues that it *doesn't matter* whether

[29] Indeed, those who merely fail to aid the state, from whatever motive, may thereby contribute to its downfall when the state is threatened by ambitious others, as Hobbes would have learned from the case, among others, of the defeat of Richard III at the battle of Bosworth due largely to the complete inaction of Northumberland, who was in command of Richard's rear-guard.

[30] EW IV, 212, emphasis added.

their action is unjust, so long as it is personally profitable, because he thinks that unless justice is profitable it "is not to be approved for good". "Justice-shmustice, forget about it" is the Foole's motto. What would be needed to incite rebellion, according to Hobbes's account, is a showing that, for instance, the sovereign could no longer protect his subjects in their obedience, and so that it was *not unjust* to rebel – or more typically, that God requires rebellion against such a (heretical, iniquitous, etc.) sovereign. The Foole offers no such argument. His iconoclastic and base approach to justice will not provide anyone with the requisite moral justification for injustice. For this reason especially, it is not plausible that the problem Hobbes sees in the Foole is that he incites rebellion by his declaration or example; and so it cannot matter essentially to the Foole's folly whether he is loud and flagrant, or only silent, except, of course, insofar as the explicit Foole is more apt to be punished, and so is even less prudent than the silent Foole. It may be true that rebellion also requires one who can "blow the trumpet" of war in service of the just cause, but the Foole, even if he is a noisy blow-hard, cannot do that job because, insisting that there is no such thing as justice, he has no means to make others believe that rebellion is just.

None of this is to deny, what Hoekstra so elegantly shows, that Hobbes had an especial aversion to loud and flagrant Fooles, just as he did to demagogues and other prideful self-promoters. But the Foole's folly does not depend on his being explicit; the silent Foole who reasons upon that faulty principle of inference, and imprudently, is already quite foolish enough.

A small but interesting further advantage of the deflationary definitional interpretation I have offered over Hoekstra's Explicit Foole interpretation is that it does a better job of explaining why Hobbes frames his discussion of the unjust fool in the Biblical language of Psalms 14:1 that evokes the atheistic fool, who has said in his heart that there is no God. Hoekstra could certainly say, as have many commentators, that the Foole *has* to be an atheist in order to support the Foole's claim that injustice may be advantageous (which would be incredible were there a God who punishes injustice). This cannot be exactly right, for the Foole could claim that injustice may be advantageous even were he only to allege doubt about whether God values justice, or about what God counts as injustice. But granting as we should that Hobbes does want to answer the Foole without relying on a threat of God's punishment, we must still ask: Why does Hobbes insist that the Foole, who has said in his heart there is no such thing as justice, is the *self-same* Foole who has said in his heart there is no God? It cannot be because of his *explicit* denial of both dogmas, because the Biblical Foole does *not* deny God's existence "with his tongue".[31] This silently atheistic Foole is foolish only if what is foolish is to believe there is no God. Our deflationary definitional account explains why Hobbes thought even silent atheism is foolish. Atheism, as Hobbes argues in chapter 11 of *Leviathan,* depends upon faulty reasoning, because anyone who sees that effects have causes and those causes prior causes "must come to this thought at last: that there is some cause, whereof there is no former cause, but is eternal, which is it men call God".[32] Atheism is, on Hobbes's account, a failure of reasoning. It is also a failure of prudence (understood as facility in extrapolating from experience), according to Hobbes's supplementary argument that "by the visible things of this world and their admirable order, a man may conceive {is certain} there is a cause of them, whom men call God".[33] In his *Answer to Bishop Bramhall* Hobbes writes,

> [I]s not atheism boldness grounded on false reasoning, such as is this, *the wicked prosper, therefore there is no God?*...I deny there is any reason...in the atheist....I say atheism is a sin of ignorance....The prophet David says, *the fool hath said in his heart, there is no God.* Is it not then a sin of folly? It is agreed between us [Bramhall and Hobbes], that right reason dictates there is a God. Does it not follow, that denying of God is a sin proceeding from misreasoning.[34]

Misreasoning, false reasoning, is folly. The faults of the unjust Foole and the atheistic Foole with whom Hobbes identifies him are thus strictly parallel on the deflationary definitional interpretation, regardless of whether those fools are explicit or silent.[35] Indeed, Hobbes

[31] As Hoekstra notes in "Hobbes and the Foole", 625.

[32] EW III, 92; T 74.

[33] Curley, ed., *Leviathan,* 62.

[34] EW IV, 292–293.

[35] Hoekstra might respond by asserting that from God's omniscient perspective, even the silent atheist's atheism is explicit, recalling Hoekstra's observation that "in the eyes of God, every act of injustice (and, indeed, every attempted or intended act of injustice) is an act of explicit foolishness" (Hoekstra, "Hobbes and the Foole", 632). Such a response would maintain a parallel between the unjust and atheistic fools,

goes on in the passage just quoted to complain of atheists that "there is no living in a commonwealth with men, to whose oaths we cannot reasonably give credit";[36] this echoes Hobbes's contention in his reply to the Foole that society will cast out those who cannot be trusted to keep their covenants, or retain them only out of error.

Nevertheless, one should not exaggerate the incompatibility between the deflationary definitional and Explicit Foole interpretations. Presented as answers to the question *What is the folly that makes the Foole?* the interpretations are strictly speaking inconsistent. But each can incorporate the essential insights of the other. The deflationary definitional interpretation can gladly agree that explicit fools are even less prudent than silent ones, for even less can they expect to deceive others about their intentions to behave unjustly. And I see no reason why the Explicit Foole interpretation could not agree with the deflationary definitional interpretation that the Foole's reasoning depends upon a faulty principle of inference and a set of imprudent expectations. At issue between them is which of these features does the heavy lifting within Hobbes's diagnosis of the Foole's folly.

Prudence, Wisdom, and the Folly of Sedition

To return to the main line of argument, there is powerful textual support for the claim that Hobbes is primarily even if not exclusively concerned with claims that attempts at sedition may accord with reason, and that in answering this claim he deploys a two-pronged strategy relying on distinct considerations, as in his reply to the Foole, both

but at the cost of *collapsing* the distinction between silent and explicit fools upon which Hoekstra's interpretation relies. How can it matter that the Foole is explicit rather than silent if it is impossible for anyone not to be explicit? And if the problem with explicitness is supposed to be that it threatens to undermine social order by inciting rebellion, how are unjust and atheistic attitudes explicit only to God supposed to incite other men to rebel? I can find no textual evidence that Hobbes thought they do. In addition to collapsing Hoekstra's distinction and undermining its explanatory power, this way of explaining why the Foole is both unjust and atheistic disables Hobbes from answering the Foole's objection in the Foole's own terms, for the Foole, who believes there is no God, *cannot be answered* by asserting that God will punish his (silent/explicit only to God) injustices. But he can be answered, as the deflationary definitional interpretation suggests, by showing him that his denials of the existence both of justice and of God rely on faulty reasoning.

[36] EW IV, 294.

from sapience and from prudence. In *De Corpore Politico,* Hobbes argues that the authors of sedition are neither wise nor prudent. He writes:

That science in particular, from which proceed the true and evident conclusions of what is right and wrong, and what is good and hurtful to the being, and well-being of mankind, the Latins call *sapientia,* and we by the general name of wisdom. For generally...only he that understandeth what conduceth to the good and government of the people, is called a wise man. Now that no author of sedition can be wise in this acceptation of the word, is sufficiently proved, in that it hath been already demonstrated, that no pretence of sedition can be right or just. And therefore the authors of sedition must be ignorant of the right of state, that is to say, unwise.... [T]hey be such, as name things, not according to their true and generally agreed upon names, but call right and wrong, good and bad, according to their passions, or according to the authorities of such as they admire, as Aristotle, Cicero, [or] Seneca.... It is required therefore in an author of sedition, that he think right, that which is wrong; and profitable, that which is pernicious; and consequently that there be in him *sapientiae parum,* little wisdom.[37]

This argument against sedition from sapience alleges that the unwise man lacks competent command of language, misunderstanding the meaning of the terms he employs in his attempted justification of sedition, and using faulty rules of inference, including the Foole's, that personal profit justifies an action, and that reliance on authority comports with reason. I shall discuss this latter error momentarily. Hobbes insists that "when men remember not how things are named, by general agreement, but either mistake and misname things, or name them aright *by chance,* they are not said to have science, but opinion, and the conclusions thence proceeding, are uncertain, and for the most part erroneous".[38]

Hobbes's argument against sedition from considerations of prudence proceeds as follows:

[T]he wisdom that proceedeth from [experience], is that ability to conjecture by the present, of what is past, and to come, which men call *prudence.* This being so, it is manifest presently, that the author of sedition, whosoever he be, must not be prudent. For if he consider and take his experiences aright, concerning the success which they have had, who have been the movers and

[37] EW IV, 210–211.
[38] EW IV, 210, emphasis added.

authors of sedition, either in this or any other state, he shall find, that for one man that hath thereby advanced himself to honour, twenty have come to a reproachful end.[39]

The examples of some few who have profited by rebellion do not vindicate the rebellious fool's actions, for he acts upon "*rash and unevident inferences,* such as are fetched only from examples, or authority of books".[40]

This two-pronged argument that "the authors of rebellion necessarily are to be men of little wisdom" precisely mirrors Hobbes's two-part reply to the unjust fool who believes rebellious violations of the foundational covenant may sometimes accord with reason. Wisdom requires the use of correct general principles, and prudence requires correct extrapolation from prior experience, but the unjust fool manages neither. While his actions may unexpectedly happen to turn out well, they do not do so "by the sole strength of his good contrivance", for he relies on a faulty general principle and owes his success to the unforeseeable errors of other men and sheer dumb luck. In *Behemoth,* Hobbes writes, "Wise, as I define it, is he that knows how to bring his business to pass, without the assistance of knavery and ignoble shifts, *by the sole strength of his good contrivance.* A fool may win from a better gamester by the advantage of false dice and packing of cards".[41] The gaming fool, like the unjust fool, *may* succeed with the assistance of knavery, but whether he does so depends on the lucky fact that his opponents make errors in not uncovering his deceptions. In no case is his success attributable to wisdom.

[39] Ibid., 210.

[40] EW III, 246; T 180. In Hobbes's discussion of crime in chapter 27 of *Leviathan,* we have further textual evidence that Hobbes took the Foole's principle to be a false one that exhibits the defect of inferring from the profitability of an action that it was reasonable, and on the basis of which men have mistakenly sought to justify injustice. There he writes,

> From defect in reasoning, that is to say, from error, men are prone to violate the laws...by presumption of false principles: as when men, from having observed how in all places, and in all ages, unjust actions have been authorized, by the force, and victories of those who have committed them...have thereupon taken for principles, and grounds of their reasoning, *that justice is but a vain word...that examples of former times are good arguments of doing the like again*...which being granted, no act in itself can be a crime, but must be made so, not by law, but by the success of them that commit it...to the perpetual disturbance of the peace of the commonwealth (EW III, 281–282; T 204).

[41] EW VI, 211, emphasis added.

A further way in which one may foolishly rest one's hopes of success on something other than one's own good contrivance is by relying on authorities rather than one's own reasoning. Hobbes faults the unjust fool for relying on hearsay to support the claim that breach of covenant may conduce to the attaining of an eternal felicity after death. In general, writes Hobbes, unless a man has science to rely upon, "to forsake his own natural judgment, and be guided by general sentences read in authors, and subject to many exceptions, is a sign of folly".[42] This is so because "words are wise men's counters, they do but reckon by them; but they are the money of fools, that value them by the authority of an Aristotle, a Cicero, or a Thomas, or any other doctor whatsoever, if but a man".[43] To blindly follow the prescriptions of authors is to succeed, if at all, by luck rather than skill.

Seeing this helps us to understand why Hobbes thinks that folly is dishonorable. We call those attributes honorable that are signs of power, power understood as means to accomplish our ends; and those dishonorable that are signs of a lack of power, or impotency. The man who can bring about his desired outcomes "by the sole strength of his good contrivance" has all the powers he needs, and his actions enjoy our admiration because they exhibit that sufficiency of power. The man who must cheat, or depend on the ignorance, or error, or help of others, or on brute luck in order for his aims to be realized, has little power, and so his actions, even insofar as they succeed, are dishonorable. In *Leviathan*, Hobbes writes, "All actions, and speeches, that proceed, or seem to proceed, from much experience, science, discretion, or wit, are honourable; for all these are powers. Actions, or words that proceed from error, ignorance, or folly [are] dishonorable... [and] craft, shifting, neglect of equity, is dishonorable".[44] Much experience is prudence, and much science is wisdom, sapience being the particular science concerned with humanity's well-being. The fool, having no moral science, must rely for his successes on craft, which term Hobbes explains thus: "To prudence, if you add the use of unjust, or dishonest means... you have that crooked wisdom, which

[42] EW III, 38; T 37.
[43] EW III, 25; T 28. Cf. EW III, 24; T 28.
[44] EW III, 79–80; T 66.

is called CRAFT".[45] Craft is crooked wisdom in the same way that a stick partially submerged in water is a crooked stick: It isn't. Both are illusions. The Foole's craft tries to impersonate wisdom, but it is just the recourse of a man of little power in pursuit of his selfish interests. We cannot esteem his actions.

Notice, however, that whether we should fault or pity him depends on our assessment of why he lacks the power to bring about his ends by the sole strength of his good contrivance. The "natural fool" has not sufficient mental facility to use language, and so cannot know general principles. Not only can he not know what time it is, because, not knowing the meanings (hence order) of number words, he counts the strikes of the clock "one, one, one ...";[46] natural fools cannot be held accountable to law at all, because, like brute beasts "they had never power to make any covenant, or to understand the consequences thereof... [and so such a person] is excused".[47] Natural fools are to be excused, not faulted, and presumably to be pitied, according to Hobbes's definition of pity as grief for the calamity of another, especially when his calamity is not the result of any wickedness on his part.

The unjust fool is however not to be let off the hook so easily, for he does have the use of language and some pretense to science, as is evidenced by his insistence on his faulty general rule of inference. He is a fool not by nature, but, presumably, by nurture. His folly arises from some defect in what we might broadly term his education. This suggests, as I shall argue below, that correcting and preventing this sort of folly depends upon a scheme of correct socialization.

Finally, we should recognize that the unjust fool's folly is more than a matter of his defect in reasoning, or his imprudence. His imprudent gamble banks on his capacity to deceive others about his true nature; and this, Hobbes argues, depends on a foolish overassessment of his capabilities relative to his fellows. It is a natural foible that men routinely suppose themselves superior in the natural qualities of mind and good sense to others, but it is a foible nonetheless. Hobbes plausibly argues that most men are not all that different with respect to their ability to deceive others, or to avoid being deceived. For this

[45] EW III, 60; T 53.
[46] EW III, 22; T 27.
[47] EW III, 257; T 187.

reason, the Foole's supposition that he can systematically deceive others is contrary to experience, and thus an imprudent folly rooted in false pride or vain glory. Hobbes writes,

> [Men who make] a false presumption of their own wisdom [are]...prone to all such crimes, as consist in craft, and in deceiving of their neighbours; because they think their designs are too subtle to be perceived....And those that deceive upon hope of not being observed,...are no wiser than children, that think all hid, by hiding their own eyes.[48]

Those unjust fools who imprudently depend on being so much abler at deception than others can add the folly of excessive pride to that of their inept reasoning. They are doubly foolish because, experience shows that "[m]en that distrust their own subtlety, are, in tumult and sedition, better disposed for victory, than they that suppose themselves wise, or crafty".[49]

Pride and Folly

How foolish is excessive pride? Hobbes maintains that it ranges from mere folly to certifiable madness. Recall that Hobbes thinks of madness as any great overvehemence of passion. It follows that there are degrees of madness which depend upon the increments of overvehemence. The man who thinks so much more of himself than others that he believes he is God, is surely mad. Those who believe themselves true prophets in direct personal communication with God are very likely mad, albeit to a lesser degree. Those who imagine their own judgment epistemically privileged, as the fools who imagine themselves able systematically to deceive their fellows, evidence an inflated self-importance that argues a degree of madness.

The relation between vain-glory and folly is explicitly mentioned in Hobbes's *Behemoth* discussion of folly and hypocrisy during the civil wars. In the opening paragraph Hobbes writes,

> If in time, as in place, there were degrees of high and low, I verily believe that the highest of time would be that which passed between 1640 and 1660.

48 EW III, 284; T 205.

49 EW III, 88; T 72. Cf. "nor when the wise in their own conceit, contend by force, with them who distrust their own wisdom, do they always, or often, or almost at any time, get the victory" (EW III, 141; T 107).

For he that thence, as from the Devil's Mountain, should have looked upon the world and observed the actions of men, especially in England, might have had a prospect of all kinds of injustice, and all kinds of folly, that the world would afford, and how they were produced by their hypocrisy and self-conceit, whereof the one is double iniquity, and the other double folly.[50]

Hypocrisy is double iniquity and it produces the injustice of sedition (and associated lesser injustices). Self-conceit is double folly, and it produces the folly of sedition (and associated lesser follies). Our deflationary definitional interpretation of Hobbes's reply to the Foole allows us to see how this characterization would be correct. The self-conceit of rebels and usurpers causes them, first, foolishly to suppose (despite their mistaken principles of inference, ignorance of concepts, reliance on authorities, and inept extrapolation from experience) that their personal judgment of what justice requires and whether it is to be "approved for good" is authoritative. This is the Job problem, that "the children of pride" arrogate to themselves the right to judge what is good and evil, which is indeed caused by a kind of self-conceit, according to Hobbes, as his discussion of the lessons of Job makes clear.[51] This first folly is then compounded by the rebels' folly in thinking themselves so much cleverer than others as to expect to succeed in grabbing and maintaining power (their designs being too subtle to be perceived, and so on). Hence, self-conceit or vain-glory, comprised of thinking one's judgment superior to others', and one's abilities to outwit others also superior is a double folly, and it causes men to do any number of foolish things, both unwisely and imprudently.

Although I have presented Hobbes's reply to the Foole as proceeding in two distinct phases, with the first arguing from wisdom and the second from prudence, we can now see how they can be understood as less distinct than may at first appear, with the prudence prong *also* evidencing a failure of right reasoning (i.e., wisdom) as the deflationary

[50] EW VI, 165.

[51] EW III, 307; T 221. Cf. his discussion of the sin of Adam and Eve, as taking "upon them God's office, which is judicature of good and evil;...as if [God] should say, doest thou that owest me obedience, take upon thee to judge of my commandments? Whereby it is clearly, though allegorically, signified, that the commands of them that have the right to command, are not by their subjects to be censured, nor disputed" (EW III, 194; T 144).

definitional interpretation contends. The unjust Foole's imprudence manifests reliance on a false principle of inference every bit as much as does his reliance on the false principle that *if an action benefits oneself, it cannot have been against reason to do it.* The Foole takes success in securing one's ends as rational vindication, and so he believes that *examples of beneficial rebellious injustice in former times are good reasons for doing the like again.* But this too is false, for the same reason that his general principle is false, namely, that not everything falling under the term "is beneficial to oneself" also falls under the term "is reasonable". Moreover, the Foole is taking notice only of past successful rebellions, and ignoring the many more unsuccessful rebellions. When it is pointed out to him that *most* rebels have failed to profit, the Foole will say that, even so, he is optimistic that his own rebellion will be among the minority that succeeds, because of his superior wit, craft, ability to deceive, and so on. But here again, the rebellious Foole makes a conceptual error, because for his optimism to provide *evidence* for his likelihood of success, it would have to be true as a general principle that *if one is optimistic that one will succeed, one is likely to succeed.* And, of course, this principle is not only not true by definition, it is empirically false; Hobbes points out that experience teaches that for every rebel who succeeds, twenty go down in defeat and ignominy, yet one of the three conditions necessary to motivate men to rebel is "hope of success", a kind of psychological optimism about their chances of success. *All* rebels think themselves more likely than others to succeed, and yet *almost all of them are wrong.* Thus the rebellious Foole errs again in embracing the principle that *if one judges oneself superior in wit, craft, etc., one is likely to succeed in rebellion.* Even the Foole's imprudence depends in the end on false general principles, and thus on a failure of wisdom, sapience, and right reasoning.[52]

On traditional interpretations of the Foole passage as intended to provide a defense of morality in terms of self-interest, Hobbes's reply to the Foole is hopelessly flawed. I have argued for a deflationary definitional interpretation of Hobbes's reply to the Foole, according to which that reply is not intended to provide an argument for the rationality of morality, but merely to answer a particular objection to Hobbes's prior demonstration that justice is a rule of reason. It does so

[52] I am grateful to Ed McCann for very helpful discussion of these ideas.

simply by discrediting the Foole's principle of inference, and showing that on a correct principle of inference, the imprudence of seditious injustice would be manifest. In this more limited aim, Hobbes's reply succeeds entirely. And it does so in a way that deprives self-interest interpretations of Hobbes's Laws of Nature of any support in Hobbes's reply to the Foole.

How do unjust fools contribute to social instability? Although it is possible that such people might do so by persuading others that they need not keep their covenant of obedience to the sovereign unless it profits them to do so, we would not expect this to be the main way in which they contribute to instability. More often they weaken the state by withholding due support, in money and services, whenever they think they can profit by doing so. Hobbes frequently complains that subjects seek to avoid paying the taxes necessary for the commonwealth's preservation; the Foole will believe himself justified in tax evasion if he thinks he can get away with it. The Foole will be the first to run from battle, or evade military service altogether, if he thinks doing so will benefit him.

But the real reason that social stability is threatened by the existence of unjust fools is not, *pace* Hoekstra, that they incite others to rebel, but that they are easily talked into rebellion by others. Because they do not think there is anything wrong with profitable injustice, they can be persuaded to rebel even without a showing that such rebellion is morally justified. One of Hobbes's three necessary conditions for motivating rebellion – "pretense of right" – is not needed to motivate unjust fools. In this way their inept command of reason makes them much easier for rebels to recruit. Or, better put, their folly makes it more likely that they will find satisfied the first and third of Hobbes's necessary conditions for motivating rebellion – discontent and hope of success. Because they are willing to be guided entirely by their sense of what would profit themselves, any discontent with their position under the existing regime will seem to them also to confer a right to rebel, and because they are foolish also in unwarrantedly assuming their ability to deceive others, they are likely to espy "hope of success" where a more reasonable person would not. The Foole and his ilk, then, are easily tricked by crafty ambitious men, for they have no standard for right apart from their contentment, and foolishly overestimate their chances for successfully overthrowing the existing regime. They do not incite rebellion, they fall victim to the siren song of those who do.

THE DUPE

Hobbes does not speak of "the Dupe" as he does of "the Foole", even though he is clearly worried about dupes, and the problems posed by dupes are closely related to those posed by fools. The reason for this, I speculate, is that while both are easily manipulated into rebellion, only the Foole is prepared to defend a general argument to give his position a pretense of rational warrant, and Hobbes is particularly keen to smack down such a pretender to wisdom. The Dupe is not so fancy as that. He is your ordinary, gullible, superstitious, under-educated, trusting, honest soul, who means to do what is right, but is easily tricked into believing right that which is wrong. Like the Foole, the Dupe is easily turned toward rebellion; but he operates not on the basis of reasoned arguments, but on the basis of his passions and trust in authorities. His trust in authorities is, as we've seen, a kind of foolishness, but considering his station in life, it would be harsh to condemn him for that. Not having science himself, he will have to depend on the authority of others; the question is just, which others? Unless the State establishes its own authority, and correctly educates him to his duty, the Dupe will be easy pickings for those who would seize power. The fault of the Dupe thus lies with the State that allowed him to be under- or miseducated, rather than with the Dupe himself. "The common people's minds", Hobbes writes, "unless they be tainted with dependance on the potent, or scribbled over with the opinions of their doctors, are like clean paper, fit to receive whatsoever by public authority shall be imprinted in them".[53]

Were noxious influences repelled, and proper education provided, the common people, despite their natural credulity, would not be duped by unjust rebels. But even innocent ignorance can quickly become a force for evil. Hobbes writes, in a characteristically subtle observation of human nature,

> Ignorance of natural causes, disposeth a man to credulity, so as to believe many times impossibilities: for such know nothing to the contrary, but that they may be true; being unable to detect the impossibility. And credulity, because men like to be hearkened unto in company, disposeth them to

[53] EW III, 325; T 233.

lying: so that ignorance itself without malice, is able to make a man both to believe lies, and tell them; and sometimes also to invent them.[54]

Dupes are unconscious conduits for destabilizing doctrine.

The magnitude of the contribution to social instability posed by dupes may be judged by how often and vociferously Hobbes remarks on men's native gullibility. In chapter 12 of *Leviathan*, Hobbes argues that humans are naturally inclined toward religious belief and that this inclination is harnessed by others who would seek to rule them. Once trusted, those leaders can induce men to believe virtually anything, "[s]o easy are men to be drawn to believe any thing, from such men as have gotten credit with them; and can with gentleness, and dexterity, take hold of their fear, and ignorance".[55] The common man's ignorance (his having no science) allows others to manipulate his fears, and presumably aspirations as well, for the ends of those seeking to incite rebellion, "[f]or such is the ignorance and aptitude to error generally of all men, but especially of them that have not much knowledge of natural causes, and of the nature and interests of men; as by innumerable and easy tricks to be abused".[56]

These passages may suggest that Hobbes counts almost everyone a dupe, at least in some matters, but that is not, or at least need not be, the case. Left uneducated, men are easily duped. But once educated, it becomes quite difficult to move them from their beliefs, no matter whether that education has been correct or incorrect,[57] and so duping them requires either miseducating them from the beginning, or gradually introducing technical jargon and sophistical reasoning to bamboozle them into believing that one's specious conclusions are actually implications of their beliefs, rather than contrary to those beliefs, as Hobbes thinks is done by the Schoolmen, and corrupt demagogues, lawyers, and clerics of all denominations. Hobbes writes,

if the minds of men were all of white paper, they would almost equally be disposed to acknowledge whatsoever should be in right method, and by right ratiocination delivered to them: but when men have once acquiesced in untrue opinions, and registered them as authentical records in their minds,

[54] EW III, 92; T 74.
[55] EW III, 103; T 82.
[56] EW III, 434; T 304.
[57] EW III, 694; T 478.

it is no less impossible to speak intelligibly to such men, than to write legibly upon a paper already scribbled over. The immediate *cause* therefore of *indocibility*, is *prejudice;* and of prejudice, false opinion of our own knowledge.[58]

Again we see that thinking we already know, makes it neigh impossible to learn better. Once duped, a person is largely lost to right reasoning, so the prospective Dupe must be handled properly from the beginning if civil stability is to be secured.

THE ZEALOT

The Zealot, again a type whom Hobbes discusses without giving this particular name, is also a dupe and a fool, after a manner. The Zealot believes that he and like-thinking others alone have God's truth in hand (a foolish overassessment of his powers of cognition and foolish underassessment of his epistemological vulnerability), relying for proof either on the authority of others (a form of folly) or on his belief that God is in direct communication with him, either through the Scriptures or supernaturally (a prudentially unwarranted vain folly). But he is more than a religious fanatic, fanaticism being excess of passion partaking of madness. The Zealot honestly believes the doctrines he espouses, so when he can be convinced that these are incompatible with civil obedience, he is prepared to rebel. His interests (unlike those of the Foole) are *transcendent.* This makes him tinder for rebellious sparks. Mere discontent will not move him to attempt rebellion; but if his religious commitments can be exploited to persuade him that rebellion is not only permissible but required, he will lead the charge, without any more concrete hope of success, perhaps, than his expectation of heavenly reward. The transcendent interests of zealots make them most dangerous of all rebel recruits, and it is Hobbes's concern about this group that explains why so much of his moral and political philosophy is devoted to clarifying and correcting religious doctrine, and expounding the proper grounds and authority for religious beliefs. Hobbes does not wish to stamp out transcendent interests – this would be undesirable even were it possible given human nature, which it is not – rather, he wishes to harness transcendent interests to reinforce

[58] EW IV, 57.

social stability instead of undermining it. He wants subjects to see that civil obedience is a part of their duty to God, and thus to be willing to die if need be in defense of the commonwealth. But to have transcendent religious interests engaged in efforts to subvert civil stability can lead to disaster.

It is noteworthy that in the review and conclusion to *Leviathan* Hobbes adds a caution against zealotry. Private zeal threatens to usurp the place of judicial decision, and this is dangerous: "There is nothing in all this, nor in any other part of the Bible, to countenance executions by private zeal; which being oftentimes but a conjunction of ignorance and passion, is against both the justice and peace of a commonwealth".[59] Like the Foole and the Dupe, the Zealot's ignorance gives improper scope to his passions; and because he believes God is with him, there is nothing he may not dare to do or risk. Unlike fools or dupes, zealots have potential to inspire rebellion by their claims that rebellion is righteous. Hobbes's systematic concern in every version of his political philosophy to discredit those who think themselves divinely inspired testifies to the gravity of the threat to social stability he sees in the Zealot.

THE HYPOCRITE

Unlike the Zealot, the Dupe, and the Foole, the Hypocrite does not really believe what he says. He says what he does not believe in order to manipulate others into serving his ends, ends that they would not willingly serve were they to see his true motives. Morally speaking, the Hypocrite is the worst of the worst, and most vile of the vile. He knows what is right, but acts against it in pursuit of his ends, and lies to others to recruit them to his service. He acts with what Hobbes calls *a seared conscience*. This is really bad. Hobbes describes the Hypocrite's behavior as "double iniquity". Because God condemns iniquity as contrary to both his natural and divine positive laws, the Hypocrite should expect to be in serious trouble upstairs. Sometimes Hobbes suggests that such hypocrites must be closet atheists, for how otherwise would they dare to behave as they do? While it is true that the Hypocrite may attempt, successfully, to incite rebellion amongst

59 EW III, 709; T 488.

Fooles and Dupes, the largest danger posed by the Hypocrite is his effect on Zealots. The Hypocrite feigns religious beliefs in order to manipulate and direct the energies of zealous true believers against the State, in order to forward his own worldly interests. He treats zealots as dupes, and succeeds because those zealots are foolish in their reliance on authority.

Hypocrites are liable to being found out, because those who rely on them will compare their words with their deeds. This makes hypocrisy foolish after a manner, because the Hypocrite must assume, along with the Foole, that he can systematically deceive others about his true character. Hobbes tells us that one of the main causes of change in religion is that the hypocritical behavior of priests causes followers to doubt their sincerity:

> That which taketh away the reputation of sincerity, is the doing or saying of such things, as appear to be signs, that what they require other men to believe, is not believed by themselves;...as injustice, cruelty, profaneness, avarice, and luxury. For who can believe, that he that doth ordinarily such actions as proceed from any of these roots, believeth there is any such invisible power to be feared, as he affrighteth other men withal, for lesser faults?[60]

To expect to be successful, the Hypocrite must suppose himself able either to hide or to explain away his unjust and otherwise unseemly actions, something it would be foolish to count on, as Hobbes's reply to the Foole makes clear. Of course, he always has available the claim, should any of his actions be found wrongful, that he sincerely believed them agreeable to God's will, which may give him some feeling of safety, and it is for this reason that Hobbes snidely remarks that "hypocrisy hath this great prerogative above other sins, that it cannot be accused".[61] But still, the Hypocrite foolishly plays at a dangerous game in pursuit of his worldly ambition:

> Hypocrites may ascend to power through craft, but they should know that power is preserved by the same virtues by which it is acquired; that is to say, by wisdom, humility, clearness of doctrine, and sincerity of conversation; and not by suppression of the natural sciences, and of the morality of natural

60 EW III, 106; T 84.
61 EW VI, 224.

reason; nor by...pious frauds; nor by such other faults, as in the pastors of God's Church are not only faults, but also scandals.[62]

The Hypocrite who purveys what he believes to be false moral and religious doctrines in the service of his own ambition has had his reason overcome. "Ambition", Hobbes writes, "and covetousness are passions also that are perpetually incumbent, and pressing; whereas reason is not perpetually present, to resist them: and therefore whensoever the hope of impunity appears, their effects proceed".[63]

Ambition is not unique to the Hypocrite, but Hobbes does seem to suppose that the Hypocrite who poses a threat to social order is politically ambitious. If such a person can make himself popular, he can pose a very serious threat because his popularity induces men to trust him, and his ambition turns that trust to his own private ends. Hobbes describes such a person's modus operandi in stark and shocking terms: "[T]his proceeding of popular, and ambitious men, is plain rebellion; and may be resembled to the effects of witchcraft".[64] When we recall that Hobbes views witchcraft as ordinary deceiving craft used to make others wrongly believe one has a special power to effect his desired outcomes, we can see why Hobbes thinks the Hypocrite so dangerous.

A GENERAL DIAGNOSIS OF DESTABILIZING CHARACTERS, AND A PRESCRIPTION FOR IMPEDING THEIR FORMATION AND MINIMIZING THEIR EFFECTS

These various problematic types are largely distinct, but they do bear a family resemblance. The Foole reasons, but wrongly, to general conclusions, thus betraying his embarrassing failure of attempted science, and insofar as he lacks science, he is ignorant. The Dupe makes no pretense to science, but his ignorance leaves him defenseless and vulnerable to the trickery of those who would foment rebellion, just as is the Foole. The Zealot, whose confidence in his doctrine outruns any possible science but depends only on his foolish reliance on authorities and unwarranted privileging of his private perceptions, believes God will vindicate his actions no matter what social havoc they wreak,

[62] EW III, 697; T 480.
[63] EW III, 285; T 206.
[64] EW III, 320–321; T 230.

his transcendent interest makes him willing to martyr himself in his cause, and he may well motivate others to rebel by his conviction and example. He is a true believer who, however misguided, is at least authentic. But he is no less foolish for that. The Hypocrite pretends to believe what the Zealot believes, or what the Foole believes, but only in order to manipulate others in his grab for temporal power. He does what he believes to be wrong, ready to act with a seared conscience in pursuit of his ambition, and is therefore doubly iniquitous, as Hobbes's introduction to *Behemoth* makes clear. All these defective types of subjects/citizens play a role in the recurrent social disorder of the commonwealth. How are such folk to be made better moral judges? How are these who light and fuel the fire of rebellion to be dissuaded from doing so?

Traditional interpretations assume that all socially disruptive behaviors and attitudes are to be handled in the same way: Threaten to punish them. Because, on traditional interpretations, Hobbesean men are egoistic, atheistic animals that put their individual survival above all else, every problematic behavior can be eradicated by credibly threatening those who would exhibit it with death. If you make them think you'll kill them, you can make them do anything.

I do not see why anyone would find it worthwhile to entertain such a view, either on its own merits, or as an appropriately charitable interpretation of Hobbes. But in any case, that answer is not Hobbes's answer. Hobbes offers an entirely different solution, in which his own writings are intended to play a part: Educate people in the truth. On the one hand, this recommendation sounds much too simple; on the other, it may seem positively Orwellian. Truth by whose lights? Are we to correct their errors, or exert mind control? Questions of the relation between coercion, ideology, and education loom large in Hobbes's moral philosophy, once we understand that he never held the naïve view that 'might makes right', or secures social order. So let us address these questions directly, as we assess Hobbes's recommendation for establishing a stable ground for social harmony through proper education.

CIVIC EDUCATION

I argued in *Ideals as Interests* that the broad aim of Hobbes's political philosophy is to bring people to recognize that they have, what are by their own lights, good and sufficient reasons to obey the commands of their effective sovereign. Hobbes attributes several basic sorts of interest to people – narrowly prudential interests in one's physical survival and flourishing; moral interests (including reasons from both obligation and natural duty); affectionate interests in the well-being of loved ones; and religious interests, both in fulfilling one's duties to God and in achieving one's own salvation and avoiding damnation (what I have called elsewhere "special prudential interests"). Hobbes aims at a confluence of reasons from these distinct interests for adhering to his principle of political obligation,[65] and accordingly mounts arguments for that principle on each of these grounds. That principle of political obligation, stated at the beginning of chapter 31 of *Leviathan,* is this: "subjects owe to sovereigns, simple obedience, in all things wherein their obedience is not repugnant to the laws of God".[66]

The narrowly prudential argument, that is, the argument from temporal self-interest, urges that it is in our interest to live in a stable state that can increase our prospects for security, ordered liberty, and a commodious life, and the principle of political obligation best suited to sustaining such a state considering human nature is Hobbes's. The moral argument holds that we have a *natural duty* not to act in a way that we would be unwilling to have others act (this is the reciprocity theorem derived as a requirement of rational agency), and that because our prudential interests dictate that we should require *others* to adhere to Hobbes's principle (because it promises maximal stability), natural duty requires us to do likewise. Moreover, if we have

65 This is part of what accounts for the difficulty of extracting "the" argument Hobbes gives for political obedience. "The" argument has appeared to many to be self-contradictory or elliptical, but this sense is reduced once we see Hobbes as offering a number of different, though intertwined, arguments converging on the same conclusion. See *IAI,* 88–94, 155–156, and 266–268.

66 EW III, 343; T 245. Hobbes continues, "There wants only, for the entire knowledge of civil duty, to know what are those laws of God. For without that, a man knows not, when he is commanded any thing by the civil power, whether it be contrary to the law of God, or not". Discovering this is the task of parts 3 and 4 of *Leviathan* (and of the corresponding sections of his earlier works), in which Hobbes concludes that "the laws of God therefore are none but the laws of nature, whereof the principal is...a commandment to obey our civil sovereigns" (EW III, 587; T 404). Our primary religious duty is to obey our Sovereign, and the willingness to do that is one of two necessary conditions for salvation (the other being faith).

either explicitly undertaken to obey our sovereign (through, say, one of the oaths of allegiance common in Hobbes's day) or tacitly done so (by openly receiving the protection of the commonwealth), then we have as well a moral *obligation* to obey in all of the conditions that Hobbes's principle specifies.[67] Hobbes offers two religious arguments for his principle of political obligation as well: the primary one from religious duty, and a supplemental one from special prudence. Our only available sources of religious knowledge – namely, natural reason, personal revelation, and Scripture – all show that our central duty to God is to obey our civil sovereign. They show further that a good faith effort to obey the civil sovereign (where God takes the will for the deed) is a necessary condition of salvation, and in our special-prudential interests. If these various arguments are accepted, and their conclusions and essential implications taught, Hobbes imagines that it may be possible to convert his "truth of speculation, into the utility of practice".[68]

What I have just described is Hobbes's argumentative strategy for persuading his readers of the truth of his principle of political obligation and motivating them to adhere, and induce others to adhere, to it. It would be a mistake to confuse this strategy with the concrete educational program Hobbes advocates for creating right-thinking and virtuous subjects who are neither fools nor dupes nor zealots. Although bringing subjects to accept that they have prudential, moral, and religious reasons for obeying their sovereign is necessary to Hobbes's strategy for addressing social disorder, teaching all subjects the central *arguments* of *Leviathan* is not necessary, but in fact would be, for every venue but the universities, overly ambitious and potentially self-defeating. *Leviathan* may profitably be taught in the universities, but the general public is better served by an educational program that teaches a manageable number of specifics including (1) the content and grounds of "the essential rights of sovereignty", (2) the Laws of Nature, (3) the sovereign's positive laws (whatever they may be), and (4) the

[67] According to Hobbes, the promise of obedience that issues in political obligation "may be either express or tacit" (EW III, 705; T 485). We have a natural duty to undertake political obligations, which we fulfill by expressly or tacitly covenanting to obey.

[68] EW III, 358; T 254.

Scriptural grounds for the sovereign's virtually absolute authority. Hobbes assumes that in addition subjects will continue to receive ordinary religious instruction from their local pastors, but only in those religious doctrines the sovereign has authorized.

"[I]n the instruction of the people in the essential rights which are the natural and fundamental laws of sovereignty", Hobbes writes,

> there is no difficulty, whilst a sovereign has his power entire, but what proceeds from his own fault, or the fault of those whom he trusteth in the administration of the commonwealth; and consequently, it is his duty, to cause them so to be instructed.... And, to descend to particulars, the people are to be taught, first, that they ought not to be in love with any form of government they see in their neighbour nations, more than with their own, nor, whatsoever present prosperity they behold in nations that are otherwise governed than they, to desire change.... Secondly, they are to be taught, that they ought not to be led with admiration of the virtue of any of their fellow-subjects,... nor of any assembly,... so as to defer to them any obedience, or honour, appropriate to the sovereign only.... Thirdly,... they ought to be informed, how great a fault it is, to speak evil of the sovereign representative.... Fourthly, seeing people cannot be taught this, nor when it is taught, remember it,... without setting apart from their ordinary labour, some certain times, in which they may attend those that are appointed to instruct them; it is necessary that some such times be determined, wherein they may... hear those their duties told them, and the positive laws, such as generally concern them all, read and expounded.... Again, every sovereign ought to cause justice to be taught,... to abstain from violence to one another's person, by private revenges; from violation of conjugal honour; and from forcible rapine, and fraudulent surreption of one another's goods. For which purpose also it is necessary they be showed the evil consequences of false judgment, by corruption either of judges or witnesses.... Lastly, they are to be taught, that not only the unjust facts, but the designs and intentions to do them, though by accident hindered, are injustice.[69]

MECHANISMS OF EDUCATION

How is this education to be accomplished? The specifics are to be taught publicly, to the common man at regular intervals from the pulpit, and to the educated in the universities. The common folk will

[69] EW III, 326–330; T 234–236.

receive most of their education from preachers. Parents will also be responsible for some of the teaching.[70]

But because preachers are educated in the universities, as are parliamentarians and others who might by their poor leadership or example corrupt the people's education, the universities must be especially carefully monitored:

the greatest part of mankind... receive the notions of their duty, chiefly from divines in the pulpit.... And the divines, and such others as make show of learning, derive their knowledge from the universities, and from the schools of law, or from the books, which by men, eminent in those schools and universities, have been published. It is therefore manifest, that *the instruction of the people, dependeth wholly, on the right teaching of youth in the universities*.[71]

It would be difficult to stress enough how important Hobbes takes the influence of the universities to be: in fact he repeatedly blames them for the English Civil War and regards their reformation as a necessary condition for the maintenance of peace. In *Behemoth*, Hobbes insists that England will never have a lasting peace until the universities, which had functioned to foment seditious doctrines, have been reformed,[72] and his interlocutors have this exchange:

B. For aught I see, all the states of Christendom will be subject to these fits of rebellion, as long as the world lasteth.

A. Like enough; and yet the fault, as I have said, may be easily mended, by mending the Universities.[73]

In addition to controlling the education of the educators such as preachers and teachers, the books they use and the actual doctrines they teach are also subject to the sovereign's direct prescreening

[70] Hobbes seems to approve of Old Testament practice in teaching civil duty: "And for the law which Moses gave to the people of Israel at the renewing of the covenant... he biddeth them to teach it their children, by discoursing of it both at home, and upon the way; at going to bed, and at rising from bed; and to write it upon the posts, and doors of their houses; and... to assemble the people, man, woman, and child, to hear it read" (EW III, 259; T 189). Cf. EW III, 589; T 406, where Hobbes writes that the ordinary cause of belief in the Scriptures is from being taught by "those that are by the law allowed and appointed to teach us, as our parents in their houses, and our pastors in the churches".

[71] EW III, 331; T 237, emphasis added.

[72] EW VI, 236–237.

[73] EW VI, 252.

and approval: "[I]t is annexed to the sovereignty, to be judge of what opinions and doctrines are averse, and what conducing to peace; and consequently, on what occasions, how far, and what men are to be trusted withal, in speaking to multitudes of people; and who shall examine the doctrines of all books before they be published".[74]

When potentially seditious works are used, like the classical republican texts, they are to be used under the supervision of state-authorized teachers. "I cannot imagine", Hobbes writes, "how anything can be more prejudicial to a monarchy, than the allowing of such books to be publicly read, without present applying such correctives of discreet masters, as are fit to take away their venom".[75] And the sovereign may select his public teachers using a litmus test, or even a catalog of what is to be taught: "It is true, that the civil magistrate, intending to employ a minister in the charge of teaching, may enquire of him, if he be content to preach such and such doctrines; and in case of refusal, may deny him the employment".[76] Hobbes is thus advocating an educational system of mandatory, state-controlled education intended to inculcate the beliefs (and purge the errors) upon which the stability of the commonwealth depend.

CIVIC EDUCATION, IDEOLOGY, AND COERCION

If the sort of educational system Hobbes recommends were put in place, we would expect to see significant thinning of the ranks of fools, dupes, and zealots. Not only would most of the general population have been deprived of those pretenses for the rightfulness of rebellion needed to motivate them to rebel, but their discontent with submitting to the burdens of government – imposition of taxes, limitation by laws, and so on – should be much reduced. While Hobbesian education will not *directly* affect those ambitious hypocrites who incite rebellion, it does profoundly affect them indirectly, by depriving them of the expectations of popular support they need in order to have that hope of success upon which their motivation to sedition depends.

74 EW III, 164; T 124.
75 EW III, 315; T 226.
76 EW III, 684; T 471.

Supposing we grant the promise of Hobbes's educational program for promoting the kind of restoration of civic character he intends, it is natural to worry that this kind of education may be morally problematic. If it criminalizes dissent and serves as a mere ideological support for a political system inimical to the fundamental interests of those subject to it, then we may wish to fault Hobbes's political theory for relying on it. To investigate this worry properly would require more extensive and detailed work than I propose to undertake in the context of our present discussion. But we can do some preliminary conceptual and textual ground-clearing work to help us in arriving at a provisional judgment of the moral permissibility of Hobbes's proposed educational system.

My approach will be to attend to the *formal features* of Hobbes's educational system, rather than to its peculiar content. In particular, I'll set aside the question whether the doctrines offered in political education are *true*. The reason is this. Any educational program that contains false doctrines will for that very reason be objectionable, and its falsehoods should be excised, or the system rejected. But acknowledging this doesn't tell us anything *systematically* interesting about *types* or *kinds* of educational systems. When we point to the objectionableness of, say, a physically coercive system, we are interested in why and how its being coercive makes it objectionable, and determining this requires that we consider how we would judge such a type of system even were it to impart only true doctrines. If we consider a system of subliminal education, our interest is in seeing whether its subliminal mode of operation is distinctively problematic, but to determine this we must abstract from its content. Similarly, if we are interested in evaluating the Hobbesian system of mandatory political education, we do best to consider it in isolation from our judgment of whether its content is true, and concentrate instead on its virtues or defects *under an appropriate formal description.*

Some examples may help to clarify what is meant by a formal description of an educational system. A liberal society might describe its educational system as "teaching all children of the society, by means of a mandatory system of publicly funded education, those attitudes, skills and true (or at least reasonable) views necessary for them to develop into independent citizens able and willing to engage in fair social cooperation". Here the description picks out the aims of the teaching, its means and scope, and our intention that it convey true/reasonable views. Contrast this with the sort of educational system depicted in the John Carpenter film *They Live.* In that science fiction world, aliens have gained control of the earth's population, unbeknownst to most humans, by means of what is best described as "a system of social saturation by subliminal messages to induce in the population a sense of private contentment and political apathy". Here there is no suggestion that the doctrines conveyed are intended as either true or consonant with the satisfaction of true human interests. To compare these as educational systems, it makes sense to set aside the question of whether the specific doctrines they teach are true and focus instead on the methods, aim, and scope of the educational systems. Further on, I isolate what I take to be a defensible formal description of Hobbes's educational system, as well as a third contrasting case, roughly characterized as Machiavellian. Both of these cases have a (similar) particular content that we may dismiss as involving false claims about how basic human interests are best served, but merit very different degrees of condemnation reflecting their quite different formal descriptions. I hope these four differing cases will make sufficiently clear this distinction between a formal description of a system and its particular content.

I'll argue that Hobbes's educational system is properly characterized, from the point of view of the sort of liberal political philosophy I find most attractive, as having acceptable formal features (even if defective content), and so is not to be condemned as immorally indoctrinating or improperly coercing those educated under it. Whether or not one is persuaded by these arguments, it should at least be possible to see that Hobbes supposes himself to be offering an effective and unobjectionable mechanism for transforming civic character and thereby realizing increased social stability. And Hobbes's critics should also concede that this educational mechanism is no more objectionable than the overtly coercive mechanism imputed to Hobbes by traditional interpretations that see him as relying entirely on coercive punishments and the threat of them.

Hobbes's educational program might be objectionable if the doctrines taught were known or with reason thought to be false, especially if they were needed to maintain a political regime that was against people's true interests and so could be accepted only if people were mistaken or deluded about the grounds of those doctrines. An educational system with those features would be purposely providing ideological support for a defective regime. It may seem on its face a crazy question even to *ask* whether Hobbes's educational system is a mere ideological tool: isn't it obvious that it *must* be, given that Hobbes endorsed Absolutism?

Suppose we grant at the outset that the political regime Hobbes favors is in fact defective, and let us assume that his educational system would in fact support it. It is still sensible to ask whether Hobbes's educational system is objectionably ideological. If it is proper to describe that system as distorting half-truths into lending support for institutional arrangements whose actual operations are, contrary to appearances, against true human interests, then we should conclude that it is objectionably ideological. But what if its proper description is quite different? Imagine, for instance, that its support for absolutist conclusions is the result of faulty internal logic or faulty causal inferences concerning the best means of satisfying basic interests, rather than of any misidentification of true human interests, dependence on half-truths, or deceptive methodology. We must allow room for some distinction between merely mistaken systems and objectionably ideological ones. The fact that the educational system conveys falsehoods is not enough to establish that it is objectionably ideological. The issue, then, is a complicated one that requires a closer examination of the formal features of Hobbes's system.

The first point to consider is, again, not whether the views Hobbes wants taught *are* true, but whether Hobbes intends his educational system to be properly describable as "disseminating only true doctrines". The textual evidence on this point is wholly unambiguous. Hobbes takes his educational system to be teaching (by a perfectly transparent mechanism), not only *true* doctrines, but doctrines whose truth is *evident* – that is to say, readily perceived – and whose recognition is *necessary* for the satisfaction of genuine human interests. Political education is to teach the science of just and unjust, and to teach a science is to "demonstrate the truth thereof perspicuously to another".[77] "Why", Hobbes asks rhetorically in his *Behemoth*, "may not men be taught their duty, that is, the science of just and unjust, as

[77] EW III, 37; T 37.

divers other sciences have been taught, *from true principles and evident demonstration;* and much more easily than any of those preachers and democratical gentlemen [during the civil war] could teach rebellion and treason?"[78]

Hobbes sees the views he is promoting as not only true, but as *evidently* true. People are gullible and *could* be made to believe almost anything; but what Hobbes wants taught are doctrines whose truth is so evident that it will be readily perceived by any unbiased listener. In a passage where he addresses the objection that the vulgar are incapable of learning the "principles of reason" that compose the essential rights of sovereignty, Hobbes insists:

> the common people's minds, unless they be tainted with dependance on the potent, or scribbled over with the opinions of their doctors, are like clean paper, fit to receive whatsoever by public authority shall be imprinted in them. Shall whole nations be brought to *acquiesce* in the great mysteries of the Christian religion, which are above reason, and millions of men be made believe, that the same body may be in innumerable places at one and the same time, which is against reason; and shall not men be able, by their teaching, and preaching, protected by the law, to make that received, *which is so consonant to reason, that any unprejudicated man, needs no more to learn it, than to hear it?* I conclude therefore, that in the instruction of the people in the essential rights which are the natural and fundamental laws of sovereignty, there is no difficulty.[79]

So the doctrines advanced by education are taken to be both true and evident.

But doesn't Hobbes famously endorse an idiosyncratic view of religious (and moral) truth that makes impossible any divergence between teaching what is really true and teaching what the state judges to be true? According to a widely received interpretation of Hobbes, those religious doctrines are true that the sovereign propounds because the sovereign's pronouncements *define* true doctrine. If this interpretation were correct, the formal feature of Hobbes's educational system that it is to convey true doctrines (including relevant religious doctrines) could not do any justificatory work. This "voluntarist" interpretation in essence collapses any distinction between this structural feature of

78 EW VI, 212, emphasis added.

79 EW III, 325–326; T 233, second emphasis added.

an educational system and its content: it would be properly formally described as "conveying true doctrines" only because whatever doctrines it conveys are said to be true by definition.

As we saw in both Chapter 2 and Chapter 6, the voluntarist interpretation misunderstands Hobbes's position, which is not that the sovereign's pronouncing something true makes it so, but is rather that Scripture requires us to regard the sovereign's judgments in matters of religion (and is all other matters) as *authoritative, whether or not they are true.* (In this way the sovereign's judgment is like that of the Supreme Court, or an umpire in a baseball game: authoritative even if "cosmically" incorrect.) True religion (the plain parts of Christian Scripture as interpreted by Hobbes) and true morality (the self-evident Laws of Nature) direct us to subordinate our judgment to that of the sovereign, even when his judgment is erroneous. This corrected reading is confirmed by Hobbes's acknowledgment that sovereigns may be *mistaken* in their religious conclusions, which would be strictly impossible if their judgments defined truth:

> [S]uppose that a Christian king should from this foundation *Jesus is the Christ,* draw some false consequences, that is to say, make some superstructions of hay or stubble, and command the teaching of the same.... *Christian kings may err in deducing a consequence,* but who shall judge? Shall a private man judge, when the question is of his own obedience?[80]

The same goes for moral judgment. If the sovereign's moral judgments may be mistaken, then his judgment cannot be what defines moral truth, yet "there is no judge subordinate, *nor sovereign,* but may err in a judgment of equity".[81] Thus Hobbes does maintain the distinction between true religious doctrine and the sovereign's pronouncements on religious doctrine, allowing that when Hobbes characterizes his educational system as teaching truths, he is saying something more than simply that it teaches what it teaches.

More important is Hobbes's insistence that true doctrines cannot urge action against humanity's general interests. Humans fundamentally need peace (securing a realm of ordered liberty) as a condition of the realization of most of their other interests. Hobbes argues that

80 EW III, 600–601; T 414, second emphasis added.
81 EW III, 263; T 192, emphasis added.

"it is annexed to the sovereignty, to be judge of what opinions and doctrines are averse, and what conducing to peace", "And though in matter of doctrine, nothing ought to be regarded but the truth; yet this is not repugnant to regulating of the same by peace. *For doctrine repugnant to peace, can no more be true, than peace and concord can be against the law of nature*".[82] So doctrine against humans' fundamental interest in peace must be false. This view is a part of what I have elsewhere called Hobbes's doctrine of the unity of reason,[83] and it resurfaces in his defense of Galileo:

> [As an instance of vain philosophy] [w]ith the introduction of false, we may join also the suppression of true philosophy, by such men, as neither by lawful authority, nor sufficient study, are competent judges of the truth.... But what reason is there for it? Is it because such opinions are contrary to true religion? *That cannot be, if they be true*.[84]

True doctrines, Hobbes maintains, cannot be contrary to the basic human interests in peace, preservation, flourishing, and piety, and all truths hang together in a perfectly coherent way. This is a consequence of God's activity in constructing the world. And so Hobbes criticizes the "vain and false philosophy" of Aristotle and the schoolmen who succeeded him on the grounds that it is "not only vain, but also pernicious to the public state".[85] This means that Hobbes *cannot* see the truths disseminated by his educational system as incompatible with the realization of our true human interests, for that would imply that they were not true.

What Hobbes apparently intends, then, is a system of education under the description "education in *evidently true doctrines that conduce to the satisfaction of basic human interests*". Furthermore, this education is to be carried out by exposing the *true grounds* of the doctrines taught. Hobbes intends his education to be transparent, requiring that not just the doctrines, but also their grounds or reasons, be taught. He writes,

> [I]t is against [the sovereign's] duty, to let the people be ignorant, or misinformed of the *grounds, and reasons* of those his essential rights; because thereby men are easy to be seduced, and drawn to resist him, when the

[82] EW III, 164; T 124–125.
[83] *IAI*, 278–279.
[84] EW III, 687; T 473–474, emphasis added.
[85] EW III, 681; T 469.

commonwealth shall require their use and exercise. *And the grounds of these rights, have the rather need to be diligently, and truly taught;* because they cannot be maintained by any civil law, or terror of legal punishment.[86]

And

Common people know nothing of right or wrong by their own meditation; they must therefore be taught the grounds of their duty, and the reasons why calamities ever follow disobedience to their lawful sovereigns. But to the contrary, our rebels were publicly taught rebellion in the pulpits.[87]

Even our obvious religious duties are better grasped once their true justifying grounds have been laid out:

All that is required, both in faith and manners, for man's salvation is (I confess) set down in Scripture as plainly as can be.... *Let all men be subject to the higher powers whether it be the King or those that are sent by him* [etc.] ... are words of the Scripture, which are well enough understood; but neither children, nor the greatest part of men, do *understand why it is their duty* to do so.[88]

On the basis of these passages it seems, then, that Hobbes believes that subjects' attachment to the doctrines will be strengthened rather than undermined if their true grounds are understood.

What all of these considerations taken together allow us to say is that Hobbes's educational system, under its proper formal description, is not obviously a mere ideological support for a defective political regime. Let us say, with Rawls, that a political system depends on ideology for its stability if it would not be stable unless people held views that they could affirm only if they were under illusions or delusions concerning the facts about the operation of the system, or its grounds, or their own interests. For Hobbes's educational system to be condemnable as simply the ideological prop for such a political regime, it would have to reliably create the necessary illusions or delusions, and in the right sort of way. But in Hobbes's system, the doctrines taught are advanced in good faith as true, and overtly argued to be doctrines squarely in line with people's interests in peace, security, flourishing, and piety, which are plausible candidates for fundamental interests. The political mechanisms that advance these

86 EW III, 323; T 232, emphasis added.
87 EW VI, 343.
88 EW VI, 230–231, second emphasis added.

interests are transparent and fully revealed by the education, and, moreover, the grounds for the doctrines are fully revealed. For this reason their acknowledgment seems not to be dependent on illusion or delusion (although, of course, they may depend on faulty inferences and thus prove mistaken). As far as Hobbes is concerned, one who sees her basic interests as they really are, can in cognizance of the actual grounds of the claims on her political obedience and the actual operation of political institutions affirm those claims as both true and proper. No illusion or delusion is needed.

Contrast this with a system that appears to be quite willing to rely on ideology. Consider the view suggested by Machiavelli's remarks in *The Discourses:*

> [I]t is the duty of the rulers of a republic or of a kingdom to maintain the foundations of the religion that sustains them; and if this is done it will be easy for them to keep their republic religious and, as a consequence, good and united. And they must favor and encourage all those things which arise in favor of religion, even if they judge them to be false.[89]

And

> If one desires or intends to reform the government of a city so that the reform will be acceptable and will be able to maintain itself to everyone's satisfaction, he should retain at least the shadow of ancient customs so that it will not seem to the people that they have changed institutions, whereas in actual fact the new institutions may be completely different from those of the past; for the majority of men delude themselves with what seems to be rather than with what actually is; indeed, they are more often moved by things that seem to be rather than by things that are.[90]

These passages suggest a view that is happy to disseminate doctrines that its author knows or believes to be false and to welcome people's erroneous assumptions about the actual character of their political institutions, all to preserve the state, and without any mention of the interests of the people. The proper formal description of such a system would seem to be as one to "create the illusion that whatever doctrines conduce to the rulers' own particular interest are true, whether

[89] Niccolò Machiavelli, *The Discourses,* in Peter Bondanella and Mark Musa, eds., *The Portable Machiavelli* (New York, 1979), 211.

[90] Ibid., 231.

or not we actually think them so". But in this respect, it is quite unlike Hobbes's system, under the appropriate formal description.

To be sure, we cannot acquit an educational system of the charge of providing ideological support for a defective regime simply by pointing to the sincerity of the belief that it is teaching evident truths, since an ideological view may be held as sincerely as any other. But insincerity of the sort that Machiavelli evidences bodes ill.

What then *would* acquit a system of the charge of ideology? It would be too much to require a demonstration that what the system teaches *actually is true;* for one thing, we cannot agree on which doctrines are true, and so requiring this would deprive the term 'objectionably ideological' of any instructive application. What we might reasonably require of a view as security against ideology is that the interests it advances be at least plausible candidates for true human goods, and that the means it uses be fairly transparent to those on whom they work, so that no wholesale illusion or delusion is needed for their successful operation. And we can require that it not take merely partial truths, and distort them to create the appearance that ends inimical to human good are in fact worth pursuing. If these are the tests, Hobbes's proposed educational system passes them.[91] So, unless we are to say that all educations endorsing (for whatever reason) views we believe false are objectionably ideological, we must recognize that the burden of proof lies with Hobbes's critic. The proper question is not what it takes to *acquit* a view of the charge of being a tool of ideology, but rather when it is reasonable to *suspect* a view of being one; and on any plausible account of grounds for suspicion, Hobbes's system should not be suspected of being one, or at least no more suspected than our own educational system.

However, it is worrisome that in Hobbes's system, people need not be taught competing doctrines and dissenting teachings need not be countenanced. Mill famously argued that the squelching of dissent or even the failure to encourage a lively debate among diverse doctrines has undesirable effects ranging from people's becoming unable to

[91] Whereas, if, for example, Marx's description of capitalism as a mode of production is correct, then its operations are neither transparent nor contributory to the satisfaction of true human interests, and so educational systems functional to the maintenance of that mode of production do fail even these weak tests.

discover the truth, or to make the truth once gained a vibrant force in their lives, to confining people to a merely imitative apelike existence unfit for progressive beings. To the extent that we accept these or other arguments to the same conclusion, we will object to Hobbes's educational system.

Two of the passages quoted earlier may suggest that Hobbes does not forbid all unorthodox teaching. In the first, Hobbes says that when the erroneous doctrines of the ancients are publicly read, they should be taught by a judicious teacher who can correct those authors' errors. This suggests that contrary views may permissibly be taught so long as they are simultaneously subjected to critical examination by someone versed in the correct view. That subjection to examination need not itself be objectionable, so long as it involves no intellectual manipulation; indeed, Millian considerations might persuade us to view it as a good thing. Still, the only likely "public" reading (i.e., institutional reading, or reading outside of persons' private libraries) of these texts would be in the universities, and so Hobbes's remarks here might not extend to public preaching. The reforming effects on state doctrine of consideration in the universities of contrary views may trickle down to the masses, but the masses themselves would not, it seems, be presented with alternative views for their consideration.

The second passage, concerning the suppression of Galileo's heliocentric view, suggests that Hobbes welcomes an open examination of nonconforming doctrines to determine the truth (which is then to be taught). The remark continues: "Let therefore the truth be first examined by competent judges, or confuted by them that pretend to know the contrary".[92] Again, however, this sort of examination might be confined to dissent prior to public dissemination of doctrines and not allowed for subsequent disagreements. These passages introduce some uncertainty about whether or not Hobbes intends to illegalize the teaching of dissenting doctrines. I am not aware of any passage in *Leviathan* that says that dissent should be made illegal, nor any in which this question is explicitly treated. We know that Hobbes intends some of the needed education to be carried out by parents, and this allows room for some discussion within families concerning the doctrines taught. But there is a passage in Hobbes's *Historical Narration*

[92] EW III, 687; T 474.

Concerning Heresy that as much as says that dissenting teachings are subject to prohibition and punishment:

[I]t is absolutely necessary, both in kingdoms and in republics, to take care lest disorders and civil wars occur. And since these are most often generated by differences of doctrine and intellectual wrangling, there must be some restraint, in the form of punishment, on those who teach, in books or sermons, things whose teaching the laws of the prince or republic prohibit.[93]

This passage tells us that if subjects teach doctrines the sovereign has made it illegal to teach, they must be punished. But it doesn't assert that the sovereign must make the teaching of some doctrines illegal, since he may refrain from issuing any laws proscribing what is to be taught. But let us assume the worst case, and ask how objectionable Hobbes's educational system would be if it were illegal to teach dissenting doctrines.

How objectionable controls on teaching are may depend on what they affect. Is their purpose to censor our thoughts – to make sure that we think only correct things – or are they intended merely to constrain our behavior in acting on our views? The latter, although involving more alienation of practice from idea, still is less personally invasive, and may for that reason be less objectionable. Throughout *Leviathan* Hobbes drives a wedge between belief and action, insisting that the state is concerned only with external obedience – that is, behavior. What subjects believe is their own business, and cannot help but be so, for

By the captivity of our understanding, is not meant a submission of the intellectual faculty to the opinion of any other man; but of the will to obedience, where obedience is due. For sense, memory, understanding, reason, and opinion are not in our power to change; but always, and necessarily such, as the things we see, hear, and consider suggest unto us; and therefore are not effects of our will, but our will of them.[94]

And so forbidding a belief "is of no effect; because belief, and unbelief never follow mens commands".[95] Although the state wishes to

[93] Thomas Hobbes, *Historical Narration Concerning Heresy,* in Curley, ed., *Leviathan,* 526; hereafter cited as *Heresy,* followed by page number.

[94] EW III, 360; T 256.

[95] EW III, 493; T 343.

affect belief through education, it may *require* only obedience, and not the belief it hopes for. Hobbes is fully explicit about this in his attack on the practice of inquisition: It is an "error" "to extend the power of the law, which is the rule of actions only, to the very thoughts and consciences of men, by examination, and *inquisition* of what they hold, notwithstanding the conformity of their speech and actions".[96] And this is true even when the doctrines held are false, for "[s]hall the law, which requires nothing but obedience, take vengeance on faulty reasoning?"[97]

Nonetheless, we might hope to say more in Hobbes's defense than that his scheme does not allow inquisition. A more promising tack is to take seriously the status of the dissenting teacher on Hobbes's view. Someone who teaches a view in opposition to the demonstrable implications of, say, the Laws of Nature is simply mistaken. His view is not partially true nor a reasonable conjecture concerning an unsolved problem, etc., but merely in error. Hobbes argues further that to permit the teaching of such errors is usually dangerous, because subjects' acting on false conceptions of political duty threatens the grave evil of social disorder. If we take seriously this trio of ideas – that teachers of dissenting doctrines are *dangerously merely mistaken* – it becomes an open question whether Hobbes would do wrong to silence them, since the stakes are very high. Would *we* allow the teaching of, for example, demonstrably false mathematics in high school engineering classes if its result were collapsed bridges? And what of demonstrably false ideas whose result were worse – say, collapsed nations?

The suggestion here is that even liberal societies, which incorporate the values Mill emphasizes in the form of protections on dissent, do nonetheless put limits on what views may be publicly acted upon, ruling out some uses of unreasonable or illiberal or intolerant views, and sometimes also of merely false ones.[98] They do not, for example, allow the teaching of racist or sectarian religious doctrine in the public

96 EW III, 684; T 471.

97 *Heresy*, 533.

98 Sometimes even of true ones. See, for example, T. M. Scanlon's argument that the Millian Principle properly endorsed by liberal states may prohibit even true expression if it is sufficiently harmful, by, for example, illegalizing the publication of a (true) recipe for nerve gas. See T. M. Scanlon, "A Theory of Freedom of Expression", *Philosophy & Public Affairs* 1 (1972): 204–226.

schools, let alone of numerology or astrology or phlogiston theory. Part of the justification for this regulation is that liberal democracies require a threshold level of tolerance and civility if they are to survive; the liberal society does not insist on securing conditions for its own annihilation. Neither does Hobbes's. So if the liberal society's regulation in public teaching of dissenting doctrines (*qua* unreasonable, false, or dangerous) is judged unobjectionable, so must be Hobbes's similar regulation.

We might nonetheless worry that for the state rather than private persons or associations to administer this education lessens people's sense of autonomy or self-determination. Even if we would in due course come to the same conclusions as those the state would teach us, our sense of self-determination is enhanced when we come to them through contact with our voluntary, or at least intimate, associations.

It is difficult to assess the force of this worry. If the underlying concern is about pressuring or coercing subjects to accept the proffered doctrine (where we imagine, perhaps implausibly, that the state, but not any lesser association, imposes such pressure), then we may from the point of view of Hobbes's theory be unable even to make sense of this worry. From Mill onward our liberal tradition has recognized the subtle arm-twisting that social opinion imposes upon individuals, although only Mill's view seeks to counter the effects of more broadly social, as opposed to strictly political, pressures to uniformity of opinion. But Hobbes's theoretical apparatus does not enable him to take up this worry, because he argues that teaching is always an activity only of *persuasion* and never of *coercion.* That is, teaching *by its nature* seeks to attract, persuade, invite, or even lure individuals to belief, but it does not (nor could it) compel them to belief. Hobbes has to hold this position in order to undermine the Roman Catholic Church's claim to have indirect sovereignty (which necessarily involves coercive power) over Christians in virtue of its authority to teach and preach. Indeed, grants Hobbes, ecclesiastical power does include authority to teach and preach, but these activities are

> compared by our Saviour, to fishing, that is, to winning men to obedience, not by coercion and punishing, but by persuasion: and therefore he said not to his apostles, he would make them so many Nimrods, *hunters of men; but fishers of men.* It is compared also to leaven, to sowing of seed, and to the multiplication of a grain of mustard-seed; by all which *compulsion is excluded*...the office

of Christ's ministers in this world, is to make men believe, and have faith in Christ; but faith hath no relation to, nor dependance at all upon compulsion or commandment; but only upon certainty or probability of arguments drawn from reason, or from something men believe already.[99]

The state's power over teaching, then, cannot by its nature be coercive. This, combined with Hobbes's express distinction between conformity in belief and obedience in action, implies that if our worry is that subjects are *more* coerced by the sovereign's teachings than they would be by those of their parents, or parish, or any lesser association, it is simply misplaced.

But the self-determination worry might be rather that self-persuasion is morally preferable to state-persuasion. I assume that there is something to this preference, although I won't attempt here to say what it is. But even taking self-persuasion to be of value, whether Hobbes's system is objectionable on this point cannot be settled without considering whether some greater good can be achieved only by a system involving state-persuasion. On Hobbes's behalf one might argue the reasonable position that state education, because uniform, provides subjects with greater confidence that others share (or at least have been exposed to and considered) their views, and so induces a greater sense of social cohesion than would be possible in a more fragmented educational system. We, in our practice of public education in civics, seek to induce allegiance to democratic ideals and decision procedures, whose widespread acceptance seems itself to be one of the most desirable outcomes of the education. Even Rawls, a political rather than comprehensive liberal, stresses the importance of publicity in the well-ordered society; of the public acceptance of both principles of justice and their grounds, and of uniform education in the essential rights and ideals of citizenship to encourage development of the political virtues of tolerance, civility, and a sense of fair play. So it is at least possible that the value of the social cement provided by uniform state teaching of basic truths outweighs the good of subjects' independent discovery of them.

If there are such reasons supporting a uniform education for subjects, Hobbes wants to argue that to permit any entity other than the

[99] EW III, 490–491; T 342, last emphasis added.

state to determine the content of education would be both harmful[100] and *unfair*.[101] In a commonwealth, no private person is subject to the authority of any other private person, and so to impose on others an educational program dictated by any merely private person would be arbitrary and hence unfair. On this point Hobbes's view is quite compatible with that of his liberal critic Mill, who writes: "Unless we are willing to adopt the logic of persecutors, and to say that we may persecute others because we are right, and that they must not persecute us because they are wrong, we must beware of admitting a principle of which we should resent as a gross injustice the application to ourselves".[102] Hobbes's own peculiar twist on the logic of persecutors (and here, obviously, he departs from Mill) is to argue that the only mutually acceptable principle is one of submission to arbitration:

> And therefore, as when there is a controversy in an account, the parties must by their own accord, set up, for right reason, the reason of some arbitrator, or judge, to whose sentence they will both stand, or their controversy must either come to blows, or be undecided, for want of a right reason constituted by nature; so is it also in all debates of what kind soever. And when men that think themselves wiser than all others, clamour and demand right reason for judge, yet seek no more, but that things should be determined, by no other men's reason but their own, it is as intolerable in the society of men, as it is in play after trump is turned, to use for trump on every occasion, that suite whereof they have most in their hand.[103]

To put Hobbes's and Mill's worry in contemporary terms, there is no *naturally given publicly available perspective* that can distinguish true views from untrue ones. And so, from the point of view of others who disagree with him, a citizen's insistence that his doctrine should

[100] The argument that it would be harmful is contained in Hobbes's broader argument against dividing the essential rights of sovereignty. For discussion of the details of this argument, see *IAI*, 81–88.

[101] It is contrary to the reciprocity theorem and to the tenth Law of Nature against arrogance to reserve to oneself any rights one would be unwilling to have extended to others. Equity thus requires that "if one be admitted to be judge, the other is to be admitted also" (the seventeenth Law of Nature). Hence, it is unfair to others to subject them to one's own merely private judgment, which action Hobbes likens to cheating at cards. See EW III, 140–144; T 107–110, and 31; T 33, which I quote below. Cf. *IAI*, 93–94.

[102] *On Liberty*, in John Gray, ed., *John Stuart Mill: On Liberty and Other* Essays (Oxford, 1991), 96.

[103] EW III, 31; T 33.

be enforced because true cannot be seen as anything more than an insistence on his own opinion. In Rawls's words,

> those who insist, when fundamental political questions are at stake, on what they take as true but others do not, seem to others simply to insist on their own beliefs when they have the political power to do so. Of course, those who do insist on their beliefs also insist that their beliefs alone are true: they impose their beliefs because, they say, their beliefs are true and not because they are their beliefs. But this is a claim that all equally could make; it is also a claim that cannot be made good to citizens generally. So when we make such claims others, who are them-selves reasonable, must count us unreasonable. And indeed we are.[104]

This pretty well captures Hobbes's position. Because everyone is in the same boat, the problem, as Mill suggests, and as Hobbes's reciprocity theorem requires, is to find a principle that subjects should not resent as unjust when applied to themselves. No grounds for preferring one private opinion over another can be justified to subjects generally. Hobbes concludes that the only fair course is to submit all controversies (including those over what subjects are to be taught) to the judgment of an impartial arbitrator, and this arbitrator must be the (universally authorized) state. Without such an arbitrator, we could not ground a commonly acceptable policy. So *if* a uniform core education is good, it is most fair for the state (as the authorized representative of each subject) to determine its content in line with its judgments of truth and the requirements of peace.

Perhaps we can agree with Hobbes that it is permissible for a society to institute a system of educating subjects in those basic truths that are necessary for the maintenance of conditions for human survival and flourishing; and the state, if it is the authorized representative of the people, is to carry out this education. And we may agree, too, that mandatory education is acceptable when people pose grave threats to one another that can be avoided only by an awareness and self-restraint that education can encourage.

This is precisely what Hobbes believes. The evil averted when subjects act on the proper political principles, namely, bloody civil war, is a horrifying evil. Indeed, Hobbes famously argues that civil war

[104] John Rawls, *Political Liberalism* (New York, 1993; paperback edition with new material, 1996), 61.

and its accompanying anarchy are such "horrible calamities" that in comparison the incommodities of political subjection "are scarce sensible".[105] Barring special assumptions (attributing, say, unsavory personal motives to particular individuals), Hobbes seems to believe that civil wars are the undesired, unforeseen effects of people's acting on false beliefs. Take by way of illustration this passage from *De Corpore:*

> [T]he utility of moral and civil philosophy is to be estimated, ... by the calamities we receive from not knowing them. Now, all such calamities as may be avoided by human industry, arise from war, but chiefly from civil war.... But the cause of war is not that men are willing to have it; for the will has nothing for object but good, at least that which seemeth good. Nor is it from this, that men know not that the effects of war are evil; for who is there that thinks not poverty and loss of life to be great evils? *The cause, therefore, of civil war, is that men know not the causes neither of war nor peace,* there being but few in the world that have learned those duties which unite and keep men in peace.[106]

Were the general population not ignorant of the causes of civil wars, troublemakers could not attract sufficient support to upset the prevailing peace. In this sense education can effectively forestall subjects' *unwittingly* eliciting the horrible evil of civil war, and is, moreover, the least coercive method of forestalling it. Hobbes's attitude toward his system of mandatory education might be understood as similar to the one we have toward public service announcements that attempt to stem the spread of contagious diseases or toward mandatory driver's education. The harms to others avoided by these sorts of compulsory education are so great that they outweigh whatever may weigh against them. The avoidance of accidental civil war is at least as great a good as either the containment of disease or road safety. So, if either of these dangers warrants prophylactic education, the danger of inadvertent civil war does.

In light of all these considerations, I am inclined to believe that Hobbes's educational system will be unobjectionable to the extent that it really is the least invasive effective method of averting a very great evil, and to believe that it is not properly criticized as objectionably ideological, or as a coercive program of mind control – at least

[105] EW III, 170; T 128.
[106] EW I, 8, emphasis added.

not under its formal description as a system of education in evident truths consonant with basic human interests by means of reasoned argument exposing their true grounds. Nor is it to be rejected as unfair to subjects. Considering only these formal descriptions of the educational system and its background psychological and social assumptions, this system does not run afoul of liberal constraints. To observe this is not to show that Hobbes espouses a liberal educational system, because, as I initially remarked, that judgment may depend on the content of the system's substantive assumptions and not just its formal features. But because its formal features are unobjectionable, if Hobbes is right to believe that his educational system would make subjects of the commonwealth better able to resist the siren song of iniquitous, hypocritical malcontents preaching views they believe false in order to incite rebellion, he will have shown us an acceptable way to make men into better moral judges.

8

The Unity of Practical Wisdom

> Reason is excellent for getting food, clothing and shelter. Reason is the very best tool kit. Nothing beats reason for keeping tigers away. But be excessively reasonable and you risk throwing out the universe with the bathwater.
>
> (Martel, *Life of Pi*, 298)

Hobbes understood that human lives are always less and always more than exercises in the individual pursuit of narrow self-interest. Although truly "generous natures" may be rare, rarer still is the person who does not find much of her life directed by her beliefs about her religious duties and moral obligations, her affectionate attachments, her sense of pride and desire to be esteemed, all operating alongside of, and sometimes pulling apart from, her narrow self-interests in temporal physical survival and material comfort. Unfortunately, these natural motivations often bring us into conflict with others, and when we hold transcendent interests in acting on them, our ensuing actions may destabilize the basic social framework that makes possible an environment conducive to the exercise of anyone's effective agency, including our own. If we were motivated solely by considerations of narrow self-interest, society could be effectually coordinated, and domestic peace maintained perpetually, by brute governmental force. The complexities of human nature being what they are, however, only a society that enjoys a critical mass of consensus in the judgment that deference to the government is licensed by the requirements of morality, honor, and affirmed religion will remain stable for long.

Hobbes develops a normative system intended to harmonize these various motivations, both within the individual and among citizens. In that system narrowly prudential interests, natural duties and binding moral obligations, religious duties both natural and revealed, and special-prudential interests in our prospects for life after death all converge on a set of practical norms for social living, ordered by a master principle of political obligation.[1] That principle is that subjects are to obey all of the commands of the effective political authority under which they live except those that would require them to violate their duties to God.[2] The sovereign interprets the Laws of Nature, embeds them in a system of civil laws designed to promote the security and prosperity of subjects, and establishes a uniform profession and practice of religion; allegiance to the whole order is reproduced by a system of education. Prudent rule removes the discontent, proper education the pretense of right, and both together the hope of success that would otherwise tempt subjects to rebel. The various requirements of practical reason are unified. The happy prospect of living in a way that satisfies our prudential, moral, and religious interests that is provided, Hobbes thinks, only by a political society in which Hobbes's principle of political obligation is affirmed and adhered to by citizens generally, and reflected in its institutional arrangements, is the consequence of God's design, or so the Christian has to believe. Our willingness to honor God requires that despite his incomprehensibility we think as highly of his goodness

[1] In *Ideals as Interests* I described Hobbes's strategy as to offer a "confluence of reasons" for affirming Hobbes's proposed principle of political obligation.

[2] Hobbes states a version of this principle in chapter 31 of *Leviathan:* "That subjects owe to their soveraigns, simple obedience, in all things wherein their obedience is not repugnant to the Lawes of God, I have sufficiently proved" (EW III, 343; T 245). The effectiveness condition appears throughout *Leviathan*. A sovereign is effective when it is able and willing to protect subjects in their loyalty. When protection of the law fails (as when suddenly accosted by a highway robber) subjects may protect themselves, subject, of course, to the sovereign's subsequent determination of whether their use of defensive force was justified. When the sovereign itself is attacking subjects (say by attempting to inflict punishment) it is not effective *with respect to them*, and so until granted freedom. For a fuller discussion of Hobbes's principle of political obligation, including its effectiveness condition and exemption, see *IAI*, 68–78.

and power as is possible, and assume that he wills our good. But doing so commits us to refusing to believe that God makes mistakes, or contradicts himself, or creates us into a world posing unavoidable practical dilemmas and tragic choices. The triple status Hobbes assigns to the Laws of Nature – as simultaneously rules of prudence, morality, and natural religion – suggests what we may call his *doctrine of the unity of practical wisdom*.[3]

One task of this final chapter is to display the unity of practical wisdom in Hobbes's system by indicating how his moral philosophy of cases in the Law of Nature is connected to his characterization of Christian religion and his political philosophy of the rights and duties of sovereigns and subjects in a commonwealth. To display these connections fully would require more extensive presentation of Hobbes's religious views and political philosophy than can be done here; but the outlines of these should suffice to establish their basic compatibility with Hobbes's moral philosophy and with each other. Using the unified theory, I'll then discuss and assess two of the most important recent efforts among philosophers to put Hobbes's normative theory to contemporary use.

RELIGION AND THE REQUIREMENTS OF MORAL AND CIVIL DUTY

One indication that Hobbes thought a proper understanding of religious duty is essential for structuring and maintaining a stable political society is the fact that he devoted an increasing percentage of each successive incarnation of his political philosophy to discussion of the profession and practice of Christianity. Hobbes also wrote several

[3] This doctrine is discussed at greater length (under the term "doctrine of the unity of practical reason") in *Ideals as Interests*, 278–288. We should note that although Hobbes is prepared to explain this unity as the effect of God's design, Hobbes presents his arguments for the convergence of the requirements of prudence and morality as reciprocity without reliance on religious premises, and so in a manner that should make possible their acceptance by nonbelievers. He then goes on to map God's positive laws as delivered by Moses in the second table onto the Laws of Nature. "There is no law of reason that can be against the law divine, for God Almighty hath given reason to man to be a light unto him", writes Hobbes in *Elements* 19.12. See, e.g., EW III, 513–514; T 357.

works devoted primarily to discussion of religion.[4] It would be safe to say that Hobbes's political and religious views engendered significant hostility. In 1666 there were threats in Parliament of an inquiry into Hobbes's religious views, and in 1683 Oxford condemned and burned *De Cive* and *Leviathan*.

Hobbes held that religion is so natural to humans as to be ineliminable. Its 'natural seeds' are a curiosity about the causes of events and a fearful desire to affect the course of events, which lead us to posit, or imagine, invisible causal agents whose actions we may hope to influence through our behavior toward them. Some have nourished these seeds of natural religion according to God's direction, but other ambitious impostors have exploited them in order to gain a following that would secure temporal power for themselves. We can assure ourselves of the bare existence of God by realizing that the causal chain of events we observe must have had an originating cause, and by observing the admirable order and design of the world. Because Hobbes holds that the religious impulse cannot be suppressed, it is essential that it be properly channeled. Although Hobbes appears to offer a somewhat deflationary account of natural religion in purely psychological terms not underwritten by a robust ontology, he does insist that his account is perfectly compatible with taking revealed religion seriously.

In order to manage the religious interests of his readers so that those interests will support rather than undermine the state's authority and operation, Hobbes attempts to show that all of the authoritative sources of religious knowledge available to Christians not only permit but also require them to submit their private judgments in all matters, including the interpretation, profession, and practice of religion, to

[4] These include his Latin poem recording the history of religion, *Historia Ecclesiastica* (1688), his *Historical Narrative Concerning Heresy and the Punishment Thereof* (1680); works arguing the compatibility of his views on free will and necessity with Christian doctrine, his *Of Libertie and Necessitie a Treatise Wherein all Controversie Concerning Predestination, Election, Free-will, Grace, Merits, Reprobation, etc. Is Fully Decided and Cleared* (1654), *The Questions concerning Liberty, Necessity, and Chance Clearly Stated and Debated between Dr Bramhall Bishop of Derry, and Thomas Hobbes of Malmesbury* (1656); a history of the English civil wars analyzed largely as resulting from religious conflict, *Behemoth* (1679); and some works attempting to defend Hobbes' own piety and doctrines, including *Considerations upon the Reputation, Loyalty, Manners, and Religion of Thomas Hobbes of Malmesbury* (1662.)

the public judgment of a civil sovereign. Hobbes argues that both natural reason and Scripture, understood as the compilation of the personal revelations of the true prophets, direct us to treat as authoritative the judgment of a single authority over temporal and spiritual matters alike. This project requires Hobbes to redescribe and rationalize his readers' religious interests, and to reinterpret Scripture. He does this through a painstaking engagement with the canonical texts of the Bible, along with philosophical analysis, for "though there be many things in God's word above reason, that is to say, which cannot by natural reason be either demonstrated or confuted; yet there is nothing contrary to it; but when it seemeth so, the fault is either in our unskilfull interpretation, or erroneous ratiocination".[5]

It is striking that across all three versions of his political theory, Hobbes increasingly expands his discussion of religion to the point that, by *Leviathan*, more than half of the book is consumed in that project. Indeed, in the final chapter of part 2 of *Leviathan*, just halfway through that work, after having laid out what most commentators regard as his complete theory of political obligation, Hobbes acknowledges that nothing he has argued so far will suffice to give us knowledge of our civil duties without our coming to a correct understanding of our religious duties. He writes:

> That subjects owe to Soveraigns, simple Obedience, in all things wherein their obedience is not repugnant to the Lawes of God, I have sufficiently proved in that which I have already written. There wants onely, for the entire knowledge of civill duty, to know what are those Lawes of God. For without that, a man knows not, when he is commanded any thing by the Civill Power, whether it be contrary to the Law of God, or not: and so, either by too much civill obedience offends the Divine Majesty, or through feare of offending God, transgresses the commandements of the Common-wealth. To avoid both the Rocks, it is necessary to know what are the Lawes Divine.

In the Dedicatory Epistle to *Leviathan*, Hobbes insists that his Scriptural exegesis is essential to his project, acknowledging "That which perhaps may most offend, are certain Texts of Holy Scripture, alleged by me to other purpose than ordinarily they used to be by others. But I have done it with due submission, and also (in order to

[5] EW III, 360; T 256.

my subject) necessarily; for they are the Outworks of the Enemy, from whence they impugne the Civill Power".

Unaided natural reason allows us to discover God's existence, but nothing of his properties: "Whatsoever we imagine is finite. Therefore there is no idea, or conception of anything we call infinite.... And therefore the name of God is used, not to make us conceive him (for he is incomprehensible, and his greatnesse and power are unconceivable); but that we may honour him".[6] To think God finite or limited in power or goodness would be to think him less than he could possibly be; while to deny his care for humanity would be to deprive us of any incentive to honor him. To honor God is to think as highly of his goodness and power as is possible. Worship is just the external expression of honor, and is naturally expressed by thanks and obedience, which praise God's goodness and magnify his power, and by prayers. These are natural forms of worship because they are the natural external expressions of those human passions – hope, love, and fear – that arise from the belief that God is infinitely good and powerful. We honor God by the same sorts of actions we use to honor human beings: obedience, thanksgiving, praise, public worship, and considerate speech. However, natural reason is silent on the question of the particular ceremonies, words, and gestures to be used in worship, and this silence suggests that these are a matter of indifference. What does matter is that worship be public, if we wish our commonwealth to be of any religion at all. Public worship requires uniformity "for those actions that are done differently, by different men, cannot be said to be a public worship. And therefore, where many sorts of worship be allowed, proceeding from the different religions of private men, it cannot be said there is any public worship, nor that the commonwealth is of any religion at all".[7] This is primarily because we worship only when we convey honor; but what conveys honor is in the eye of the beholder, and so if the ceremonies used by various sects and factions seem ridiculous to each other, none will have succeeded in worshipping God before the public.

Natural reason requires obedience to God's laws, but what does it tell us about the content of those laws? To summarize our previous

6 EW III, 17; T 23.
7 EW III, 355; T 252–253.

argument, Hobbes holds that natural reason instructs us to form political communities by authorizing a single public judgment – a sovereign – to interpret all laws and adjudicate all disputes, including those concerning the proper public profession and practice of religion. Recall that Hobbes distinguishes between prudence and sapience, or wisdom. Prudence is correct extrapolation from experience to predict future events or to identify past causes of current events. This sort of practical know-how depends upon experience, is also possessed by many nonhuman animals, and is, like claims based on occurent sensory experience, fallible. Sapience is scientific knowledge of what conduces to human good, and science is a system of demonstrated truths deduced from universal propositions that are true by virtue of the definitions of their component terms. Hobbes defends a conventionalist view of science as a purely formal system modeled on Euclidean geometry, with the addition of indubitable introspectables (propositions that, although not analytic, are indubitable upon introspection by every person who considers them).

"The science of the Lawes of Nature is the true Morall Philosophie", according to Hobbes, and these Laws of Nature are those of God's laws discernible by unaided natural reason. Using the method just described, Hobbes argues that human beings are rational, and that rationality requires offering justifying considerations for one's actions; but to offer considerations as justifying one's own action commits one to accepting those same considerations as justifying the like actions of others, *ceteris paribus*. Thus the reasons we offer to others for imposing constraints on their actions, we too must accept as imposing the same constraints on our own. Hobbes conceives of this reciprocity requirement of rational agency as the 'sum' of the Law of Nature, and says that it is captured in "that law of the Gospell; Whatsoever you require that others should do to you, that do ye to them. And that Law of all men, *Quod tibi fieri non vis, alteri ne fecris*".[8]

From this core Law of Nature Hobbes argues that a rational person is required to submit to government. The situation that would result if every person remained free to exercise their 'Right of Nature' to do whatever they think useful for their own preservation is so dangerous

[8] EW III, 118; T 92.

to the lives, fortunes, liberty, and effective agency of others that no rational person can be willing to allow others such an extensive right. Each must demand that others transfer a portion of their natural right to a political authority who is authorized and empowered to adjudicate disputes and enforce decisions over contested matters; but what one demands of others one must also do oneself, hence Hobbes's second Law of Nature: "That a man be willing, when others are so too, as farre-forth, as for Peace and defence of himselfe he shall think it necessary, to lay down this right to all things; and be contented with so much liberty against other men, as he would allow other men against himself"[9]. This is done by authorizing a Sovereign. In this way natural reason tells us that God requires us to submit to government. Hobbes argues further that any effective government must necessarily enjoy the right to interpret all laws and adjudicate all disputes over contended matters, including those concerning the profession and practice of religion, and indeed must insist on uniformity in religion if the Commonwealth is to exhibit the public worship natural religion demands.

Personal revelation and prophecy are the other known sources of religious knowledge. Both are forms of supernatural revelation; in the first, God speaks to a person immediately; in the second, he speaks to her by the mediation of some other person, to whom he has formerly spoken immediately. The methods by which God reveals his will to individuals are dreams and visions resulting from the immediate intervention. This makes revelation *essentially private,* and *inaccessible* to others. Because most dreams and visions have perfectly naturalistic causal explanations, people are entitled to doubt whether one who claims to have received a personal revelation has, in fact, done so; Scripture explicitly directs that we should reject such claims unless the claimant both performs miracles and teaches the established religion. A miracle, as Hobbes defines it, is "a work of God (besides his operation by the way of nature, ordained in the Creation,) done for the making manifest to his elect, the mission of an extraordinary minister for their salvation".[10] God does not make mistakes, and does not change his mind (according to the required assumptions of omniscience

[9] Ibid.

[10] EW III, 432; T 303.

and benevolence), so he is not going to direct his prophets to preach against the religion he has formerly established. And because God wants us to *believe* his prophets – and since what we believe is a function of our reason and experience – he requires the performance of an experience for which our reason can give no naturalistic account. And so, "it is manifest that the teaching of the religion which God hath established, and the shewing of a present miracle, joined together, were the only marks whereby the Scripture would have a true prophet, that is to say, immediate revelation to be acknowledged; neither of them being singly sufficient to oblige any other man to regard what he saith".[11]

However, there have long since ceased to be any miracles, Hobbes asserts, and so we are no longer required to acknowledge the doctrine of any pretended prophet "farther than it is conformable to the Holy Scriptures, which since the time of our Saviour, supply the place, and sufficiently recompense the want of all other prophesy".[12] Because what counts as naturalistically inexplicable to one person may not so count to another of greater scientific sophistication, and because frauds may conspire to stage apparent miracles to dupe innocent onlookers for their own gain, the individual's judgment of whether a miracle has been performed is unreliable. If we can't know a miracle when we see one, it is as if, for us, miracles had ceased; and miracles ceasing, we can no longer be assured that anyone who now claims to be a prophet truly is. To settle a judgment about whether something we have witnessed or heard tell of is or is not a miracle, "we must have recourse to God's Lieutenant, [sovereign] to whom in all doubtful cases wee have submitted our private judgments".[13] And because judgment of whether the new doctrine alleged does or does not conform to the established religion also properly belongs to the Sovereign, personal revelation ceases to be, for all practical political purposes, an independent source of religious knowledge.

Although a person who genuinely believes that God has immediately spoken to her ought to do whatever she believes she has been directed to do, such permission can have little effect on social stability

[11] EW III, 365; T 259.
[12] Ibid.
[13] EW III, 435; T 305.

when the rest are justified in following her only if the Sovereign approves her claim. She may permissibly, and perhaps ought to follow her conscience even against the law if she has the intestinal fortitude to endure her martyrdom. "It is true", Hobbes writes, "that God is the soveraign of all soveraigns, and therefore, when he speaks to any subject, he ought to be obeyed, whatsoever any earthly potentate command to the contrary".[14] But ordinary subjects who have not enjoyed immediate divine revelation need have no scruples of conscience in obeying even the erroneous religious commands of their sovereigns, for those commands are the sole responsibility of the Sovereign; whereas the responsibility of the Subject is, as analysis of Scripture shows, first and foremost to obey the civil sovereign in all of its commands. Of course, *if* obeying a sovereign command would damn one to eternal death, "it would be madnesse" to obey. But Hobbes argues from Scripture that the necessary conditions for salvation are but two: belief that Jesus is the Christ, and a will to obey God's laws, which will we exhibit by the internal intention to comply, and repentance for our failures. God accepts the will for the deed, so faith in this single article, along with a will to obey, including to obey our sovereign are all that God requires of us.

In his extended interpretation of Scripture, Hobbes aims to show that this source of religious knowledge, when properly interpreted, confirms rather than undermines civil authority. He seeks to prove out of Scripture (1) that one's duty to God is properly identified by an appropriate religious authority, and thus that everyone ought to profess and practice religion as that appropriate religious authority dictates, (2) that any given group of Christians is subject to only one authority in both civil and religious matters, and (3) that the appropriate authority in both secular and religious matters is one's national civil sovereign. In fact, Hobbes's arguments carry him only so far as (3′) that the appropriate authority is *either* one's national civil sovereign *or* the Pope understood as the sovereign of a universal commonwealth of Christians; but considering his English audience, and his subsequent efforts in part 4 of *Leviathan* to unmask Catholic pretensions as biblically unsupported power grabs, conclusion (3′) suffices for his purpose.

[14] EW III, 366; T 260.

There are, however, limits on credible claims as to the content of revealed religion. As noted, natural reason, along with our experiences, "are the talents which He hath put into our hands to negotiate till the coming again of our blessed Saviour, and therefore not to be folded up in the napkin of an implicate faith, but employed in the purchase of justice, peace, and true religion".[15] This commitment shapes Hobbes's Scriptural interpretations. If the Bible offers mutually contradictory accounts of some concept, we are to interpret at least some of those accounts metaphorically, because our readiness to honor God requires that we refuse to believe that God makes mistakes or contradicts himself. So, for instance, we should not take literally the biblical claim that Hell is a bottomless pit in the earth, because no thing of finite size (as is the Earth) could contain anything of infinite size. Surveying all the conflicting characterizations of Hell he finds in Scripture, Hobbes employs his own natural reason to conclude that 'Hell' must be a metaphor for *final* death.

Hobbes interprets Scripture to say that humans do not by their nature have immortal souls existing separately from their bodies. "The soule in Scripture", writes Hobbes, "signifieth always, either the life, or the living creature and the body and soule jointly, the body alive".[16] It is true that had Adam not sinned, he and his posterity, eating from the tree of life, would have lived eternally in their bodies on the earth; but since by sinning Adam forfeited eternal life, God has withheld from humans the tree that would have allowed them to overcome their natural mortality. Jesus cancels that forfeiture of eternal life for those who believe in him, and at the Second Coming they will be resurrected, body, brain, and mental life, to live in their incorruptible bodies on the earth forever. Establishing this conclusion is essential to Hobbes's political project of showing that there can be only one sovereign at a time over any given Christian because there do not exist two coexistent realms, one spiritual and the other temporal: "It is true that the bodies of the faithful, after the resurrection, shall be not onely spirituall, but eternall: but in this life they are grosse, and corruptibile. There is therefore no other government in this life,

[15] EW III, 359–360; T 255–256.
[16] EW III, 615; T 425.

neither of state, nor religion, but temporall".[17] Furthermore, a correct interpretation of Scripture shows that the commission of ecclesiastics was merely to convert people to belief by teaching, and so never included coercive authority, such as must be held by sovereigns. Citing Peter's admonition to, in Hobbes's words, "obey the king and his governors, for this is God's will" (1 Peter 2: 13–14), and Paul's instruction to "put men in mind to be subject to their principalities and powers, and to obey magistrates" (Titus 3: 1) even though they were infidels, Hobbes argues that Scripture established that Christians are to recognize the judgments of their civil sovereigns in all matters, religious and civil, as authoritative, whether those judgments are ultimately correct or incorrect. God will sort the wheat from the chaff.

Hobbes insists that part of the problem of the Schools is that they demand that Christians abandon their natural reason to embrace conceptual impossibilities, such as the bodiless body that they term 'immaterial substance'. These sorts of nonsensical concepts that defy natural reason are designed, Hobbes argues, by the Schools as weapons of war against civil authority. Many of these are imported out of Aristotle, whom Hobbes systematically condemns as employing nonsense concepts that have perverted Christian doctrine. The now familiar engraving Hobbes commissioned for the frontispiece of *Leviathan* (Figure 8.1) pithily to depict its theme of the problem posed for peace by the duplication of temporal and spiritual sovereignties contains under the title banner a frame showing various "verbal forks".

The far left figure in the spiritual frame depicting the church's weapons has the word 'syllogisme' written on it, divided into three parts, to correspond to the structure of a syllogism. The next three figures are what Hobbes calls "verbal forks". Verbal forks are "distinctions that signify nothing, but serve only to astonish the multitude of ignorant men" used by the schoolmen for "the trick of imposing what they list upon their readers, and declining the force of true reason".[18] The verbal forks depicted here are the temporal/spiritual distinction, which, Hobbes insists, "makes men see double, and mistake their lawfull soveraign", and the direct/indirect distinction, which was used to assert the church's authority over those civil matters thought to affect

[17] EW III, 460; T 322.

[18] *B* 41; cf. EW III, 316; T 226.

FIGURE 8.1. Frontispiece to Leviathan, 1651.

spiritual matters. Hobbes sarcastically remarks on this distinction that Cardinal Bellarmine's fourth conclusion "That the pope has (in the dominions of other princes) the supreme temporall power INDIRECTLY'...is denyed; unlesse hee mean by indireclty, that he has gotten it by indirect means [e.g., fraud or theft]; then is that also granted".[19] But he adds in earnest that this distinction of "temporall, and spirituall power is but words. Power is as really divided, and as dangerously to all purposes, by sharing with another indirect power, as with a direct one".[20]

The right-hand-most verbal fork is the esse reale/esse intentionale distinction that makes possible the church's use of the Aristotelian doctrine of separated essences to support its doctrines of the immortality of the soul, transubstantiation, and the infusion of qualities, all of which Hobbes attacks as diminishing the civil authority. In the bottom of the frame we have Hobbes's wry comment on these distinctions – he has labeled a set of *horns* from which the temporal/spiritual distinction springs "Di-lem-ma".

The reason different people embrace differing religious views is that they have been differently taught, or trained. Hobbes thinks that because our beliefs result from our experience and education in conjunction with our bodily constitutions, *what* we believe will be a fairly straightforward function of *whom* we believe, and so shaping the content of religious belief is importantly a matter of having one's authority accepted. This implies that uniformity of religious education will be essential for the maintenance of sovereign authority in any commonwealth, and so Hobbes expends considerable effort discussing how religious education ought to be conceived and disseminated. "The greatest part of Man-kind...received the notions of their duty chiefly from Divines in the pulpit...and the Divines...derive their knowledge from the Universities....It is therefore manifest, that the instruction of the people dependeth wholly on the right teaching of Youth in the universities".[21] It is the duty of the Sovereign under the Law of Nature to procure the good of the people, and so to educate all subjects in the fundamentals of religious duty contained in those

19 EW III, 572; T 394.
20 EW III, 574; T 396.
21 EW III, 331; T 237.

laws. This duty to educate does not, however, imply that the Sovereign must inquire into subjects' religious beliefs and root out dissidents and disbelievers, nor even that such inquisition and persecution are permissible under the Law of Nature. They are not permissible. Belief not being subject to the will, the most a Sovereign may reasonably require from subjects is outward conformity in profession and practice. "There ought to be no power over the consciences of men, but of the word it selfe, working faith in every one... according to the purpose of God himself", Hobbes writes, particularly because "it is unreasonable of them who teach there is such danger in every little error, to require of a man endued with reason of his own, to follow the reason of any other man".[22]

The most difficult structural issue in understanding Hobbes's religious views is thinking about how Hobbes reconciles Natural Divine Law and the possibly whimsical pronouncements of any Sovereign's positive law. As we saw in Chapter 3, Hobbes is not a value subjectivist. He notes that most people 'call' right and wrong, good and bad, by their own likings and dislikings, but he expressly disapproves of that use of language and condemns the "Schools of the Grecians" for it in these words: "Their morall philosophy is but a description of their own passions. For the rule of manners, without civill government, is the Law of Nature; and in it, the law civill; that determineth what is... good and evill: whereas they make the rules of good and bad by their own liking and disliking: By which means, in so great diversity of taste, there is nothing generally agreed on; but every one doth (as far as he dares) whatsoever seemeth good in his owne eyes, to the subversion of commonwealth".[23]

There is an objective fact of the matter about what is right or wrong, good or evil; people may "*misrepresent*" to others what is good as evil or vice versa, and even though they judge conscientiously, may "*err*" on such matters. Hobbes explicitly acknowledges that the Sovereign may, in fact, err on such matters: "There is no judge, subordinate, nor sovereign, but may erre in a judgment of equity";[24] and "Suppose that a Christian king should from this foundation *Jesus is the Christ*,

[22] EW III, 696; T 480.
[23] EW III, 669; T 461.
[24] EW III, 263–264; T 192.

draw some false consequences...and demand the teaching of the same.... *Christian kings may err in deducing a consequence,* but who shall judge? Shall a private man judge, when the question is of his own obedience?"[25] God's Laws of Nature tell us that no private man is to judge. Despite the fallibility of all sovereigns, God prefers that we should comport ourselves in compliance with the commands of even so fallible an authority, than that we should march each to our own different drummer headlong into others.

God will burn away the erroneous "superstructions of hay or stubble", correct from incorrect inferences, in due time, and it is not the subjects' business to try to make that judgment. Hobbes titles his major political treatise "*Leviathan*", drawing on the Book of Job, precisely because he wishes to humble us prideful humans. Each of us supposes that our own private judgments are authoritative, that we know right from wrong, good from bad, righteous from wicked, and that we are justified in fighting for the claims of our little conscience, no matter the costs to other people, to peace, to civilization. Hobbes insists that we are not justified. Such behavior is unreasonable, for the private judgments of others merit no less deference than our own. It is also arrogant. We were nowhere when God laid the foundations of the world, we cannot know his purposes or judge his justice. To think otherwise is mere hubris. A Leviathan is needed to rule "over all the children of pride".

But how can a Christian, in good conscience, obey commands concerning religion that they believe with full conviction to be wrongful? As argued in Chapter 6, Hobbes asserted a *hierarchy of responsibility,* according to which subjects are answerable to God for their obedience to the commands of their governors, while those governors are answerable to God for their substantive commands. In his discussion in *Leviathan* explaining how Naaman, a Christian, could guiltlessly bow before his master's heathen gods, Hobbes explains that whatever one does in obedience to the command of constituted authority is blameless, so long as one holds in one's heart a different belief, and obeys only because commanded to do so by an authority whom God requires him to obey, whether the command is substantively right or wrong. (Indeed, Hobbes goes further, arguing that to deny a

[25] EW III, 601; T 414.

"Mohemetan" the same protection of conscience and action against a Christian master would be to violate both the Law of Nature requiring reciprocity and the Savior's directive under the Golden Rule.)

Some will dismiss this position of Hobbes as a form of *Nuremberg defense*, a claim that anything goes for those who were "just following orders". Such a judgment would not be fair to Hobbes. For Hobbes, the uniquely correct interpretation of the authoritative Christian religion directs us to submit our private judgment to the public – whether we think it right or wrong – *as a matter of religious principle.* There is thus a *self-effacing* character to Hobbes's religious argument, of the sort we noted in his argument concerning law generally: both the Law of Nature and divine positive law as revealed in Scripture direct individuals to treat as authoritative the interpretations of those laws' requirements laid down by their civil sovereigns.

How did Hobbes reconcile his naturalistic, scientific, determinist conception of the world with morality and Christian theology? This study has not sought to connect Hobbes's normative theory with his speculative philosophy, but here the connection is illuminating. Hobbes held that every event is strictly determined in a causal chain beginning in the actions of God. Most of these actions are set in motion by God's ordination of natural physical laws, others by his extraordinary suspension of those laws. But all are strictly causally necessitated. This fact neither abridges human freedom nor invalidates human practices of praise and blame. A free human person is one who is not stopped by external impediments from doing that which she has the will and capability to do. A person is responsible – and so liable to praise or blame – for those of her actions that result from her will, that is, from her own deliberation. Although a person is not free to choose how she wills, she is properly said to be free when she can do as she wills, and is properly held responsible for those of her doings that result from her willing. Hobbes articulates a genuinely compatibilist position, judging that no other position permits us to honor God as both omnipotent and just.

Hobbes's tone in writing has prompted many readers to wonder about the sincerity of his religious beliefs, and whether he adequately appreciated the sensibilities of religious persons with regard to religious duty and virtue. Seeing Hobbes's mode of operation in systematically viewing religion with an eye to establishing and maintaining civil authority, one may reasonably wonder whether Hobbes was himself a Christian believer.[26] He always insisted that he was, and his biographer Aubrey provides some evidence for his claim.[27] But even Hobbes's definition of religion in chapter 6 of *Leviathan* invites the question. Hobbes defines 'RELIGION' thus: "Feare of powers invisible, feigned by the mind, or imagined from tales publiquely allowed, RELIGION; not allowed, SUPERSTITION", although adding that "when the power imagined, is truly such as we imagine, TRUE RELIGION".[28] This talk of what we "imagine" seems already deflationary, even before we notice that on this account, even true religion would count as superstition in any society in which it was not authorized. However, attention to Hobbes's concern with disagreement in private judgments, as just discussed, permits us to interpret these remarks consistently with the possibility of veridical religion.

It is not clear to me how we could decisively settle the question what Hobbes believed in his heart of hearts. I doubt that anything important turns on settling that question. How could it, when we have his actual arguments before us?[29] What *is* important is to recognize that Hobbes's analysis of the problem of social disorder takes seriously the religious interests of citizens (as a matter of political sociology, if nothing else), and his solution depends crucially on managing those

[26] Hobbes resisted accusations of atheism and defended his position that subjects should defer to the judgment of their civil sovereign in matters of religion in remarks like this one from his *Six Lessons to the Professors of the Mathematics:* "But do not many other men, as well as you, read my *Leviathan*, and my other books? And yet they all find not such enmity in them against religion. Take heed of calling them all atheists that have read and approved my *Leviathan*. Do you think I can be an atheist and not know it? Or knowing it, durst have offered my atheism to the press?... You that take so heinously that I would have the rules of God's worship in a Christian commonwealth taken from the laws, tell me, from whom would you have them taken? From yourselves? Why so, more than from me? From the bishops?... why from them rather than from me?... From a consistory of presbeters...? Why from them rather than from me, or from any man else?" (EW VII, 350).

[27] Brief Lives, Chiefly of Contemporaries, set down by John Aubrey, between the Years 1669 & 1696, ed. from the author's mss, by Andrew Clark, 2 vols. (Oxford, 1898); cited in Curley (1994).

[28] EW III, 45; T 42.

[29] Some have suggested that Hobbes's arguments concerning religion are not to be taken at face value, but rather as using irony and other devices to lead elite readers to reject Christian doctrine altogether. Were that so, important aspects of Hobbes's theory would turn, not on Hobbes's personal religious beliefs, but on his intentions in offering his interpretations of religious doctrines.

interests in a way acceptable on principled grounds to their proponents. No civil order that counterposes itself to its citizens' religious interests, or merely wishes them away, or attempts to stamp them out of existence, can possibly remain stable in the long run.

Hobbes's anticlericalism is absolutely clear and undeniable, as is his hostility to the "Romish" religion. Was Hobbes a respectable Lutheran, a would-be, if unconventional, orthodox Protestant Christian, a Deist, an early advocate of religious toleration, or a closeted atheist with designs to pull down an evil empire? Hobbes scholars part company on this question. Some have argued that he was an orthodox Anglican, or Lutheran; others that he was a skeptic; still others that he intended to overthrow religious belief altogether by a sneaky program of rhetorical "avowal by disavowal". This question need not be settled in order to appreciate the compatibility of Hobbes's expressed views on religious, moral, and political obligation.

But it is interesting to consider why Hobbes proceeds the way he does. He opts for authoritarianism in religion rather than for toleration. This may seem to us to be unnatural, and we may wish to inquire why. Hobbes seems wistfully to have acknowledged the attractions of toleration and free faith in his remark in chapter 47 of *Leviathan* that "the independency of the primitive Christians to follow Paul, or Cephas, or Apollos, every man as he liketh best,... if it be without contention... is perhaps the best". Still, Hobbes did not believe that the psychological commitments required to sustain a system of toleration existed in his day. Religious toleration is a significant achievement of human society. It requires us to respect and protect those whom we think mistaken about the most fundamental matters, as a point of principle, and not just because we cannot stably impose our beliefs on them. Hobbes saw no prospect for this for his own society. In the same way that we might suppose that some barbarous peoples will fight themselves out of existence unless their passions are tamped down by a strongman, so Hobbes seems to have believed that until humanity follows the train of its God-given natural reason, it does best in a sort of receivership, parented by a trustee certified by the Divine Court.

THE INDEPENDENCE OF POLITICAL THEORY

The Laws of Nature, with their triple status as dictates of narrow self-interest, moral duty, and natural religion, stand as the pivot of Hobbes's unified normative theory of practical wisdom. It would be natural to suppose that if practical wisdom enjoys a unity, its distinct elements must exhibit some interdependence. But it is a matter of some complexity to sort out the relations of dependence within Hobbes's system between the demands of prudence, morality, and political obligation. As we noted in Chapter 5, although the reciprocity theorem that grounds all Laws of Nature does not depend on any assumptions about the particular ends of rational agents, the derivation from it of a natural duty to submit to government does depend on the unwillingness each of us finds herself to have to live in a world of unrestricted private judgment. The moral duty to submit to an effectively enforced system of mutual arbitration of all disputes – to sovereignty, in Hobbes's term – is in this limited sense parasitic on the nonarbitrary personal concern of any rational agent to establish and maintain the necessary social conditions for the effective exercise of her agency. To characterize that relation as one of the dependence of political obligation on prudence would be misleading, at best, because the sort of prudential interest at issue – preserving agency *tout court* – is a broader interest of anyone deliberating practically, even outside of her narrowly self-interested ends.

But Hobbes steadfastly operates to show the independence, not only of moral theory from metaphysics and epistemology,[30] but also of political theory from moral theory. One of the most striking features of Hobbes's view is its conviction about independence on the basis of what may appear to be purely methodological fiat. Hobbes was scrupulously self-reflective and fastidious about philosophical method (as we noted when unfolding in Chapter 5 his definitional derivation of the Laws of Nature), and, as he simply said in another context, "anyone who sees what I am doing may easily perceive what I think".[31]

We can just look at what he was doing. Hobbes famously detached *De Cive*, discussing civic duties and the rights and duties of sovereigns

[30] In his summary of "lessons of *Leviathan*", Kavka concludes that "Hobbes's moral and political theory is essentially independent of his materialist-determinist metaphysics"; *Hobbesian Moral and Political Theory* (Princeton, NJ, 1986), 447.

[31] EW III, 332; T 237. Hobbes makes this remark in the context of his critique of the education provided in the universities, as a response to the imagined question of whether the universities of England are not already learned enough to teach the youth correctly. At the end of *Leviathan* Hobbes famously recommends that *it* be taught in the universities (EW III, 713; T 491).

and subjects, from what should have been the prior discussions of man in *De Homine*, and of a grounding speculative philosophy of bodies before that. He insisted that his political philosophy did not stand in need of the prior sections, and, the practical urgency of the time being what it was, he saw no problem in offering the political philosophy independently (or as we would now say after Rawls, as a "free-standing" doctrine). This is the most robust possible expression of the independence of political philosophy. But when we notice also his insistence that we have no scientific knowledge of human nature (nor the nature of the "smallest creature living") and so *cannot* found a civil philosophy on that (nor need we any "science" of human nature because the conclusions of indubitable introspection suffice), and his own method (declared at the beginning of part 2 of *Leviathan*) of settling political rights and duties solely out of the *definition of a commonwealth*, it becomes impossible to doubt Hobbes's belief in the independence of political theory. Even his chart of the sciences in chapter 10 of *Leviathan* places moral science and the science of politics (or commonwealths) in different branches of knowledge, with the latter not a sub-branch of the former, nor of any of its ancestor sciences. Civil science studies the properties of commonwealths, which are artificial creations, and the relations of subjects and sovereigns, neither of which exists as such in nature.[32]

CONTEMPORARY USES OF HOBBES'S NORMATIVE PHILOSOPHY

It is not uncommon that commentaries on Hobbes's moral and political philosophy conclude with an account of the allegedly useful lessons we might take away from our study. Because interpreters by and large do not accept Hobbes's argument mandating the establishment of an absolute, unlimited, and undivided sovereign power, nor his description of life without government, nor what they take to be his conception of human nature, nor his interpretation of Christian

[32] Presumably, *nonhuman* beings of sufficient sophistication – extraterrestrials, or artificial intelligences, or chimeras we might create or that evolved *might* under imaginable circumstances find that it accords with reason for them to institute relations of subject and sovereign among themselves or with us. Nothing in those relations requires that they hold only among humans.

doctrine, finding the salutary lesson can prove challenging. Negative lessons, drawn from Hobbes's errors, have dominated.[33] But numerous commentators have found in Hobbes's work a valuable embryonic germ of methods or views they find attractive and wish to defend in a more developed form of their devising.[34] Although they may not actually have arrived at those attractive views by studying Hobbes, finding in Hobbes the seed of their views provides a resource for situating, clarifying, and in some cases further motivating their views. These cases do not so much draw lessons from Hobbes as they put Hobbesian insights to use for a contemporary purpose. Among these fall two of the most celebrated analytical approaches of present-day political philosophy – namely, Rawls's Political Liberalism, and Gauthier's Moral Contractarianism – both of which claim Hobbes as their first illustrious ancestor.[35]

[33] For instance, Gauthier concludes that it is fortunate that men are not as intractable as Hobbes asserted, because if they were, the sovereignty necessary for security would not be attainable; and since they are not, no such sovereignty is needed, *pace* Hobbes; *The Logic of 'Leviathan': The Moral and Political Theory of Thomas Hobbes* (Oxford, 1969), 169–170. Gauthier maintains of Hobbes's theory that "the content is, as we have shown in the case of the moral theory, and will show in the political theory, inadequate. But the conceptual structure may provide us with insights into the construction of a more adequate theory" (133). J. W. N. Watkins praises Hobbes, however faintly, for his "interconnected system of ideas, all of them fallible, most of them controversial, and some of them outrageous", asserting that it is "just because Hobbes tried, unsuccessfully, to demonstrate his conclusions, he succeeded in elaborating a richly criticizable philosophy – which is what we should ask from a political philosopher"; *Hobbes's System of Ideas* (London, 1965), 169, 163. Edwin Curley draws the more substantive, if somewhat humdrum moral that we "still need to learn the negative lessons of part III of *Leviathan*, as well as the more positive lesson of part II: though we may be as deeply divided in our values as we are in our religious beliefs, we need civil society if we are to survive and to have even a tolerably comfortable existence"; Introduction to *Hobbes Leviathan*, Edwin Curley, ed. (Indianapolis, 1994), xlvi.

[34] Kavka, in a section entitled "lessons of *Leviathan*", sees in Hobbes an original diagnosis of the problems of anarchy and a source of our theory of public goods, and arguments that hypothetical consent can ground political obligation, that moral requirements must be consistent with our motivations, and that moral and legal requirements must work together if peace is to be sustained. He concludes, "That morality and justice are effectively and lastingly realizable only within the State is an antianarchist theme of *Leviathan* that is worth taking to heart" (*Hobbesian Moral and Political Theory*, 446–452, 452).

[35] David Gauthier, *Morals by Agreement* (Oxford, 1986), hereafter referred to as *MA*. John Rawls, *Political Liberalism* (New York, 1993). From at least the late 1980s Rawls had been considering whether Hobbes in fact had espoused a form of political

At first it seems clear enough why both of these approaches should regard themselves as descended from Hobbes: despite their essential antipathy, each is a variety of social contract theory, and we understand Hobbes to have undertaken the contractarian task of justifying political arrangements by appeal to the agreement that informed and rational occupants of a prepolitical state would make to advance their interests by the means that reason specifies. This generally accepted characterization of Hobbes's project is sufficiently neutral to render Hobbes a resource for both Rawls and Gauthier. Political Liberalism emphasizes Hobbes's use of what Rawls calls *reasonable* (as opposed to merely rational) constraints on the set-up of the contractors' choice situation and on their reasoning in it, such as the presumption of equality in the contractors' moral standing and bargaining position, and the requirements of reciprocity, mutual benefit, and fairness in the terms agreed to which are imposed by Hobbes's Laws of Nature – his laws forbidding, for example, injustice, iniquity, and partiality – where these laws are conceived as reasonable directives. In particular, Hobbes's requirement of *reciprocity* among persons understood as free and equal,[36] in the face of disagreement in interests, beliefs, and judgments as to the correct conduct of common life,[37] invites the suspicion that Hobbes may have developed a fledgling political liberalism.

Gauthier, in calling Hobbes the greatest advocate of moral contractarianism, instead stresses Hobbes's atomistic conception of the person as moved by sociable precepts like the Laws of Nature only to the extent that those are recommended by the self-interested calculations of a maximizing rationality. In contrast to Political Liberalism, Gauthier's Moral Contractarianism characterizes Hobbes's moral

liberalism, and in April 1993 he wrote to me asking whether Hobbes was "the first political liberal".

36 On this equality see *Leviathan:* The question who is the better man, has no place in the condition of meer nature; where, (as has been shewn before,) all men are equall.... If nature therefore have made men equall, that equalitie is to be acknowledged: or if nature have made men unequall; yet because men that think themselves equall, will not enter into conditions of peace, but upon equall termes, such equalitie must be admitted. And therefore for the ninth law of nature, I put this, *That every man acknowledge other for his Equall by Nature* (EW III, 141; T 110).

37 E.g., at L 79: "And divers men, differ not onely in their judgement, on the senses of what is pleasant, and unpleasant to the tast, smell, hearing, touch, and sight; but also of what is conformable, or disagreeable to reason, in the actions of common life".

norms as consequences, rather than conditions, of the contractors' deliberations. "In Hobbes we find the true ancestor of the theory of morality we shall present", writes Gauthier, but "to the conceptual underpinning that may be found in Hobbes, we seek to add the rigor of rational choice".[38]

Hobbes would probably have been pleased to imagine twentieth-century philosophers fighting to claim him as one of their own; in his own day he was called everything from a "supercilious dogmatist" of "magisterial pomposity" to a purveyor of "horrid and execrable opinions" and "pander to bestiality". But neither patrimony suit turns out to be defensible. Exposing the difficulty with Moral Contractarianism's claim depends upon showing that the theory it purports to take from Hobbes is not in fact Hobbes's, and that Hobbes's theory properly understood renders inapplicable the particular model for rational choice Gauthier defends. Disinheriting Political Liberalism involves showing that Hobbes's actual view prohibits the use of an argumentative device Political Liberalism cannot do without. In the process of arguing that what is of real philosophical interest in Hobbes's view cannot be what Gauthier thought it to be, nor quite what Political Liberalism would take it to be, I'll suggest what I take to be the primary philosophical interest of Hobbes's political theory, the part that is true and good and marvelously useful.

Gauthier's doctrine of Morals by Agreement employs what has become over the last several decades the standard philosophical interpretation of Hobbes's political theory. That is not surprising since Gauthier himself was a major contributor to that interpretation,[39] introducing the refinements of game theory into the interpretive tradition passed from Laird through Strauss, J. W. N. Watkins, Nagel, and Plamenatz, and via Gauthier's innovation, developed to what must surely have been its zenith by Hampton and Kavka.[40] This interpretation identifies Hobbes's

[38] Gauthier, *Morals by Agreement*, 10.

[39] See David Gauthier, *The Logic of 'Leviathan'*.

[40] Peter Vanderschraaf has since developed this school of Hobbes interpretation. See John Laird, *Hobbes* (London; 1934); Leo Strauss, *The Political Philosophy of Hobbes* (Chicago, 1952); J. W. N. Watkins, *Hobbes's System of Ideas* and his "Philosophy and Politics in Hobbes", in K. C. Brown, ed., *Hobbes Studies* (Cambridge, MA, 1965), 237–262; Thomas Nagel, "Hobbes's Concept of Obligation", *Philosophical Review* 68 (January 1959): 68–53; John Plamenatz, "Mr. Warrender's Hobbes", in K. C. Brown,

solution to the problem of social disorder as the erection of a political power that coerces obedience by credibly threatening to punish disobedience. The power to punish operates to secure order because, says the standard interpretation, humans are egoists who care above all about self-preservation and the avoidance of bodily harm to themselves. Given this preservation-centered conception of human nature, the fear of death, and of the punishments that may well lead to death – wounds, imprisonment, or the deprivation of goods or livelihood – may be expected to motivate compliance with the sovereign's commands. Denuded, then, of its game-theoretic fancy dress, the standard interpretation's central claim is that "might plus fright makes order".

It asserts further that Hobbes derives his preservation-centered conception of human nature from a mechanistic materialism that analyzes men as bits of matter in motion, attracted or repulsed by external stimuli proportionately to the increase or decrease of internal vital motion produced by the impingement on them of these stimuli. "From [Hobbes's] account of vital and voluntary motion it follows", writes Gauthier, "that each man seeks, and seeks only, to preserve and strengthen himself. A concern for continued well-being is both the necessary and sufficient ground of human action. Hence man is necessarily selfish".[41]

The standard interpreters take this to imply that no irreducibly moral or religious consideration can motivate action. For example, Watkins writes that "since the vital motions of the heart can only be excited by the prospect of some bodily change in its owner... merely moral considerations unrelated to such a change cannot affect behavior".[42] This suggests, what the standard interpretation asserts, that Hobbes will have to hold a subjectivist and personally relativist moral theory that analyzes moral utterances in terms of personal affinity or aversion. And it suggests further that theism will be irrelevant to Hobbes's system, because the requirements of religious duty *per se* will also be motivationally inert, as will even the requirements of what might be called "special prudence" – of salvation – if these

ed., *Hobbes Studies;* Jean Hampton, *Hobbes and the Social Contract Tradition* (Cambridge, 1986); and Kavka, *Hobbesian Moral and Political Theory.*

41 Gauthier, *The Logic of 'Leviathan'*, 7.

42 Watkins, "Philosophy and Politics in Hobbes", 252.

involve the death of one's present physical body. Thus we have, on the standard interpretation, a theory that attempts to move from a physical-scientific account of man as matter in motion to a preservation-centered egoism that precludes the motivational efficacy of religious and moral requirements as such, to a "might plus fright makes order" solution to social unrest. Such a reading might naturally attract those who believe that only a materialist and nontheistic political theory can have any real philosophical interest in the modern world.

There are two major reasons for thinking that the theory just sketched is improperly attributed to Hobbes. The first is that it fits extremely poorly with Hobbes's text, as I hope is by now clear; the second that it makes Hobbes's theory conceptually incoherent.[43] I regard these considerations as decisive against the standard interpretation.

a. Textual Inadequacy

The first reason for thinking that Hobbes did not espouse the theory the standard interpreters attribute to him is that fully half of Hobbes's masterwork *Leviathan,* his political theory in its mature form, is devoted to a detailed discussion of religious doctrine, practice, and history, a fact for which the standard interpretation cannot adequately account. The theory it ascribes to Hobbes does not attend to religion, and it makes no reference to material contained in the half of *Leviathan* devoted to discussion of religion. But it is fair to ask, since so much of *Leviathan* is about religion, Why does Hobbes obsess about religion?

It is *not* plausible to suppose that Hobbes included the discussion of religion in order to make an essentially irreligious political theory easier for a religious audience to swallow, because the content of that discussion was extremely inflammatory, drawing the most scathing attacks from Hobbes's contemporaries, and Hobbes quite clearly anticipated that reaction. We can see this from his remarks in *Leviathan* concerning its accounts of religious doctrines: they "will appear to most men a novelty"[44] and "That which perhaps may most

[43] Both of these lines of objection are developed in my *Ideals as Interests,* chapter 1.
[44] EW III, 444; T 311.

offend are certain texts of Holy Scripture alleged by me to other purpose than ordinarily they used to be by others".[45] Had Hobbes been intending his discussions of religion as "window-dressing", an effort to prettify the theory by disguising its atheism, he would surely have had the sense to employ a less scandalous religious position.

It is marginally more plausible to imagine that the half of the book Hobbes devotes to religion is included solely to address people's self-interested concern to secure their own salvation. It is unfortunate that this account, which reduces all religious motives to special prudence, seems to rely on an impoverished conception of what it is to have religious concerns, and sits poorly with the fact that many of Hobbes's intended readers were Calvinist predestinarians who did not believe it possible for them to affect their own salvation, and thus would not have been open to persuasion by a reductionist argument. But unfortunate or not, if the standard interpretation hoped to include the half of *Leviathan* on religion as a working part of Hobbes's theory, its egoism assumption would compel it to understand that half as about a longest-run self-interest in salvation, despite the obvious tension between that account and its assumption of mechanistic materialism. The larger difficulty for the standard interpretation is that if it were true that Hobbes had devoted half his book to the issue of salvation, that would suggest that he regarded people's interest in their own salvation as an *extremely important source of social disorder*. But how could it be, given the state's threats of capital punishment, unless that interest were often and widely given *priority* over people's interest in securing their temporal bodily preservation? Obviously, if the interest in salvation didn't *override* fear of bodily harm, then it would not need to be dealt with for Hobbes's "might plus fright makes order" solution to work. But if the interest in salvation does need to be confronted, then it must be that people's action on that interest can jeopardize order, which could happen only if their interest in salvation could override their concerns to avoid bodily harm. If the concern to secure one's own salvation were overriding in this way, then the sovereign's threat to inflict such comparatively minor harms couldn't possibly provide the fundamental foundation for political obedience, as the standard interpretation insists it does.

45 EW III, Epistle Dedication; T 3.

Notice that this will be true even if the society in question includes many people who themselves have no religious interests and who *would* be deterred by a credible threat of capital punishment. So long as there are enough *others* who do have overriding religious concerns that they can disrupt social order, the reasons for obedience of even atheistic egoists are undermined. If the state can neither protect them nor credibly threaten to punish them, as it may not be able to do if religious resisters impede its functioning, then they have no reason from narrow prudence to obey it, even though they themselves have no religious interests. (In homely terms, a few rotten apples can spoil the whole barrel.) So the standard interpretation is in a bind. If religious interests do *not* pose any serious threat to social order, then Hobbes's extended treatment of them becomes an inexplicable mystery. It could not have served as window dressing, and it is no working part of the theory. But if those interests *do* pose a serious threat, it is because they can override fear of the bodily harm the sovereign's punishments threaten, and that would make the standard interpretation's proffered solution for social disorder no solution at all. So it appears that if that interpretation renders the half of *Leviathan* on religion a working part of the theory, its foundation crumbles. This may explain why the standard interpreters line up behind Leslie Stephen's condescending claim that Hobbes's system "would clearly be more consistent and intelligible if he simply omitted the theology altogether".[46]

Still – and here's the point – *Hobbes* didn't think so: after acknowledging in the Epistle dedicatory that his unorthodox interpretations of Scripture are of all his ideas the most likely to offend, he explains, "but I have done it with due submission, *and also (in order to my subject) necessarily;* for they [the orthodox understandings] are the outworks of the enemy, from whence they impugne the civill power".[47] And later, in the *Six Lessons*, commenting on the writing of *Leviathan* and speaking of the clergy, Hobbes said explicitly that "The cause of my writing that book was the consideration of what the ministers and before and in the beginning of the civil war, by their preaching and writing did contribute thereunto".[48] Later still, in his *Seven*

[46] Leslie Stephen, *Hobbes* (London, 1928), 152.
[47] EW III, vi; T 3, emphasis added.
[48] EW VII, 335.

Philosophical Problems, he says of *Leviathan*, "It was written in a time when the pretence of Christ's kingdom was made use of for the most horrid actions that can be imagined; and it was in just indignation of that that I desired to see the bottom of that doctrine of the kingdom of Christ, which divers ministers then preached for a pretence to their rebellion".[49]

b. Conceptual Incoherence

The second reason for doubting that the view the standard interpretation ascribes to Hobbes really is his is that on no plausible construal of the problem Hobbes was addressing could that problem be solved by the solution the standard interpreters attribute to Hobbes. The standard reading represents the disorder of the state of nature as the product of rational egoists trapped in a prisoner's dilemma, to be solved, as we've seen, by erecting a sovereign power to change the payoffs of noncooperation through threat of punishment. If this were right, Hobbes's solution would be capable of *originally* establishing order from the anarchy of the state of nature. But what analysis shall we give of *recurrent* disorder – of the recurring collapses of order within established societies? This, after all, is the problem Hobbes was addressing: He writes, "long time after men have begun to constitute commonwealths, imperfect, and apt to relapse into disorder, there may principles of reason be found out, by industrious meditation, to make their constitution (excepting by externall violence) everlasting. And such are those which I have in this discourse set forth".[50]

These principles of reason are principles to prevent domestic rebellion, for, as Hobbes writes, "in those nations whose commonwealths have been long-lived, and not been destroyed but by forraign warre, the subjects never did dispute of the sovereign power".[51] So recurrent disorder caused by rebellious subjects is the problem that engages Hobbes. Can the standard interpretation give a plausible account of rebellion compatible with the solution it attributes to Hobbes?

49 EW VII, 5.
50 EW III, 324–325; T 232.
51 EW III, 195; T 145.

If original disorder were the result of the actions of rational egoists trapped in a prisoner's dilemma, then once the payoff matrix is changed, disorder ought to have been permanently eradicated. Rational egoists will be deterred from rebellion by the sovereign's threatened punishments. That's just what it means to say that the payoff matrix has been changed. If, then, subjects rebel in the face of the sovereign's credibly threatened punishments, bringing a state of *order* to collapse (and assuming none of those "externall factors" Hobbes has excluded from his discussion – foreign invasion, natural disaster, plague, etc.), rebellious subjects must be experiencing either a *failure* of rationality or the intrusion of *extra*-rational forces that undermine or override their rational self-interest. If the proper account of recurrent disorder is a failure of rationality pure and simple, then one could hardly expect the standard interpretation's solution to restore order – the threat of punishment will motivate only self-interested persons who correctly identify their self-interest; it cannot be expected to have any salutary effect on self-interested people who are so irrational as to fail to see the imprudence of rebellion even in the face of credibly threatened punishments of sufficient severity.

On the other hand, if rebellion results from *perturbations* of reason such as the passions associated with religious zeal, moral indignation, and personal pride, these must be forces capable of overriding rational self-interest (that is assuming, as the standard interpretation does, that the avoidance of punishment is in one's rational self-interest), and be forces capable also of overriding one particular sort of passion, namely, the fear of death. Otherwise they couldn't motivate disobedience in the face of credibly threatened capital punishment. But we can see that if recurrent disorder is caused by forces that override rational self-interest and fear of death, the standard interpretation's solution by appeal to rational self-interest and fear of death cannot be expected to solve the problem. For the standard interpretation, changing the payoff matrix ought to do it – for good; and if it doesn't, that interpretation has nothing further to offer. Given the solution it attributes to Hobbes, and the analyses of Hobbes's problem available to it, the problem of recurrent disorder is either negligible or insoluble, and Hobbes's solution is either unnecessary or useless. So unless we are to conclude that Hobbes himself was, to use his own favorite term of abuse, an "egregious blockhead", a conclusion the principle of charity in interpretation requires us to resist, we should reject the standard interpretation.

The transcendent interests interpretation of Hobbes's political philosophy begins by taking at face value Hobbes's remark that "The most frequent praetext of sedition and civil war, in Christian commonwealths hath a long time proceeded from a difficulty, not yet sufficiently resolved, of obeying at once both God and man, then when their commandments are one contrary to the other".[52] And in *Behemoth*, Hobbes's history of the English Civil War, Hobbes writes, "If it be lawfull then for subjects to resist the king, when he commands anything that is against the Scripture, that is, contrary to the command of God, and to be judge of the meaning of scripture, it is *impossible* that the life of any King, or the peace of any Christian kingdom, can long be secure".[53] These remarks strongly suggest that people's opinions may contribute to disorder. Hobbes confirms this suspicion, writing that "the actions of men procede from their opinions, and in the well governing of opinions, consists the well governing of mens actions, in order to their peace and concord.... It belongeth therefore to him that hath the soveraign power, to be judge, or constitute all judges of opinions and doctrines, as a thing necessary to peace, thereby to prevent discord and civill warre".[54] Because people's opinions about their religious duty are particularly problematic, stability requires that the sovereign *must* control religious doctrine, since, "if he give away the government of doctrines, men will be frighted into rebellion with the feare of spirits".[55] So people's religious beliefs *can* cause rebellion.

But can't the sovereign prevent rebellion by threatening punishment? The sovereign's rights, Hobbes insists,

> cannot be maintained by any civill law, or terrour of legal punishment. For a civill law that shall forbid rebellion... is not... any obligation, but by virtue onely of the law of nature that forbiddeth the violation of faith; which naturall obligation if men know not, they cannot know the right of any law the soveraign maketh. And for the punishment, they take it for an act of hostility;

[52] EW III, 584; T 402.

[53] Hobbes's *Behemoth or the Long Parliament*, edited by Ferdinand Tonnies with an introduction by Stephen Holmes (Chicago, 1990), 50.

[54] EW III, 164; T 125.

[55] EW III, 168; T 127.

which when they think they have strength enough, they will endeavour by acts of hostility, to avoyd.[56]

In a Christian commonwealth like Hobbes's, the sovereign's civil power depends "on the opinion men have of their duty to him, and the fear they have of punishment in *another* world",[57] not, that is, on their sovereign's coercive threats (nor even merely on fear of God), but also on their opinions of what God expects of them. They must be brought to see civil obedience as their duty, for, as Hobbes asks, "If men know not their duty, what is there that can force them to obey the laws? An army, you will say. But what shall force the army?"[58] Hobbes presumably thinks that *nothing* shall force the army, and so that order cannot be maintained by force, all the way down, so to speak. This explains his view that "The power of the mighty hath no foundation but in the opinion and belief of the people".[59]

If order depends on the subjects' believing themselves duty-bound to obey their sovereign, responsibility for disorder is, it seems, naturally to be laid at the door of those who persuade subjects that obedience is not due to their sovereign, or is rather due to someone else. This is precisely where Hobbes deposits it, the lion's share with ecclesiastics who urge that fulfilling our supreme duties to God may require disobedience to the civil sovereign. In his *Behemoth* account of the cause of the English civil wars, Hobbes blames primarily the Presbyterian ministers, who, aided by (as he calls them) Papists, and various independent sects, promulgated religious doctrines inimical to the sovereign's authority, for example, the doctrine that "the present church now militant on earth is the kingdom of God" and so that its commands have priority over the civil sovereign's; that "whatsoever a man does against his conscience is sinne", making each man's own judgment in matters of religion authoritative; and that "every private man is judge of good and evil actions", including the actions of his sovereign. All of these doctrines encourage subjects to regard some judgment *other* than the sovereign's as authoritative (that is, to regard

[56] EW III, 324; T 232.
[57] EW III, 539; T 373.
[58] *Behemoth*, 59.
[59] Ibid., 16.

some *private* judgment as authoritative), and to obey it in defiance of constituted public authority.

Once subjects believe these disruptive doctrines, the sovereign's coercive threats will be useless. In *Leviathan* Hobbes writes that

> the emperours, and other Christian soveraigns, under whose government these errours and the like encroachments of ecclesiastics upon their office, at first crept in to the disturbance of their possessions, and of the tranquillity of their subjects... might have hindered the same in the beginning: But when the people were once possessed by those spirituall men, there was no humane remedy to be applied, that any man could invent.[60]

It is essential that civil sovereigns establish their authority in religious matters because "It is impossible a commonwealth should stand, where any other than the soveraign, hath a power of giving greater rewards than life; and of inflicting greater punishments than death. [And] eternall life is a greater reward, than the life present; and eternall torment a greater punishment than the death of nature".[61]

For this reason, we cannot expect to avoid rebellion in Christian commonwealths like Hobbes's until "preaching be better looked to, whereby the interpretation of a verse in the Hebrew, Greek, or Latin Bible, is oftentimes the cause of a civil war".[62] It matters what preachers preach, "for ambition can do little without hands, and few hands it would have, if the common people were as diligently instructed in the true principles of their duty, as they are terrified and amazed by their preachers, with fruitless and dangerous doctrines".[63] It begins to sound very much as though preventing rebellion requires overcoming any division between civil and religious authority.

Let's return to our discussion of *Leviathan*'s frontispiece. Certainly everyone has noticed that the figure of the king is wearing armor composed of many small people, signifying that the sovereign's power consists in the combined strength of his subjects. He holds the civil sword in his right hand, and the church staff in his left. Above him is written a quotation from Job 41: 33 (the citation is to the Vulgate), "Upon earth there is not his like", which refers to God's creature

[60] EW III, 693–694; T 478.
[61] EW III, 437; T 307.
[62] *Behemoth*, 181.
[63] Ibid., 70.

Leviathan. This kingly figure represents the human approximation to Leviathan.

Now notice the two sets of smaller drawings on either side of the title banner. These represent the division of authority with which the book is primarily concerned, the counterposition of the ways and means of temporal versus spiritual rule that Leviathan overcomes. The first depicts the seat of power, the temporal castle on the left, and the spiritual church on the right. The person in whom authority is vested is signified in the second frame by the crown on the temporal side, and the bishop's miter on the spiritual. The third set of drawings contrasts the type of force exercised in temporal rule – physical force, as symbolized by the cannon, with the wrath of God, the threat of excommunication and damnation, symbolized by lightning bolts.

The fourth set of pictures takes as its subject the weapons and equipment of war: temporal rule uses guns, bayonets, standards, and drums; spiritual warfare is conducted by means of arguments and distinctions, the verbal forks we discussed earlier.

The final set of scenes depicts the battlefield on which each side struggles – the site of its conquests. The temporal frame shows an ordinary battlefield, with soldiers engaged in combat. The spiritual frame is a scene from a university disputation among divines, where doctrines conducive to the church's independent power are developed, and their supporting verbal forks devised. In the Epistle Dedicatory to *Liberty and Necessity*, Hobbes inquires:

> What, I pray, is the effect of so many... disputations, conferences, conventicles, printed books, written with so much distraction and presumption upon God Almighty, and abuse of his Holy Word? Marry this: it is the seminary of many vexatious, endless, and fruitless controversies, the consequence whereof are jealousies,... the introduction of factions and national quarrels into matters of religion, and consequently all the calamities of war and devastation.[64]

Clausewitz famously remarked that war is the continuation of politics by other means. *Leviathan*'s frontispiece shows Hobbes to have affirmed a kind of twisted anticipation of that celebrated dictum: according to Hobbes, ecclesiastical politics is the continuation of war by other means.

[64] EW IV, 233.

The frontispiece is, then, a symbolic representation of Hobbes's theory of social disorder, disorder as generated by conflict between civil and religious authorities. Hobbes tells us in the *Six Lessons* that "though the competition of the papal and civil power be taken away now, yet the competition between the ecclesiastical and the civil power hath manifestly enough appeared very lately".[65] And so, Hobbes concludes,

> When therefore these two powers oppose one another, the common-wealth cannot but be in great danger of civill warre, and dissolution. For the civill authority being more visible, and standing in the cleerer light of naturall reason cannot choose but draw in all times a very considerable part of the people: And the spirituall, though it stand in the darknesse of schoole distinctions, and hard words; yet because the fear of darknesse, and ghosts, is greater than other fears, cannot want a party sufficient to trouble, and sometimes to destroy a common-wealth.[66]

The problem here is not one of merely superstitious fears, of some irrational pneumatophobia. Our religious duties *should* trump the civil when in conflict.[67] "It is manifest enough", Hobbes writes, "that when a man receiveth two contrary commands, and knows that one of them is God's, he ought to obey that, and not the other, though it be the command even of his lawfull soveraign", and "if the [sovereign's] command be such as cannot be obeyed without being damned to eternall death, then it were madnesse to obey it".

In this light we can see that Hobbes's problem of social disorder cannot be solved by threatening civil punishment for disobedience. People simply aren't the bodily preservation-centered egoists needed to make that sort of threat motivationally reliable. Rather, they are religious believers who count salvation and the fulfillment of their duties to God as a part of their good, and who may embrace martyrdom for their faith, or resist their government on the ground of conscience. They have interests that may *transcend* their interest in

[65] EW VII, 345.

[66] EW III, 317; T 227.

[67] "It is manifest enough", Hobbes writes, "that when a man receiveth two contrary commands, and knows that one of them is God's, he ought to obey that, and not the other, though it be the command even of his lawfull soveraign", and "if the [sovereign's] command be such as cannot be obeyed without being damned to eternall death, then it were madnesse to obey it" (EW III, 585; T 403).

temporal bodily preservation, interests for the sake of which they may be willing to risk death, or even to embrace death. Hobbes says of the clergy that "by the canonization of saints, and declaring who are martyrs, they assure their power, in that they induce simple men into an obstinacy against the laws and commands of their civill soveraigns *even to death*".[68] That makes proper management of these transcendent interests indispensable to the maintenance of order. And that means that "the right of judging what doctrines are fit for peace and to be taught to the subjects, is...inseparably annexed...to the soveraign power civill....For...men that are once possessed of an opinion that their obedience to the soveraign power will bee more hurtfull to them, than their disobedience, will disobey the laws, and thereby overthrow the commonwealth, and introduce confusion, and civill war".[69]

So the bodily preservation-centered conception of human nature the standard interpretation attributes to Hobbes is not in fact Hobbes's. This snag is a serious problem for that interpretation, because if we pull on this thread we can watch the standard interpretation unravel in both directions. The bodily preservation-centered egoism was said to be derived from Hobbes's physical-scientific account of man as matter in motion, and together with it to form the account of man from which the political theory is derived. But that psychological conception is *not* derived from Hobbes's physical science. Hobbes insists that "in this naturall kingdome of God, there is no other way to know any thing, but by naturall reason; that is, from the principles of naturall science; which are so farre from teaching us any thing of Gods nature, *as they cannot teach us our own nature*, nor the nature of the smallest creature living".[70] Preservation-centered egoism receives no support from Hobbes's natural science because that natural science cannot in practice ground *any* conception of human nature, nor through it a political philosophy.

Could it do so in principle, at least? If we think back to Hobbes's own chart of the sciences, we can see that civil philosophy, that is, the science of politics, is a distinct branch of philosophy and not a subfield

[68] EW III, 692; T 447, emphasis added.
[69] EW III, 537; T 372.
[70] EW III, 353–354; T 251–252.

of the study of bodies, including men, and their natural properties, physical or psychological. He is committed to the independence of political philosophy.

Of course, in some sense a study of the properties of states would have to be related to a study of the properties of humans, because the states we know of have all been in some sense composed of humans. But if, as Hobbes's chart indicates, a science of politics is not a branch of the science of natural bodies, then it seems likely that Hobbes's natural science is not meant to provide what we would think of as deductive grounding for his political argument. If that were Hobbes's intention, we would expect the chart to be configured quite differently.

If, upon seeing this, we are curious to know why the natural science is included at all, we have only to pay attention to what Hobbes actually does with it. He uses it to correct mistaken accounts of sense perception, dreams, and visions, because

> This nature of sight having never been discovered by the ancient pretenders to naturall knowledge... it was hard for men to conceive of those images in the fancy, and in the sense, otherwise than of things really without us... Daemons. As if the dead of whom they dreamed were not inhabitants of their own brain, but of the air, or of heaven, or hell... and by that means have feared them.[71]

This bad natural science made plausible the Schoole's doctrine, importing Aristotle, of separated essences, which Hobbes declares

> would fright [men] from obeying the laws of their countrey with empty names.... For it is upon this ground, that when a man is dead and buried, they say his soule (that is his life) can walk separated from his body; and a great many other things that serve to lessen the dependance of subjects on the soveraign power of their countrey.[72]

Such erroneous doctrines, made plausible only by a misunderstanding of natural science, position the church to claim that it has jurisdiction over men's spirits or souls at the very same time that men's bodies are under the sovereign's civil jurisdiction. This duplication of authorities over men is precisely what Hobbes is concerned to avoid.

71 EW III, 637–638; T 440–441.
72 EW III, 674–675; T 465.

In short, Hobbes's remarks on natural science are present in order to correct several identifiable disruptive religious errors, and not, as the standard interpretation would have it, to ground some general psychological theory, and through that, a political theory. That is why Hobbes's physical science is so thin and patchy, and is abandoned after only a few short chapters. And it also explains why in each revision of his political theory, although Hobbes vastly expands his *religious* discussion – from twenty-nine pages or about 12 percent of *The Elements of Law*, to 116 pages or 36 percent of *De Cive*, to a whopping 357 pages, exactly 50 percent of *Leviathan* – he never feels the need to develop the rudimentary physical science that serves in his political writings. It is not that Hobbes is generally uninterested in science; he wrote many scientific works and engaged in many scientific debates. *But not in the service of his political theory*. There the science had a sharply limited, nonfoundational, role. We need not doubt that Hobbes had confidence that should the future bring us a fully developed science of human nature, that science would support his political theory. But his political theory had no need to wait on the development of that science.

As for the standard interpretation's claim that Hobbes must have affirmed a subjectivist and personally relativist moral theory because that is implied by bodily preservation-centered egoism, once the egoism goes, the nonobjectivism is no longer necessary, unless there is compelling independent textual evidence for it. As it happens, there is not. As we noted in Chapter 6, Hobbes *disapproved* of subjective or relativized uses of moral terms. Recall that he *criticized* the schools of the Grecians on this ground:

> Their morall philosophy is but a description of their own passions. For the rule of manners, without civill government, is the Law of Nature; and in it, the law civill; that determineth... what is good and evill: whereas they make the rules of good and bad by their own liking and disliking: By which means, in so great diversity of taste, there is nothing generally agreed on; but every one doth (as far as he dares) whatsoever seemeth good in his owne eyes, to the subversion of commonwealth.[73]

Hobbes is here indicating that it is *incorrect* to suppose that private appetite is the measure of good and evil. In a state of nature the proper

[73] EW III, 669; T 461.

measure of good and evil is the Law of Nature; and in a commonwealth, the proper measure of good and evil is the civil law, because the Law of Nature requires us to take it for such. We may observe that in a state of nature people do in fact use their differing private appetites as the measure of good and evil (partly because there are difficulties in applying and enforcing the Laws of Nature), but even there, it is *not the correct* measure. It is *never* the correct measure.

In fact, Hobbes's famous state of nature argument is best understood as a *reductio* of the use of private judgment; he writes "And therefore so long a man is in the condition of mere nature, (which is a condition of war), as private appetite is the measure of good and evill".[74] Note carefully that this passage does *not* say (as the standard interpretation would have it) that *so long as* people are in the condition of mere nature, their private appetites *are* the measure of good and evil; what it says is that so long as private appetite is *the measure* of good and evil, people will remain in the condition of mere nature, which is a state of war. What it *is* to be in a state of nature is to be every man measuring good and evil by his own private appetite. Government by individual appetite – private judgment of good and evil – is the *defining* characteristic of a state of nature in which, as we all know, life is said to be "solitary, poore, nasty, brutish and short". Such a state can obtain in the absence of all government, but it can also occur in the presence of government if there is another authority, say, a *church*, which challenges the government's authority so that individuals must use their private judgments to decide which authority to obey, with the prospect of them deciding, some of them one way, others another, in a dispute that cannot be settled by peaceful means.

As I suggested in Chapter 1, a state of nature can obtain even in the presence of a single, sovereign authority, if people reserve to themselves a right to decide whether or not to obey their government, since they may withhold their obedience, to the paralysis of effective government. Hobbes warns:

Take away in any kind of state the obedience (and consequently the concord of the people), and they shall not onely not flourish, but in short time be dissolved. And they that go about by disobedience to doe no more than

[74] EW III, 146; T 111.

reforme the common-wealth, shall find they thereby destroy it; like the foolish daughters of Peleus (in the fable), which desiring to renew the youth of their decrepit father, did by the counsell of Medea, cut in him pieces, and boyle him together with strange herbs, but made not of him a new man.[75]

No new man indeed. Both divided sovereignty and limited sovereignty necessitate the use of private judgment to adjudicate or evaluate the claims of pretenders to authority. That is why Hobbes disapproves of them.

"And thus", concludes Hobbes at "wee fall again into the fault of taking upon us to judge of good and evill; or to make judges of it, such private men as pretend to be supernaturally inspired, *to the dissolution of all civill government*".[76] Taking it upon ourselves to judge of good and evil is imprudent, but it isn't merely imprudent; it is also explicitly prohibited by God's positive laws as revealed in Scripture, for "the Scripture teacheth [that] it belongeth... to the soveraigne to bee judge, and to praescribe the rules of discerning good and evill".[77] The text thus shows that personal relativism is out.[78]

Hobbes's remarks on science, morality, language, and so on must be taken in context. What appears at first to be a motley hodgepodge of disconnected topics in part 1 of *Leviathan* turns out to be a catalog of most of the root sources of disorder in Hobbes's commonwealth, and a first pass at correcting disruptive errors at their source. Not all

[75] EW III, 327; T 234.
[76] EW III, 311–312; T 223–224.
[77] EW III, 192; T 143.
[78] Nor should we imagine that Hobbes took moral judgment to be relative to at least one person, namely, the sovereign, and that sovereigns, by their pronouncements, define good and evil. If sovereigns defined good and evil, it would be impossible for them to err in their moral judgments. But Hobbes says in plain language that it *is* possible for sovereigns to make moral mistakes: "[T]here is no judge subordinate, *nor sovereign*, but may erre in a judgment of equity" (EW III, 263; T 192, emphasis added). Cf. EW III, 601; T 414, where Hobbes indicates that Christian kings may issue mistaken religious directives. As we noted in Chapter 6, Hobbes's point is not that one's sovereign defines right and wrong, or is for some other reason normatively infallible; it is rather that one ought to accept one's sovereign's judgment as authoritative, whether or not it is correct. To refuse to do so would be to create the need for a further authority to arbitrate the dispute between oneself and one's sovereign. But what if one also believes *that* authority's verdict erroneous? Reciprocity disallows the refusal to submit to authoritative judgment, because one cannot be willing to permit all our fellow subjects also to refuse, for this implies one's effective agency generally, in all areas of life.

errors stem from bad natural science, but some do; hence an early four chapters on errors grounded in faulty science. Numerous other disruptive errors rely on mistakes about the use of language, and a failure to distinguish distinct ideas; hence another seven chapters on errors from the abuse of language. Religious errors are a *major* source of disorder; so Hobbes includes a preliminary corrective discussion of religion. The natural tendencies toward pride, fearfulness, and acquisitiveness, when we make private judgment the rule of our actions, can cause disorder; hence an expose of the perils of private judgment. A misunderstanding of the most basic norms of social life causes people to offend one another and to advance contentious moral claims, so Hobbes devotes two chapters on the Laws of Nature to clarify these norms. A misunderstanding of persons and authors leads subjects to resist their public representative, sometimes on the ground that they will be held responsible for the sinful actions he commands, other times on the ground that they have not authorized the powers he exercises; hence Hobbes includes a corrective chapter on authorization.

These are the primary sources of disorder identifiable by unaided natural reason. The remainder of the sources of disorder are presented in part 4, where Hobbes discusses the root causes of those religious errors that most severely threaten order, a task that could not be completed until Hobbes had established (in part 3) what true religion properly involves, and so what should be counted as an error.

Parts 2 and 3 of *Leviathan* carry out the compositive, or constructive, portion of Hobbes's project. In part 2 he aims to derive the rights and duties of subjects and sovereigns from the concept of a commonwealth,[79] and by the end of part 2 Hobbes sums up his accomplishment thus far in these by now very familiar words:

> That subjects owe to sovereigns simple obedience in all things wherein their obedience is not repugnant to the laws of God, I have sufficiently proved in that which I have already written. There wants onely, for the entire knowledge of civill duty, to know what are those lawes of God. For without that, a man knows not when he is commanded any thing by the civill power, whether it be contrary to the law of God or not; and so, either by too much civill obedience, offends the divine majesty, or through feare of offending God,

[79] For an account of how this is done, see *IAI*, chapter 2.

transgresses the commandements of the commonwealth. To avoid both these rocks, it is necessary to know what are the lawes divine.[80]

That project is carried out in part 3. So parts 1 and 4 discuss the causes of disorder, while parts 2 and 3 devise a remedy. Parts 1 and 2 employ exclusively natural knowledge, while parts 3 and 4 make additional use of prophetic or supernatural knowledge. The parts have different functions, but *none* of the parts is dispensable to Hobbes's project. *Pace* Stephen, it is not the case that Hobbes's system would be more consistent and intelligible if he omitted the theology altogether. To omit the theology would leave it incoherent and of no practical relevance.

The textual evidence indicates that the standard interpretation, with its attribution to Hobbes of an attempted logical progression from mechanistic-materialism to preservation-centered egoism to personal relativism to the "might plus fright makes order" remedy for rebellion stalls on every count. Its Hobbes is a fiction; a reassuringly modern and in some ways philosophically interesting one, but a fiction nonetheless.

And now the reason why Gauthier's Moral Contractarianism cannot properly claim Hobbes as an ancestor is clear. It relies on the standard interpretation's Hobbes to model the deliberations of its contractors – on a narrowly egoistic Hobbes devoid of overriding religious concerns that impose constraints on bargaining strategies and desirable ends. Ruling out these kinds of interest is required by the rational bargaining model, which seeks to generate, rather than to import, normative constraints on action. But in Hobbes, everything depends on acknowledging the existence of such constraints, and their effect on the reasonableness of social cooperation.

For Hobbes, to imagine narrowly egoistic interest-maximizing deliberators stripped of their transcendent, non-negotiable, religious commitments would be to abstract away from the very features of persons that generate the most serious problems for social stability. To appreciate Hobbes's point, consider not just Christian martyrs in ancient Rome, or various Medieval sects, but today's Hamas, or Al Qaeda engaged in a project of Islamic Jihad. Members of such groups

80 EW III, 343; T 245.

identify their religious interests in ways that can make the sacrifice of their temporal (bodily) self-preservation acceptable, so long as they judge their actions to substantially contribute to their transcendent ends. These interests may threaten social order, since if those who have them are willing to die in pursuit of them, it is difficult to see how they could be deterred from destabilizing action by threat of state force.

We can give greater rigor to our intuitive understanding of this point. The more fastidious way of putting it is that Hobbes analyzes social disorder as primarily the result of transcendent religious interests,[81] which divide into two basic interests: the interest in fulfilling one's duty to God, and the interest in obtaining salvation and avoiding damnation. But the model of rational choice Gauthier employs and wishes to credit, at least embryonically, to Hobbes cannot accomodate interests of this transcendent (i.e., temporal bodily-preservation overriding) character. Gauthier insists that one of the necessary conditions on preference required for an interval measure of the satisfaction of preferences is *continuity*, that for three possible outcomes, A, B, and C, such that A is preferred to B and B to C, there is one (and only one) lottery, with A and C as prizes, that is indifferent to B. That is, assuming these preferences, there exists a probability p such that

$$Pu(A) + (1 - p)uC = u(B).$$

But this continuity condition is not met by the preference orderings of those who have transcendent religious interests as Hobbes conceives of these. It is true that in Hobbes's view, the seventeenth-century Christian believer might prefer eating fruit to eating gruel, and will prefer eating gruel to experiencing eternal damnation; but he is certainly not understood to be indifferent as between the certainty of eating gruel and a gamble with fruit and damnation as the stakes. Similarly, the believer will prefer attaining salvation to eating fruit, and fruit to gruel, but he is not understood to be indifferent as

[81] He also recognizes transcendent interests in honor, reputation, the good of loved ones, and the pursuit of moral ideas or ends. But these play a secondary role in his analysis of the English disorder. We can well imagine him giving these sorts of transcendent interests a more central causal role in certain ancient or eastern civil disorders.

between fruit now and some gamble on salvation. To be indifferent between these sorts of things – culinary preferences versus eternal prospects – would be *certifiably insane*, in Hobbes's view.[82] So continuity is *not* assumed to hold for these kinds of cases.

Gauthier's response to cases like this that indicate the failure of continuity is to say that these are, quoting here from *Morals by Agreement*, "perhaps best handled by limiting the contexts in which continuity is expected to hold by exempting 'extreme' cases".[83] This response might do fine for some purposes. But for Hobbes's project, the "extreme" cases are central. They are *ineliminable* from his account of disorder, and so cannot be excluded from any model of rational cooperation adequate to address that problem. No model that required their exclusion could be in a relevant sense Hobbesian.

The same can also be said of the transcendent interest in fulfilling one's duty to God, which also fails to satisfy the continuity condition, although apparently for a different reason. The most natural account of the failure of continuity for the case just considered of interests concerning salvation and damnation is that to these outcomes we attach an infinite utility or disutility, in the specific sense that we are *unwilling* to consider any bargain at all concerning them. (The problem there was not that one could not, in principle, do the math, since in nonstandard analysis one can deal with such quantities, but rather that some possibilities, such as damnation, are ruled out of court – unacceptable, full stop – no matter what the result of the mathematician's calculation.) The difference in this case of transcendent interests in fulfilling our duties to God is that given Hobbes's view that, when it comes to fulfilling one's duties to God, *the will is the deed*, the probability of achieving that outcome if chosen can never be less than 1, so no point of indifference between it and the next best outcome can ever be established.

Hobbes argues for the view that "The obedience required at our hands by God, that accepteth in all our action the will for the deed, is a serious endeavour to obey him.... Whosoever therefore unfeignedly desireth to fulfill the commandements of God... hath all the obedience necessary to his reception

[82] I mean this quite literally. It would show an extreme "over-vehemence of passion" for fruit or gruel!

[83] Gauthier, *Morals by Agreement*, 46.

into the kingdome of God".[84] And again, "[the laws of nature/God], because they oblige onely to a desire and endeavour...are easie to be observed. For in that they require nothing but endeavour; he that endeavoureth their performance, fulfilleth them; and he that fulfilleth the law, is just".[85]

This means that if one selects to do one's duty to God, one automatically succeeds, with complete certainty, in doing so. Uncertainty, or risk, is eliminated. So it is impossible to assign to one's most preferred outcome A a probability that could allow for indifference between B and a lottery between A and C. If A is chosen, the probability of achieving it is 1, and so the expected utility of that action must, by hypothesis, be greater than that of the next preferred outcome B. If A is not chosen, the probability of achieving it is 0, and so the expected utility of one's action is just the utility of C, which is, by hypothesis, less than that of B. But in neither case can it be equal to that of B. *Continuity fails.*

So the continuity condition, which Gauthier insists is essential to his model for rational choice (the refinement he intends to introduce into Hobbes's theory), is one that Hobbes's central problem requires him to reject. And seeing this gives us a more precise way of explaining why the standard interpretation of Hobbes was not equipped to give an account of disorder that could even in principle be solved by the remedy it attributed to Hobbes. Its suggested solution is to increase the probability of bodily harm (via punishment) to alter the payoff matrix for disobedience; but no such increase will be adequate to force a reordering of preferences if continuity fails. And it does fail, where transcendent interests of the character Hobbes describes are what generate disorder.

Hobbes would thus have judged Gauthier's facile elimination of the "extreme case" of transcendent religious interests from his model of human deliberation to be a particularly egregious example of throwing out the baby with the bathwater. His reason throws out the universe with the bathwater, and can't even keep tigers away (according to Pi). Hobbes is no forefather, nor even friend, to Gauthier's Moral Contractarianism.

[84] EW III, 586; T 404.
[85] EW III, 145–146; T 110.

In contrast, our emerging sense of Hobbes's actual concerns makes it easier to understand why the political liberal would see a friend in Hobbes. Hobbes was addressing the problem of maintaining social order in the face of fundamental religious and moral disagreement over how people should live and thus over the state's proper ends and operations. Hobbes's problem, to use the modern parlance of Rawls's Political Liberalism, was one of how to ensure stable social cooperation in the face of competing comprehensive doctrines. Rawls's Political Liberalism addresses a closely related problem, the problem of discovering how a just democratic system of social cooperation might reproduce its own support among those who affirm competing and irreconcilable comprehensive doctrines. Both philosophers are attempting to respond to the fundamental problems posed by pluralism: Hobbes to the problem of order simpliciter assuming brute pluralism, and Rawls to the problem of establishing a just social order that could endure within a reasonable pluralism. Both problems arise when people within a society disagree in their comprehensive doctrines, and either cannot or will not allow each person free reign to act on his or her own comprehensive doctrine. Indeed, we can see both problems as generated by the same pair of conditions:

1. A collapse of consensus on values, interests and ends as articulated by a comprehensive doctrine

and

2. The unwillingness to tolerate others' pursuit of comprehensive doctrines of which one disapproves, along with the willingness to use state power to enforce compliance with one's own comprehensive doctrine.

Together these conditions give rise to problems both of social order and of social justice, for both Hobbes and Rawls. So we can understand why Rawls might find a resource in Hobbes.

Nonetheless, although their problems are related, it is their approaches to a solution that distinguish them, and these are what matter for our purposes. Hobbes's strategy for resolving his problem of order is to overcome (1), diversity in comprehensive doctrines, by reconciling them through a process of correcting disruptive religious errors, and redescribing religious duty so that formerly competing religious factions can be brought to affirm one and the same substantive conception of their religious duties, a conception that reinforces social order. This is a complicated process on which Hobbes spends some 300 pages of *Leviathan*, and I shall not attempt to recount it here further than the sketch I've already given.[86] It involves identifying commonly acceptable resources for settling doctrinal disagreement, and then arguing that these support a unique conception of religious duty fully compatible with civil obedience. Through this process Hobbes aims to move all of his intended audience from their idiosyncratic beliefs to a single comprehensive doctrine, and then to use the full force of the state's power to enforce and to reproduce allegiance to that comprehensive doctrine. Clearly, this is a fundamentally illiberal strategy.

In contrast, the liberal solution to the problem of justice focuses on overcoming, or limiting, (2), people's intolerance of competing doctrines. It attempts this by appealing to the political values of reciprocity among equals, liberty, and individuality, by separating church and state, the public and associational realms, and most importantly in the case of Rawls's political liberalism, by emphasizing the primacy of citizens' interest in securing the necessary conditions for the exercise of their capacities to form, revise, and pursue a conception of the good, and to have and act from a sense of justice (what Rawls calls their powers of moral personality). Rawls gives greater emphasis to citizens' interest in securing conditions for the exercise of these powers than to their interest in actually pursing the substantive comprehensive doctrines they actually affirm at any given time. Citizens' representatives in the Original Position select principles of justice that best protect the exercise of these capacities, but they do so in ignorance of the actual content of the comprehensive doctrines affirmed by those whom they represent. Roughly speaking, instead of pressing for the requirements of your comprehensive doctrine, they press for conditions that would allow you to pursue the requirements of any reasonable comprehensive doctrine you may affirm, or may come to affirm. Hobbes would not have understood how we could realistically expect people to be satisfied with that. The "zeal to embody the whole truth in politics" still characterized many competing religious factions in

[86] I offer a detailed account of Hobbes's argument in *IAI*, chapter 3.

Hobbes's day, and indeed remains difficult for many persons today to resist.[87]

So Hobbes takes aim at the problem of pluralism, seeking to forge uniformity in belief, while Rawls, assuming the fact of pluralism, seeks to delegitimize the use of state power in enforcing intolerance of differing, although reasonable, comprehensive doctrines. Given their fundamental difference in approach, should Rawls's Political Liberalism claim Hobbes as one of its own?

Insofar as overcoming intolerance requires Rawls to rely on the distancing device of the veil of ignorance to abstract away from the particular content of people's transcendent interests, his theory will be, like Gauthier's, dancing around the very problem that Hobbes thought an adequate political philosophy must grapple with directly. We can see from what he was doing that Hobbes firmly believed that "the devil is in the details"; that political instability is generated by the actual details of the particular religious views citizens actually affirm. And remedying disorder requires direct attention to these particularisms. Hobbes demonstrates the required attention in the half of *Leviathan* he devotes to religious issues. Indeed, the painfully thorough way in which he works through every competitor to his own interpretation of religious duty may partially explain why until recently so few contemporary readers have had the patience to study the half of *Leviathan* devoted to religious argument. Hobbes allows himself no broad brush strokes of high theory, no abstractions that gloss over the points of contention among combatants. People can be moved to a new position only by arguments that stem from where they are. And there is no guarantee in advance that even the most ingenious philosopher can build a sound argument to his desired conclusion when starting from the particular beliefs of the persons he seeks to move. (If you want to make a meringue from his ingredients, you'd better hope what he's holding is an egg and not a potato.)

But Rawls's use of a veil of ignorance to defuse the problem posed by intolerance precisely *precludes* doing what would be necessary to

87 Rawls insisted that "the zeal to embody the whole truth in politics is incompatible with an idea of public reason that belongs with democratic citizenship". John Rawls, "The Idea of Public Reason Revisited," in Rawls, *The Law of Peoples: with "The Idea of Public Reason Revisited"* (Cambridge, MA, 1999), §1.1, 132–133.

eliminate diversity. One cannot expect to move people from the views they hold without dealing with the content of those views; yet Rawls's device prevents his deliberators from even knowing what those views are, except in the most general terms. Of course, the Original Position is not designed to create consensus on comprehensive doctrine; it is designed to select principles that could settle the fair and reciprocal terms of cooperation among equals, despite the fact that those equal citizens do not enjoy consensus on a single comprehensive doctrine. But if some such distancing device as the veil of ignorance is indispensable for defending the kind of principles of justice Rawls seeks (namely, principles that could gain the support of an overlapping consensus in a society well ordered by them), then Hobbes's approach, which disallows this sort of abstraction, is probably not an appropriate resource for Political Liberalism.

However, this argument goes a bit too fast, because it does not reflect how subtle are the differences between Hobbes and Rawls, large although we'd normally think them to be. First, Hobbes cannot escape resort to a distancing device of his own. Hobbes argues that our religious duties are properly specified by the judgment of a religious authority, and that we ought to profess and practice as the appropriate authority in matters of religion dictates (whatever the content of its dictates). This is an abstraction of sorts, because it transforms the question of what religious doctrines are true into the question of whose judgment God requires us to regard as authoritative on religious questions. The only truth that really matters is the truth about whose judgment we are to treat as authoritative. Consensus on this is a very thin, contentless, consensus, and it is all Hobbes really needs.

But one important difference between Rawls's distancing device and that employed by Hobbes is that Hobbes's distancing move away from characterizations of religious duty as requiring particular profession and practice, toward one requiring whatever profession and practice the appropriate religious authority may dictate, is argued to be *actually sanctioned by, rather than foreign to,* the comprehensive doctrines it seemingly disempowers. That is why Hobbes has to attempt to create consensus across the vast swaths of Judeo-Christian doctrine needed to establish the crucial contentless consensus. It is not at all clear that the same can be said of Rawls's distancing device, and this seems to me to be a very important difference. Even should Rawls's principles of justice find direct support in the comprehensive doctrines that make up an overlapping consensus, it is still highly unlikely that all of Rawls's *machinery*, including, especially, the Original Position, will enjoy such support. So if the use of the Original Position's veil of ignorance is required in order to settle on Rawls's principles of justice, his Political Liberalism will depend upon an abstraction Hobbes would have viewed as impermissible.

But here again, the contrast is not so sharp, because Rawls's device of representation is not just cut from whole cloth entirely unrelated to our existing normative beliefs. It embeds what are said to be our shared conceptions of society as a system of social cooperation on fair terms for mutual benefit and of citizens as free and equal with the moral powers to have and act from a sense of justice, and to form, revise, and pursue a conception of the good (along with higher order interests in exercising these powers.) These core ideas – "fundamental intuitive ideas" – are said to be both latent in the public political culture of our democratic society and also ideas that "we, here and now" accept. Furthermore, it embeds certain shared principles of practical reasoning, such as the requirements that like cases be treated alike, and that equals are to be situated fairly (and the principles that issue from it are to be brought into reflective equilibrium with our shared considered convictions about justice – such as the conviction that slavery is wrong). This is quite a robust basis of normative agreement, even though it falls far short of agreement in comprehensive doctrines. So it is not as if the conceptions and principles that shape Rawls's Original Position machinery are entirely foreign to the normative views citizens already hold. Indeed, if they were, the prospect of developing an overlapping consensus on the principles of justice selected by reasoning from the Original Position would be seriously damaged. The difference then between Hobbes and Rawls on how far we are to distance ourselves from our substantive normative commitments is merely a matter of degree.

Second, there is a noteworthy similarity in the reasoning behind Rawls's insistence on a "freestanding" justification for his principles of justice, and Hobbes's care to provide a multiplication of reasons from different comprehensive views for adherence to his principle of political obligation; after all, to show one's principles justified without dependence on *any* comprehensive doctrine, and to show them justifiable from within *many* comprehensive doctrines, are different ways of showing one's principles to be not dependent upon the affirmation of some *privileged* comprehensive doctrine. When Hobbes offers converging arguments from narrow self-interest, morality, religious duty, and special prudence for his principle of political obligation, we can imagine that each of these may provide the core of a comprehensive doctrine for some people: morality for the nonreligious, self-interest for the sorts of egoists Hobbes deemed fools, special prudence for purely egoistic religionists, and religious duty for others.[88] If so, the justification for his principle of political obligation will not depend on privileging any particular comprehensive doctrine – just as the justification for Rawls's principles of justice does not – and this is a very big plus under conditions of pluralism. I believe it was actually precisely this similarity that Rawls found so striking as to prompt him to wonder whether Hobbes may have been the first political liberal.

One might discount this striking commonality between the two theories on the ground that in Rawls's theory, there is the common core of normative agreement just mentioned among the citizens of liberal democratic societies, and that it is precisely this shared core that makes it possible to justify principles without dependence on any privileged comprehensive doctrine. Rawls has enough common ground to work with that political principles can be generated independently. *But so too does Hobbes, in the Laws of Nature.* The triple status of the Laws of Nature as precepts of prudence, requirements of morality, and dictates of natural religion provides a substantial area of overlap among virtually all comprehensive doctrines, which could support Hobbes's principle of political obligation without further reliance on any controversial aspects of sectarian doctrine.

We now have in hand the best case I am able to make for the claim that Hobbes was a political liberal, but it is not enough. It is not enough for the simple reason that Hobbes was not enough a liberal. Although he viewed all men and women as equal and free by nature, as reasonable and bound by a principle of reciprocity, insisted on

[88] On the confluence of reasons for supporting Hobbes's principle of political obligation see *IAI*, 279; for a discussion of the requirement that the argument for principles of justice be freestanding, see Rawls, *Political Liberalism*, 10–12, 140, 144.

equality before the law and held that democracy was a perfectly fine form of sovereignty, and was tempted toward religious toleration – all respectable liberal ideas – his authoritarianism refuses to institutionalize guarantees of such seemingly essential liberal rights as freedoms of expression, religion, and association. He may have been politically liberal in the senses just discussed that his theory was *political* rather than comprehensive; but if political liberalism requires also that the view be liberal, we should probably conclude that Hobbes didn't quite make it to the mountaintop.[89] So the real Hobbes cannot be used to support the admittedly philosophically interesting projects of Gauthier or Rawls. But there is, to my mind, a philosophical problem at least as interesting as theirs to which the real Hobbes speaks directly, and that is the problem of how to address disorder generated by competing transcendent interests. This is perhaps the most pressing problem of our world. Many of the religious conflicts, and ethnic conflicts, and pride and blood feuds we confront every day seem to have the "force resistant" character of transcendent interests. So we need a theory that addresses disorder fueled by transcendent interests, and Hobbes was the first to have made significant progress toward designing such a theory. The real Hobbes brought an astounding intellect to bear on one of the most pressing problems of human life, and suggested what, to my knowledge, is the most promising *strategy* for solving it.[90] The central feature of Hobbes's insight that gives it promise as a solution is its insistence on our developing out of our various *existing ideals and interests* a *principled* attachment to settled mechanisms for adjudication of our disputes.

That Hobbes's theory selected as the appropriate mechanism a sovereign authority explains why it is so terrifying. Deference to authority *is* dangerous. No one wants to subject herself to the power of others. Machiavelli says we care much less for exercising power over others than we do for escaping their exercise of power over us. For almost all of us that is true, and so Hobbes's solution could not be anything but terrifying. But civil war is also dangerous. And there is plenty of

89 Perhaps Rawls, whose commitment to learning from the history of philosophy, and humility in the face of his predecessors, failed to realize that in fact, *he* was the first political liberal.

90 I try to explain how we might adapt Hobbes's general method to the particular features of the conflicts that concern us in *IAI*, chapter 9.

conceptual room in Hobbes to design a system of sovereign government that contains constitutional constraints and the balancing of power to check arbitrariness and corruption. There is room to design a safer system. The only real requirement of Hobbesian sovereignty is that we be able to resolve every question. It must be a system sufficiently nimble to provide a *complete resolution mechanism* for every dispute. The buck must stop somewhere. And we must share a *principled* commitment to accept that public authority. Failing that, we'll have no choice but to "appeal to heaven"[91] by fighting it out.

But whether people will see themselves as having sufficient reason to defer to their political authority, and be motivated to do so, depends upon their ideals and their conception of their interests. For practical purposes, we can regard their ideals as interests. Continued stable social cooperation requires engaging their interests and linking the satisfaction of those to deference to a political authority. It requires this because, as Hobbes insists, societies of equals cannot be maintained by sheer coercion without the free and willing cooperation of their members. The acceptable terms of that cooperation are constrained by the requirement of reciprocity, because equals demand reciprocal consideration from one another. This requirement, articulated again and again in various forms by the Laws of Nature, settles a minimal framework for social cooperation that can be expected to be widely acceptable on the basis of our common human reason.

While the Laws of Nature give a symmetrical form and minimal content to the basic framework for social cooperation, sustaining that framework requires attention to people's embraced interests. It may be possible to convince people to affirm interpretations of those interests that better comport with the needs of social stability; how this effort is carried out will also be morally constrained by the requirement of reciprocity.

Happily for us, every moment of every day, new individuals roll onto the moving sidewalk of civil life, while intransigent elders exit it. This makes reform of our society possible because we can affect the formation of the ideals and interests in which our progressive projects

[91] The phrase is Locke's in his *Second Treatise of Government* II, section 168 (ed. C. B. Macpherson [Indianapolis, 1980]): "The people have no other remedy in this, as in all other cases where they have no judge on earth, but to *appeal to Heaven*".

will have to find their support. We can affect the character of citizens toward greater attachment to liberal democracy, *if* we can persuade enough of the existing factional idealists – by means the reciprocity principle would approve – that they have what they can see to be a principled interest in the needed reforms.

Hobbes saw that motivating human action depends as much on engaging our ideals as it does on serving our pedestrian interests. Because we make judgments about whether to pursue what we desire or need, and do so according to our conceptions of moral and religious duty, inducing us to submit to political authority and to act in socially salutary ways will require addressing our principled convictions. Hobbes alerts us to this in his liveliest of ways, and provides us important conceptual tools and guiding examples for how to deal with the most basic fact of human social life. That fact is: Our ideals are an ineliminable part of our interests.

Bibliography

Primary Sources

Behemoth or The Long Parliament (1990). Ferdinand Tonnies, ed., with an introduction by Stephen Holmes. Chicago.

The Collected English Works of Thomas Hobbes (1839–1845). Sir William Molesworth, ed., 11 volumes. London.

Attributed to Hobbes. "A Discourse of Laws" (1995), in Noel B. Reynolds and Arlene W. Saxonhouse, eds., *Thomas Hobbes: Three Discourses.* Chicago.

Hobbes's 'Leviathan', Leviathan with selected variants from the Latin edition of 1668 (1994.) Edwin Curley, ed. Indianapolis.

Hobbes's Leviathan (1996). Richard Tuck, ed. Cambridge.

Man and Citizen (1978). Bernard Gert, ed. Gloucester, MA.

Secondary Sources

Aeschylus (1977). *The Oresteia,* trans. Robert Fagles. Harmondsworth, UK.

Allison, Henry E. (1998). "Morality and Freedom: Kant's Reciprocity Thesis", in Paul Guyer, ed., *Kant's Groundwork of the Metaphysics of Morals: Critical Essays,* 273–302. Lanham, MD.

Angeles, Peter A. (1987). *Dictionary of Philosophy.* New York.

Annas, Julia (1981). *An Introduction to Plato's Republic.* Oxford.

Barry, Brian (1989). *A Treatise on Social Justice, Volume 1: Theories of Justice.* Berkeley, CA.

Baumgold, Deborah (1988). *Hobbes's Political Theory.* Cambridge.

Boonin-Vail, David (1994). *Thomas Hobbes and the Science of Moral Virtue.* Cambridge.

Brown, K. C., ed. (1965). *Hobbes Studies.* Cambridge, MA.

Cohen, Joshua (1986). "Structure, Choice, and Legitimacy: Locke's Theory of the State", *Philosophy and Public Affairs* 15: 301–324.

Coleman, Jules, and Brian Leiter (1999). "Legal Positivism", in Dennis Patterson, ed., *A Companion to Philosophy of Law and Legal Theory*, 241–260. Malden.

Cooper, John M. (1994). "Introduction to Hobbes's *Leviathan*", in E. Curly, ed., *Leviathan*, viii–xliv.

(1999). "Plato on Human Motivation", in Cooper, *Reason and Emotion: Essays on Ancient Moral Psychology and Ethical Theory*, 118–137. Princeton, NJ.

Darwall, Stephen (1995). *The British Moralists and the Internal "Ought", 1640–1740.* Cambridge.

(2000). "Normativity and Projection in Hobbes's *Leviathan*", *Philosophical Review* 109, no. 3: 313–347.

Deigh, John (1996). "Reason and Ethics in Hobbes's *Leviathan*", *Journal of the History of Philosophy* 34: 33–60.

Dietz, Mary G., ed. (1990). *Thomas Hobbes and Political Theory.* Lawrence, KS.

Ewin, R. E. (1991). *Virtues and Rights: The Moral Philosophy of Thomas Hobbes.* Boulder, CO.

Gauthier, David P. (1969). *The Logic of 'Leviathan': The Moral and Political Theory of Thomas Hobbes.* Oxford.

(1969). *Morals by Agreement.* Oxford.

(1987). "Taming Leviathan", *Philosophy and Public Affairs* 16: 280–298.

(1990). "Thomas Hobbes and Contractarian Theory of Law", *Canadian Journal of Philosophy* Supp. 16: 5–34.

Gert, Bernard (1967). "Hobbes and Psychological Egoism", *Journal of the History of Ideas* 28: 503–520.

(1988). "The Law of Nature and the Moral Law", *Hobbes Studies* 1: 26–44.

(1988). Review of Kavka, *Hobbesian Moral and Political Theory, Political Theory* 16: 159–163.

(1996). "Hobbes on Law", in Tom Sorell, ed., *The Cambridge Companion to Hobbes*, 274–304.

(1996). "Hobbes's Psychology", in Tom Sorell, ed., *The Cambridge Companion to Hobbes*, 157–174.

(2001). "Hobbes on Reason", *Pacific Philosophical Quarterly* 82: 243–257.

Hampton, Jean (1986). *Hobbes and the Social Contract Tradition.* Cambridge.

Hoekstra, Kinch (1997). "Hobbes and the Foole", *Political Theory* 25: 620–654.

(1999). "Nothing to Declare? Hobbes and the Advocate of Injustice", *Political Theory* 27: 230–235.

(2003). "Hobbes on Law, Nature, and Reason", *Journal of the History of Philosophy* 41: 111–120.

Hood, Francis C. (1964). *The Divine Politics of Thomas Hobbes.* Oxford.

Johnston, David (1986). *The Rhetoric of 'Leviathan': Thomas Hobbes and the Politics of Cultural Transformation.* Princeton, NJ.

Kavka, Gregory S. (1986). *Hobbesian Moral and Political Theory.* Princeton, NJ.

Laird, John (1934). *Hobbes.* London.

Lloyd, S. A. (1992). *Ideals as Interests in Hobbes's 'Leviathan': The Power of Mind over Matter.* Cambridge.

(1994). "Family Justice and Social Justice", *Pacific Philosophical Quarterly* 75: 353–371.

(1997). "Coercion, Ideology, and Education in Hobbes's *Leviathan*", in Andrews Reath, Barbara Herman, and Christine Korsgaard, eds., *Reclaiming the History of Ethics*, 36–65. Cambridge.

Lloyd, S. A., ed. (2001). "Special Issue on Recent Work on the Moral and Political Philosophy of Thomas Hobbes", *Pacific Philosophical Quarterly* 82, nos. 3 & 4: 285–308.

Locke, John (1980). *Second Treatise of Government*. C.B. Macpherson, ed. Indianapolis.

Machiavelli, Niccolò. (1979). *The Discourses*, in Peter Bondanella and Mark Musa, eds., *The Portable Machiavelli*, 167–418. New York.

Macpherson, C. B. (1968). "Introduction", in Macpherson, ed., *Leviathan*, 9–63.

Martel, Yann (2001). *Life of Pi*. Orlando, FL.

Martinich, A. P. (1992). *The Two Gods of Leviathan: Thomas Hobbes on Religion and Politics*. Cambridge.

(1999). *Hobbes: A Biography*. Cambridge.

(2005). *Thomas Hobbes*. London.

McNeilly, F. S. (1968). *The Anatomy of Leviathan*. New York.

Mill, J. S. (1991). *On Liberty*, in John Gray, ed., *John Stuart Mill: On Liberty and Other Essays*, 5–128. Oxford.

Murphy, Mark (2000). "Desire and Ethics in Hobbes's *Leviathan*: A Response to Professor Deigh", *Journal of the History of Philosophy* 38: 259–268.

(2000). "Hobbes on the Evil of Death", *Archiv für Geschichte der Philosophie* 82: 36–61.

Nagel, Thomas (1959). "Hobbes's Concept of Obligation", *Philosophical Review* 68 (January): 68–53.

Okin, Susan Moller (1994). "Political Liberalism, Justice, and Gender", *Ethics* 105: 23–43.

Pasquino, Pasquale (2001). "Hobbes, Religion, and Rational Choice: Hobbes's Two Leviathans and the Fool", *Pacific Philosophical Quarterly* 82: 406–419.

Pettit, Philip (2008). *Made with Words*. Princeton, NJ.

Plamenatz, John (1965). "Mr. Warrender's Hobbes", in K.C. Brown, ed., *Hobbes Studies*, 73–87.

Raphael, D.D. (1977). *Hobbes: Morals and Politics*. London.

Rawls, John (1955). "Two Concepts of Rules", *Philosophical Review* 64: 3–32.

(1971). *A Theory of Justice*. Cambridge, MA.

(1993). *Political Liberalism*. New York.

(1999). "The Idea of Public Reason Revisited," in Rawls, *The Law of Peoples: With "The Idea of Public Reason Revisited"*, 129–180. Cambridge, MA.

Rogers, G.A.J., and K. Schuhmann (2003). *Thomas Hobbes Leviathan*. Bristol.

Ryan, Alan (1986). "A More Tolerant Hobbes?", in Susan Mendus, ed., *Justifying Toleration*, 37–59. Cambridge.

Scanlon, T. M. (1972). "A Theory of Freedom of Expression", *Philosophy & Public Affairs* 1: 204–226.

(1999). *What We Owe to Each Other*. Cambridge, MA.

Schneewind, J. B. (1997). *The Invention of Autonomy: History of Modern Moral Philosophy*. Cambridge.

Shapin, Steven, and Simon Schaffer (1985). *Leviathan and the Air Pump.* Princeton, NJ.

Shelton, George (1992). *Morality and Sovereignty in the Philosophy of Hobbes.* New York.

Simmons, A. John (1993). *On the Edge of Anarchy.* Princeton, NJ.

Skinner, Quentin (1996). *Reason and Rhetoric in the Philosophy of Hobbes.* Cambridge.

Sommerville, Johann P., ed. (1991). *Robert Filmer: Patriarcha and Other Writings.* Cambridge.

(1992). *Thomas Hobbes: Political Ideas in Historical Context.* New York.

Sophocles (1984). *The Three Theban Plays.* Translated by Robert Fagles. New York.

Sorell, Tom (1986). *Hobbes.* London.

Sorell, Tom, ed. (1996). *The Cambridge Companion to Hobbes.* Cambridge.

Stephen, Leslie (1928). *Hobbes.* London.

Strauss, Leo (1936). *The Political Philosophy of Hobbes: Its Basis and Genesis.* Oxford.

(1952). *The Political Philosophy of Hobbes.* Chicago.

(1965). "The Spirit of Hobbes's Political Philosophy", in K. C. Brown, ed., *Hobbes Studies,* 1–29.

Taylor, A. E. (1965). "The Ethical Doctrine", in K. C. Brown, ed., *Hobbes Studies,* 35–55.

Tuck, Richard (1996). "Introduction", in Tuck, ed., *Leviathan,* ix–lxv.

Tuck, Richard, and Michael Silverthorne, eds. (1998). *On the Citizen.* Cambridge.

van Mill, David (2001). *Liberty, Rationality, and Agency in Hobbes's Leviathan.* Albany, NY.

Waldron, Jeremy (2002). *God, Locke and Equality.* Cambridge.

Warrender, Howard (1957). *The Political Philosophy of Hobbes: His Theory of Obligation.* Oxford.

Watkins, J. W. N. (1965). *Hobbes's System of Ideas.* London.

(1965). "Philosophy and Politics in Hobbes", in Brown, ed., *Hobbes Studies,* 237–262.

Williams, Garrath (2000). "Normatively Demanding Creatures: Hobbes, the Fall and Individual Responsibility", *Res Publica* 6, no. 3: 301–319.

Index

Lightning Source UK Ltd.
Milton Keynes UK
UKHW012322050320
359878UK00001B/87

9 781107 629899